The complexity of complexity – the authors reveal how the system components interact in multiple, interdependent ways. They develop a picture on how Homo sapiens in our age of the Anthropocene crosses thresholds of Earth's safe-operating space for humanity, describing the disastrous impact of Homo faber on climate, water, biodiversity, migration or international relations. Solutions and loopholes, emphasizing the importance of education, science, technology and innovation, make the book a "must" to read.
– *Walter J. Ammann, Founder, Global Risk Forum GRF Davos*

Control of complexity is the central parameter of evolution. Extremely long, error-free messages are needed for control. Science is humanity's best means for such messages and is thus the *sine qua non* of power in the 21st century, as this book shows.
– *Jesse Ausubel, Director, Human Environment Project,*
Rockefeller University, USA

The scale and scope of Erdelen's and Richardson's book is truly remarkable. Tracing the impact of human activity on the planet's complex ecosystem and the resulting environmental problems, their broad and interdisciplinary systems approach embraces both history and foresight. The resulting linked, insightful essays culminate in the key question for the future of *Homo sapiens*: Do we have the ability to moderate our behavior so that we live with more measured consumption while continuing to reap considerable rewards from education, science and industry?
– *Colin Blackman, Centre for European Policy Studies; Editor of* Digital Policy, Regulation and Governance; *Former Editor of* Futures & Foresight

Science must be an essential component of any effective strategy leading to sustainable development. As the authors emphasize, science clears the mind, sobers our views and leads to robust decisions. Wise counsel from the UN's new Scientific Advisory Board should help member nations prioritize the most important challenges ahead. Science thus assumes a major role in solving global

and interlinked problems related *inter alia* to poverty, food security and public health, water management, and biological diversity.
— Vladimir Y. Fortov, *Russian Academy of Sciences*

This book is much needed today to help us understand the complexity of the challenges facing all Earth's inhabitants. It advances solutions to learning how to live in harmony with Nature and with each other. Erdelen and Richardson bring years of experience to a survey which should be required reading for everyone working on the quest for sustainability.
— Julia Marton-Lefèvre, *former Director-General, International Union for Conservation of Nature (IUCN)*

Two international investigators, a social scientist and a life scientist with extensive leadership experience in UNESCO, take a well-researched new look at the human stance in a world of growing complexity and risk of existence. The authors unravel human pursuit in exploiting nature as one root of growing disharmony in "human/environment relationship," up to present-day global climate change, massive migration and loss of biodiversity. Core chapters highlight education, science and philosophy (especially ethics) as key "tools" to combat, should "humankind . . . sustain its further development." This compact, highly-readable and challenging book will deserve a wide and receptive audience.
— Kurt Pawlik, *Emeritus Professor of Psychology, University of Hamburg, Germany; former President, International Social Science Council*

We have entered the sustainable development decade where to achieve the desired goal, we should examine every programme from the point of view of social and economic and environmental sustainability. I am glad that this book brings out very clearly the complexity of the world problems and the strategies to face them. I hope the book will be read widely.
— Prof. M. S. Swaminathan, *Founder Chairman, M. S. Swaminathan Foundation*

Managing Complexity: Earth Systems and Strategies for the Future

Managing Complexity: Earth Systems and Strategies for the Future introduces and explores systems and complexity in relation to near-synchronous world and environmental problems. These relate to but are not limited to water, biological diversity, worldwide climate change, trade and conflict, global migration and the quest for sustainable development. Complemented by discussion of the new era of the Anthropocene, its many manifestations and Earth system properties such as planetary boundaries and tipping points, this book offers practical suggestions for how a sustainable future for humanity can be realized.

Specifically discussed in *Managing Complexity: Earth Systems and Strategies for the Future* are innovation, education and capacity building, application of the natural and social sciences and new paths toward sustainability based on industrial development and engineering, as well as in diplomacy and foreign aid. The book's conclusions discuss the ambitious yet vital reforms the authors propose as routes to a sustainable existence. This book will be of great interest to students and scholars of sustainability, sustainable development and complexity theory.

Walter R. Erdelen is an ecologist and biogeographer with extensive international experience. Development of vision, concepts and strategies, targeted capacity building and networking have been essentials of his policy-related scientific work. He was previously Assistant Director-General for Natural Sciences of the United Nations Educational, Scientific and Cultural Organization (UNESCO).

Jacques G. Richardson is an author and journalist concentrating on the sciences and engineering, and has also worked extensively in strategic analysis and planning. He spent 13 years at UNESCO as head of its Science and Society Section.

Routledge Studies in Sustainability

Aesthetic Sustainability
Product design and sustainable usage
Kristine H. Harper

Stress, Affluence and Sustainable Consumption
Cecilia Solér

Digital Technology and Sustainability
Engaging the paradox
Edited by Mike Hazas and Lisa P. Nathan

Personal Sustainability
Exploring the far side of sustainable development
Edited by Oliver Parodi and Kaidi Tamm

Sustainable Modernity
The Nordic model and beyond
Edited by Nina Witoszek and Atle Midttun

Towards the Ethics of a Green Future
The theory and practice of human rights for future people
Edited by Marcus Düwell, Gerhard Bos and Naomi van Steenbergen

Sustainability Transitions in South Africa
Edited by Najma Mohamed

Strongly Sustainable Societies
Organising human activities on a hot and full Earth
Edited by Karl Johan Bonnedahl and Pasi Heikkurinen

Managing Complexity: Earth Systems and Strategies for the Future
Walter R. Erdelen and Jacques G Richardson

www.routledge.com/Routledge-Studies-in-Sustainability/book-series/RSSTY

Managing Complexity: Earth Systems and Strategies for the Future

Walter R. Erdelen and
Jacques G. Richardson

LONDON AND NEW YORK

from Routledge

First published 2019 by Routledge

2 Park Square, Milton Park, Abingdon, Oxfordshire OX14 4RN

52 Vanderbilt Avenue, New York, NY 10017

Routledge is an imprint of the Taylor & Francis Group, an informa business

First issued in paperback 2020

© 2019 Walter R. Erdelen and Jacques G. Richardson

The right of Walter R. Erdelen and Jacques G. Richardson to be identified as authors of this work has been asserted by them in accordance with sections 77 and 78 of the Copyright, Designs and Patents Act 1988.

All rights reserved. No part of this book may be reprinted or reproduced or utilised in any form or by any electronic, mechanical, or other means, now known or hereafter invented, including photocopying and recording, or in any information storage or retrieval system, without permission in writing from the publishers.

Trademark notice: Product or corporate names may be trademarks or registered trademarks, and are used only for identification and explanation without intent to infringe.

British Library Cataloguing-in-Publication Data
A catalogue record for this book is available from the British Library

Library of Congress Cataloging-in-Publication Data
A catalog record for this book has been requested

ISBN: 978-0-367-00006-6 (hbk)
ISBN: 978-0-367-50044-3 (pbk)

Typeset in Goudy
by Apex CoVantage, LLC

To our wives, Amina and Erika, who bore the brunt of endless dialogue about system dynamics, self-adaptation, stumbles, chaos and resilience.

Contents

Foreword by Hon. Margaret E. Austin   xi
Preface   xiv
Acknowledgments   xviii
List of abbreviations and acronyms   xix

1 Introduction: setting the scene   1

2 The Anthropocene and planetary boundaries: conditioners of sustainable development   15

3 Foresight and innovation: searching for the right future   28

4 Education: towards universal understanding   41

5 Science: the complexity of searching the truth   57

6 Industry, engineering, further complexity: steam engines and more   73

7 *Philosophia moralis*: systems stretched to the breaking point   88

8 Water: simple matter of special complexity   103

9 Biological diversity: bountiful Mother Nature   118

10 Global climate change: humanity's supreme challenge   133

11 Diplomacy and foreign trade: weaving the web of international intercourse   160

12 The military: risk management-plus, not perversity 180

13 Migration: when exit becomes exodus 195

14 Sustainable development: *Homo sapiens*' Holy Grail 210

15 Risks, new departures, global solutions: challenges of a complex frontier 229

Further reading 242
Index 245

Foreword

Managing Complexity: Earth Systems and Strategies for the Future is a significant and welcome contribution to the issues facing humanity. The reader is presented a wide range of examples from which to draw conclusions about systems and the role of agencies in finding pathways for the future and, at the same time, contributing to ensuring an informed public capable of comprehending and advocating the issues confronting humanity.

This book helps the reader to understand the complexity of the problems; it should be widely read by people everywhere and especially by decision makers in government and business, member nations and staff of the United Nations (UN) and its institutions as well as NGOs of all description.

It must be asked whether *Homo sapiens* can conceive of a world where energy, water, mineral and biological resources are managed sustainably for future generations or will the race for increased GDP by wealthy nations and the desire of the developing world to catch up, take precedence and allow humanity to continue to plunder and exploit without consideration for the 22nd century and beyond?

Throughout this important debate, readers will traverse interrelated systems of the past and the present in a way which will allow consideration of the efficiency and effectiveness of many of the systems in place. Barring catastrophe, the necessities of living sustainably will be available with safety assured and the care needed will be forthcoming. This does not mean that many citizens will not encounter very complex situations requiring analysis and considered decisions to find solutions.

Nations and peoples have to set targets and goals to achieve aims, whether they be personal or for humanity and the environment. Acceptance of the problem, complex or not, is the first step but only by relentless perseverance along with international collaboration will *Homo sapiens* be able to leave its legacy with confidence. The days of belligerence must be set aside, the environmental threats are of too great a moment to be left to chance – population pressure, availability of water, rising sea levels with drastic consequences for millions of people living in low-lying areas, soil degradation – all require systematic and long-term examination and evidence-based decision making to which nations must subscribe and implement.

The problems beg committed solutions. Nothing is simple, as this book clearly illustrates in drawing attention throughout to "complexity." Finding solutions is essential if humanity is to be sustainable into the future. The current generation cannot and must not be the architect of the eventual demise of *Homo sapiens*.

The authors rightly draw attention to humanity having entered a new era, the Anthropocene. How will humanity react? Surely not by overseeing further extinction of fauna and flora or greater air and water pollution – the new era requires vision, direction and action to achieve the newly adopted Sustainable Development Goals of the UN.

This is not fantasy – it is reality. People must question and engage in rigorous examination but reject skepticism when the evidence is placed in front of them. The "new shoes" will be comfortable if people of all ages, rural and urban, are open-minded and receptive to change even if there are some obstacles and stumbles along the way.

If the purpose of education is the initiation of the young into those spheres of knowledge which cannot be left to chance, then a broad-ranging *thematic* approach to the "Delors Pillars" of learning (learning to know, learning to do, learning to live together, learning to be) are essential. Thematic approaches to curriculum engages the learner at the center and moves away from discrete disciplines; it provides open learning environments conducive to cooperation between teachers and between teachers and students. In such environments young people can explore, be inspired and give rein to their creativity and eventually be led into sustainable economic and social futures.

Only with lifelong opportunity will people escape the poverty trap, achieve their potential and at the same time sustainable development for humanity. There is no room here for selection, labeling and privilege and as C. E. Beeby asserted as New Zealand's director of education and UNESCO's first head of education, "every person whatever his/her level of ability, rich or poor, living in town or country, has a right as a citizen to a free education of the kind that fits them to the very fullest of their powers."

Science and the community of scientists have an awesome responsibility, despite the increasing complexity and minutiae of their findings, to embrace collegiality and recognize the contribution not only of natural and environmental sciences but also of social science and the humanities. The science community must become effective communicators if people are to become scientifically literate. This is the message cogently set out in Chapter 5 on science and its uses.

The authors go to some length to comment on the great industrial advances of recent times and draw attention to the extreme effects on the environment of disasters subsequently causing apprehension for the future. There is no room for negligence, unethical practice or a repetition of the fraudulent practices or corruption of the past. These resulted in many of today's inequalities.

Sound evidence-based decisions must be applied to water as the most essential commodity for life on Earth so that Goal 6 of the 2030 Agenda for Sustainable Development is achieved as a means to contributing to poverty eradication, gender equality and enjoyment of the human right to water and sanitation – while conserving finite and vulnerable water resources for the future. The same principles apply to biodiversity. Chapter 9 outlines the Aichi Targets for Biodiversity and promotes intergovernmental panels to meet yet another very complex challenge.

A major problem contributing to "complexity" revolves around climate change, yet there remain numerous skeptics refusing to acknowledge the link between greenhouse gas concentrations, global warming and sea-level rise. The authors rightly outline the significance of the 2015 Paris Agreement in leading nations and their public to adopt policy changes for the future. To achieve these changes will require astute international diplomacy where there is no room for pursuit of power through warfare and the pressures it induces for migration.

Humans have the means, but have we the will? Taking on board the information in these 15 chapters the reader will be obliged to confront the reality of each person's significance as a voter and therefore a determinant of purpose, direction, perseverance, information and application and actions together with the world's citizenry with hope.

Margaret E. Austin

Hon. Margaret E. Austin
Former Minister of Research, Science and Technology,
Arts and Culture and Internal Affairs
Government of New Zealand

Preface
The critical need to stimulate better management of our future

1

Today humanity stands precariously on the brim of a vast canyon, puzzled by how its surroundings have changed radically in so little time. We stare blankly while wondering what the future holds. Experts tell us that the global population will grow to over nine billion within a generation. Climate change is more than evident in every land and ocean. The air is contaminated, we question future supplies of water and food, and we confront new epidemics which researchers strain to banish.

The problems are real and many. We struggle to understand them as major complications, while we seek ways and means to cope with them and strive to avoid making them worse. They are part of the complexity of today's world; we want, we demand that they be confined in order to limit or eliminate the extent of their ravages. We seek a return to the good life or, that not being available, at least to a level of control by the very force that has created the current unease: the human species. We are now well into the era of the Anthropocene (human-generated) as we search Earth and, for many, heaven as well for leavening influences and happy results.

Are we up to the challenge, capable of dealing with systems gone awry, understanding what complexity means? To grasp how this condition can be exploited to full advantage, the authors look closely in this book at past, present and some future forms of complexity and how most wisely to prepare to set goals, manage new potential, seize emerging opportunities and do better than we have done in the past.

Readers will find an alternation of some major problem areas (water, biodiversity, climate change) with factual recalls of significant challenges of the past in other areas (industry, migration, military activity) and how their actors responded to persistent complexity.

Our fascination with non-controlled or leaderless movement is endless. We find "disorganized" motion in ant colonies, galactic gases, investment markets, the body's immune system, Saharan drought or monsoon flood, Brownian movement, the cerebrospinal nervous system, fast-moving clouds of cumuli or starlings, even competitive research on a new remedial molecule. Such activity often appears to be without method and chaotic; it may possess extraordinary dynamism and bewildering force. Systems they are, nonetheless, often far from simple and thus what we choose to call complex.

2

Is complexity good or bad? A system may develop into one or the other. Visualize a surgical theater where a trained team is about to clean and repair a patient's seriously infected heart valve. The officiating surgeon, anesthetist, consulting cardiologists and a neurologist, surgical nurses and several instrument technicians are all scrubbed and waiting. Complexity binds their individual tasks into working unity. The patient is wheeled in and – suddenly there is an electrical power failure. All subsystems come to a halt, complexity is turned on its head. There is still no electricity; emergency generators are inadequate. The patient can no longer be treated.[1] Complexity passes from professional promise to inability to cope.

Specialists who study complex developments, their oddities and consequences, speak of *complexity theory*. Complexity theory holds that in the evolution of a system a series of things happen, non-linear as well as linear, resulting in cause-and-effect sequences. The feedback from such emergences tends to test the self-organization, adaptation, resilience and ultimate stability of the system as a whole. As systemic complications intensify and multiply, they may edge toward system breakdown and, in the worst case, failure. The ability of a living system to resist wreckage is a confirming test, in turn, of the system's durability.

Does every system have the potential of encountering complexity? The reply is affirmative, as we shall see in detail throughout this book's many concrete (rather than abstract) examples. Weather and climate are favorites for complexity analysis. So are vehicular circulation and queuing for the ordering and delivery of foodstuffs, medicines and other priority needs. Timetables of most kinds (commercial transport and the launching of astronauts or aerospace instrumentation, among other examples) are their own watchdogs against over-complexifying, an impasse that ties down resources and impairs effectiveness. The value of sports to our physical and psychological well-being is undisputed. The quadrennial Olympic Games, both summer and winter, usually cost their sponsoring cities or regions deficit spending. Yet organizers realize the long-term advantages accruing in good will, better foreign relations and expanded tourism and trade. These are frontiers more easily managed today than yesterday.

There is little reason to doubt that our natural environment cannot benefit from such public enthusiasm. Nature is one of the best examples of complexity around and "within" us. Global awareness of our impacts on the environment is an emergent conscience only a few generations old. The industrial revolution spoiled the atmosphere and continental waters of parts of Europe, America and, ultimately, Asia. Still, the 19th century saw the birth of protected areas such as national parks, nature-conscious associations and a spreading concern for active defense of the planet's ambience. While "green" political parties, with few exceptions, have shown little muscle in this direction – largely because their main antagonists are well-financed industrial lobbies, there is enormous room for improvement in non-governmental support for a better life for all. Such consciousness has by now permeated much of the world. Still deficient, however, is dedicated leadership in civil society as a whole.

The public has become sensitive, on the other hand, to the dramatic loss of biological diversity. Species of many groups of organisms, in particular of the most complex ecosystems such as tropical rainforests and coral reefs, disappear at a rapid rate. Global climate change, essentially a result of anthropogenic (human-caused) origin is now universal. The melting of glaciers, the thawing of subterranean zones under permafrost, extreme weather events and sea- level rise are just a few of the multiple changes we are already experiencing. With environmental degradation now a fact of life itself, the UN stepped on stage. With major conferences held in 1972 (Stockholm) and 1992 (Rio de Janeiro) and a long regional series since then, the UN assumed the role of midwife in the nascence of major projects at world level to combat the degradation of nature. And today, the UN remains the major agent for sufficiently drastic change.

Our treatment of complexity also looks into the problems faced and solved by industry, often through political pressure. The "greening" of industry and trade has begun with the adoption of rational strategies at sectoral and corporate level. Not much new effort is required to avoid the excesses to which complexity in modern business practice may lead. Sound political decision at both national and global levels should remain the prime mover in simplifying complexity; shortcuts and other tactical expedients may be necessary to save our environment.

3

Conservation and sustainable development, especially when related to life, water and energy, are proving to be workable solutions, necessitating reinforced determination *to do something now*. The need for action means that past and present negligence must not become schematic of the future. The new generations deserve well-being and peace, new knowledge through education and unfettered communication and the urging of progress and justice for life on the planet. These are not unattainable needs. They are real, heavily risk-laden, but pressing.

The pathways to paradise are paved, to vary the usual bromide, with flaws and misjudgment. The already complex world of international relations is itself a convoluted cultural brew. Take, for example, criminal justice sought by sovereign states having among them incompatible judiciaries. Or the intergovernmental headache of rogue states and a handful of other resistants to reasoned, systematic and negotiated agreement. The overarching process of the UN is the tested way forward despite its vulnerability to national or regional obstinacy, if not selfishness – the undermining of consensus.

Other vital aspects of international relations and diplomacy are a) international trade (in the globalized world, tantamount to the basis for most political agreements) and b) foreign aid offered for national development. These key extensions of the foreign relations of a sovereign state have become indispensable to inter-nation intercourse.

We have not excluded the military context. It imposes itself since well before the annals of Thucydides on the Peloponnesian wars. We examined warfare through a functional microscope of its own. Complexity in military operations implies a contradiction in outcome. Complexity for one side usually means victory for that side (good decisions were made), defeat for the other (bad decisions prevailed). These effects may be reversed in a subsequent conflict. This system translates itself into a structured game, usually vicious but replete with lessons for the future. Difficult as this may be, such complexity is an unwelcome adjunct of life and living.

Fortunately, many other complexities provide satisfaction and even pleasure or delight by their felicitous resolution.

Walter Erdelen and Jacques Richardson

Note

1 Precisely these conditions befell a friend of one of the authors, scheduled to be treated in a Manhattan surgery early in the morning of 11 September 2001 when, extraneously but collaterally, terrorist-piloted commercial aircraft struck New York City. With the power failure, the inoperable patient died shortly after.

Acknowledgments

We are grateful for the encouragement by Hon. Margaret Austin, who reviewed chapters and agreed to prepare the Foreword. We also thank Wilhelm Konle for assisting with layout, his technical astuteness and knack for rectifying matters once that we got stuck with our own computer systems. As to the substance of our thesis, we thank Sidney Passman and his perceptive information service, helping us better understand the role of scientists and engineers in coping with large-scale problems not usually confronted by diplomats.

We had also the wisdom of specialists who commented on individual chapters: Janos Bogardi, Han Qunli, Chuck Hopkins, Dominique Livet, Jan Visser, Jan Zalasiewicz. Alain Dyèvre wondered unceasingly about the novelty of complexity, asking, "What do we know of the simplicity of nature before the Big Bang?" And Misha Taniuchi lent us her talents as technical editor with rigorous copyediting and insistence that our message be as clear as crystal. We also credit our charming editors at Routledge, Rebecca Brennan, Leila Walker, and Jennifer Bonnar with her colleagues, for their thorough professionalism. All became generous partners in a single endeavor to popularize complexity and its effects on systems.

We are grateful to all friends and colleagues who – upon our request and with almost relativistic speed – sent us information, materials or reprints of their publications.

Of course, any errors and deficiencies, as well as the opinions and interpretations expressed, remain the authors' responsibilities.

Abbreviations and acronyms

AAAS	American Association for the Advancement of Science
BECCS	Bioenergy with carbon capture and storage
BP	British Petroleum
CBD	Convention on Biological Diversity
CDR	Carbon dioxide removal
CITES	Convention on International Trade in Endangered Species of Wild Fauna and Flora
CLA	Causal layered analysis
CMS	Convention on the Conservation of Migratory Species of Wild Animals
COMEST	World Commission on the Ethics of Scientific Knowledge and Technology
COP	Conference of the Parties
DDT	Dichlorodiphenyltrichloroethane (synthetic insecticide)
DESD	Decade of Education for Sustainable Development
EEAS	European External Action Service
EFA	Education for All (program)
ESD	Education for Sustainable Development
ESSP	Earth System Science Partnership
ETC	ETC Group, Action Group on Erosion, Technology and Concentration, an international civil society organization (CSO)
EU	European Union
FAO	Food and Agriculture Organization (of the UN)
GAP	Global Action Plan (on Education for Sustainable Development)
GATT	(UN) General Agreement on Tariffs and Trade
GBO	Global Biodiversity Outlook
GCOS	Global Climate Observing System
GDP	Gross domestic product
GHG	Greenhouse gases
GNP	Gross national product
GPS	Global positioning system
GUNI	Global University Network for Innovation
ICIMOD	International Center for Integrated Mountain Development

Abbreviations and acronyms

ICSU	International Council for Science
ICT	Information and communication technologies
IGBP	International Geosphere-Biosphere Program
IGO	Intergovernmental organization
IHDP	International Human Dimensions Program on Global Environmental Change
IHP	International Hydrological Program
IIASA	International Institute for Applied Systems Analysis
IISD	International Institute for Sustainable Development
INSERM	Institut National de la Santé et de la Recherche Médicale
IOM	International Organization for Migration (a UN agency)
IPBES	Intergovernmental Platform on Biodiversity and Ecosystem Services
IPCC	Intergovernmental Panel on Climate Change
IPPC	International Plant Protection Convention
ISSC	International Social Science Council
IT	Information technology
ITPGRFA	International Treaty on Plant Genetic Resources for Food and Agriculture
IUCN	International Union for Conservation of Nature
IUGS	International Union of Geological Sciences
LDCs	Least developed countries
MDGs	Millennium Development Goals
MEA	*Millennium Ecosystem Assessment*
MOOC	Massive online open course
NASA	National Aeronautics and Space Administration
NATO	North Atlantic Treaty Organization
NETs	Negative emission technologies
NGO	Non-governmental organization
OECD	Organization for Economic Cooperation and Development
OR	Operational research (operational analysis)
PDA	Personal digital assistant
PLA	(Chinese) People's Liberation Army
RAF	(British) Royal Air Force
R&D	Research and development
SAB	Scientific Advisory Board (of the UN Secretary-General)
S&T	Science and technology
SCBD	Secretariat of the Convention on Biological Diversity
SD	Sustainable development
SDG	Sustainable Development Goals(s)
SIDS	Small Island Developing States
SRM	Solar radiation management
SSC	Species Survival Commission (of IUCN)
STEM	Science, technology, engineering, mathematics
STI	Science, technology and innovation
SUNY	State University of New York

TBR	Transboundary Biosphere Reserve
TTIP	Transatlantic/Transpacific Trade and Investment Partnership
UN	United Nations
UNCCD	UN Convention to Combat Desertification
UNCED	UN Conference on Environment and Development
UNDESA	UN Department of Economic and Social Affairs
UNDP	UN Development Program
UNEP	UN Environment Program
UNESCO	UN Educational, Scientific and Cultural Organization
UNFCCC	UN Framework Convention on Climate Change
UNHCR	UN High Commissioner for Refugees
USD	United States dollars
VW	Volkswagen (People's Car)
WCED	World Commission on Environment and Development
WCRP	World Climate Research Program
WCS	World Conference on Science
WHC	World Heritage Convention
WIPO	World Intellectual Property Organization
WMO	World Meteorological Organization
WSSD	World Summit on Sustainable Development
WWF	World Wide Fund for Nature

*ICSU and ISSC have merged and are now the International Science Council (ISC).

1 Introduction
Setting the scene

This book's title has three integrated components, *complexity, system and strategy*. The authors apply these terms by keeping them in mutual context, here defined. Strategy is an overall plan for estimation, organization, and implementation of action according to circumstances. In his book of 1982, *Science sans conscience* (best translated as Knowledge without Conscience), sociologist Edgar Morin referred to system as *concept* and to complexity as *paradigm*. Morin has pioneered in introducing the complexity phenomenon to social scientists, educators and philosophers (see e.g. Morin 2001). We believe that his terminology should stand.

A system is a regularly interacting or interdependent group of items forming a unified whole. By use of the term of Earth systems, we include the systems conceived by *Homo sapiens* and put to its use. Every system has spatial and temporal boundaries, surrounded and influenced by its environment, described by its structure and purpose, and expressed by its function(s). System, implying movement or action, embodies probably universally the cause-and-effect relationship.

The term *system* derives from the Greek σύστημα (*sustēma*): a "whole concept made of several parts or members." The word "system" derives from the Greek "sunhistanai" which means "to place together."

As Fritjof Capra observed in *The Web of Life* (1997), "a system has come to mean an integrated whole whose essential properties arise from the relationships between its parts" and that "systems cannot be understood by analysis" but "only within the context of the larger whole." This upsets the Cartesian paradigm that, in complex systems, the behavior of the whole can be understood entirely through the properties of its parts.

We find systems almost everywhere: In culture and economics, logic, information theory and computer-related models, in numerous other scientific disciplines, management. We refer, moreover, to organic systems in medicine, to complex or conceptually formal and non-formal systems, to subsystems, metasystems and even systems of systems as well as hybrid systems. Sufficiently trained in mathematics, your authors prefer not to wonder what lies on either side of a complexity equation's equal sign.

Evidence of complexity and its effects intrigue us immensely. We exclude debate on complexity theory by what researchers D. Chu, R. Strand and R. Fjelland stressed in an earlier treatise, "Theories of Complexity" – namely, "that whatever definition one might one day agree on, contextuality and radical openness are essential features of complexity. Both properties are clarified by means of [. . .] example and implications for a future theory of complexity" (see Chu et al. 2003).

Applying a systemic view seems most appropriate for this book's chapters relating to Earth, climate, water, biodiversity, the UN, diplomacy, education, science, innovation, politics, migration, trade, the military and philosophy.

Complexity (and complex systems)

Second, complexity. This alludes to something with two or more parts interacting with each other in multiple ways and creating a high order of emergence, an idea commonly referred to as "greater than the sum of its parts." In complex systems, "emergent properties at any level must be consistent with interaction specified at the lower level(s)" (Holland 2014). Also emerging at the time were human-made, truly complex systems for application in information theory, supersonic flight, aerospace exploration, instantaneous telecommunications and remote medical therapy.

A familiar quotation states, "There is no absolute definition of complexity, there is only consensus that there is no agreement about the definition of what complexity means." What is considered *complex* or *simple* is relative and changes with time. What is complex can be typified, nevertheless, through a number of different but rigorous approaches to the observation. Complexity, including networks (as perceived through analysis of nodes-and-links arrangements) may lead to seemingly extreme disorder (chaos theory).

There is agreement that complex systems may be unique in their individual attributes, yet have many interconnected components. There does not exist, however, a universal definition of a complex system. It is nevertheless possible to use, in addition to mathematical equations, narrative and methods allowing identification, design, exploration and interaction among such systems – and these appear throughout the present volume.

Complex systems may be further characterized through their *self-organization* into patterns, *chaotic behavior* (small shifts in initial conditions give way to large changes), *fat-tailed behavior* (rare events occur more frequently than would be predicted from a normal or bell-shaped distribution), *adaptive interaction* (interacting agents modify their strategies diversely as experience accrues), and *emergent behavior* (Holland 2014).

The authors seek to familiarize concerned readers with the particular nature of some systems, both natural and human-made, their interrelationships and results as well as (often) second-order consequences. Citing scores of practical cases, the authors describe especially utilitarian measures together with algorithms for the handling of specific problems. Treatment is interdisciplinary, intercultural and international in scope. We introduce to the non-scientific reader the new geological era of the Anthropocene.

Among the themes selected are major issue challenges: water management, biological diversity, climate change, public security, migration, foreign relations, innovation and planning for the future. The prevention of incapacitating war is treated by drawing on major lessons from recent history.

Within disciplines or other broad sweeps of human endeavor, this book reflects a multidisciplinary approach, differing from the mode in other books on procedural complexity. There is emphasis on the intervening role of *Homo sapiens*, whose agency is often at the root of large-scale obstacles or constraints.

Existing books on complexity concentrate on popularization for general and younger readers, but are suitable for university-bound readers. *Theories* on complexity, as we have suggested, may exceed empirical accounts. Pedro Ferreira of MIT turned a seminar on complexity theory into a valuable volume, *Tracing Complexity Theory*. Elsewhere, Jens Jäger and his colleagues have put complexity to work on, for example, marketing-oriented value networks. Journals specializing in systems and complexity will help the reader satisfy his or her curiosity about particular complications.

Our clientele comprises generally educated adults who are required to recommend or make decisions, propose policy, plan and apply strategy or are simply curious to learn about the condition of our planet, its interaction with the human species and our combined future. The last aim mentioned leads the reader to grasp not only what can be done about what lies ahead but realistically what has been achieved in terms of organization contrived since the UN Conference on Environment and Development (the "Earth Summit") held in Rio de Janeiro in 1992.

Complexity by selected themes

Complexity is part, therefore, of life's entire dynamic model. We emphasize here, and repeat later, that all its possibilities cannot be treated in a single volume. Is the system we call democracy, for instance, limitless in its development, or inherently hobbled by systemic fragility? System advantages and shortcomings may be counterbalanced, or lapse into puzzling inertia. In response to varying pressures, natural and human systems may thereby function well or poorly.

Complexity is recognizable yet difficult to define. It cannot be measured, nor necessarily be the cause of wonder, frustration or reaction. The authors, avoiding higher mathematics and grand hypotheses, note that complexity has been the object of numerous theories during the past century. They present an amalgam of systems typifying how nature works, uniting or dividing humanity. Humans react more and more to nature's ways, in the era that specialists have named the Anthropocene. One result is that, as the "superiors" among Earth's many living things, humans are now dominating all biota and even the planet's own systems.

The authors take their views beyond analysis. They present solutions, especially regarding education, scientific research and technological advance. They explain the means proposed, globally through guidance provided by the UN system, confronting head-on (for example) climate change and sustainable development with pragmatic algorithms to minimize complexity.

Climate change prevails, the world over, tomorrow as today. It is the boldest challenge to us all. It means facing the future with humility, the best of our cerebral potential, and perseverance. All these defiances, complications in themselves, lead the authors to plead *Save System Homo sapiens*!

Not forgotten are activities in which contest and competition abound: industrial initiative and innovation, political policy, ethical concerns springing from egotism and corruption, the pressures of international relations and the strategic roles of military action. These spheres teem with complexity, with which humanity strives to cope by calling upon enquiring cognition, good sense and patience.

Systems and complexity – historical remarks

The brief history of systems approaches and thinking that follows can at most be a sketch of a highly diverse transdisciplinary development involving many outstanding personalities and scientists. Early roots of systems thinking date back to the ancient Greek philosophers, and the later Renaissance and Romantic periods.

Science in the 20th century revealed that analyses or analytical thinking do not lead to an understanding of living systems, not even physical systems (e.g., classical physics vs. the "new physics" including the full structure of the atom, quantum mechanics, statistical causality).

We speak of a "Gestaltproblem" in the sense of the Austrian philosopher Christian von Ehrenfels. The German term "Gestalt" was introduced into the English language and reflected what is commonly referred to as "the whole is more than the sum of its parts." This thinking triggered the movement of "Gestaltpsychologie." In parallel the new discipline of ecology – the term was coined by the German biologist Ernst Haeckel – emerged, creating notions such as food web, ecosystem and biosphere, ultimately culminating in the Gaia concept or hypothesis (Lovelock 1995).

The term or concept of a network was intimately associated with early ecological thought and led to new models at all levels of biological organization. The science of networks was born, so well-illustrated in Albert-László Barabási's book *Linked* (Barabási 2003). In nature, ultimately, networks interact with networks. We speak of nested, non-hierarchical or – as in particular in ecosystem ecology – hierarchical systems (overview in O'Neill et al. 1986).

During the first half of the 20th century the Russian researcher Alexander Bogdanov ("Tectology;" published 1912–1917) and the Austrian biologist Ludwig von Bertalanffy developed what is now known as General Systems Theory. This was followed in the late 1940s and 1950s by Norbert Wiener's and others' work in the new field of *cybernetics* (Wiener had coined the term), commonly defined as the science of control and communication of humans, other living organisms and machines.

Terms such as feedback loop and input/output have since enriched our vocabulary. With the availability of powerful computers new areas such as artificial intelligence and robotics were included in modern cybernetics. Ilya Prigogine, famous for his *dissipative structures*, benefiting from new mathematical methods available for the study of complexity, continued what Bertalanffy had already worked on: a new thermodynamics of open systems. Thermodynamically, living organisms may indeed be seen as open systems.

Complexity theory or non-linear dynamics are "mathematical manifestations" of complexity. As pointed out and further discussed by Capra and Luisi (2016), "Complexity theory is not a scientific theory, but rather a mathematical theory." Relationships and patterns form the backbone of this new branch of mathematics, as illustrated by terms such as strange attractors in chaos theory and fractals of fractal geometry. Complexity theory has proven a tool highly useful in many fields such as organizational change and learning, management including knowledge management, market dynamics (overviews, e.g., in Gleick 1987, Mandelbrot 2008, Senge 1990). A thought-provoking paper of the early 1990s was titled "Chaos in Ecology: Is Mother Nature a Strange Attractor?" (Hastings et al. 1993). Our new powerful computers have allowed us not only to solve non-linear equations ("numerically") but also to visualize complex systems and their behavior. Fractal geometry and chaos theory have indeed led to a reexamination of the concept of complexity itself. As Capra and Luisi (2016) put it, "The understanding of pattern is crucial to understand the living world around us, and that all questions of pattern, order, and complexity are essentially mathematical."

Complexity and systems, or "revisiting" this book's philosophy

Complexity does not offer new, methodical approaches to analyzing complex systems nor does it penetrate scientific and other theories of systems, complexity and related terminology. Rather, the book explores exposure of the human species to complex systems in diverse contexts. Emphasis is on pressing challenges to critical needs.

Discussion of a select number of themes is meant to illustrate the dilemma of today's global society: The major obstacles of our time cannot be understood in isolation; they are systemic – i.e., interconnected and interdependent, and at the same time our worldviews may be outdated in an urbanized, overpopulated and highly interconnected world. The new worldviews may (need to) be holistic and ecological. A change of paradigms is required, possibly more radical than the Copernican revolution. We need a new kind of thinking, "systemic thinking," or "systems thinking," focusing on relationships, patterns and total context (Capra and Luisi 2016).

All topics presented in this volume may be seen as a window on nature's diversity of manifestations of complexity and complex, networked systems; they are all essential for sustaining the human species on its limited resource base: planet Earth. As said in a 2005 issue of *Scientific American*, "Depending on how we manage the next few decades, we could usher in environmental sustainability – or collapse."

Complex systems form the background of our discourse. The link between theory and practice is reflected in the need to develop better functioning of the science-policy interfaces. They put our understanding of complexity and complex systems into practice – into decision-making processes, international politics and into a global governance context. The latter is massively shaped by efforts of the UN system, its organizations and constituency, the member states. The system's framework is defined through the global community's striving toward sustainable development at a time of immense challenges but also immense opportunity.

The main message here, therefore, is that a better understanding of complexity and complex systems is *sine qua non* for a sustainable and successful trajectory of humanity's journey forward. Humans will continue to seek a future ensuring them well-being – even the highest quality of life, founded on sustained resources. This must include biodiversity and its services. Education, research and a global effort to assure necessary capacities must be targeted at improving global literacy. Emphasis should be stressed on a thorough understanding of our planetary system of systems and *Homo sapiens*' impact during "its age," the Anthropocene.

Why an entire book on complexity?

Would not a journal article suffice? Complexity is obviously remote from what we call simplicity. Recognizing and dealing with the complex is one way of recognizing and assessing the challenges of living. Often a matter of routine, complexity is a permanent companion of us all. In this book, we shall look at wide-ranging examples of complexity, which we hope will lead our readers to rethink their own perceptions of and relationship with thoughts and things complex.

Would a magazine or journal article not suffice? The most decisive or divisive moments at board meetings, conferences and workshops are not always those of presentations or vote-taking but the informal exchanges over lunch or a beverage. In a similar manner, it was during a lunch in Sermaise, France when the idea of digging deeply into the many phenomena of complexity struck us as a compelling effort. This volume is the result.

Although we had worked together at UNESCO on a book (*Sixty Years of Science at UNESCO, 1945–2005*) on research and engineering fostered by that UN agency, our professional backgrounds were different. Yet we found shared ground, even many common denominators, in complexity – perceiving and understanding it and its sometimes awesome defiance.

There are reasons for complexity. Our choice of subject was not random, or something we aired lightly as our lunch progressed. Instead, we found the topic of complexity worth dissecting in pragmatic terms: comparing our perceptions and ideas, and expanding the effort to translate it all into a joint "product." We were confident, too, that there is a broadening public interest in the issues raised.

We should add that the impulse grew to embark on this endeavor in order to understand better the relevance of complexity (or its lack) in the future of the human species. More specifically, we sought to craft a critical nexus joining the sciences (both natural and social), technological advancement and political evolution. All of these form the core of our combined interests.

Omnipresent features of complex systems are "tipping points," almost always inherent in complex situations. A simple example is sterile water as it approaches zero degrees Celsius, turning the liquid to ice, or approaching 100°C, when fluid water changes state to become vapor.

Tipping points may also be less clearly conspicuous, as was the "July crisis" affecting Europe in 1914. Assassination in Montenegro of the presumptive heir to the Austro-Hungarian throne was seen by Vienna as cause for war with the assassin's homeland, Serbia. Germany's emperor, its president and its war minister put unrelenting pressure on Austria's feeble emperor of 84 years and his own war minister to declare hostilities. After a month of repetitive indecision, Austria opted for war. The cumulative tipping points also dragged on – through treaties or pangs of solidarity – for France, Russia and Germany itself. Most of Europe with the British and Ottoman empires, and much of the rest of the world found themselves drawn into a maelstrom whose effects remain discernible today. The initial complexity had tipped over into one worse by far.

There is more commentary on tipping points in Chapter 2 and farther on.

Evaluating the human enterprise

Complexity seems to be everywhere, simplicity has become rare. Many of our daily decisions seem linked to a process of selecting carefully among multiple alternatives. In fact, the life we share with our loved ones and friends is often characterized by complex patterns of behavior and competing objectives as opposed to exclusive aims, as well as day-to-day routine.

Complexity, in other words, is a fixture of life, not only in quantum physicist Erwin Schrödinger's enormous sense (see his *What is Life?* of 1944) but also in an individual sense: What is *my life* all about? The Austrian scientist's wonderment emerged about a decade after early, convergent research in biology and physics wedded with microbiology, virology and biochemistry to form the new subdiscipline of molecular biology. The aim was to understand life in its earliest forms and functions. Today, we are still trying to understand the mixed bag of personal behavior: Why do we choose to do *this* instead of *that*?

British-born archeologist and historian Ian M. Morris of Stanford University has concentrated his work on pivotal initiatives in the development of *Homo sapiens*. Paraphrasing key ideas taken from three of his many published works,[1] the salient actions of humankind are

- *Organizational ability*, from agriculture to commerce to government to urbanism (as examples),
- *Energy capture*, whether from plants or animals and their derivatives (and ulteriorly from renewable sources),
- *Processing and communicating information*, and, regrettably,
- *The capacity to make war* – i.e., turning the first three achievements toward aggression and devastation.

It is from these four key domains of human effort that we seek, in this book, to break down the anatomy and physiology of complexity. Treading our way through Morris' four domains, we meet simplicity perhaps less often than we like, complications more frequently, and complexity (especially when inauspicious) on more occasions than expected.

What philosopher Karl Jaspers, in *Vom Ursprung und Ziel der Geschichte* (On the Origin and Goal of History) of 1949, termed the Axial age – roughly the millennium before the birth of Christ – witnessed the creation of what he called the core of modern civilization. This was the era in which the four action domains proposed by Ian Morris most likely solidified in shape, functions, complexity and effects of durable groupings of activity that we call systems. This is consequently the world which we inhabit today and, one earnestly hopes, for a long time ahead.

The motivating elements of the Axial age are compassion, the Golden Rule, discovery of morality, non-violence and equal access by everyone (hypothetically, at least) to the new understanding. As values representing the quality of life, all the elements have not always been present, yet their existence has assured a continuing ambience that has been, all in all, more peaceful than aggressive or violent.

Expanding the system concept

These codes of belief and guidance date most probably, according to Jaspers, from when humans took on a consistency of behavior in an expanding geocultural context. Lasting character was largely influenced in the East by Confucian and Taoist texts, in South Asia by Buddhist and Jain teaching, and in the West by the Hebrew Bible, Greek philosophy, the New Testament and (in the 7th and 8th centuries) by the Qu'ran. The system, or systems, of humankind continued to assume complication of form and complexity of application, intra-action and, inevitably, interaction and effect.

As complexity broadened, so did system fragility and often, the very opposite: surprising robustness. Today, system infirmity remains perplexing, frequently without remedy. Why, for instance, do some countries vote in favor of UN resolutions and then consistently contravene or fail to apply them? Vulnerable mechanisms include plant and animal health; sustained biodiversity; the ocean-weather complex; water conservation, distribution and management; economic inconsistencies; competitive social goals; and mutual disrespect of religions.

The concepts of complication and complexity have much the same imagined configuration: influences, immediate cause, setting, incremental advance, effects, potential consequences (even indirectly) and impacts on public opinion. The essential difference between the two constructs is that complication is relatively simple to perceive and manage, whereas complexity is often utterly complicated and commensurately difficult or impossible to accept and resolve.

The Roman road system, for example, begun during the Axial age and reaching its height of performance during the centuries of the Roman Empire, dealt with the complications of building straight highways, somewhat elevated in surface –

"high-crowned" – for quick drainage, as well as resistant to the ravages of wind, flooding, vehicular weight, trampling and other wear and tear of its hardened surfaces. The system also satisfied the need for the rapid conveyance of troops, in the shortest time possible, between geographic points widely separated and often plagued by hostile peoples or roving bandits and bad weather: the very complexity of a road network. Roman army engineers built a fabric of 80,000 kilometers of roads, usually 12 meters in width, not only westwards in Europe but also southwards in North Africa and as far east as present-day Iraq.[2] Many of their stone bridges survive, two millennia after their construction. By contrast the Romans failed to dominate wholly the Germanic tribes to the north because of their heavily forested habitat that lacked even the first rutted tracks of a road web.

Systems already complicated become more intricate

Roughly a millennium later, in the Andes of Peru, civil and hydraulic engineers (without those designations) devised and built the sanctuary community of Machu Picchu at an altitude of 2,400 meters (almost 8,000 feet). The sole access route was mastered along steep mountainsides by carefully studied grading and surfacing, and the storage and distribution of sufficient fresh water supplies was skillfully arranged by the accurate localization of underground sources and the construction of stone-lined storage "fountains" that were virtually leakproof.

Perhaps a satisfying way to compare and contrast complication and complexity is to take an historical incident and describe it according to two major abstractions: a proffered would-be explanation, and the truth. Our example is the loss of a Russian commercial aircraft, en route from Sharm el Sheik in Egypt to St. Petersburg, Russia, on 31 October 2015. Recounting the story emphasizes the expanding international implications (complexity) of what happened. At first limited to an action involving two countries, its ripples spread far and wide.

Some 45,000 Russian tourists were vacationing in and around the Sharm el Sheik resort on the shores of the Red Sea. Early in the morning of 31 October 2015, 224 passengers and crew boarded an 18-year old Airbus A-321, which (according to Russian statements) had recently been inspected mechanically. The Russian-owned airliner was scheduled to arrive in St. Petersburg later the same day. Less than half an hour after takeoff, in clear weather, the Airbus exploded in midair. The aircraft fell in fragments, its debris spilling over an area some 4 kilometers in diameter. Everyone aboard perished.

Searchers soon found the plane's two "black boxes," sent immediately to Egyptian technical authorities for examination and analysis. A week's study of recorded performance data and crew conversations indicated a sudden loud noise heard aboard the aircraft, and silence thereafter. The world's media assumed the loud sound was caused by an explosive device illicitly placed inside the aircraft, yet Russian and Egyptian denials continued until the Russian president ordered the return of all Russian holiday makers in Egypt.

For the Egyptians, their vital tourist economy was at stake; they preferred avoiding mention of bombs. American and British sources confirmed, however, that satellite imagery had recorded a brilliant explosion in the sky above the Sinai Peninsula's desert in the morning of 31 October. Less than three weeks after the disaster, Russian sources admitted that there had been an explosion, detected through fragments found on a soft-drink container bearing traces of expended explosive.

One assumes, therefore, that there was introduction of an explosive device aboard the Airbus: it was likely a relatively simple procedure since the airport at Sharm el Sheik was known for its almost total lack of physical and technical security. The ill-fated aircraft had been parked overnight near a terminal building, without adequate guards and, in the words of a retired employee of the installation recorded by French radio journalists, the plane could easily have been boarded by anyone bribing airport guards and even police in order to visit the vacant airliner.

We can speculate that the destructive system installed at Sharm el Sheik was a fairly closed one not requiring ignition from a distance and thus relatively simple to manage. A band of terrorists, probably jihadists, objecting strongly to President Vladimir Putin's decision to commit Russian resources to fight the enemies – including the self-styled Islamic State, or Daesh – of the Syrian president, Bashar al Assad, decided to act. Motivation was therefore strong. The terrorists' leadership opted for reprisal and, mindful of the worldwide reaction a year earlier when a Russian-made missile destroyed a Malaysian airliner over the battlefields of Ukraine, decided on a similar assault.

Coping with complications already known

We continue our hypothesis. Orders were accordingly passed to local subordinates, probably avoiding communication by the Internet and its social networks in order to preclude electronic interception. A local team or individual, selected for proximity to the Russian aircraft target, was ordered to obtain explosives, survey and assess the target's configuration, and finally board the plane, select an appropriate niche to conceal the explosive, set its timer for a mid-morning hour and then leave the target – very likely unchallenged and undisturbed during the job being done. Whatever *complications* were foreseen, they were met and resolved immediately and ultimately had the desired effect.

We have thus felt our way and explored some of the intricacies arising from interaction between individuals and their social sets – another one or more human beings acting in concert, but inside specific boundaries and with specified aims. In our example, the system was, in other words, self-adjusting.

Also we need to consider, besides methods of work, the interactions between people and the tools and services they require to finish a piece of handiwork, or to adapt a tool or other application to facilitate work and duly exploit the energy needed to do the job. The simplest task may go wrong for a number of technical reasons so that complicated work may face combinations of delay requiring adaptation by executants. These are pragmatic risks. One professional source lists nearly a dozen such shortcomings, as follows next.[3] We have altered the sequence of potential anomalies for the purposes of our aircraft-destruction example. In addition to these structural handicaps, unexpected human intervention may frustrate planning, such as the arrival of a cleaner or alert watchman.

1. Design errors or design deficiencies
2. Improper, poor selection of materials
3. Casting discontinuities
4. Manufacturing defects
5. Improper heat treatment
6. Errors of assembly
7. Unforeseen operating conditions
8. Misuse or abuse
9. Inadequate quality assurance
10. Improper or inadequate maintenance
11. Inadequate environmental protection/control

The authors of this list of defects are apparently mechanical engineers, who add that failure by fracture of materials may also occur because of static overload (too much mass to handle), leading to fracture. Other causes of device or functional fault may appear as buckling of material, misalignment, overloading of other components, poor yield (output), failure of construction materials chosen, shock, excessive wear and corrosion. If we extend these shortcomings to system scale, the probability of error or failure rises accordingly.

Deficiencies of the kinds suggested do not necessarily occur in natural systems, those not created by humanity. They may be identified, however, by engineers, textile designers, architects, inventors of many sorts, surgeons, astronomers, naval architects, dietitians or deep-sea divers, among many others. Faults thus occur – as does success – through human agency, whatever its quality, running along a scale extending from the zeal to achieve downwards through casual handling to inexcusable sloppiness. Some humans at Sharm el Sheik applied zeal to their murderous work, and it was surely zeal that produced the results desired in the case of the A-321 overflying the Sinai Desert.

Wanton use of the machine

The cargo ship *Modern Express*, launched in South Korean shipyards in 2000, is 164 meters long, diesel-powered and registered in Panama. Owned by Asians, the ship served some years as a ferry shuttling passenger cars and trucks between East Asian ports. The vessel's hold is cavernous and not intended for the stowage of heavy materials in bulk. The ship and its Philippine crew were leased to European importers of fine tropical wood to transport 3,600 tons of tree trunks and assorted materials-handling equipment (tractors, log claws) from Gabon in West Africa to the Channel port of Antwerp, a routine operation in the fine-timber trade. A first complication was a poor choice of transport for the type of cargo.

Put to sea during the typically perturbed Atlantic Ocean of mid-January (2016), the *Modern Express* encountered extremely bad weather: the second complication as it steamed from African waters northwards past the Iberian Peninsula. The vessel was battered by waves sometimes 15 meters high, and began to list severely without redressing itself: a third complication, probably caused by improperly stowed and shifting cargo. And, despite a reserve of 300 tons of fuel oil, the engines were failing as the crew became nervous and inattentive: a fourth complication. Spanish and French coast-guard frigates stood by, while helicopters from the two nations watched from overhead. By 26 January, worsening conditions in the Bay of Biscay justified removal of captain and crew by helicopter. This was the fifth complication that, legally, could presage abandonment of the vessel to any who would take possession of it.

Attempts by professional divers, sent to the ship via helicopter to attach a cable weighing 35 kilograms per meter, failed because the steel strands broke: the sixth complication. High seas, gale-force winds and driving rain persisted. The idea now was to tow the incapacitated vessel to the nearest port for adjustment of stowed cargo and probable repairs and partial refitting.

The ship's owners arranged to obtain a highly resistant polyurethane towline with two special divers brought from salvagers in the Netherlands, aboard an ocean-going tug. The duo of new divers succeeded in attaching the plastic line to the *Modern Express*, all but abandoned in the Atlantic with a precipitous list of 50°, but still floating. The series of major complications had, as mentioned, culminated in the crew's evacuation – leaving a dauntingly complex of mess for all concerned. The luckless ship was towed to Bilbao, Spain, where the port is equipped with sufficiently powerful cranes to re-stow cargo correctly. This was a potentially injudicious decision, which could have generated even more complications: grounding of the vessel in shallow waters along Europe's coastline, leaving a hazard to coastwise shipping and a possibly new source of pollution if the ship's fuel reserves had leaked into the sea. Worst, a total loss of both ship and cargo could have followed. But they succeeded. Finally, the *Modern Express* survived its repeated trials.

Systems and scale

No man is an island . . . nor is a system. A large commercial carrier belonging to an airline or a shipping firm is part of a worldwide system whose operational norms are set by competent agencies (the International Civil Aviation Organization and the International Maritime Organization) of the UN system. Member nations of these bodies have their own codes of organization, hierarchy and regulation and so may have an airline's or shipping company's ownership and management. Communication control is assured by radio, radar and for strayed or lost aircraft or ships direction-finding means. Aircraft manufacturers have their own, tamper-proof radio surveillance of in-flight performance.

The security of airports and harbors as well as their terminals and transfer facilities are a local responsibility – all of which makes a *complex* and tangled combination of obligations, problems and challenges that demand their intelligent resolution. Among the responsibilities are those of protection of passengers and crews; legal and financial commitments in case of accident or death, damage or destruction of accommodating infrastructure; and second-party (passengers, cargo and their delivery dates) as well as third-party liability.

The executants of the terrorist act striking the Russian Airbus A-321 may have been too preoccupied with their own immanent *complications* to give thought to the nature of the *complexity* or indeed of the consequences in which they were key players. This complexity involved official and public opinion in Russia, Egypt and elsewhere as in the case of the 20,000 British tourists left stranded as a consequence of the Russian catastrophe, opinion in other countries patronizing Egypt's unique tourist attractions, and economic stability within Egypt and neighboring Jordan and Tunisia of a tourist industry serving as a major source of foreign revenue.

Scale, therefore, may be a major element separating complication from greater complexity, whose respective consequences embrace subsequent impacts whether immediate or delayed and even longer-range results.

President Putin announced and may have believed that there was no criminal explosion aboard the A-321, but he did not hesitate to make transport aircraft sufficiently available for the immediate return from Egypt of all Russian tourists once the causes of the October tragedy were clear. His action was a meaningful gesture of a second kind in reassuring his nation that the Moscow government protects its people and communicating to the world that the Russian president would not yield to attackers of Russians abroad.

How to profit from complexity

A system may appear to be singular, independent and isolated (hammer and nails, knife and fork, clinical thermometer), but it remains associated in part or in whole with other systems. Holistic approach, systems theory, network analysis, Earth system science, food webs, chaos and many other terms are associated with the complexity phenomenon. They lead us to problem analyses and the potential to discover resolutions exemplified in the chapters that follow.

Is complexity thus a science? This is one of many questions intriguing us, possibly a "strange attractor" in itself, to use the jargon of chaos theory. As already phrased so nicely by physicist Neil Johnson in 2009, the phenomenon might be summed up by the quip, "Two's company, three is complexity." Johnson even argued, "We can justifiably think of complexity as a sort of umbrella science – even the Science of all Sciences."

These thoughts are our point of departure on a wide-ranging adventure in complexity. We shall deal with typical, but real, problems deriving from complexity: how some of them have been resolved, others are still puzzles needing attention as well as further methods for responding to ever larger worries.

The reader will be astonished by the imaginative work of many good minds exercising both theoretical and practical cognition. They represent the dedicated fabric of the UN system, governments, education, applied research in industry and the service sector. Their combined efforts have set global goals and pinpointed demanding tasks to be accomplished, once again earning Earth's riches – while learning better to interact with ourselves.

Before heading into the more complex topics of the Anthropocene and planetary boundaries, play a little game with us.

Question: In our account of the innocent travelers aboard a Russian airliner, what is the most likely moment at which the future of the terrorist mission was assured?

Answer: When the aircraft was last checked in and out for criminals and concealed explosives.

Q: What is the most likely tipping point in the trajectory of the Modern Express cargo vessel before it sailed from Africa?

A: This was probably at the moment when its owners decided to allot the ship its mission of delivering improperly stowed round and heavy tree trunks.

Do readers agree?

Now, come along with us to Chapter 2.

Notes

1 *Why the West Rules – For Now: The Patterns of History, and What They Reveal About the Future* (2011); *The Measure of Civilization: How Social Development Decides the Fate of Nations* (2013); and *War! What Is It Good For? Conflict and the Progress of Civilization from Primates to Robots* (2014).
2 Roman conquests via good roads included Caesar's victory over the Celtic chief Vercingetorix at Alesia (52 B.C., in Gaul) and domination over all Celts from Austria to Spain and then in Britain.
3 Malone, M. A., M. S. Salis, *Materials Selection and Design*, Berlin: Springer, 2013, Chap. 2.

References

Barabási, A.L. 2003. *Linked. How Everything Is Connected to Everything Else and What It Means for Business, Science, and Everyday Life.* Penguin, London.
Capra, F. and P.L. Luisi 2016. *The Systems View of Life: A Unifying Vision.* Cambridge University Press, Cambridge.
Chu, D., R. Strand and R. Fjelland 2003. Theories of complexity. Common denominators of complex systems. *Complexity* 8: 19–30.
Gleick, J. 1987. *Chaos. The Amazing Science of the Unpredictable.* Minerva, London.
Hastings, A., C.L. Hom, S. Ellner, P. Turchin and H.C. Godfray 1993. Chaos in ecology: Is mother nature a strange attractor? *Annual Review of Ecology and Systematics* 24: 1–33.
Holland, J.H. 2014. *Complexity: A Very Short Introduction.* Oxford University Press, Oxford.
Lovelock, J. 1995. *The Ages of Gaia: A Biography of Our Living Earth.* Norton, New York.
Mandelbrot, B.B. 2008. *The (Mis)Behavior of Markets. A Fractal View of Risk, Ruin and Reward.* Profile Books, London.
O'Neill, R.V., D.L. DeAngelis, J.B. Waide and T.F.H. Allen 1986. *A Hierarchical Concept of Ecosystems.* Princeton University Press. Princeton.
Senge, P.M. 1990. *The Fifth Discipline. The Art & Practice of The Learning Organization.* Century Business, London.
von Bertalanffy, L. 1968. *General System Theory: Foundations, Development, Applications.* George Braziller, New York.

2 The Anthropocene and planetary boundaries
Conditioners of sustainable development

Preservation of our natural milieu has not always been a priority. In the Introduction we cited typical examples of everyday complexity, some of them curious indeed and not connected with nature. The present chapter is a nuts-and-bolts tally of what *Home sapiens* has done to nature, whether unwittingly or fully aware of the changes imposed by our species. For deniers of global change, protesting against those who try to protect the planet, naming and calculating the damage may provide a thought-provoking perspective.

Earth in the intellect: new concepts and terminology

This chapter deals with two aspects of complexity reflecting the increased diversity and extent of interactions between humans and their environment. These are the notions of the Anthropocene and of planetary boundaries.

Impacts of the human species on Earth systems have become so severe that scientists propose a resultant new geological epoch, the Anthropocene. Human-induced system stresses have created awareness that this evolution may ultimately backfire on us in unpredictable ways. Systemic stress should not be pushed to states beyond certain thresholds to ensure a safe operating space for humanity. These thresholds we call the planetary boundaries.

Humans have added their footprint to nature's complexity. They have also induced changes which may shape the lives of future generations. This is reflected in the new terminology and in, *inter alia*, explorations of a global development agenda by the UN system. We discuss in this overview what may be disastrously at stake, based on recent insights into how we have been treating Mother Earth.

The novel term *Anthropocene* has been widely recognized since around the year 2000. The concept has "enjoyed a truly meteoric career" since that time (Malm and Hornborg 2014). The new term is meant to characterize the time demarcating a new period in the stratigraphy (geological history) of our globe. This has proved to be a thoroughgoing transformation of Earth by the human species, outcompeting what many call the traditional natural forces: human impact versus the "Great Forces of Nature" (see Steffen et al. 2015a, for a more recent overview).

In a seminal paper on global change, Steffen et al. (2011b) emphasized,

> Over the past century, the total material wealth of humanity has been enhanced. However, in the twenty-first century, we face scarcity in critical resources, the degradation of ecosystem services, and the erosion of the planet's capability to absorb our wastes. Equity issues remain stubbornly difficult to solve. *The situation is novel in its speed, its global scale and its threat to the resilience of the Earth System.*
>
> (Italics ours)

The impoverishment of traditional analysis

The novel term *Anthropocene* came to the world's scientific circles when Paul Crutzen, Nobel Laureate in chemistry and well reputed for his work on the hole in atmospheric ozone, used it during a meeting of the International Geosphere-Biosphere Program (IGBP) in 2000 (Crutzen and Stoermer 2000). He mentioned the *Anthropocene* while discussing the current geological period, the Holocene. Crutzen stated,

> We are no longer living in the Holocene, because the Holocene is characterized by relatively little influence of humans on the environment which no longer applies to the present. A new epoch has started: the Anthropocene, the age of man on the planet.

Following the IGBP conference Crutzen and his American colleague Stoermer suggested renaming the current geological period Anthropocene (Crutzen and Stoermer 2000). In a contribution to the prestigious journal *Nature* entitled "The Geology of Mankind," this was reiterated by Crutzen in 2002, as follows:

> The rapid expansion of mankind in numbers and per capita exploitation of the Earth's resources has continued apace. . . . Unless there is a global catastrophe – a meteorite impact, a world war or a pandemic – mankind will remain a major force for many millennia. A daunting task lies ahead for scientists and engineers to guide society towards environmentally sustainable management during the era of the Anthropocene.

As Joseph Stromberg, a science reporter, stated in the *Smithsonian Newsletter* of January 2013,

> According to the International Union of Geological Sciences (IUGS), the professional organization in charge of defining earth's time scale, we are officially in the Holocene ("entirely recent") epoch, which began 11,700 years ago [. . .] But that label is outdated [. . .] because humankind has caused mass extinctions of plant and animal species, polluted the oceans and altered the atmosphere, among other lasting impacts.

Realizing that humans are the dominant factor shaping the future of planet Earth had been recognized earlier. In the 19th century the outstanding impact of humans on the environment was already realized as a "new telluric force which in power and universality may be compared to the greater forces of Earth," terms such as "anthropozoic era," "noösphere" and others were suggested. (See also Steffen et al. 2011a, Zalasiewicz and Waters 2015).

There has been considerable criticism of the term Anthropocene, including of the use of this term to formally label a new interval of Earth's history. Meanwhile the term has become an environmental buzzword and is widely used in scientific literature (using Google to search for publications related to the Anthropocene shows this clearly). Such comments apply not only to the many environmental challenges we face but also to disciplines covering *Homo sapiens* as a component of socio-ecological systems and the quest for the resilience of these systems. In 2013,

> the word picked up velocity in elite science circles: it appeared in nearly 200 peer-reviewed articles, the publisher Elsevier has launched a new academic journal titled Anthropocene, and the IUGS convened a group of scholars to decide by 2016 whether to declare officially that the Holocene is over and the Anthropocene has begun.
>
> (Stromberg 2013)

Earth in its mass: knowledge found in layers

Autin and Holbrook (2012) advance the introduction of the Anthropocene as a new geologic epoch serving to identify the period since humanity became an Earth system driver. These authors highlight problems associated with

- identification of a basal boundary for the Anthropocene and its validation with a global stratigraphic marker, and
- the question of amending the formal time nomenclature by the inclusion of the newly suggested epoch.

The beginning of the Anthropocene is associated with different events in human history. Ruddiman (2013) uses the time when humans abandoned hunter-gatherer lifestyles for subsistence settlement, animal domestication and cultivation agriculture, commonly referred to as "early Anthropocene" (see also the Palaeoanthropocene of Foley et al. 2013). Crutzen and Stoermer proposed the time since the onset of the Industrial Revolution – i.e., the latter part of the 18th century (Crutzen 2002). Steffen et al. (2011a) suggested the period following the Second World War, as did Zalasiewicz et al. (2015), and the evidence collated in Waters et al. (2016) was consistent with such a level.

Autin and Holbrook (2012) put it thusly:

> Before we amend our stratigraphy and end the Holocene, it would be best to settle the question of where in the stratigraphic record to drive the golden

spike that defines when humanity became one of the preeminent forces of nature.

In their response to Autin and Holbrook, Zalasiewicz et al. (2012) highlighted that

> the issue here is not the presence or absence of human traces in the strata. It is whether Earth's stratigraphic record – and the processes that shape it – have changed sufficiently to make a new unit justifiable and useful and, if so, to seek the most effectively traceable boundary horizon for it.

Without doubt humans meanwhile have left stunning marks on the planet since the Paleolithic period. Terms and concepts like anthromes, technofossils and technosphere, archeosphere and anthroturbation have become center stage of discussions of human impacts (overview in Zalasiewicz and Waters 2015). These markers reflect the most recent changes in humans' production and consumption patterns related to biomass, natural resources and goods produced creating new patterns of global energy flow as needed to sustain complex modern societies (Williams et al. 2016).

Zalasiewicz and Waters (2015) have provided stunning information of how humans changed the Earth's face since mid-20th century: Since about 1950, the world has produced almost 500 million tons of aluminum. This metal could coat the United States and parts of Canada in standard kitchen foil. Novel minerals include boron nitride (harder than diamond), tungsten carbide (for ball-point pens), special garnets (for lasers) and graphene. Some 6 billion tons of plastic, invented early in the 1900s, have been produced during the same decades. New rock forms have been devised: modified concrete, fire-resistant brick, cinder and cement blocks and improved macadam. The total amount of concrete poured comes to 1kg for every square meter of Earth's surface. The global road network is about the distance between Earth and Mars (*circa* 50 million km). Human burrowing (or anthroturbation) penetrates Earth up to several kilometers in-depth. The total length of oil boreholes may be equal to that of the global road network. Since 1945, radionuclides have been dispersed worldwide, essentially a result of nuclear testing and major nuclear accidents such as in the United Kingdom, Ukraine and Japan.

We hesitate to elaborate these abuses. Perhaps the major obstacle to introducing the Anthropocene is that it cannot be viewed with the hindsight applicable to other geologic epochs. On the contrary, we can use only the insight provided by our presence in the midst of current circumstances. In sum, the Anthropocene is a new conception; its discussion reflects work in progress (see Box 2.1).

Last but not least the concept itself reflects an "add-on" to Earth system behavior and environmental processes that have not only increased the complexity of the Earth system of systems immensely but also may seriously affect the future of the major driver itself – humankind.

As pointed out by Braje and Erlandson (2013), the most important attribute of the Anthropocene may be its use as a public communication tool and the "esoteric debate over 'stratigraphic nomenclature' . . . may be less important than the message it conveys to our global community and the future of human-environmental interactions."

Box 2.1 Dissension in scientific ranks

Many stratigraphers criticize the anthropocenic idea: clear-cut evidence of a new epoch simply isn't there. "When you start naming geologic-time terms, you need to define what exactly the boundary is, where it appears in the rock strata," says Whitney Autin, a stratigrapher at the SUNY College of Brockport. He suggests Anthropocene is more about pop culture than hard science. The crucial question, he says, is specifying exactly when human beings began to leave their mark on the planet: The atomic era, for instance, has left traces of radiation in soils around the globe, while deeper down in the rock strata, agriculture's signature in Europe can be detected as far back as AD 900. The Anthropocene, according to Autin, "provides eye-catching jargon, but from the geologic side, I need the bare bones facts that fit the code."

Some Anthropocene proponents concede that difficulty. But don't get bogged down in the mud, they say, just stipulate a date and move on. Will Steffen, who heads Australia National University's Climate Change Institute and has written articles with Crutzen, recommends starting the epoch with the advent of the industrial revolution in the early 1800s or with the atomic age in the 1950s. Either way, he says, the new name sends a message: "[It] will be another strong reminder to the general public that we are now having undeniable impacts on the environment at the scale of the planet as a whole, so much so that a new geological epoch has begun."

To Andrew Revkin, a *New York Times* reporter (now blogger) who suggested a similar term in 1992 that never quite caught on ("Anthrocene"), it's significant that the issue is being debated at all. "Two billion years ago, cyanobacteria oxygenated the atmosphere and powerfully disrupted life on Earth," he says. "We're the first species that's become a planet-scale influence and is aware of that reality. That's what distinguishes us."

Source: Excerpt from Stromberg (2013)

Challenges for the global environment

Human-induced environmental changes are not a new phenomenon. Most of the biosphere has been transformed into anthropogenic biomes (*anthromes*), and anthropogenic alteration of the terrestrial biosphere has been significant for at least the last 8,000 years (Box 2.2). Recently, however, the "majority of the terrestrial biosphere has been transformed into intensively used anthromes with predominantly novel anthropogenic ecological processes" (Ellis 2011).

> Less than a quarter of Earth's ice-free land is wild; only 20 percent of this is forests and over 36 percent is barren land, and more than 80 percent of all people live in densely populated urban and village biomes.
> (Ellis and Ramankutty 2008)

The world population will probably reach 8 billion by the year 2030. In 2050, around 10 billion humans may inhabit the planet. The median projection is 9.6 billion; its range is 8.3–11.0 billion; see references in Bradshaw and Brook (2014). Energy consumption by humans, largely exploiting fossil fuels, has little or no precedent in Earth history. The resultant CO_2 buildup in the atmosphere has reached levels "not seen since Pliocene times" (Zalasiewicz et al. 2012). The current debate on climate change discusses scenarios of global warming between 2°C and 4°C until the end of the current century (see chapter on climate change). Perturbation, or disordering, of the nitrogen cycle has been enormous, transcending nitrogen's planetary boundary (see Steffen et al. 2015b). Scientists speak of a sixth mass extinction with regard to present rates of species extinction (Barnosky et al. 2011; Kolbert 2014; an overview of defaunation is given in Dirzo et al. 2014; see also this book's chapter on biodiversity).

Box 2.2   Chronology of major human impacts on the biosphere

Human stone tools	2.5 mybp
Anatomically modern humans	c. 200 kyr
Culturally modern humans	70–50 kyr
Domestication of plants and animals	c. 14 kyr
Anthromes subsuming natural landscapes	10 kyr
Beginning of urbanization	8 kyr
Jethro Tull and mechanized farming	1701
Industrial-scale use of fossil fuels	1709
Gregor Mendel and genetics	1856
Concentration of humans in huge cities	1900
Haber-Bosch ammonia synthesis	1909
Green revolution	1950s onwards
Human population exceeds 7 billion	2011

Source: Williams et al. (2016)

The biosphere of the Anthropocene is characterized by four major components (see also Box 2.2): The global homogenization of biota, humans as the single species shaping net primary production and energy flow, human-directed evolution of species, and creation of a rapidly evolving "technosphere," increasingly interacting with the biosphere (Williams et al. 2015).

The Anthropocene and planetary boundaries

Only one year after the ground-breaking paper on planetary boundaries had been published by Rockström et al. (2009a), Zalasiewicz et al. (2010) pointed out the link between the Anthropocene and the concept of planetary boundaries. The Anthropocene was mentioned in the two key papers by Rockström et al. (2009a, 2009b), possibly a result of the co-authorship and exchange of ideas among major proponents of the idea of the Anthropocene in the monographs on planetary boundaries.

The concept of planetary boundaries may be a logical extension of perceiving "the human factor" as a major driver of current Earth system processes and the resulting quest to identify major processes. For this, it is necessary to define planetary boundaries and quantify the respective safe operating spaces for humanity.

In other words, human activities may push the Earth system or its subsystems outside the stable states they were in during the Holocene, with large-scale detrimental or catastrophic consequences. The Earth's systems are clearly complex systems which may react smoothly to changing pressures. They may also react in non-linear and abrupt fashion around threshold levels. Crossing such thresholds may trigger shifts into a new state with enormous consequences (for details, see Rockström et al. 2009b).

In their classical papers on planetary boundaries Rockström et al. (2009a, 2009b) identified nine planetary boundary categories. Of these, seven were quantified (numbers 1 to 7).

1   Climate change
2   Rate of biodiversity loss
3   Interference with nitrogen and phosphorus cycles
4   Stratospheric ozone depletion
5   Ocean acidification
6   Global freshwater use
7   Change in land use
8   Chemical pollution
9   Aerosol loading of atmosphere

For the last two, no boundary levels have yet been presented. As explained in *Big World Small Planet*, a book of 2016 by Johan Rockström and the photographer Mattias Klum, the major reason why these two factors are difficult to quantify is their enormous complexity. They depend on many parameters, such as the vast range of chemical compounds and pollutants involved. Because chemical pollution is determined by chemical compounds of anthropogenic origin, the boundary for this type of pollution is now assigned to the category "new entities." Steffen et al. (2015b) define these as "new substances, new forms of existing substances, and modified life forms that have the potential for unwanted geophysical and/or biological effects." The authors note that more than 100,000 such substances are in global commerce, a list which would be even longer if nanomaterials and plastic polymers were included. Worldwide production of chemicals and their diversity are increasing at an enormous rate.

Since the original publication of 2009, two major new developments are notable. First, boundaries are not equal but show a hierarchical pattern. Climate change and biosphere integrity (earlier called biodiversity loss) are core boundaries, connected to all other boundaries; through these two, the other boundaries operate. The boundaries in their entirety operate interdependently, connected through stabilizing or destabilizing feedback loops to the Earth system. As pointed out by Steffen et al. (2015b), "This has profound implications for global sustainability, because it emphasizes the need to address multiple interacting environmental processes simultaneously."

Secondly, the importance of local and regional levels is recognized. For every global planetary boundary, regional boundaries have been identified. This allows applying the concept of planetary boundaries at the most important policy levels: national, regional or even system-relevant level (such as a river basins). Thus a process is fostered which may facilitate policy coherence and coordination. This is prerequisite for successful top-down and bottom-up implementation of global policies. To make the boundary concept operational, control variables and associated indicators have been identified, but need not be further discussed here.

Four of the nine planetary boundary-system elements have already exceeded critical thresholds: climate change, biodiversity loss, land-system change and interference with the nitrogen and phosphorus cycle. Boundaries may soon be reached for global freshwater use and ocean acidification (for details see Steffen et al. 2015b). More recent analysis and updates for all nine boundaries are available in Rockström and Klum (2016), Steffen et al. (2015b).

Planetary boundaries, tipping points, Earth systems

Most recent discussions of the concept of planetary boundaries centered on their relation to *thresholds* or *tipping points* at various scales and for a variety of Earth systems. These debates are not only of an academic nature. They relate directly to how we manage planetary systems without risking irreversible regime shifts which may put our own future at risk. As the dynamics sketched here are intricately linked to stability concepts, a short retrospective on stability thinking will be useful.

Community or ecosystem stability has been related to complexity for decades. In ecology, complexity was in many cases related to biological diversity, in particular the number of species and/or their interactions, as related to food chain or food web structural attributes (e.g., Stuart L. Pimm's and Joel E. Cohen's work on food webs and niche space).

In the 1950s and 1960s, empirical and theoretical observations suggested that complexity may be directly linked to system stability. This was aired in the pioneering Brookhaven Symposium on *Diversity and Stability in Ecological Systems*, held in 1969, in the report of the first international congress of ecology titled *Unifying Concepts in Ecology* (1975), in ecology textbooks such as that of Begon et al. (first edition published in 1986) and many other titles.

Terms like constancy, elasticity, resilience, resistance, local, global and cyclic stability, fragility and robustness were used extensively in the ecological sciences. Complexity-stability discussions have meanwhile extended their scope from ecological/environmental to social and economic systems thus encompassing not only a wider range of systems but all the so-called pillars of sustainable development.

In sum, many of the current ideas on fragility of the Earth and its systems were already anticipated decades ago by ecologists. In parallel, this was complemented by progress in cybernetics, systems science and complexity science; notions from thermodynamics of closed and open systems enriched the debate (see introduction). *Tipping point* and *attractor* have been terms commonly used in (modern) studies of complex systems. The former gained unexpected popularity through Gladwell's book "The Tipping Point," published in 2000 and subtitled "How Little Things Can Make a Big Difference." Tipping points are points of systems' states where small changes make big differences or where a small perturbation triggers a qualitative state shift ("regime shift") of the system under study. Authors differ in their views as to whether such change generally occurs rapidly or slowly (e.g., discussion in Lenton and Williams 2013).

The debate on complexity and stability, or rather instability or collapse, gained further momentum after introduction of the concept of planetary boundaries by Rockström and collaborators (2009a; 2009b; see the aforementioned). Progress in Earth system science over the last decades facilitated development of the concept for "keeping world development within a safe operating space" (Rockström 2015). A planetary boundary is "a specific point related to a global scale environmental process beyond which humanity should not go. The position of the boundary is a normative judgment, informed by science but largely based on human perceptions of risk" (Steffen et al. 2011c). The boundaries are positioned to allow for buffering space, a "zone of uncertainty," before any threshold may be reached. They do not directly relate to singular thresholds of a specific boundary and its control or response variables but rather are placed upstream to allow for timely action (see Steffen et al. 2015b, in particular Fig. 1 and Table 1). Science can and should warn if systems approach thresholds or show other signs of critical change. Time lags in Earth systems complicate the process of avoiding the crossing of thresholds: from a within-system perspective to the provision of robust scientific evidence, to eventual societal action or reaction.

The concept had instigated new discussion of eventual tipping points at various scales and for different Earth subsystems, including our societal systems. A focus issue of the journal *Trends in Ecology & Evolution* discussed the question, "Is there a global tipping point for planet Earth?" In their contribution to the debate, Hughes et al. (2013) elaborated on the complexity of relating major shifts in ecosystems, tipping points or thresholds, and incremental progress of regional- and planetary-scale responses during regime shifts to (an eventual) global collapse. The seemingly simple question revealed the multifaceted nature of what determines system dynamics and how this may be related to most recent human activities (overviews, for example, in Barnosky et al. 2012, 2016; Galaz et al. 2012; Lenton and Williams 2013; Walker and Salt 2006).

What has become clear is that "there are many uncertainties, warranting a precautionary approach to guiding future planetary trajectories" (Hughes et al. 2013). What is at stake is more than clearly illustrated through the interlinkages among tipping elements in the climate system (see Fig. 2.2 in Lenton and Williams 2013). These are, however, only part of a bigger picture: The highly dynamic and still poorly understood Earth system of systems which may be in serious trouble.

A few functional, final remarks

Anthropocene and planetary boundaries are both concepts which have provoked rethinking of the human/environment relationship. Anthropocene has become an important heuristic concept and tool for science, society and philosophy; the human factor is now center stage at environmental discussions.

Both terms fostered a systemic perception of Earth systems and their inherent properties and interactions. It is perhaps needless to add that boundary definition and measurement of the current state of Earth parameters, as included in classical papers, may incite political action and decision making. The planetary boundary concept is not a static construct. It is highly dynamic: new parameters may be included in the analyses and boundaries themselves may vary in regard to the "safe operating space." Finally, parameters for which boundary conditions may be identified may interact themselves, thus adding a further dimension to complexity.

In sum, the intertwined concepts of Anthropocene and planetary boundaries not only reflect the complexity of the systems we are dealing with; they also foster awareness and scientific study of system properties for future informed (i.e., science-based) and sound decision making. The latter is of particular importance in an era during which the world community has set itself a new development agenda – Agenda 2030 and its Sustainable Development Goals. In fact, the Anthropocene poses specific challenges for design and formulation of the Goals, which ultimately determines how strong and legitimate these will be as successors to the Millennium Development Goals (MDGs). In other words, the "purpose of the United Nations-guided process to establish SDGs is to galvanize governments and civil society to rise to the interlinked environmental, societal, and economic challenges we face in the Anthropocene" (Norström et al. 2014).

Our modern world is characterized by an unprecedented degree of interconnectedness. This embraces the environmental, economic, cultural and political arenas. The existence of this expansively globalized social system has to meet the urgent need for better understanding of the Earth systems and their complexity as well as the complexity inherent in the activities of a human population already surpassing the 7 billion mark and possibly reaching ten billion by 2050. "We are dealing with complex systemic impacts, requiring a more comprehensive conceptual framework as well as newly emerging research priorities" (Oldfield et al. 2014). It is not only innovative approaches that are needed for sustaining humankind's future. Also essential are more holistic approaches transcending responsibilities and competencies of individual institutions and traditional scientific disciplines. In short, a new world needs both transdisciplinary and transinstitutional initiatives.

In the chapter following, the reader is invited to examine the indispensable roles of foresight and innovation: how we humans look ahead, but with precaution, and how change the abstract into the concrete.

References

Autin, W.J. and J.M. Holbrook 2012. *Is the Anthropocene an issue of stratigraphy or pop culture?* GSA Today, Vol. 22. Doi:10.1130/G153GW.1.

Barnosky, A.D. and E.A. Hadly, J. Bascompte and 19 co-authors 2012. Approaching a state shift in Earth's biosphere. *Nature* 486: 52–58.

Barnosky, A.D., P.R. Ehrlich and E.A. Hadly 2016. Avoiding collapse: Grand challenges for science and society to solve by 2050. *Elementa: Science of the Anthropocene* 4: 000094. Doi:10.12952/journal.elements.000094.

Barnosky, A.D., N. Matzke and S. Tomiya and 9 others 2011. Has the Earth's sixth mass extinction already arrived? *Nature* 471: 51–57.

Begon, M., J.L. Harper and C.R. Townsend 1986. *Ecology: Individuals, Populations and Communities.* Blackwell Science, Oxford.

Bradshaw, C.J.A. and B.W. Brook 2014. *Human population reduction is not a quick fix for environmental problems.* www.pnas.org/cgi/doi/10.1073/pnas.1410465111.

Braje, T.J. and J.M. Erlandson 2013. Looking forward, looking back: Humans, anthropogenic change, and the Anthropocene. *Anthropocene* 4: 116–121.

Crutzen, P.J. 2002. Geology of mankind. *Nature* 415: 23.

Crutzen, P.J. and E.F. Stoermer 2000. The "Anthropocene." *IGBP Newsletter* 41: 17–19.

Dirzo, R., H.S. Young, M. Galetti, G. Ceballos, N.J.B. Isaac and B. Collen 2014. Defaunation in the Anthropocene. *Science* 345: 401–406.

Ellis, E.C. 2011. Anthropogenic transformation of the terrestrial biosphere. *Philosophical Transactions of the Royal Society* A 369: 1010–1035.

Ellis, E.C. and N. Ramankutty 2008. Putting people in the map: anthropogenic biomes of the world. *Frontiers in Ecology and the Environment* 6: 439–447, doi: 10.1890/070062.

Foley, S.F., D. Gronenborn, M.O. Andreae, J.W. Kadereit, J. Esper, D. Scholz, U. Pöschl, D.E. Jacob, B.R. Schöne, R. Schreg, A. Vött, D. Jordan, J. Lelieveld, C.G. Weller, K.W. Alt, S. Gaudzinski-Windheuser, K.C. Bruhn, H. Tost, F. Sirocko and P.J. Crutzen, 2013. The Palaeoanthropocene – The beginnings of anthropogenic environmental change. *Anthropocene* 3: 83–88.

Galaz, V., F. Biermann and B. Crona and 7 co-authors 2012. 'Planetary boundaries'- exploring the challenges for global environmental governance. *Current Opinion in Environmental Sustainability* 4: 80–87.

Gladwell, M. 2000. *The Tipping Point. How Little Things Can Make a Big Difference*. Back Bay Books, New York.

Hughes, T.P., S. Carpenter, J. Rockström, M. Scheffer and B. Walker 2013. Multiscale regime shifts and planetary boundaries. *TREE* 28: 389–395.

Kolbert, E. 2014. *The Sixth Extinction: An Unnatural History*. Henry Holt and Company, New York.

Lenton, T.M. and H.T.P. Williams 2013. On the origin of planetary-scale tipping points. *TREE* 28: 380–382.

Malm, A. and A. Hornborg 2014. The geology of mankind? A critique of the Anthropocene narrative. *The Anthropocene Review* 20: 1–8.

Norström, A.V., A. Dannenberg, G. Mc Carney and 14 others 2014. Three necessary conditions for establishing effective Sustainable Development Goals in the Anthropocene. *Ecology and Society* 19: 8. www.ecologyandsociety.org/vol19/iss3/art8/.

Oldfield, F., A.D. Barnosky, J. Dearing, M. Fischer-Kowalski, J. McNeill, W. Steffen and J. Zalasiewicz 2014. The anthropocene review: Its significance, implications and the rationale for a new transdisciplinary journal. *The Anthropocene Review* 1: 3–7.

Rockström, J. 2015. *Bounding the Planetary Future: Why We Need a Great Transition*. Great Transition Initiative (April 2015).

Rockström, J. and M. Klum 2016. *Big World Small Planet*. Ullstein, Berlin. (German Edition)

Rockström, J., W. Steffen and K. Noone and 26 others 2009a. Planetary boundaries: Exploring the safe operating space for humanity. *Ecology and Society* 14: 32. [online] www.ecologyandsociety.org/Vol14/iss2/art32/.

Rockström, J., W. Steffen and K. Noone and 32 others 2009b. A safe operating space for humanity. *Nature* 461: 472–475.

Ruddiman, W.F. 2013. The Anthropocene. *Annual Review of Earth and Planetary Sciences* 41: 45–68.

Steffen, W., J. Grinevald, P. Crutzen and J. McNeill 2011a. The Anthropocene: Conceptual and historical perspectives. *Philosophical Transactions of the Royal Society A* 369: 842–867.

Steffen, W., A. Persson, L. Deutsch and 13 others 2011b. The Anthropocene: From global change to planetary stewardship. *AMBIO* 40: 739–761.

Steffen, W., J. Rockström and R. Costanza 2011c. How defining planetary boundaries can transform our approach to growth. *Solutions: For a Sustainable & Desirable Future* 2: 59–65.

Steffen, W., W. Broadgate, L. Deutsch, O. Gaffney and C. Ludwig 2015a. The trajectory of the Anthropocene: The great acceleration. *The Anthropocene Review* 2: 81–98.

Steffen, W., K. Richardson, J. Rockström and 15 others 2015b. Planetary boundaries: Guiding human development on a changing planet. *Science* 347. Doi:10.1126/science.1259855.

Stromberg, J. 2013. *What is the Anthropocene and Are We in It?* Smithsonian Magazine January 2013. www.smithsonianmag.com/science-nature/what-is-the-anthropocene-and-are-we-in-it-164801414/#4pXOzBYtQLjlJ92O.99.

Walker, B. and D. Salt 2006. *Resilience Thinking. Sustaining Ecosystems and People in a Changing World*. Island Press, Washington.

Waters, C.N. and J. Zalasiewicz, C. Summerhayes and 22 others 2016. The Anthropocene is functionally and stratigraphically distinct from the Holocene. *Science* 351: 137. http://dx.doi.org/10.1126/science.aad2622.

Williams, M., J. Zalasiewicz, C.N. Waters and 22 others 2016. The Anthropocene: A conspicuous stratigraphical signal of anthropogenic changes in production and consumption across the biosphere. *Earth's Future* 4: 34–53. Doi:10.1002/2015EF000339.

Williams, M. and J. Zalasiewicz, P.K. Haff, C. Schwaegerl, A.D. Barnosky, E.C. Ellis 2015. *The Anthropocene biosphere.* The Anthropocene Review 2: 196–219.

Zalasiewicz, J., A. Cearreta, P. Crutzen and 13 others 2012. Response to Autin and Holbrook on "Is the Anthropocene an issue of stratigraphy or pop culture? *GSA Today* 22. Doi:10.1130/GSATG162C.1, p. e21.

Zalasiewicz, J., C.N. Waters, M. Williams and 23 others 2015. When did the Anthropocene begin? A mid-twentieth century boundary level is stratigraphically optimal. *Quaternary International* 383: 196–203.

Zalasiewicz, J. and C. Waters 2015. *The Anthropocene. Oxford Research Encyclopedias: Environmental Science.* Oxford University Press, Oxford.

Zalasiewicz, J., M. Williams, W. Steffen and P. Crutzen 2010. The New World of the Anthropocene. *Environmental Science & Technology* 44: 2228–2231.

3 Foresight and innovation
Searching for the right future

Introduction

After noting the re-designation of the fast-moving era in which we live, the Anthropocene, we now consider the sociocultural processes that accompany, with the passage of time, human development in general. We comment on the capacities of *Homo sapiens* to look ahead intelligently and create the new.

Why should we relate complexity to foresight, however, and why is this important? Visionary projections of future perfection appear in the holy scriptures of many of the world's religions. Glimpsing the good to come has challenged the mind to foresee the worst along with the best. The unsurpassed sweetness and peace of afterlife (Paradise) contrasts brutally with sudden and durable condemnation forever (wars or rumors of wars, the Apocalypse, perhaps lasting chaos). The Berber (today Algerian) Saint Augustine is remembered for his prophecies of the 4th and 5th centuries AD. Humanity's visionary outlook runs the scale, in other words, between most desirable and the most inescapable – from success and joy to stumbling and tumbling.

Until recently, forecasting what might be was largely the domain of foreseers of a better world: fabulists and oracles, fantasy essayists and dramatists, authors of science fiction. Today, that is to say, will prove to be better than yesterday, tomorrow even more provident and rosier. All the while, the scientific and industrial revolutions assumed reality, inciting the work of Jules Verne, Ernst Bloch, Albert Robida and H. G. Wells. These enthusiasts of technological fiction were strongly influenced by 19th-century technical advance and that of the First World War (aircraft, tanks, early radio), and then those of the Second World War (jets, ocean-wide naval encounters, early penicillin, DDT).

There followed the information and communication revolution, now integral to our lives. Compared with the science of the 18th and 19th centuries, science of the 20th–21st centuries is characterized by many new tools and better understanding of physics, chemistry, materials science and biology. We begin to ask and solve problems which were, until the 21st century, the stuff of pure fiction. The borders between science and science fiction began to blur. Social systems wandered and erred. New -isms were tried, seldom successfully. Sometimes we misused or abused new devices and services or combinations of these, inducing mechanical woes that are neither natural evolution nor human error.

A recent example, related to works of other science fiction authors, is Frank Schätzing's novel *The Swarm*, published in German in 2004. The story describes threats imposed on humanity by an unknown, intelligent marine-life form. It is written *almost scientifically* and provides insight into real problems in marine biology, geology, behavioral science and artificial intelligence. We cite here science fiction writer Robert A. Heinlein, who asserts in a book of 1959 that

> a handy short definition of almost all science fiction might read: realistic speculation about possible future events, based solidly on adequate knowledge of the real world, past and present, and on a thorough understanding of the nature and significance of the scientific method.

It is noteworthy that a book (1969), titled *The Andromeda Strain* by Michael Crichton, a graduate of Harvard Medical School, and a film (1971), based on Crichton's novel and directed by Robert Wise, correspond nicely to Heinlein's prescription.

More currently, indicative examples of imminent societal change are *The New Yorker magazine's* articles by Jon Lee Anderson on algorithmic creativity in Silicon Valley and the philosopher Eric Sadin published an essay in 2015 decrying the "Silicolonization" of the world.

[1]In the latter, the French philosopher condemns one-click solutions to all the world's problems. Sadin protests against over-admiration for the digitalized office, factory and laboratory or home whose computerized controls could be easy prey to viruses and other system intruders.

Practicalities of foresight analysis

Successful fiction can prove very close to futures analysis and strategic foresight, especially since science fiction is underpinned by reason and introduces elements which are realizable on the basis of known science and technology. Spaceflight, for example, or elements of future evolution, or teleportation are often featured in plausible fiction. Arthur C. Clarke, famed for his daring technical fiction, predicted two decades beforehand the orbiting of geostationary satellites – "geolocalizing" instruments without which our life today would be significantly different. One should add that the long-running film series "Star Wars," created by George Lucas, marked worldwide its fortieth anniversary in 2017.

Leaving aside the fantasizing aspect of science fiction, let's see how strategists and planners – many of whom, by the way, are experienced economists – view the predictive approaches evident in foresight. One fundamental outlook is based on what experience relates: if a population of x million consumed y million pairs of footwear over the past z years, can one reasonably accept a similar rate of production in the foreseeable future of $z + n$ years? This is simple interpolation; it is usually sound guidance in the planning of innovative competition (or, conversely, in the disappearance of competitors) within the same market. The competition may consist of new firms or new product lines, perhaps exploiting novel materials produced by existing competitors. These are routine complications with which professional competence can usually deal effectively.

Still in the same footwear industry, will the application of newly developed designs for walking comfort using recycled materials prove to have entirely different consumer appeal? A new type of footwear may suggest to marketers a broadened clientele – e.g., a female market for what was originally reserved for males? This is a cause-and-effect approach, sometimes so drastic in its evolution that it justifies investing in new manufacturing machinery, marketing campaigns and changes in wholesale and retail distribution patterns. Plastic boots for rain and snow displaced, in this way, heavy rubber overshoes to protect against rain and snow. Here the only "science" applied is simple arithmetical projection, and the only fiction remaining is, *we have yet to test the new markets available.*

The modern approach to systematic foresight probably began with American Secretary of Commerce Herbert Hoover's call, during his appointment (1921–1928), for a complete survey of his country's energy resources: fossil fuels, the hydrological cycle (rain, mountain streams, river networks, dams and subterranean reserves) and forest cover. Hoover, a geological engineer, had also acquired valuable managerial experience as director of Allied initiatives to help feed Europe's hungry populations suffering from the ravages of the First World War and the years immediately following.[2] Hoover's professional knowledge and administrative record had made it possible for his relief operations to feed the hungry, whereas his energy inventory primed a continuing concern on the part of the American and other governments for storing strategic supplies for the future.

The Hoover energy study was complexity analysis whose main omission was mention of renewable resources: sunlight, ocean, wind and geothermic potential: these natural forces had not yet become accessible. Hoover was elected president in 1928 but lost re-election to Franklin Roosevelt in 1932, when the country turned to a full-time economic struggle against the Great Depression. Little attention was paid to energy reserves until new pressures were felt with the advent of the Second World War, the later increased construction of cars, trucks and elaborately designed highways. Later came the petroleum crisis of 1973. With this, unexpected complexity arrived in the economics of fuel for automotive transport.

Foresight as life saver

In his autobiographical *Disturbing the Universe* (1979), physicist Freeman Dyson tells of his wartime work in Britain as a statistician for the Royal Air Force's Bomber Command. As a young mathematician, his task was to find the causes of the loss of substantial numbers of trained flight crews during nightly raids over German-occupied Europe. Dyson and his colleagues practiced the applied mathematics of *operational analysis*, also called *operations research*. OR is the process used to estimate precisely, for example, the quantities required and the timing of deliveries of essential materials to build public works, skyscrapers and fleets of vehicles or aircraft (among other mass production).

Foresight and innovation 31

The RAF's OR analysts concluded that the position of fuselage gunner aboard the Lancaster heavy bomber was inordinately vulnerable to attack by enemy fighter aircraft and should be eliminated. The time required to redesign the lower fuselage of the Lancaster and put the changes into production was such, however, that the war ended before the modifications could be realized – while the air force continued to lose valuable crews and aircraft. Despite this tragic failing, OR confirmed its utility as a combination of logic and understanding system complexity, as well as combining foresight and innovation. Today's towering buildings, oceanic superliners, high-speed trains and motor expressways could not materialize, in terms of cost, without OR techniques and their calculations necessary to cope with complexity.

Options in foresight studies

Interpolation may have been the first statistical method used to estimate a future level of change. Surely one of the best-known statistics today is that of the UN's estimated world population for the year 2050 of between 9.4 and 10 billion human beings. This is roughly the midway point between a deliberately (over)estimated maximal number possible (worst-case scenario, in this case) and a deliberately (under)estimated minimal number (best-case scenario). The worst-case assumption, carried to *reductio ad absurdum*, could envisage no births at all. More than unlikely as a prospect, this simple case of educated guesswork remains a way of *visioning* future demographic growth. (The 2050 estimate was recalibrated in early 2017 to 9.8 billion, according to a UN release.)

The year 2050 is also the temporal goal of a modeling strategy being developed by the International Institute for Applied Systems Analysis in Laxenburg (Austria). Called "The World in 2050: Pathways Towards a Sustainable Future," the project collaborates with the University of Stockholm, Columbia University's Earth Institute and the Alpbach-Laxenburg Group for applied research. The quest for sustainable development has seen the birth of research networks such as *Future Earth*, the UN's own Millennium Development Goals and many other entities, official and non-official, dedicated to futures research and the applications of innovation to a better life for humankind.

It is essential that future options not be whimsical. The ten highest national birthrates of 38.3+ per thousand population, all in Africa, remain fairly constant. Also based on UN projections, the global rate remains, when averaged, constant at 18.7 births per thousand population. These bracketing extremes are watched closely through the UN's actuarial calculations and provide a more than plausible projection of the world's demographic estimates for several decades hence. Scenarios can be altered, combined or wholly replaced, depending on their type of anticipation and possible (or probable) changes in ambient conditions.

A Royal Dutch Shell look ahead

A strategic analysis of long-term planning for the Royal Dutch Shell petroleum extraction and distribution giant at the end of the 20th century has become a milestone of this type of looking ahead. Authors Paul Schoemaker (of Decision Strategies International, a Chicago consultancy) and Cornelius van der Heijden (professor of business administration at the University of Strathclyde, Scotland) summarized their findings in a 1992 issue of Planning Review.[3] The authors' study enabled Shell to develop new methods to make the planning scenarios meaningful to line management. Shell also adopted measures to integrate the learning experience acquired within the strategic business unit (or sbu) that is often part of a corporate system of planning. As a result, new ideas emerged as new Shell product lines and services, but without the sensational (often environmentally harmful) results of new departures publicized by some major competitors.

A significant shift in major strategy came 23 years after the article published in Planning Review, when Shell announced that it would concentrate on the exploration and exploitation of liquefied natural gas. In order to accomplish this, Shell announced the completion of its U.S. $70-billion acquisition of the British-owned BG Group. Of this sum, $30 billion would come from the sale of both Shell and BG Group assets during the years 2016–2018.[4] This major change in planning can be seen as an essential characteristic of strategic foresight: not only how the future *could* but also *can*, bring change in its train.

In the contemporary French school of *la prospective*, best translated as prospecting the future, a goal is first declared, after which arguments pro and con are advanced. The originator in the 1950s of this type of futures analysis, Bertrand de Jouvenel, favored advancing strong arguments to support the objective to be attained. The method resembles somewhat the best/worst scenario model. The Jouvenel argumentation uses well-quantified data tending to emphasize self-correction and sustainability. The principle is applied today by son Hugues de Jouvenel and his colleagues at *Futuribles*, a professional consultancy with clients in government, industry and academia. The company also publishes a lively monthly journal, also called *Futuribles*, a term derived from the words "*future*" and "*possible*."

Complexity may produce insight too

Germany's entry as a combatant in the First World War, on the other hand, is almost uniformly attributed to the German Imperial General Staff's intentions to apply a particular plan of assault to a campaign against Belgium and France. We include it here not because of its military nature, but because of the storm the plan's conception and origins raised, as a result, in both history and historiography.

The Schlieffen Plan, as it became known universally, was the creation of Alfred von Schlieffen, field marshal and head of the General Staff (1891–1900 and again in 1905–1906): an all-out attack to overwhelm France in record time. This was the scheme's supposed foresight. Instead, the hostilities expanded geographically and with enormous casualties, the butchery lasting almost four and a half years. Germany met defeat. Postwar civil servants in the State Records

Office (*Reichsarchiv*) and other chroniclers attributed the plan-gone-wrong thesis to its faulty application by Schlieffen's successor, Colonel-General Helmut von Moltke the Younger. While this remains conceivable, it is essential to recall that the General Staff's theorizing throughout the 19th century held that the success of a military campaign is unforeseeable – much as today's futurists reject prediction.

But another school of retro-strategy places the blame elsewhere. This view contends that the plan was never a war plan, but a strategy devised during the non-belligerent decades following the Franco-Prussian War of 1870–1871. In the terminology of war planners, the Schlieffen model was a "war game," a large-scale drill intended primarily as an exercise in preparedness and ready response. A recent book by William D. O'Neil recapitulates, with supporting documentation, this explanation that a strategy not intended for implementation went dreadfully wrong when called into concrete use.[5] The Schlieffen Plan may have been little more than an invention by German patriots in the 1920s to exonerate senior commanders who had managed so disastrously Germany's war effort a decade earlier.

Behavior among prelates of a major church

Pope Francis assumed his functions in 2013 at a moment when the Roman Catholic Church faced internal problems of corruption and turpitude requiring a reordering of priorities in the governance of its worldwide clergy. Marriages between members of the same sex, the possibility of remarriage by divorced members of the faith, scandals of sexual abuse of minors by members of the clergy, homosexuality within the clergy, the reduced appeal of clerical life for aspiring young men and women: The list itself is a study in complexity in the moral ramifications of recruitment, professional training, ordination, deployment and ministration.

The origin of this knot of problems stretches back to the Nicene Creed of 325 AD, declaring that ordained priests were forbidden to marry. Centuries later the First Lateran Council (1123 AD) confirmed that marriage of a priest was not authorized – an obligation later extended to other clergy. Part of the reasoning was that marriage and a family presented distractions of purpose as well as economic complications for members of religious orders. In his probing of the causes of scandal by the otherwise faithful, Pope Francis has had little hesitation to call a spade a spade and undertake corrective measures, including disciplinary injunctions (see Box 3.1).

To continue our brief pseudo military diversions, as a general commanding a strong corps of lesser generals and colonels (the cardinals and bishops) not always in agreement with their chief, Francis's insight must contend with due attention to tradition, custom and quotidian processes now well ingrained among his senior clergy. Insight may lead to foresight. The Pontiff's work of significant, if not drastic, reform remains to be accomplished.

> **Box 3.1 Nearly 80 and going strong**
>
> [Pope Francis] is tough, still sturdy at 78, intensely focused on making the most of his allotted time. He is also a shrewd politician; his early shuffling of the cutthroat ranks of the Curia [is] proof enough of that; he has kept the old guard of the Vatican guessing and off balance while quietly installing a vanguard of his own.
>
> Source: *Time*, 23 September 2015

The application of foresight when contending with issues of system or subordination may come easily to experienced problem-solvers. Foresight may also present, in its turn, levels of complexity even more difficult to resolve. Some months after his first criticism of some of the church's professionals, the Pope visited the Greek island of Lesbos where he greeted hundreds of migrants awaiting entry into Europe. He took back with him four Syrian families (all Muslims), in an act of humanitarianism, to the protection of the Vatican. When asked why, the Pope replied publicly that he was concerned about the "globalization of indifference" toward the world's refugees.

Futures analysts use alternative methods to try to understand how a problem of today might unfold tomorrow or next year. These techniques include *framing* (understanding attitudes about both present and future), *leadership analysis* (are the right people in charge?), *decision-making impediments* (functional obstacles), *horizon scanning* (whence the brightest ideas lying beyond the next hill?), *rejecting the assumed and accepted* and *cultural clash existing among forecasters* themselves.

Visioning technique

Visioning is a method sufficiently different from the approaches just mentioned and requires a combination of openness of mind, contesting established assumptions, day-dreaming and even fantasizing, probing and endless testing (for instance, Edison and his winning of 1,093 patents).[6] There is daring, sometimes to the point of near-recklessness (Scott at the South Pole in 1912 or Felix Baumgartner's 2012 aerial dive by parachute from 38,000 feet). Not overlooked are the patience-testing development of Salk and Sabin vaccines (against polio), creating the totally unknown (the mechanical reaper by McCormick) and the Worldwide Web (or www, by Berners-Lee and his pioneering predecessors). Johann Wolfgang von Goethe, civil servant, essayist and minor aristocrat, may have been the first war correspondent writing dispatches directly from the battlefield (1790s). This vocation grew with the descriptive reports of the Crimean War (1853–1856) by William H. Russell of *The Times* of London.

These innovators all saw well ahead and exercised their imaginations, risked failure and sometimes their lives. Rachel Carson, marine biologist and conservationist, accelerated exponentially society's concern for disappearing species with her book, *Silent Spring* (1962), and created an infectious public concern for environmental pollution, at the time in particular through the global effects of DDT, and the sustenance of biota of all kinds and in all climes. Carson's concern for disappearing species has become an element of today's quest for sustainable development.

For all these innovators and more, insight translated into foresight and the impulsion to go much further in refining design, inventing new objects or systems, and (typically among commercial and industrial start-ups) services of profitable kinds, especially those employing young adults.

Today, almost a half century after the appearance of *The Limits to Growth*, can we not punch our powerful computers to measure the restraints to be enforced so as to keep global temperature rise below 1.5C degrees? Gordon Moore (of Moore's law) states that our computers are today 3,500 times more performing than they were in 1965. These machines have indeed been put to work to help us understand the constraints to be accepted, if not enforced, so that the 1.5C degree limit is not exceeded. See the chapter on climate change for specific compendia of such data already carefully researched and compiled. Models for global warming have been used extensively for IPCC reports; the restraints mentioned may be too many and too complex, however, for modeling.

Complex transition from foresight to innovation

Tomorrow's innovation had its forerunners yesterday and today. Let us take the computer (another originally military-aided device). It emerged through the two main analytical branches of radio-signal intelligence – i.e., traffic analysis and content analysis. The first is understanding how enciphered communications are sent by whom, to whom, how frequently, in what volume, and how answered. The second, content analysis, requires the ability to decipher the messages being sent or answered, often in a language not the same as the analyst's. More abstractly, patience, perseverance and an understanding of the adversary's mentality are almost obligatory.

Humans had tried for long to understand the essentials of language itself, and then to comprehend communication via language. In the 1920s, specialists at the Bell Telephone Laboratories made the first attempts to bring order to research on language and its communication. In the late 1930s, mathematician Alan Turing provided the basic theoretical analogies in what would shortly become the electronic computer. The Bell Laboratories' formulations of *information theory* were completed in 1948 by Claude Shannon, a 32-year-old mathematician and electrical engineer at the Massachusetts Institute of Technology. The uneven pathway to the information age was now clear.

In the 1840s, George Boole had broken words and syllables into *bits*, later expressed as combinations of 0s and 1s. Claude Shannon brought Boolean algebra into his research, an extension of Aristotelian true/false logic and notions of probability. After Shannon, these became the encoded expressions of small fragments of thought and expression, much as had the *dits* and *dahs* of Morse's international telegraphic code of a century earlier. Simplicity of symbols soon took on complications, and then a complexity, of its own. Without information theory, today we would probably not have high-performing software, social networks and "cloud" reserves of massed data in temporary storage. Concurrently with much of the successful interception of enemy communications achieved during the Second World War, improved electronic transmission of information and radar detection have made possible the continuing revolution in information and its conveyance.

Good ideas abound in many societies, even those where discovery, invention and innovation are not pillars of the national culture or economy. Edison, who simultaneously with Britain's Sir Joseph W. Swan, invented the ultimately ubiquitous electric light bulb, credited the inventor's results far more to perspiration than inspiration. Edison made endless trials of incandescence with filaments, both vegetal and metallic, to be illuminated by electrical current. He selected, although not a final choice, the metal tungsten as the most dependable and durable at the time.

Newness in plenitude

Innovating men and women let inspiration guide mind and hand to devise new things, concrete or immaterial, practical and almost always serviceable. Intellectual challenge and gamesmanship are the rewards of Indian-Persian chess and Chinese-Korean-Japanese go games – defeated in our times by advanced computers. All contenders, whether human, playing board, computer or their combined configurations, may be the epitome of resolving complexity. In our time only, the Internet has attained network intricacies that may be exceeded only by the complexity of the brain or galactic systems.

Innovators have made possible the creation of artifacts so numerous as to defy their count: from the hammer to the clock or watch assembled by robotic assistance, from "wooden legs" to reliable dental and aural prostheses to artificial limbs joined to the human body's neurological and muscular networks, from Leonardo da Vinci's primitive telescope to nanotechnology supported by subelectron microscopy and radio/radar communication with research vessels exploring outer space. And yet nuclear reactors, desalination of seawater and captured solar radiation are preventing neither water shortages nor the spreading of desert sands in Africa and China.

Pakistan-born lawyer Ram Jakhu teaches at McGill University's Law School in Montreal. A former collaborator with the World Economic Forum, Jakhu has made a specialty of space law applicable to security in extra-atmospheric space. He perceives this effort as a precursor to the advent of space diplomacy, or an application of the discretionary arts and discipline to factors well beyond the quotidian.

Humankind's search for new art forms, labor-reducing devices and materials is equally endless, as are the applications of new thought to musical form and instruments and their sounds. Novelty, sometimes shocking, extends to opera and musical comedy, new tonalities from old instruments, to wide-stage scenography and wraparound acoustics, to cleverly animated films and infographic-loaded documentaries intended for learning or entertainment. And in domains remote from the arts, the expressions "waste management" and "wealth management" were non-existent three generations ago. There seems no end to both pragmatic and pleasurable possibilities in the world of innovation.

Although there are errors, snarls and traps lying in wait, the innovation train seems to be moving along an evolving track that promises more marvels than disappointments – providing that we not let our imaginations fail us.

Humans generate the innovation that transforms

Search and research are daily activities in humanity's quest for answers to problems besetting the human race. North Korea decided, decades ago, that the nuclear bomb would settle the country's differences with much of the rest of the world, leading it to develop its own nuclear and then missile-launching capabilities. Most of the rest of the world knows that it would be utter folly to be beguiled by the potential of thermonuclear weapons as a means to end disputes with neighbors,[7] because it stills those disputes and all progress.

Thus, as shown schematically below, the cause-and-effect process applied by humans in the conception and creation of effective novelty, especially societal and technical advancement, may harbor risks and pitfalls all along an often unpredictable way.

Foresight ➜ Trials, Stumbles ➜ Complications ➜ Further Stumbles ➜ Insight ➜ Innovation

---

Every effort needs to be made to avoid, or at least minimize, stumbles. Putting aside nuclear arms, the effort and yield endemic to intellectual property, especially in its material manifestations, are normally affected with the benefit of patent or copyright protection. This is essentially a matter of jurisprudence intended to safeguard the proprietary interests of creative individuals or enterprises: a legal defense of the initiative to create or improve.

Protection hinges on

- agreement as to who filed patent papers first or who produced first the thing for which patent is sought,
- how long should last the patent coverage on vital products such as pharmaceuticals and certain foodstuffs, or
- why copyright should be renewable after a given number of years.

Improvement in patent processes, more so than copyright restrictions, is currently a work in progress around the globe. Their knots and quirks are monitored and normalized internationally by an arm of the UN, the World Intellectual Property Organization (WIPO) based in Geneva. WIPO cooperates with national equivalents where they exist.

Since the formulation in Venice of the first patent statute in 1450, some societies have been traditionally more productive than others, with notable leadership coming from the western world. Today, the global mass of patent documents numbers 48 million, a figure that grows as more innovators produce more patentable ideas. In recent decades, applications have increased considerably in Japan, China, the Republic of Korea, India and Brazil, for example – nations with impressively high export levels.

There are anomalies in the protection of intellectual property. Sensitive military arms and defensive systems are usually not patented for obvious reasons, while dual-purpose (civil as well as military) applications have given us the Internet and global positioning by satellite. Individual experimenters, small enterprises (start-ups included) and the large, R&D-based corporations seek, find and patent something new every day. The field is ruled by competition, intense rivalry and commercial advantage; it is an area that should not stop expanding and providing the entire world with all manner of useful novelty. The future output of Silicon Valley and the Chinese IT laboratories bear close watching for surprises. Civil requirements may be the first served by industry, but the military are not lagging. In 2018, the U.S. Army created the first Futures Command, an R&D survey-and-evaluation/procurement agency meant to equip field forces rapidly "to fight multiple types of wars at the same time," as assessed by the *New York Times*.

Innovation versus economic stagnation

Among the advanced societies practicing innovation is France, a country that has been anything but a laggard in scientific research and discovery or invention. We need think only of the early understanding of optics, the first attempts at controlled flight and the findings of Louis Pasteur in microbiology. Yet France has found inordinate difficulty, especially during the 20th century, in transforming new ideas into marketable products or services (the cause, in part, of its festering unemployment). French economic progress based on innovation is conspicuously behind the steady progress made by her immediate neighbor, Germany.

To combat economic stagnation, the French government has vigorously bolstered innovative approaches since the end of the Second World War; it remains fairly generous with financial assistance in various research-inducing initiatives. The country's National Commission for the Evaluation of Innovation Policies produced a study of R&D behavior during a 15-year period, 2000–2015, a decade and a half reflecting a governmental investment of €10 billon in R&D, at an annual rate of 0.5 percent of gross domestic product. Initial subsidies and other financial aid went more or less directly to innovators through 30 different agencies. Today, financial action is more indirect, however diffused via 62 different mechanisms, supposedly better to cover aspiring inventors throughout the population of 65 million.

Foresight and innovation   39

Findings of the National Commission: At the first five-year mark of financial incentives, the average research scientist or engineer was plodding along. By the next five-year mark, many aspects of research proved more promising and the innovator manifested less doubt about his/her efforts. The Eureka moment usually occurred at about the 15-year mark, justifying the accumulated investment of public money in innovative research.

Some runners-up

Russia, traditionally slow in most of the innovative processes beyond the extractive industries, space technology and military R&D, caught the attention in 2015 of Stratfor, a U.S. publisher and global intelligence company. (Stratfor stands for Strategic Forecasting, Inc.) This group concluded that the Russian Federation was outstripping the United States in the production and sales of liquefied natural gas. Sales depend on price per cubic meter, of course, and despite a glut in fossil-fuel supply, the Russian lead could last until 2020.[8]

In the case of India, the energy required for electrification of its enormous and fast-growing population of 1.32 billion (2016) will depend on exploitation of the solar source. "There is no other," Jean-Joseph Boileau, an expert on the Indian economy, told the Parisian public radio broadcaster France Inter, on the occasion of a visit to India by President François Hollande and 50 industrial leaders to conclude a sale of French military aircraft.[9]

The realities of foreseeing and perceiving complexity and then applying both to innovation inevitably require material support. How much of a nation's gross product should be allotted to research and development? During the 1960s, there was near-consensus among research circles in the advanced countries that the rate for a developed, industrial economy should be 2.5–3.0 percent, a figure only erratically met in a few national budgets.

With respect to gross domestic expenditures on R&D today, a half century later, the 41-country (including associates) OECD provides some surprising answers. From 2000 until 2014, the Republic of Korea raised its proportion from about 2.2 percent to 4.29 percent, nearly twofold. Israel increased its percentage from 2.2 to 4.11 percent, while Japan went from an already high 3.0 percent to 3.58 percent. Germany followed at 2.8 percent and the United States with a variably stable 2.5–2.7 percent all along the 15-year path. China's rate rose from about 1.7 to 2.05 percent, just a notch under the OECD average of 2.33 percent. The average rise for the then 28 nations of the EU was 1.94 percent, hindered by the lesser rates of the Balkan members and Eastern Europe. The EU projects, recent figures notwithstanding, a rate of 3.0 percent by the year 2020.[10]

A truly magisterial undertaking in statistical analysis, the OECD's efforts could serve future understanding of how innovation functions through its many inputs (of need, education and training, skills, productive talent and opportunity) as seen by leaders of the EU and those of other geo-economic regional groupings (Asia-Pacific, Latin America-Caribbean, African and Middle Eastern) not currently equipped to do so.

We have seen how the creative world is capable of productive innovation of many sorts, much of its product being tangible, functioning and of extensive service to humans. But invention, manufacture, distribution and putting new artifacts to best use require the thinking and synthesis resulting from sound teaching and learning. Education at the preschool, primary and secondary levels is the *sine qua non* for the formation of a nation's curiosity, culture and practical achievements. The following chapter explores the why and how of acquiring essential knowledge.

Notes

1 Pundits of emerging technology are especially watchful of novelty produced by Silicon Valley and China's R&D establishments.
2 Bernard Cazes, a former director of long-range planning at France's Commissariat au Plan, recounts this episode in his *Histoire des futurs* (The Story of Futures), Paris: Seghers, 1986.
3 See "Integrating Scenarios into Strategic Planning at Royal Dutch Shell," *Planning Review*, Vol. 20, No. 3 (1992), pp. 41–46.
4 Reported widely in the world's business media in the days following Royal Dutch Shell's announcement of 3 November 2015.
5 O'Neil, W. D., *The Plan that Broke the World: The "Schlieffen Plan" and World War I* (2d ed.), Washington, DC, 2014. This self-published volume is marked ISBN 1481955853.
6 Artur Fischer (1919–2016), a German-born locksmith holding more than 1,100 patents, conceived the electronically synchronized camera-flash and the drywall plug for embedding metal bolts in plasterboard.
7 See the January 2016 issue of *The Bulletin of the Atomic Scientists*.
8 The intelligence consultancy Stratfor, "Russia Outcompetes the U.S. When It Comes to LNG," 17 March 2015. It is fair to add, however, that stunning innovation in literature and music, in chemistry, and in early theory of flight flourished in the 19th-century Russian Empire.
9 See also Boileau, J.J., *L'Economie de l'Inde*, Paris: La Découverte, 2009.
10 Cumulative data released by OECD on 3 February 2016. Exhaustive data are presented in OECD Science, Technology and Industry Scoreboard 2015, Innovation for Growth and Society, Paris, OECD, 2016, a handy compendium of statistics on the types, modes and processes of innovation.

4 Education
Towards universal understanding

Building knowledge

We have reviewed the highlights and low points of the newly baptized Anthropocenic epoch of Earth. All of us alive today and tomorrow are part of this dynamic age. The patience-demanding processes of teaching and learning by those who will follow have become ever more complex since the Bohemian theologian Jan Hus set out in the 14th century to organize children and keep them attentive. The youngsters were exposed to the fundamentals of religious faith. From the scriptures, too, they learned to count accurately as well as read and write.

Today globalization and its derivative problems pose enormous challenges to educational structures. This applies to all forms of learning and in particular to children and adult education. A specific challenge is educating or, in other words, capacity building for policy makers.

The term *literacy* has thus become a buzzword with new meaning. We speak especially of scientific or mathematical literacy. This is pertinent in the teaching of science, the environment, climate change and particularly so in educating for sustainable development. Education about complex issues, complex systems and complexity itself has become a major obligation in an increasingly interconnected world. Adaptable education is now vital as we improve capacity to shape societies to meet the world's needs and aspirations.

Education is therefore *the* door opener to how the world meets and surmounts the most difficult problem confronting us: *devastating environmental change*. The principal guidance is the UN's 2030 Development Agenda, specifically its Sustainable Development Goals (SDGs). Modern education may need to address evolving problem areas – international mobility, the spread of diseases, political disputes, terrorism and inter-nation warfare.

Education has been dramatically affected by a revolution in two interrelated fields: the information and communication technologies (ICT) and social networks (Facebook, Flickr, Twitter, for example). Education-relevant information is available in quantity and quality as never before. An emerging task combines ensuring information of quality with retrieval of data germane to a given purpose, efficiently and effectively. Very often, including while preparing this book, many admit confrontation with the sensation of being deeply lost in information.

What is the endeavor we call education?

Education is the process of facilitating learning. Knowledge, skills, theory and practice, values, beliefs and group habits are transferred to others through discussion, story-telling, teaching, training, research and informed speculation. Education frequently takes place under the guidance of educators or tutors, but learners may also educate themselves through the autodidactic or self-learning method. Any experience that has a formative effect on the way one thinks, senses or acts may be considered instructive. If we borrow terminology from the economists, the outgoing learning process may be perceived as micro-education; they formed the student to think like his congeners. The new learning process we describe next is macro-education; the student begins to absorb how "everything influences everything else."

Education today is divided, commonly and formally, into orderly stages such as preschool, primary, secondary and then college/university, post-graduate or else vocational apprenticeship. In exceptional cases there is also home learning. The methods of teaching are called pedagogy (teaching the teachers). The right to education is recognized in Article 26 of the Universal Declaration of Human Rights, adopted by the UN's General Assembly in 1948.

Early human societies were largely dependent on lifestyles of hunter/food gatherer and subsistence farmer. In these settings, transfer of knowledge and skills from adults to the young was a requisite for sustaining family and clan. With increasingly complex societies and the need to accommodate for more information and diversity of skills, imitation was no longer the means to build successfully the knowledge capacities and astuteness needed. Formal education replaced artisanal (craft) learning. The most important prerequisite was the development of counting and writing systems; these emerged about 3500 BC in various civilizations of the Eastern Hemisphere.

The first schools were established in Egypt, Greece and China. After the fall of the Roman Empire the Roman Catholic Church became the only guardian of scholarship in Western Europe. The church established schools and cathedral universities which anticipated the founding of Europe's modern universities. Of particular importance during the Middle Ages was the surging of astronomy and mathematics in Islamic societies of the Middle East. A quantum leap forward was triggered by the Renaissance in Europe and the subsequent global spread of European concepts of education through the spreading European empires. Missionaries and scholars provided a reverse exchange: new ideas from China, Korea and India reached Europe. By the late 19th century, formal systems of education were widely introduced in Europe, North America, Japan and parts of Latin America. Their focus, however, was essentially on primary education; secondary education was open to the more affluent socioeconomic classes.

For what is education intended?

There are endless reasons why we need education and – in particular – why education has become ever more important for both present and future. Rather iterating the many, we look at the current, global situation. This is eloquently summarized in *Transforming Our World*, the new 2030 Development Agenda for Sustainable Development, a UN document of 2015. Under the heading of *Our World Today*, this agenda describes the situation today as follows (italics ours).

> Billions of our citizens continue to live in *poverty* and are denied a life of dignity. There are rising *inequalities* within and among countries. There are enormous disparities of opportunity, wealth and power. *Gender inequality* remains a key challenge. *Unemployment*, particularly youth unemployment, is a major concern. *Global health threats*, more frequent and intense *natural disasters*, spiralling *conflict*, violent *extremism*, *terrorism* and related humanitarian crises and *forced displacement* of people threaten to reverse much of the development progress made in recent decades. *Natural resource depletion* and adverse impacts of *environmental degradation*, including desertification, drought, land degradation, freshwater scarcity and loss of biodiversity, add to and exacerbate the list of challenges which humanity faces. *Climate change* is one of the greatest challenges of our time and its adverse impacts undermine the ability of all countries to achieve sustainable development. Increases in global temperature, sea level rise, ocean acidification and other climate change impacts are seriously affecting coastal areas and low-lying coastal countries, including many least developed countries and Small Island Developing States. The survival of many societies, and of the biological support systems of the planet, is at risk.

A veritable register of grief! Yet this is precisely where education comes into play. For much of this despair, education does not provide the solutions but the pathway toward educated and literate societies. In the same document, which essentially highlights the new global development goals, one of them is exclusively related to education. Goal 4 is to "ensure inclusive and equitable quality education and promote lifelong learning opportunities for all."

Our quotation about the purposes of education, mirroring today's world, echoes what environmentalist and teacher David W. Orr emphasized in 1991 in a paper entitled, "What Is Education For?" There Orr wrote, "All education is environmental education." The education most needed is education which teaches students in the widest sense – from preschool to adult ages – that they are part of our natural world. Education may need to overcome curricula which represent a world fragmented artificially into "bits and pieces called disciplines and subdisciplines." Paraphrasing Orr, the science we need in modern society is one of synthesis rather than its dissection into subordinate topics.

Urging that students have an "integrated sense of the unity of things," Orr speculated that humankind may become more ignorant of the things it should know to live well and sustainably on our planet. Isn't this somehow reflected in our struggle to come to grips with sustainable development as illustrated in the latest effort toward this end: the international community's casting of the new 2030 Agenda? And are not our major problems, linked to making sustainability become reality, partly the result of the need to improve educational systems?

44 *Education*

These have not (yet) produced the knowledge societies with citizens literate in *all matters* related to sustainability.

There is an educational system-inherent aspect tending to be often overlooked. As Stephen Sterling of Plymouth University in Britain has expressed it, "Education can build lasting change – that is, sustainable change – when it is owned by the learner" and "education and learning can reach the hearts and minds" (Sterling 2014). Ultimately, education is an intergenerational process too. It should shape following generations in order to cope with the challenges they are going to face, real or potential: building literate societies among increasingly interconnected and interdependent nations.

This is reflected in many international activities, in especially those linked to UNESCO which has, since its inception, the strongest focus on education. (UNESCO comprises five major program sectors: education, natural sciences and engineering, social and human sciences, culture and communication.)

Since its foundation in 1946, education has been UNESCO's first priority. Below is a sketch of the most pertinent, ongoing global program: Education for Sustainable Development (ESD).

Past shaping future in education

> The real and urgent threats to peace and international security are exclusion, poverty and underdevelopment and all the woes that accompany them. Yet, yesterday as today, education is among all the best responses – sometimes the only response – that society has to offer: education for all, education for development, education for justice and liberty and peace.

These remarks were written in 1996 by biochemist Federico Mayor, then head of UNESCO, in *50 Years of Education*, marking that organization's half-century anniversary (UNESCO 1997). This volume stressed the UN agency's efforts in the educational field. In the same volume the eminent biologist Julian Huxley (UNESCO's first head) is cited, who regarded his organization's topmost challenge the "existence of immense numbers of people who lack the most elementary means of participating in the life of the modern world."

Other key publications contributed to addressing the world's educational challenges. One of these was *The World Educational Crisis: A Systems Analysis* (1968), published by the first director of UNESCO's International Institute of Educational Planning, Philip H. Coombs. This volume not only used the modern term *systems analysis* but it "shocked the international education community," as recalled in a later edition of the same book published in 1985.

The underlying thought, already expressed in Coombs' book, is how educational systems could be up to date in view of changing environments at national and international levels. Two intergovernmental commissions had been chaired by Edgar Faure (politician, historian) and Jacques Delors (economist, politician), respectively. They produced two guiding documents, *Learning to Be* and *Learning: The Treasure Within*. The former was published by the Faure Commission in 1972 and reissued by UNESCO in 2013, the latter by the Delors International Commission on Education for the Twenty-First Century in 1996. Both publications were visionary, and they specifically emphasized the need for global and lifelong education. They may even be considered examples of how much we can learn for the future by at least occasionally looking into the past. A quotation from the Faure Report, already written in 1972, reads almost as if written these days (see Box 4.1).

Box 4.1   Excerpt from *Learning to Be* (UNESCO 1972)

Education must recognize itself for what it is: it may be the product of history and society, but it is not their passive plaything. It is an essential factor in shaping the future, particularly at the present moment, since in the last resort education has to prepare mankind to adapt to change, the predominant characteristic of our time.

There are many, complex changes. Varying greatly in nature, they affect virtually every human community, and they are equivocal, opening new vistas and creating new threats.

Education, in this context, also has two dimensions. It has to prepare for changes, show people how to accept them and benefit from them, create a dynamic, non-conformist, non-conservative frame of mind. Concurrently, it has to play the part of an antidote to the many distortions within man and society. For democratic education must be able to provide a remedy to frustration, to the depersonalization and anonymity in the modern world and, through lifelong education, reduce insecurity and enhance professional mobility.

These aspects of educational action are all too often neglected, although it is unreasonable to expect more of education than it can give or count on education alone to produce solutions to the basic problems of our time. But this does not in the least diminish the importance of efforts undertaken to renew methods of education and rethink its functions, duties and ultimate aims. On the contrary, the real dimensions of these efforts will be enhanced if they are seen against the background of this age of man and its challenging drama.

Subject-specific approaches in education

Overview

The UN, other governmental and NGOs have varying approaches to meet education needs. These include, of course, different modes of the educational process, from teaching children to lifelong learning.

Specific approaches include education in science, technology, engineering and mathematics ("STEM Education"); the Education for All movement; and issue-related education, which may embrace water, climate change, biodiversity or desertification. The last three themes fall into the context of the three Rio Conventions, dating from the Earth Summit of 1992 in Brazil. Today, substance-oriented teaching of this type is closely linked to those environmental conventions.

The Global Action Program (GAP) on Education for Sustainable Development is the follow-up to the UN Decade (2005–2014) of Education for Sustainable Development. Its policy-support mechanism relates to the Rio Conventions. The mechanism is one of the (five) priority actions forming the "roadmap" for implementing the GAP just mentioned (reference in UNESCO 2014b).

Climate change education

International concerns about global warming led to the establishment of the United Nations Framework Convention on Climate Change (UNFCCC) in 1992. UNFCCC was a major outcome of the 1992 UN Conference on Environment and Development, the famous "Rio Earth Summit." The Convention covers educational needs with regard to climate change in its Article 6 on education, training and public awareness (Box 4.2).

Box 4.2 Education, training and public awareness (Article 6, UNFCCC)

Promote and facilitate at the national and, as appropriate, sub-regional and regional levels, and in accordance with national laws and regulations, and within their respective capacities:

(i) The development and implementation of educational and public awareness programs on climate change and its effects;
(ii) Public access to information on climate change and its effects;
(iii) Public participation in addressing climate change and its effects and developing adequate responses; and
(iv) Training of scientific, technical and managerial personnel.

Cooperate in and promote, at the international level, and, where appropriate, using existing bodies:

(i) The development and exchange of educational and public awareness material on climate change and its effects; and
(ii) The development and implementation of education and training programs, including the strengthening of national institutions and the exchange or detailing of personnel to train experts in this field, in particular for developing countries.

With the aim of aligning the diversity, expertise and specifics of the UN system into a single endeavor, secretary-general of the UN Ban Ki-moon urged the UN System "to deliver as one." This initiative was set in motion during the COP 13 conference of the UN Expert Committee on Climate Change (Bali, Indonesia, 2007). Its objective was "to maximize existing synergies, eliminate duplication and overlap, and optimize the impact of collective effort of the UN System" (UNESCO 2010).

UNESCO at that time had put in place an "intersectoral platform" to deliver a unity of effort. This included climate change. A mapping exercise revealed that over 40 climate change activities were already borne within that organization. Still lacking was an internal coordinating mechanism. The new platform provided both a strategy and an integrated approach for UNESCO. Ultimately, the platform was targeted at positioning the organization within the UN System's effort to "deliver as one." With platform implementation (in the 2008–2009 biennium), Education for Sustainable Development and UNESCO's action on climate change were separate platforms.

UNESCO's World Conference on Education for Sustainable Development, held in Bonn, Germany (2009), reaffirmed climate change as a key action-theme of the Decade of Education for Sustainable Development (DESD). More concretely, the Conference requested the intensification of "efforts in education and training systems to address critical and urgent sustainability challenges such as climate change, water and food security by developing specific action plans and/or programs within the UN DESD umbrella and partnership framework" (sic).

Subsequently, education related to these specific fields, including environmental education, was streamlined during DESD. ESD has since become possibly one of the most important movements in teaching during the new century. More importantly, it will underpin and enable activation of the new 2030 Agenda for Sustainable Development and its development goals.

Education for Sustainable Development

Agenda 21 was one of the major outcome documents of the UN "Earth Summit" held in Rio de Janeiro (1992). It is a comprehensive action plan for sustainable development at global, national and local levels including the UN, national governments and local stakeholders. Already prior to the preparation of Agenda 21 the synergies between the *Education for All* efforts and sustainable development were seen. It was clearly understood that there is no development let alone sustainable development without an educated and understanding citizenry (Hopkins, pers. comm.). Agenda 21 considered education as a cross-cutting theme, mentioned in each of its 40 chapters.

Its Article 36 focuses specifically on education. It is entitled "Promoting education, public awareness and training." This points out the necessity of "reorienting education towards sustainable development." Education was subsequently also included in the so-called Rio Conventions on climate change, biological diversity and desertification.

As outlined *inter alia* in UNESCO's sourcebook on Education for Sustainable Development (2012), ESD comprises four thrusts of emphasis, derived from Chapter 36:

(1) Improving access and retention in quality basic education
(2) Reorienting existing educational programs to address sustainability
(3) Increasing public understanding and awareness of sustainability
(4) Providing training to all sectors of the workforce

The first and second thrust essentially relate to formal education, the third and fourth to non-formal and informal education thus including all sectors of education. The interrelationship between ESD and quality education has recently been summarized in a synthesis of studies carried out in 18 countries (Laurie et al. 2016).

This process of reorienting education toward sustainable development was massively scaled up during the UN DESD (2005–2014). The Rio+20 Summit in 2012 reinforced the importance of DESD. In the outcome document, *The Future We Want*, member states supported a continuing effort beyond the Decade. This resulted in the Global Action Plan on ESD as a follow-up to the Decade. UNESCO was the UN's lead agency for this decade in which over 20 UN entities were involved.

UNESCO had released its final DESD monitoring and evaluation report (UNESCO 2014a). The document highlights achievements during, and challenges at the end, of DESD as well as action taken at local, national, regional and global levels, and it touches all areas and levels of education. The organization initiated a roadmap for implementing an action plan as follow-up to the Decade (UNESCO 2014b). It now houses the secretariat for this Global Action Plan.

This was a timely release not only in view of the decade's coming to a close but also on the concluding negotiations of the global post-2015 development agenda. Its SDGs were to succeed the MDGs. The report assessed "progress towards embedding ESD into education systems and into sustainable development efforts."

DESD was a very ambitious undertaking (Box 4.3). It aimed at "integrating the principles and practices of sustainable development into all aspects of education and learning, to encourage changes in knowledge, values and attitudes with the vision of enabling a more sustainable and just society for all" (from Executive Summary in UNESCO 2014a). This echoes the important connotation that ESD is education *for* and not simply *about* sustainable development. Moreover, as pointed out by Jan Visser (pers. comm.), it would be interesting to see what this encouragement process means in practice, how it is measured and whether it leads to fundamental improvement in learning and education systems.

Box 4.3   What is Education for Sustainable Development (ESD)?

ESD empowers learners to take informed decisions and responsible actions for environmental integrity, economic viability and a just society, for present and future generations, while respecting cultural diversity. It is about lifelong learning, and is an integral part of quality education. ESD is holistic and transformational education which addresses learning content and outcomes, pedagogy and the learning environment itself. It achieves its purpose by transforming society. ESD has the following dimensions:

- **Learning content:** Integrating critical issues (such as climate change, biodiversity, disaster risk reduction, and sustainable consumption and production) within the curriculum.
- **Pedagogy and learning environments:** Designing teaching and learning in an interactive, learner-centered way that enables exploratory, action-oriented and transformative learning. Rethinking learning environments – physical as well as virtual and online – to inspire learners to act for sustainability.
- **Learning outcomes:** Stimulating learning and promoting core competencies, such as critical and systemic thinking, collaborative decision making and taking responsibility for present and future generations.
- **Societal transformation:** Empowering learners of any age, in any educational setting, to transform themselves and the society they live in.

    - Enabling a transition to greener economies and societies.
        – Equipping learners with skills for "green jobs."
        – Motivating people to adopt sustainable lifestyles.

    - Empowering people to be "global citizens" who commit themselves to active roles, both locally and globally, to face and to resolve global challenges and ultimately to become proactive contributors to creating a more just, peaceful, tolerant, inclusive, secure and sustainable world.

Source: http://en.unesco.org/themes/education-sustainable-development/what-is-esd; accessed 30 April 2016

Teaching, learning and the 2030 Agenda

The World Education Forum was held 2015 in Incheon, Republic of Korea. With over 1,600 participants from 160 countries, this was one of the largest recent educational gatherings. The Forum's affirmation, the *Incheon Declaration for Education 2030*, presents a new vision for education for the years 2015–2030. The Declaration reflects "the commitment of the education community to Education 2030 and the 2030 Agenda for Sustainable Development, recognizing the important role of education as a main driver of development" (UNESCO 2015b).

Goal 4 of the SDGs exhorts, "Ensure inclusive and equitable quality education and promote lifelong learning opportunities for all." This stand-alone task is indicative of the importance that education is assigned for realizing sustainable development. As stated in the Incheon Declaration and its Framework for Action: "Education is at the heart of the 2030 Agenda for Sustainable Development and essential for the success of all SDGs." Moreover, the same document stresses that Education 2030 is "universal and is owned by the entire world, developed and developing countries alike."

This renewed impetus for education is a result of remarkable progress but only partial successes in the education domain since the year 2000. At that time the Education for All (EFA) goals and the MDGs had been agreed upon by the world community. EFA goals and education-related MDGs have at most been reached partially. As regards ESD, the final report on the DESD says that only 50 percent of UNESCO's member states have integrated ESD into official policy (UNESCO 2014a). It would be important to learn more about the implications of this integration process at national level, what subject-specific difference it may have made, and whether the 50 percent figure is likely to increase globally in the near future.

As a result, reaching the education SDG means both attending to unfinished business from the years 2000–2015 as well as attending to global challenges such as climate change and biodiversity loss. There also remain associated educational needs (see the following) to be addressed by the post-2015 Agenda. This poses enormous challenges to governments: implementation of Education 2030 and SDG 4 signifies responsibilities for action. Nevertheless, globalization, interconnectedness and in particular the availability of the latest ICT may bolster education efforts at all levels.

In the future, national education systems may no longer operate at the national level only but, increasingly, be part and parcel of global efforts toward education for all segments of society within a lifelong learning framework. International exchange programs, the internationalization of tertiary education and online courses, as well as "virtual universities," may provide unprecedented opportunities for educating responsible citizens.

All of this means that this mainstreaming of education into the 2030 Agenda may risk loss of specific areas in our learning systems. There is today erosion in faculty within the social sciences and humanities, even in countries of the north. Likewise, the strengths of environmental education may have been lost in the process of its streamlining into ESD. For instance, Kopnina (2011) argued,

> ESD replaces a problem orientation associated with environmental education and shifts the focus to the inclusion of social issues and economic development. ESD masks its anthropocentric agenda and may in fact be counterproductive to the efficacy of environmental education in fostering a citizenry that is prepared to address the anthropogenic causes of environmental problems.

We may need a comprehensive rethinking and eventual recasting of our educational systems to achieve a new literacy. The diversity of needs and aspirations at different scales, from local to global, and the fast-changing situations at these very scales may demand highly adaptive and dynamic education systems. ESD may thus form the framework but its filling would require dealing with the diversity of global challenges; it would also need to anticipate new challenges.

The development of new visions of learning and the rethinking of education and its complex learning environments is certainly one of them, in particular in our increasingly globalized and interconnected world of the Anthropocene (overview in Visser 2016).

The ICT revolution: how it affects macro-education

A revolution indeed took place when modern ICTs' role and importance for education was recognized and widely applied. In their article in the German weekly *Die Zeit* of 24 September 2015, headed "Humboldt versus Orwell," Jörg Dräger and Ralph Müller-Eiselt observed that digitalization may lead to profound change in education systems, comparable to the invention of printing and the introduction of mandatory schooling. A fundamental change encompasses much more than the use of tablets and Smart Boards in school or at university. The authors mention the online high school "Coursera" with an enrollment of some 15 million students. This is six times the number of students at all institutions of higher education in Germany. Coursera is an education platform partnering with top institutions worldwide. Currently, it has 145 partner institutions of higher education from 28 countries, and it offers some 2,000 different courses (www.coursera.org, accessed 20 June 2016).

In 2014, investment into education technology start-ups amounted to almost $2 billion. The digital revolution in learning turns upside down how we teach and learn. Exclusivity in learning in the Western world is increasingly being replaced by mass products. Unified learning that follows a rigorously designed curriculum gives way to support for everyone. Institutions for elites are replaced by modern ones building upon individual competencies of students.

Many are worried about these changes in the educational landscape. As the authors write, in Germany people speak of a digital tsunami which destroys the education and learning ideals of Wilhelm von Humboldt. They also point out, however, that Humboldt was a staunch supporter of the "education for all" ideal and that he would have been favorable to the idea of digitalization. This would have facilitated his introduction of compulsory school attendance. Dräger and Müller-Eiselt depict problems with opportunities for further democratizing education systems. Take, for example, the decoupling of education from societal background of the individual. In Germany, they argue, digitalization is still seen as burden rather than part of the solution to bigger classes and, therefore, to a much more heterogeneous community of learners. The German educational system could risk missing the boat, especially when competing with its European neighbors and, more pronouncedly, with very advanced Asian countries.

In the same *Die Zeit* article, the elite American Stanford University was reported to construe its free introductory course via Internet in artificial intelligence as a

MOOC (massive open online course). A total of 160,000 persons from 190 countries subscribed to the course. 23,000 students passed the final exam and received a certificate. Addressing such a body of students would have been impossible during the lifetime of the two Stanford professors responsible for the course.

The most unexpected outcome of this MOOC was not the number of participants, but the results: The best Stanford student ranked 413th. In other words, 412 participants surpassed Stanford's best students. Even an 11-year old Pakistani girl passed the exam: A computer, fast Internet, patience and a few mouse clicks opened the door for her to most advanced knowledge. As outlined in the article, the "new classroom" method allows digitally communicated yet personalized learning through a diversity of pedagogic tools. These include automated engagement, video presentations, learning software and group work. Engagement comprises daily short, online tests which are analyzed through a central computer. The tests tell the student what he/she still needs to work on, which of the pedagogical tools used works best for her or him. Personalized learning, new opportunities through the use of "Big Data," and the appropriate use of computer games may save time for teacher-student personal interaction. Such use should allow for flexibility in the timing of teaching, provide new opportunities for students with "non-academic" parents, or even for finding the best candidate for a specific job opening.

Major progress could thus be achieved through decoupling learning and education from a student's social environment and financial background. Through digitized education and learning systems the North/South divide between the so-called developing and developed worlds may be overcome to a significant extent. However, as indicated in "Humboldt versus Orwell," such systems may resemble George Orwell's vision of a totalitarian or authoritarian state as described in his novel *1984*.

The interface between education and ICT was addressed in the International Conference on ICT and Post-2015 Education, held in May 2015 in Qingdao, People's Republic of China (UNESCO 2015c). As stated in the *Qingdao Declaration* of the Conference: "Equitable and inclusive access to quality education for all across life is an imperative for building sustainable and inclusive knowledge societies, and as a key means of implementation to achieve **all of the SDGs**" (bold ours). In other words, education, through SDG 4, is thought to be an enabler for reaching all SDGs. The *Qingdao Declaration* states, "To achieve the goal of inclusive and equitable quality education and lifelong learning by 2030, ICT – *including mobile learning* – *must be harnessed to strengthen education systems, knowledge dissemination, information access, quality and effective learning, and more efficient service provision*" (italics ours).

The conference report reiterates a great advantage of modern ICT: People can learn anything, anytime, anywhere, in any way selected. Learning and working in our ICT-based environments, however, requires well thought-through plans and strategies for the educational systems under national master-plans. ICT have the potential to scale up worldwide teaching efforts, both in quality and quantity.

Education 53

They carry risks, as already discussed. At the same time, they have become essential in day-to-day life.

Is education in a crisis of complexity?

Despite years of widespread educational efforts since the Second World War and creation of the UN, the status of education around the world is less than satisfactory. Its major defects continue to be

- access (or rather effective access) to education by everyone and retention,
- the need to improve education quality,
- making learning more effective, and
- using resources effectively.

In addition to these it would be worth examining how successful efforts have been in making education more holistic. Since the release of Agenda 21 education has gone through a re-orientation process, from the traditional focus of individual well-being of the individual to the inclusion of concepts such as global citizenship and responsibility (Hopkins, pers comm.). Both are intimately related to making sustainable development become reality.

This discussion has continued and is reflected in the results presented in UNESCO's 2015 Global Monitoring Report for Education for All (EFA; UNESCO 2015a). This summary of EFA achievements during 2000–2015 came up with interesting conclusions of a more systemic nature. When the MDGs became the key element of the global development agenda (2000), EFA efforts were almost sidelined in favor of the MDG on universal primary education. This target, as well as the EFA Goals, was not reached. Secondly, conferences as means for accountability of national and international commitments to education have not proved to be functioning well.

Education systems are facing challenges at all levels. Hazelkorn (2011) noted three big challenges for higher education, irrespective of the specificities of each country and each institution. First, "ensuring sustainable higher education systems at the same time that public funding is decreasing and competitiveness is increasing." Second, "improving the quality of the total student experience even as the demand for participation is growing," and third, "strengthening knowledge and innovation as drivers of growth while ensuring that multi- and cross-disciplinary critical inquiry is maintained."

Education challenges are complex, multifaceted and they relate to all major elements of the educational process, its capacities and related socio-political environments. This situation extends to even more complex patterns if discussed at levels above the national level and in the context of today's global challenges. Complicating things further are highly dynamic challenges at all levels, local to global. How can education systems keep pace with the ongoing process of thorough changes in teaching and learning? The challenges bear a similarity, in fact, to conservation problems.

Complex socio-ecological, even socio-political systems, are of a nature related to so-called wicked problems. These usually lack clear solutions, each problem is linked to others. The characterization of each cannot be isolated. A public policy issue such as the modification of school curricula is of small scale within the broader context of education. This is a wicked problem. (For details, see the seminal paper of Rittel and Webber 1973).

In virtually all contexts, there is discussion of the need to review and evaluate. Yet there exist unprecedented means of communication through ICT. Furthermore, we often fail to consult the essential stakeholders for their feedback on improvement. These are the students, parents and the teachers with longevity (sometimes decades) of experience. Consultation could prevent frustration and lead to better problem solving. Modern exchange programs, underpinned by information from the Internet, can also help foster improved education and thus responsible citizenship. These goals are linked to improved international mobility of both teachers and students, as stressed in the Faure Report of 1972.

Philip Coombs, in his 1968 book on *The World Educational Crisis: A Systems Analysis* (already mentioned), highlighted a major issue with regard to global development and education systems.

> Since 1945, all countries have undergone fantastically swift environmental changes, brought about by a number of concurrent worldwide revolutions – in science and technology, in economic and political affairs, in demographic and social structures. Educational systems have also grown and changed more rapidly than ever before. But they have adapted all too slowly in relation to the faster pace of events on the move all around them. The consequent disparity – taking many forms – between educational systems and their environments is the essence of the worldwide crisis in education.

A half a century after this publication we still recognize the disparity between the dynamics of education systems, including all their different dimensions, and the dynamics of their "environments." Nowadays the latter change much more rapidly. The gaps left are widening. ICTs offer a unique set of tools to align education systems with the social, environmental and political surroundings and the rapid evolution in the sciences, technology and innovation.

In her outstanding article of 2016 on higher education Cristina Escrigas, adviser to the Global University Network for Innovation (GUNI), argued,

> To address the rapid evolution of knowledge, the prevailing educational paradigm needs to shift from a focus on *knowing* to one on *being*. This involves preparing students to discern the differences between information, knowledge and wisdom and teaching them how to deal with uncertainty and ambiguity in a volatile world. It means helping students to search, synthesize and apply knowledge from different sources and different cultural backgrounds to understand complex problems. It means showing students

how to integrate feelings, values, and emotions with facts, a task for which the humanities are essential.

This reflects precisely what we discuss in this book: complexity versus monolithic thinking, acting and capacity building. Our world is in great transition and transformation. At the same time, it experiences global challenges which may affect humanity in its entirety. The greatest challenge for education is that humanity seizes upon its two main conflicts, *sensu* Escrigas: coexistence with nature and coexistence with each other.

We close with a few questions

Education will continue to play a primary role in the further development of mankind. We have noted that virtually all the SDGs of the new 2030 Agenda concern education. So there are key questions to be asked.

How can we optimize interrelationships among the different stages in educational systems, ranging from preschool to tertiary levels? How can education, in all its different settings, foster the augmented need for lifelong learning in the new ICT-based knowledge societies? In this age of knowledge explosion, how can we accelerate the process of including newly created knowledge into education systems? How should "relevant" information be selected from a vast pool of options? What are the most adequate governance solutions for the education systems of the future? Will we still struggle with national or even intra-national autonomy regarding education matters? More generally, to what extent will our future education systems reflect national priorities or global challenges?

Lastly, but most importantly, will education ultimately become a key driver for building inclusive, just and peaceful societies, producing world citizens aware of their responsibilities to coming generations?

References

Coombs, P.H. 1968. *The World Educational Crisis: A Systems Analysis*. Oxford University Press, New York.
Coombs, P.H. 1985. *The World Crisis in Education. The View from the Eighties*. Oxford University Press, New York.
Dräger, J. and R. Müller-Eiselt 2015. "Humboldt gegen Orwell." *DIE ZEIT*, No. 39, 24 September 2015, pp. 75–76.
Escrigas, C. 2016. *A Higher Calling for Higher Education*. Great Transition Initiative (June 2016). www.greattransition.org/publication/a-higher-calling-for-higher-education.
Hazelkorn, E. 2011. Three key challenges facing higher education and policy makers. In: *Libraries at Webscale. Appendix A: World Views*, pp. 43–44. *OCLC Online Computer Library Center, Inc*, Dublin, OH.
Kopnina, H. 2011. Revisiting Education for Sustainable Development (ESD): Examining anthropogenic bias through the transition of environmental education to ESD.

Sustainable Development. John Wiley and Sons, Ltd and ERP Environment. Doi:10.1002/sd.529.

Laurie, R., Y. Nonoyama-Tarumi, R. McKeown and C. Hopkins 2016. Contributions of Education for Sustainable Development (ESD) to quality education: A synthesis of research. *Journal Education for Sustainable Development* 10: 226–242.

Morin, E. 2001. *Seven Complex Lessons in Education for the Future.* UNESCO, Paris.

Rittel, H.W.J. and M.M. Webber 1973. Dilemmas in a general theory of planning. *Political Science* 4: 155–169.

Sterling, S. 2014. '*Learner Drivers' for the Future: A Different Education for a Different World.* http://documents.routledge-interactive.s3.amazonaws.com/sustainability/thematic/Education%20Thematic%20Essay.pdf.

UNESCO 1972. *Learning to be. The World of Education Today and Tomorrow.* UNESCO, Paris.

UNESCO 1996. *Learning: The Treasure Within. Report to UNESCO of the International Commission on Education for the Twenty-First Century.* UNESCO, Paris.

UNESCO 1997. *50 Years of Education.* UNESCO, Paris.

UNESCO 2010. *Climate Change Education for Sustainable Development.* UNESCO, Paris.

UNESCO 2012. *Education for Sustainable Development. Sourcebook.* UNESCO, Paris.

UNESCO 2014a. *Shaping the Future We Want. UN Decade of Education for Sustainable Development (2005–2014).* Final Report. UNESCO, Paris.

UNESCO 2014b. *Roadmap for Implementing the Global Action Programme on Education for Sustainable Development.* UNESCO, Paris.

UNESCO 2015a. *A Global Monitoring Report 2015. Education for All 2000–2015: Achievements and Challenges.* UNESCO, Paris.

UNESCO 2015b. *World Education Forum 2015. Education 2030. Incheon Declaration and Framework for Action.* UNESCO, Paris.

UNESCO 2015c. *Leveraging Information and Communication Technologies to Achieve the Post-2015 Education Goal.* Report of the International Conference on ICT and Post-2015 Education, 23–25 May, Qingdao, People's Republic of China. UNESCO, Paris.

United Nations 2015. *Transforming Our World: The 2030 Agenda for Sustainable Development.* United Nations, New York.

Visser, J. 2016. Human Learning and the Development of Mind in the Anthropocene: Reflections against the Backdrop of Big History. *Origins, the bulletin of the International Big History Association* VI: 1–12.

5 Science
The complexity of searching the truth

Setting the scene

In the last chapter, we reviewed what the professional educator seeks to contribute as means of thinking about and solving some of the major problems confronting humanity today. In the present chapter, we dip into comparable efforts made by the world of scientific researchers, engineers and technicians: in other words, the world of science, both theoretical and applied. Science is knowledge of nature and the cosmos and how they function. An engineer acquaintance of the authors has remarked jokingly, "With the recent discovery of the Higgs boson, suddenly there was complexity. Before that, all was simplicity."[1]

Not quite. Science is an elaborate enterprise reserved (thus far) for *Homo sapiens*. Other biota devise the simplest tools to help feed and shelter themselves, keep warm or cool and assure protection against predators, even use passively Earth's magnetic field in avian navigation. Science is the derivation of systematized knowledge from observation, study, trial and experimentation in order to determine the nature and principles of what is being studied (adapted from *Webster's New World Dictionary*). How do science and complexity relate, each with the other? One view is that complexity itself is a scientific field with many branches (e.g., Holland 2014). Another view is that complex systems, systems with many interconnected components, have become an increasingly important constituent of science.

Complex systems may be natural such as tropical rainforests, or man-made such as market systems or the Internet. A principal characteristic of complex systems is *emergence*, when these systems show properties which cannot be deduced from analysis of only the system's components. This is commonly stated as *the whole is more than the sum of its parts*.

Complex systems may also be characterized by features such as *self-organization*, *chaotic behavior*, *"fat-tailed" behavior* and *adaptive interaction* (Holland 2014). The world of complexity plays a central role in 21st-century science because science has "reacted" to its new environment and developed tools and methods to analyze complex systemic problems.

This chapter can neither discuss developments in all the different scientific disciplines nor can it highlight the many aspects relating science to society. Rather, we put emphasis on "global science" and major efforts of the scientific community to improve the standing of science in international debates. More specifically, we concentrate on the global challenges humankind faces. A most important aspect of the future of science or preferably, science, technology and innovation (STI), is proper recognition of their roles in realizing sustainable development. Some of these aspects are found in detail in other chapters.

Science as we use the term here includes the natural and environmental sciences, engineering, the social sciences and humanities. The importance of the latter is well articulated in the *2013 World Social Science Report* with its (quite unexpected) subtitle "Changing Global Environments" (ISSC and UNESCO 2013). We perceive, furthermore, theoretical and applied science not only related to all these disciplines but also as end points of a continuum instead of discrete fields within science.

Science in the new century

Science in the 20th century and its tools available were used to examine "simple" phenomena and structures (elementary particles and their excitations) and led to the design, synthesis and characterization of small molecules for production of numerous materials, including catalysts and pharmaceuticals. Science in the 21st century focuses, on the contrary, on interactions among simple structures to create new phenomena, designs large and complicated structures – atom by atom – meaning that we build on the successes of the past century and now confront questions previously the stuff of science fiction.

The prime interrogations science will face to are sometimes summarized in a "will we?" list projection of humankind's (ultimate) research agenda (Box 5.1).

Box 5.1   The "will we?" of science, visions of the 21st century

Will we travel to the stars?
Will we clone a dinosaur?
Will a killer asteroid hit the earth?
Will the brain understand itself?
Will we travel in time?
Will we meet ET?
Will we discover another universe?
Will we control the weather?
Will we have a final theory of everything?
Will there be anything left to discover?

Source: Time.com, 3 April 2000

Science in context

The complexity of systems in the scientific domain, particularly in regard to the science-policy interface, demands changes in the production and use of research. This was stressed by Gallopin et al. (2001). The complexity is more than evident in, for instance, biodiversity, climate change and sustainable development.

The challenge is echoed in efforts to devise new ways of reacting to pressing science-policy matters – as in the functioning of the Intergovernmental Panel on Climate Change (see chapter on climate change) or the Intergovernmental Platform on Biodiversity and Ecosystem Services (see chapter on biodiversity).

Current environmental challenges also pose new need for setting policy and making decisions. A few of these interlinked adaptations are listed in Box 5.2.

Box 5.2   Interlinked problems of environmental change

Enormous impacts recently on the atmosphere
Health risks from ground-level ozone, smog and fine particulates
Overexploitation of surface-water resources and aquifers
Increasing threats to biodiversity
Increasing exploitation and depletion of stocks of wild fish
Worsening soil degradation, especially in developing countries
Fragmentation and degradation of forest ecosystems
Increase in frequency and intensity of natural disasters
Climate change and its impact everywhere

The World Conference on Science (WCS) held in Budapest in 1999 was convened by the UN Educational, Scientific and Cultural Organization (UNESCO) and the International Council for Science (ICSU). The conference, in its own words

> established what efforts should be invested to make science advance in response to both social expectations and the challenges posed by human and social development . . . it negotiated a new 'social contract' for science as we enter the 21st century.

The meeting's results are summarized in two documents. First, the *Declaration on Science and the Use of Scientific Knowledge* stressed the political commitment needed to science and, through science itself, the science-society interface. Second, the *Science Agenda – Framework for Action* specified the needs for capacity building in research and the applications of science to sustainable development. The latter identified several major needs (Box 5.3; for further details see UNESCO 2000).

> **Box 5.3 World Conference on Science (1999) – framework of guiding principles and scientific commitment: the "needs"**
>
> Need for drastic changes of attitude and approach to problems of development, especially to their social, human and environmental dimensions.
> Need to improve, strengthen and diversify science education, formal and non-formal, at all levels and for all sectors...
> Need to strengthen the national S&T base, refurbishing national science policies, increasing scientific personnel and ensuring a stable and supportive research context...
> Need to break traditional barriers between natural and social sciences and to adopt interdisciplinarity as a common practice.
> Need to open scientific matters to public debate and democratic participation, so as to reach consensus and concerted action.
> Need to broaden scientific cooperation, regional and international, through networking and institutional arrangements with IGOs, NGOs and research and education centers.
>
> *Source*: UNESCO (2000)

The needs sketched in Box 5.3 are those not fully met. The complex landscape within which science operates today is characterized by a highly dynamic setting with new challenges. Examples: (1) politics is no longer internal or external, (2) the global emergence of civil society, characterized by multinational firms and the dynamics of stock markets worldwide, (3) evolution of our ICT and (4) recognition of global problems – e.g., the north/south debate, ethical questions, and how these are affected by climate change.

Responses to these much more complex environments in which science takes place, the "sciences" both natural and social, result in paradigm shifts as to how science is practiced today. A few models will illustrate this formidable process of change.

New terminology can be a good indicator of changes in the way science works. Examples are the new "interdisciplinarities," such as *biodiversity, biocultural diversity, ecological economics, bioinformatics* and *bioethics*. Tremendous changes in science resulted from the knowledge explosion in genetics, molecular biology and the biotechnologies. At the same time our ignorance of the natural world remains amazing. Biodiversity loss continues, yet we still do not know the order of magnitude of species living on Earth. The deep sea and its ecosystems are less well known than the surface of the Moon.

In view of the complex environment of modern science, the rigorous distinction between *basic* and *applied sciences* has given way to a concept of continuum in research covering "pure" basic and applied aspects and all shades in between. The Budapest Conference also ignited controversial dialogue on science versus "other systems of knowledge." Indigenous and local knowledge systems have become an essential add-on to modern science (see Erdelen 2001, for an overview). Modern ICT allow for new ways of retrieving and sharing information and lively networking among institutions at all geographic levels.

Many of our environmental issues are *transboundary* issues. Rivers and other ecosystems often transcend political boundaries at national level and therefore require transnational approaches to address questions of system conservation, management and sustainable development. Terms such as the "river continuum concept" and "transboundary protected areas" illustrate the need for operating beyond national levels – i.e., on systems levels.

Scientific literacy

In their book *Science Matters* (2009), earth scientist Robert Hazen and physicist James Trefil identify scientific literacy as "the knowledge you need to understand public issues." This means being able to understand scientific questions as they appear in news media and online. News items may report science concerning developments in the ecological, oceanic, geological, climate sciences, in energy or in physics, astronomy, biology, public infrastructure and even daring engineering design.

Frequently not properly understood, scientific literacy refers to *using* science rather than *doing* science. For example, scientific and technological literacy does not include how to operate a smartphone.

Then, there is a whole range of magazines which present popular science such as *Scientific American* (Box 5.4). Contributions in such reviews offer an advanced level of science from different fields such as astronomy, physics, biology, anthropology or biotechnology. Some scientific journals specialize in a scientific discipline – e.g., simply chemistry or herpetology. Within the world of technical media, there are differences in specialization whereby the scientific knowledge needed to understand prevails. Besides these, leading international publications such as *Science* or *Nature* may carry articles which even practicing scientists may not understand fully.

Box 5.4   Communicating science to non-scientists

Politics, economy, sports and entertainment may be the higher-ranking issues in popular media. Good presentations of science are found in the printed media, documentary films, radio and television reporting. Some media recapitulate annually topics covered the previous year, and many journals and magazines are accessible via the Internet. To be most effective, writing should be transdisciplinary and clear, avoiding use of unfamiliar scientific or engineering terms. For good models, see Britain's *New Scientist*, the French *Sciences & Avenir* or the German *Spektrum*. Science is cosmopolitan, so an excellent medium will diversify its material, with little hesitation about offering varied and attractive styles. In a single edition of the *Scientific American Weekly Review* (April 2016; available only online) the subjects reported and illustrated included the following:

- New Clues Show Out-of-Control Synapse Pruning May Underlie Alzheimer's
- The Addictive Personality Isn't What You Think It Is
- Mysterious Gravitational Tug on Orbiter May Help Find Planet Nine
- Zika Vaccine Could Solve One Problem While Stoking Another
- Archeologists Uncover Another Branch of the Silk Road
- What Really Killed the Dinosaurs?
- New Frontiers in Cancer Treatments
- Is Swearing a Sign of a Limited Vocabulary?
- How Cultural Differences Affect Autism Diagnoses
- It's Square Root Day! Prepare to Be Somewhat Underwhelmed . . .
- Lasers Could Hide Earth from Prying Aliens
- Do Lobsters Need Ear Plugs?
- Twin Birth Proposed for Colliding Black Holes that Produced Gravitational Waves
- The Sexual Brain

A relaxed style of expression, accessible to all, avoids long sentences and unexplained references, and the ranking or topical formatting found in professional presentations. Text should be accompanied by videos, photographs, infographics, simple statistical tables and pie charts and occasionally by rough hand-sketches or cartoons as well as poetry and music.

Scientific literacy is not a luxury but a necessity for survival of the living. Science is becoming ever more important for understanding our world better, and to understand the grave challenges humankind faces. Literacy is basic to analyze critically developments in research and technology and to comprehend debates in areas affecting us all. Examples are the fields of genetic engineering, the use of genetically modified crops to feed man and beast, and using synthetic fertilizers and pesticides in agriculture. Added to these somewhat passive worries are the pressing environmental threats (Box 5.2). There is much to be made "literate," scientifically speaking.

If scientific literacy is increasingly important for modern society, education in science and technology becomes equally more relevant for the average citizen. This is reflected in terms such as ICT (information and communication technologies), R&D (research and development), S&T (science and technology) and STEM (science, technology, engineering, mathematics) education. Evolving ICT facilitate the process of becoming scientifically literate. Information from Wikipedia and other platforms is available virtually everywhere at all times. They can be consulted on almost any scientific subject.

From this short excursion into scientific literacy it becomes clear how inextricably we are linked to our knowledge and educational systems, ultimately to worldwide challenges. Recent dialogue among many specialists results in complexity readily apparent. Assessment of scientific literacy itself has led increasingly to an overall systemic view. Such perspective corroborates further the fact that Earth systems cannot be fully understood through traditional content-related disciplines still prevalent as recently as the 1990s.

Sciences in the third millennium

A few thoughts

What science do we need in view of the fast-evolving environment and humankind's reactions in the new millennium? This question was raised almost two decades ago by Walter Erdelen and marine biologist Howard Moore (see their 2005 ref.). They observed as follows.

But what are the features – the kind of science – that we should be encouraging in our world of the Third Millennium? It is clear that we need a science that would, first and foremost, meet basic human needs throughout the world, such as primary health care, sanitation, provision of food, clean water and energy and generally improve the quality of life for all. It would allow greater understanding of the major global environmental processes, a more sustainable use of natural resources and the mitigation of natural disasters. It would be more equitable in terms of access to information and knowledge, and provide fairer opportunities for entering and pursuing scientific careers. In addition, it would provide a balance between the freedom to pursue research without hindrance of a political or economic nature, and the ethical responsibilities that are incumbent upon the individual researcher.

Science certainly needs to play a much greater role than hitherto in addressing some of the most pressing global challenges such as poverty, environment and health, availability of water and food security. This underlines the need for increased international cooperation on global and long-term projects. If the science of the 21st century is to confront complex problems of a truly global scale it will need to be interdisciplinary in approach, drawing on not only the natural sciences but also the social sciences and the humanities. We can see today how the major successes in molecular genetics and biotechnology owe so much to the advances made in physics, chemistry and biology. Environmental problems – we now understand – can only be thoroughly investigated through the concerted efforts of geologists, chemists, biologists, engineers, economists and others.

As spelled out in the same paper, and ever more relevant today,

> big problems demand big solutions, and the power of interdisciplinarity coupled with innovative methods will be needed to help the resolution of the complex issues that span wide temporal and spatial scales. There must also be effective bridges between policy, management and science, as well as closer links between the public and private sectors.

And some developments

The last few years have seen impressive efforts to broaden science at international level. The encouragement continues, notably in 2012 during the International Council for Science's Planet Under Pressure Conference in London. At the same time, preparatory activity for the Rio+20 Summit played an essential role in catalyzing the process for a new, global scientific initiative called *Future Earth*. A newly established UN body should be significant in recognizing the contribution of science to implement the 2030 Development Agenda. The body is the UN Secretary-General's Scientific Advisory Board.

The Planet Under Pressure Conference

The Global Environmental Change Programs,[2] together with the International Council for Science, organized this gathering (Box 5.5). This major meeting, held in London, took place during the run-up to the UN's Rio+20 summit (see the chapter on sustainable development). With the subtitle *New Knowledge Towards Solutions*, the London gathering, held 26–29 March 2012, thus indicated its major objective. This was to assess the state of our global home by exploring solutions to impending crises, as reported in its *State of the Planet Declaration*.

Lying behind initiating the conference was the realization that scientific research had shown that the future functioning of the Earth system of systems is at risk if urgent action is not taken. Research was linked to our understanding of global climate change. This change is recorded in the reports of the Intergovernmental Panel on Climate Change (IPCC) and related reporting on water, food and biodiversity. The influence of the planetary boundary concept together with that of the Anthropocene epoch have been instrumental in publicizing an alarming situation – and not only within the scientific community.

As stated in the *State of the Planet Declaration*, "In one lifetime our increasingly interconnected and interdependent economic, social, cultural and political systems have come to place pressures on the environment that may cause fundamental changes in the Earth system and move us beyond safe natural boundaries." The text continues in a more optimistic tone: "But at the same time interconnectedness provides the potential for solutions: new ideas can form and spread quickly, creating the momentum for the major transformation required for a truly sustainable planet."

The lofty conference goal is of course not achievable in a single conference. Rather, it is indicative of the urgent need for new solutions. These are related to progress in STI and the quest for a transformation of values, beliefs and aspirations to "sustainable prosperity." This is stated in the conference's Declaration, which also suggests a "new contract between science and society" based on a strengthened and coherent science-policy interface. A major research initiative is proposed, labeled *Future Earth: Research for Global Sustainability*.

An important aspect of this conference was its timing. Insights from the meeting were targeted at inclusion in the deliberations of the Rio+20 Summit, so the scientific community to gain more weight in the UN-led process leading to sustainable development. Science was to be no longer left at the door.

Box 5.5   Vision of the Planet Under Pressure Conference

The global scientific community must deliver to society the knowledge necessary to assess the risks humanity is facing from global change. It must provide knowledge of how society can effectively mitigate dangerous changes and cope with changes we cannot manage.

Based on the latest scientific evidence, the London Planet Under Pressure Conference will provide a comprehensive update of our knowledge of the Earth system and the pressure our planet is now under. The London conference will focus the scientific community's and the wider world's attention on climate, ecological degradation, human well-being, planetary thresholds, food security, energy, governance across scales and poverty alleviation.

The conference will discuss solutions, at all scales, to move societies on to a sustainable pathway. It will provide scientific leadership toward the 2012 UN Rio +20 conference, also in 2012.

Guiding the direction for the conference is the International Council for Science's five grand challenges for global sustainability research: observations, forecasting, thresholds, governance and economic requirements, and innovation (technological, political and societal). The conference will also support international assessment processes, for example the IPCC and the new biodiversity assessment, plus the MDGs.

The program will be designed to attract senior policy makers, industry leaders, NGOs, young scientists, the media, health specialists and academics from many disciplines.

Source: www.planetunderpressure2012.net/

As stated in an editorial in the journal *Science*, "UNsustainable?," Carlos A. Nobre, former chair of the IGBP, expressed hope that three major global changes, emerging during the last two decades, should affect the outcome of the Rio+20 Summit: These influences are interconnectedness among nations, the concept of the Anthropocene, and the critical role that developing economies will play in future global sustainability agendas (Nobre 2012).

Along the same lines the declaration *The Future We Choose*, an outcome of a High-Level Dialogue on Global Sustainability and signed by a number of leaders of the world's scientific community (including UN entities), declared: "A fully integrated science-based approach is necessary to tackle the very real risks that confront us" and that "we need to reconnect human societies with the biosphere."

And yet representatives of the science community at Rio+20 were disappointed with the results of the Summit. This is reflected in a statement made by ICSU entitled "Science was short-changed at Rio+20, but informal actors did generate momentum for sustainable development." Major criticism in the ICSU statement centered on the following:

- Throughout the preparatory process for Rio+20 ICSU and the global environmental research programs had presented strong scientific evidence on changes in our environment and the need to act with urgency. The latter is not reflected in the document *The Future We Want*.
- Governments have failed to recognize that (1) the latest scientific knowledge is vital to developing solutions for the sustainability challenges that humanity faces, and (2) there is a strong interrelationship between scientific research, knowledge, development and innovative technologies.
- Technological innovations are an important part of the solution, but they will not suffice. It is knowledge from across both natural and social sciences that is needed to identify, validate and monitor new technologies and to introduce new, "green" economic models.

On the more positive side ICSU acknowledged that the Rio+20 findings provide opportunities for further strengthening the science-policy interface but also highlighted that the real achievements of the Summit were made by so-called "coalitions of the willing," the networks of governments, businesses, scientific organizations, NGOs and other members of civil society. This leads to possibly one of the most important conclusions from the conference, reflected in its outcome document: *Governments cannot deliver Sustainable Development alone!*[3]

During Rio+20 a disconnect was observed between civil society and governments. Governments showed a profound interest in preserving the integrity of multilateralism. People have become aware, however, that governmental institutions have experienced damage because of their failure to "produce solutions that rise to the moment, effectively integrate latest scientific evidence, and address the world as it is and not as it once was," as expressed in the analysis of the Rio+20 Summit and presented in the Earth Negotiations Bulletin of the International Institute for Sustainable Development (IISD). This is echoed in the declaration *The Future We Choose*: "Such an integrated model, which reflects the scientific consensus and is guided by the principles of responsibility and equity will and must provide a **systemic solution** [bold ours] that ensures the wise stewardship of the planet and its peoples."

Future Earth

Future Earth, announced at the Rio+20 Summit, has since established its distributed structure and corresponding administrative bodies (see www.futureearth.org and Box 5.6). *Future Earth* mainstreams major global change programs and builds on their over 20 years of collaboration. The DIVERSITAS program website announced that it is opening a new era of integrated sustainability science. As a result of this mainstreaming, the communiqué titled *ESSP Transitions into "Future Earth,"* stated in December 2012 that the Earth System Science Partnership (ESSP) "will close and transition into 'Future Earth' as it develops over the next few years." DIVERSITAS and the IGBP transferred all their activities to the new *Future Earth* program. IHDP[4] was dissolved in July 2014. The World Climate Research Program now continues, but contributes to Future Earth.

Time will show whether this organizational reshuffle and mainstreaming process, respectively, will bring Earth system related science to the fore and into international debates on sustainable development – essential for, and in, the future.

Box 5.6   *Future Earth*: a ten-year international research initiative

Announced: June 2012, at Rio+20 Summit
Timeline: Through 2025
April 2015:   Permanent secretariat established, with global hubs acting as a single entity, located in Canada (at Montreal), France (Paris), Japan (Tokyo), Sweden (Stockholm), United States (Colorado). Complemented by regional hubs

Research Themes: 1   Dynamic planet
 2   Global development
 3   Transformations toward sustainability

Sponsored by: Science and Technology Alliance for Global Sustainability comprising
International Council for Science
International Social Science Council
Belmont Forum (of funding agencies)
UN Educational, Scientific, and Cultural Organization
UN Environment Program
UN University
World Meteorological Organization

Source: www.futureearth.org

UNESCO and the UN Secretary-General's Scientific Advisory Board

UNESCO is the only UN entity with a mandate for science. Science at UNESCO includes not only the natural sciences (including engineering, biotechnologies, as well as the Earth, water, ocean and environmental sciences) but also the social sciences and humanities. This is reflected in the Organization's five program (action) arms.

As a result, UNESCO has long sought to increase the prominence of science within the overall activities of the UN in general and, more specifically, in the context of sustainable development. The idea of better positioning of science in the international debate, including its policy dimensions, has been at the heart of UNESCO's activities in science.

The Organizations' flagship publication has been the *UNESCO Science Report*, a series of reports launched in 1993. They occupy a unique niche by "mapping science, technology and innovation (STI) around the world on a regular basis." Six issues have appeared to date, the latest published in 2015 and, subtitled *Towards 2030*, a clear indication of its link to the 2030 Agenda for Sustainable Development (UNESCO 2016a, for the revised edition).

In 2012, along with the release of the report *Resilient People, Resilient Planet* by the UN Secretary-General's High-Level Panel on Global Sustainability (the "GSP" below), the notion of a more formal anchoring of science throughout the entire UN system received the recognition long deserved: a Scientific Advisory Board (SAB) of the UN Secretary-General was created. UNESCO's director-general was requested to establish, chair and house the SAB's secretariat.

As specified in its terms of reference,

> the central function of the board will be to provide advice on science, technology and innovation (STI) for sustainable development to the UN Secretary-General and to executive heads of UN organizations. The Board will bring together in a coherent manner the collective capacity of all relevant scientific fields, with due regard to social and ethical dimensions of sustainable development. The fields will span a broad spectrum, from the basic sciences, through engineering and technology, social sciences and humanities, ethics, health, economic, behavioral, and agricultural sciences, in addition to the environmental sciences, which are more commonly associated with sustainability.

A key role in this advisory capacity will be assigned to the science (meaning research) policy responsibility alluded to elsewhere in this and other chapters. It is not only the sheer number of disciplines with which the SAB should deal, but the functions it is supposed to fill.

These are (from SAB's terms of reference):

- strengthening the linkage between science and policy;
- ensuring that up to date and rigorous science is appropriately reflected in high-level policy discussions within the UN system;

- offering advice, in cooperation and consultation with the UN agencies concerned, on how the many organizations in the UN system with a science, technology, engineering and humanities mission in the area of sustainability can work together more effectively, avoid mission creep and overlap, and curb counterproductive competition;
- offering recommendations to the Secretary-General on priorities related to science for sustainable development that should be supported or encouraged within or by the UN system, including for the post-2015 development process;
- carrying out relevant intellectual work including providing advice to the UN Secretary-General on up-to-date scientific issues relevant to sustainable development, including advice on "assessments and digests around concepts as 'planetary boundaries,' 'tipping points' and 'environmental thresholds,'" as indicated in Recommendation 51 of the report of the GSP. This will allow the Secretary-General to articulate scientific issues which have attracted widespread attention in contemporary affairs;
- identifying knowledge gaps that could be addressed outside the UN system by either national or international research programs – e.g., the emerging *Future Earth* program;
- identifying specific assessment needs that could be addressed by ongoing assessments (e.g., IPCC or the IPBES) or new assessment activities to be developed within the UN system;
- advising on issues related to the public visibility and understanding of science;
- offering insight on democratic global governance, focused on sustainability and the responsible and ethical development of science.

Within this extremely broad and demanding mandate, the secretary-general has defined the following *Focus Areas* for the new Board. These are as follows:

1 Ideas on how to strengthen the high-level political forum on sustainable development – i.e., how to improve the synergy between science and decision making.
2 Advice on climate change ahead of the 2015 Paris Climate Conference, where the international community hopes to adopt a new climate agreement (which in fact happened; see chapter on climate change).
3 Contributions to the data revolution for sustainable development.
4 Advice on other scientific concerns about the future of both people and planet, to be brought to the attention of the Secretary-General.

The prospects may raise eyebrows. How realistic should be the expectations evoked by such a board?

The future will show whether the SAB can meet all expectations. We have the impression that these are beyond what a small group may be able to achieve, unless it is part of broader resources such as the existing expertise within the UN system. Ultimately, this effort may transform itself into a heavier and bureaucratic structure (logistically housed at UNESCO).

The process of creating a body such as SAB is indicative of a more profound issue (see UNESCO 2016b). Science has not gained sufficient prestige in the UN machinery that it needs. Science will be vital for confronting the major crises humankind will face, pressures clearly stipulated in the present and other chapters. Modern technologies and a paradigm shift toward a green and circular economy need to underlie processes keeping humanity within the well-labeled safe operating space of the Anthropocene.

Some conclusions

We wish to finish this chapter with two quotations from the epilogue of Gregory N. Derry's book of 1999, *What Science Is and How It Works*, but in an order that is not that of the author:

> How science works: starting with ideas and concepts you know, observing the world, trying different things, creating a coherent context, seeing patterns, formulating hypotheses and predictions, finding the limits where your understanding fails, making new discoveries when the unexpected happens, and formulating a new and broader context within which to understand what you see.
>
> I would like to end with some pithy aphorism that sums up in a few words my understanding of what science is. But I don't believe that's possible. Every brief attempt I've seen to define science has failed to capture some crucial element of the total picture.

Many important aspects characterizing science could not be taken up here. We mean, for example, how science is practiced and the problems inherent to specialized education at all levels, to university and test-bench careers, to the social status of scientists and more.

One hopes that science will help provide the knowledge base for decision makers, for a society possessing full sensitivity to the immense challenges all of us must meet. Science permeates virtually all of civilization, including the use of natural resources to meet society's demands in an increasingly globalized and urban world. Ethical and moral concerns weigh, furthermore, on the great majority of *Homo complexus*; such conscience is part of us. STI are, in the broadest interpretation, facets of knowledge more needed than ever before.

As stated in the policy brief of the SAB for the 2015 Climate Summit,

> Scientists are often not familiar with the complexities and practical problems associated with policymaking and the outcome of specific decisions. Conversely, decision makers do not always understand scientific phenomena, which often do not lend themselves to ease of matching with practical decision making frameworks.

The same policy document also notes,

> Closer interaction between the two communities would ensure that scientists frame the results of scientific research to match the needs of policy makers in a manner that demystifies science and makes it universally applicable. It can also ensure that scientists recognize the gaps in the political understanding of issues, and can set scientific agendas more closely attuned to ongoing policy processes.

The global community can no longer afford such disjointed rapport. This is a situation necessitating attention urgently. The circumstances seek a paradigm shift in the thinking and practice of scientists and deciders. Communication, education and cultural involvement of civil society are essential for a shift in model that is long overdue.

Notes

1 The Higgs boson, first suspected to exist in the 1960s, is one of 17 particles forming the Standard Model of physics: infinitely small building blocks of matter energized by four forces: strong, weak, electromagnetic and gravitational. Most research was conducted at the CERN laboratories near Geneva, Switzerland.
2 DIVERSITAS, the International Geosphere-Biosphere Program (IGBP), the International Human Dimensions Program on Global Environmental Change (IHDP), and the World Climate Research Program (WCRP).
3 One should add that governments, despite their assent in UN resolutions, are beset by their own problems, limiting both budgetary ability and adequate human resources. Of the 38 Islamic states (almost 20 percent of the UN membership), only Tunisia has emerged from the Arab Spring of 2011 to a condition of near-democracy. The other 37 states are at war, combatting insurrection or civil war, or so preoccupied with other priorities that sustainable development is illusory.
4 The International Human Dimensions Program on Global Environmental Change (IHDP) was a research effort that studied the societal aspects of the phenomenon of global change. IHDP was initiated as the Human Dimensions Program (HDP) in 1990 by the International Social Science Council (ISSC). It was established under its closing name, International Human Dimensions Program on Global Environmental Change, by ISSC and the International Council for Science in 1996.

References

Derry, G.N. 1999. *What Science is and How It Works*. Princeton University Press, Princeton and Oxford.
Erdelen, W.R. 2001. *Opening Address*. International Conference "Science and Tradition: Roots and Wings for Development." Royal Academy of Overseas Sciences and UNESCO, 14–19.
Erdelen, W.R. and H. Moore 2005. Science, yes – but what kind? *UNESCO Today* 2/2005: 32–36.
Gallopin, G.C., S. Funtowicz, M. O' Connor and J. Ravetz 2001. Science for the twenty-first century: From social contract to the scientific core. *International Social Science Journal* 168: 219–229.

Hazen, R.M. and J. Trefil 2009. *Science Matters: Achieving Scientific Literacy*. Anchor Books, New York.

Holland, J.H. 2014. *Complexity: A Very Short Introduction*. Oxford University Press, Oxford.

ISSC and UNESCO 2013. *World Social Science Report 2013. Changing Global Environments*. OECD Publishing and UNESCO Publishing, Paris.

Nobre, C.A. 2012. UNsustainable? *Science* 336: 1361.

UNESCO 2000. *World Conference on Science – Science for the Twenty-First Century: A New Commitment*. UNESCO, Paris.

UNESCO 2016a. *UNESCO Science Report: Towards 2030*. Revised edition 2016. UNESCO, Paris.

UNESCO 2016b. *The Future of Scientific Advice to the United Nations. A Summary Report to the Secretary-General of the United Nations from the Scientific Advisory Board*. UNESCO, Paris.

6 Industry, engineering, further complexity
Steam engines and more

Biodiversity shows up, curiously transformed, in individual and group behavior on the part of *Homo faber*: the human who makes. In the world of education, economic anthropology teaches that the human species has sought from its start to improvise, adapt, improve and perfect tools, and what these produce. Implements make work more responsive to need and easier for the human body to handle. During the inventive 19th century alone, our minds learned to measure accurately and gave birth to still newer implements and techniques. These often yielded their own complexities and opportunities for additional advance. Here we illustrate such perplexities, complementing the earlier chapter on foresight and innovation.

The enduring quest for better working aids

We learned to control fire to work the hardest metals, melt and process glass and came to use light as the prime tool of telescopy and photography. The camera and photomicrography opened doors to molecular, cellular and other finely detailed biology. Black-and-white photography integrated radiology (X-rays), discovered color manipulation and instant processing, made possible Skype and smartphones, and combine with radar to probe distant galaxies.

Tools and their users compete with others, are sometimes surpassed by rivals, fail or fall into disuse. Such are the habits of the Anthropocene: the recently named anthropological period in which the human being came to control (or abuse) the natural environment in a continuing effort to manage nature's resources.[1] The innovative era began about 1850, was joined by nuclear energy a century later, and has since led to a permanent process of innovation (see Tab. 6.1).

George Eastman's profitable marketing of the one-dollar Brownie box camera in the 1890s revolutionized still photography: it put the medium directly in the hands of an eager public. By the late 1940s, Edwin Land's Polaroid technology made available to amateurs almost instant photographic prints. Enthusiasts no longer depended on days-long photofinishing to enjoy the results of their click-and-flash moments. But the Eastman "Kodak" and Land Polaroid ventures both encountered system stumbles that had vital consequences for both firms.

74 Industry, engineering, further complexity

Table 6.1 Evolution of four emergences in the continuing industrial revolution, reckoned by the World Economic Forum in Davos (Switzerland)

Revolution	Year	Information
1	1784	Steam, water, mechanical production equipment
2	1870	Division of labor, electricity, mass production
3	1969	Electronics, IT, automated production
4	?	Cyber-physical systems

Dates vary with different authorities. The year 1969 was marked by the (still) longest distance covered by humans communicating via radiotelephony: between Earth and Moon and return, 768,800 km. Klaus Schwab, head of the Davos group, views this evolution's unsparing impact equally on the worlds of business and government as well as on the population as a whole. Development of cyber-physical systems includes, if proved, the complexity of several governments accused of hacking others' communication facilities in an effort to disrupt national election campaigns. If confirmed, this will prove to be a new form of international political warfare in violation of standing policies of non-interference. As Klaus Schwab said on occasion of the opening of WEF's innovative Center for the Fourth Industrial Revolution (in 2016), "Given the accelerating change brought on by innovation, continuous public-private cooperation on a global level is needed more than ever" and therefore [the Center] "will serve as a global platform for dialogue and collaborative action on the most important questions related to the impact of emerging technologies."

Kodak's evolving management, while meeting extraordinary success with the manufacture of photographic films and papers as well as portable motion-picture cameras and equipment, hesitated too long in deciding to enter the field of digital-image creation. The company was forced to file for bankruptcy in 2012, divesting itself of more than a half-billion dollars in plant sites, sold chiefly to the large digital-system designers and builders. In effect, these were the technological interlopers responsible for the downfall of a once world-famous, highly prosperous undertaking.

The Land Polaroid firm had financed its instant-camera research with profits from sunglasses and night-seeing optical equipment for the military. Diverting its energy and resources to R&D of color and sound capabilities for the then popular 8mm home-movie market, the company overextended itself financially and ultimately failed. Both the Eastman and Land misadventures were abundantly reported in their time. The essential causes of failure were systemic: the wandering of market-researched innovation and resulting products (according to some of Land's severest critics), insufficient managerial control over diversified development and exploitation of product, insufficient adaptability to fast-evolving technology and a fatal let's-wait-and-see mentality. Victor K. McElheny's biography of Land, *Insisting on the Impossible* (1998), is the most recent on this self-taught, imaginative and tireless inventor.

From photography to telephony

Consider the impact of the choices that were also not made by a major manufacturer of portable telephones. These became an item of business news circulating worldwide in 2010. The introduction three years earlier of Apple's iPhone coincided with testing a similar touch-screen device for use on the Internet by the Finnish IT firm Nokia. Several former employees of Nokia told the business press that, as early as 2004, Nokia had customer-tested a prototype, but "management . . . killed it" because of its production costs. This inertia allowed the Canadian firm BlackBerry, Korea's Samsung and LG (all three of them dynamic rivals) "to steal a beat in a main battle for the industry's future."[2] In late 2015 BlackBerry announced that it would integrate Google's mobile Android into its new telephones.

Ever ready to respond to novelty, BlackBerry introduced in 2014 its Classic smartphone, equipped with keyboard and trackpad to appeal to consumers less interested in advanced tactile technology. The device did not do well in the marketplace, and Ian Austen of the *New York Times* reported on 7 July 2016 that the Canadian manufacturer was discontinuing the Classic. Introduction of BlackBerry's PRIV telephone was seen by market analysts as perhaps a test of the firm's long-range plans to remain in the telephone sector, Avast Software in Prague reported. (About one million portable telephones existed worldwide in 1990; by early 2015 this figure rose to between five and six billion.[3] The market still broadens.)

A former specialist at Finland's Nokia firm reported that he had recommended

> a 3-D user interface for [Nokia's] Symbian handsets, which at that time would have been unique . . . He said his proposal [was] rejected because the needed software would have added $2.05 each to the cost of producing a telephone.

He compared Nokia's design approval process to a "Soviet-style bureaucracy." Another former worker reported that he "was still upbeat about his former employer but thought it had lost its creative momentum and would take a couple years to respond to the Apple iPhone." It is also interesting for complexity specialists to note the relevance expressed here between decision making and the creative spirit. Each year Nokia's engineers file roughly a thousand new patent applications, spanning a remarkable range of some 11,000 "families" of intellectual property. A patent application can be easily derailed by insoluble emerging complexities of both technical and commercial nature.

Nokia then found itself with a new chief, Stephen Elop of Canada – the firm's first non-Finnish chief executive – busily restructuring the firm's global workforce of 129,000: a staff grown, according to former and current employees, bureaucratic and too dependent on a multitude of managerial decisions made by committee. Within a month, President Elop was able to announce an impressive balance for the firm's fiscal third-quarter, exploiting "a new software application development tool called Qt to speed the creation of applications for its Symbian and MeeGo handsets, and the reduction-in-force (3 percent) of some 1,800 staff."[4]

When feasibility thwarts the will

We have mentioned rationality giving way to expediency: a contrary motivation for getting things done. A remarkable case of expediency is to be found within the U.S. defense establishment's logistical system. This has involved, among other logistical calculations, a continuous resupply of engine fuel for the many vehicles engaged in the Afghanistan intervention. Combat conditions meant that a single liter of gasoline costing the American taxpayer $0.025 required a further expenditure of $400 to move the fuel to where it was needed. What could be done?

One solution tried by the military was resorting to renewable energy. A major challenge, of course, was to overcome the fixed-site characteristic of (for example) most solar panels. The authority for funding was explained by Elisabeth Rosenthal of the *New York Times*:

> While setting national energy policy requires Congressional debates, military leaders can simply order the adoption of renewable energy. And the military has the buying power to create products and market. That, in turn, may make renewable energy more practical and affordable for everyday [civil] uses.[5]

On land, the 150 troops of "I" Company of the U.S. 5th Marine Regiment experimented with solar power for computers (panels that fold into boxes) and habitable shelter (tent shields providing shade and electricity) in ambient temperatures of as much as 49°C. This renewable technology can cost $70,000, but the investment is amortized once the costs of fossil fuel and its transport are calculated. At sea, the U.S. Navy introduced in 2009 a Wasp-class assault ship of a hybrid type, the *Makin*. This amphibious vessel, running at less than 10 knots, saved some 3,500,000 liters of fuel on its first voyage between Mississippi and California. The choice here obviated, rather clearly, the fallacious reasoning behind maintaining total reliance on fossil-fuel supply; it also facilitates increased dual use – both military and civil. Out of complexity (and cost), relative simplicity.

Still in the energy domain, a recent conjugation of different and practically unassociated technologies brought energy relief and for some, unexpected profits. *Directional drilling* – of a water, brine, petroleum or other well – is a rather well-known technique dating from the 1920s, when corrective shifting of an oil-well drill was sometimes necessitated because of illegal trespass on a neighbor's underground oil reserves. "Slant" drilling became, indeed, a *casus belli* in 1990 when Iraq charged neighboring Kuwait with doing just that to retract, from wellhead through tortuous borehole, Iraqi oil stocks underground.

Hydraulic fracturing (fracking)

This technique has been known since the earliest moments of petroleum extraction on a commercial basis, the 1860s. In the United States, fracturing is regularly used for 90 percent of gas drilling, a complicated process whereby enormous amounts of water mixed with sand and catalytic chemicals are pushed underground under high pressure. The pressing causes rock structures impeding the otherwise free passage of gas (and now petroleum) to rupture, releasing the "black gold" toward the surface for collection, further processing and distribution. The chemicals used risk causing pollution when stored at the surface or left below ground after drilling has ended. These methods are in themselves complications, but they risk triggering serious complexity in subterranean rock structures and, hypothetically at least, aggravated tectonic movement. The technique is better known today as "fracking."

Thus two models of extraction system were combined, especially in the shale fields of the United States and the tar sands of Canada, to change drastically global exploitation of oil and gas from underground reserves. The price-per-barrel of oil dropped by 50 percent in a few months of winter 2014–2015, holding promise of remaining low for a few years. Energy guru Daniel Yergin reviewed this remarkable shift in resource economics in the *New York Times*.[6]

There may be no final word in the attempt to call upon alternative energy sources to provide for both civil and military needs. In January 2011 the RAND Corporation published an evaluation of substitute fuels for the armed services, *Alternative Fuels for Military Application*. RAND concluded that "it is uncertain how much these [substitute] fuels will cost and what effect they may have on the environment, particularly in terms of greenhouse-gas emissions." The report also noted, surprisingly, that "current efforts by the services to test and certify alternative fuels are far outpacing commercial development, and that certain efforts are directed at fuels with a very limited potential for sustainable production."[7] In view of its carbon dioxide emissions, fracking technology promises to remain hotly debated.

Preventive action is seldom assured

British Petroleum's notorious oil spill of April 2010 became a weeks-long preoccupation in the international news. Upwelling oil and gas caused a conflagration that destroyed completely BP's offshore drilling platform, *Deepwater Horizon*. Public sympathy for the loss of 11 lives among the operating crew and around 40 injured workers compounded a growing fear of lasting environmental damage to the flora and fauna of the Gulf of Mexico region. The nearly one billion liters of petroleum lost seemed also to portend immeasurable damage to life *beneath* the Gulf's surface – an environmental complexity of high order.

What happened? A primary accident, a blowout of oil and gas at the level of the "Macondo" wellhead some 1,500 meters (5,000 ft.) beneath the ocean's surface caused explosions and a devastating fire on the drilling platform and its equipment. Safeguard systems either were not activated in time or, once in action, proved inadequate to control the cataclysm.

Two events, consecutive but near-simultaneous, occurred. The wellhead erupted on the seabed, totally out of control; escaping oil and gas ignited, then destroyed the platform at sea level. The incendiary fury took lives, injured more workers and left drilling and emergency equipment immediately inoperable. "The worst of the explosions," reported the *New York Times*, "gutted the Deepwater Horizon from stem to stern." The newspaper, citing the official report of the National Commission on the BP Deepwater Horizon and Offshore Drilling, wrote of "indecision and fear." Death and injuries followed because "every one of the Horizon's defenses failed on 20 April."[8]

One element in the unfolding drama seemed to carry much of the burden of doubt that prevailed immediately after the first explosion of gas and liquid petroleum. That was the role played by a young bridge officer named Andrea Fleytas. Twenty-three years old and trained to respond manually to set off a general-evacuation alarm, Ms. Fleytas watched her computer console as mud flew thickly around her workstation and gas and oil sensors activated warning lights on her console.

Both Ms. Fleytas and her supervisor nearby, Yancy Keplinger, said they were fully aware of what was happening and could have shut down the emergency system – which would have turned off ventilation fans and slowed the flow of gas. They could have used the emergency plans

> to turn off electrical equipment and limit ignition sources. They could have even used [them] to shut down the engines. They did none of these things . . . The Deepwater Horizon [thus] had a number of defenses against blowouts. But members of the crew hesitated at critical moments and failed to coordinate a response in three key areas,

reported another medium, the *New York Journal*. As complexity combined within more complexity, uncertainty sat at the controls.

Giovanni Pezzulo and Martin Butz state in their book *The Challenge of Anticipation* that it is commonly believed that "all motor control [in the human organism] is mediated by internal predictive models that permit the emulation of the environment."[9] This predictive model failed, in final effect, to emulate the instantaneous shift in environment aboard *Deepwater Horizon*. Nor could this mode apply. Incidentally, neither to the exploding batteries in Samsung's Galaxy Note 7 smartphone six years later, nor to the defective airbags supplied (and later recalled) by the Takata Corporation to Japanese automobile builders.

As to the prospective sequels to this major incident, a widely respect journal of the chemical-engineering industry commented on the special Commission's recommendation: "[A] jump in funding for enforcement, oversight, and Gulf environmental restoration and [a call for] creation of a new industry-funded organization to develop industry-wide standards of excellence." Thus Gulf environmental groups, fishing interests and citizens' associations backed the report; industry groups did not. The American Petroleum Institute claimed the Commission had not recognized recent petroleum company and government reforms and was citing a single incident to judge the industry as a whole. Foresight can indeed have conflicting interpretations.

By July 2015, BP's management reached an agreement with federal and state officials to pay an indemnity totaling $18.7 billion for the oil spill affecting Alabama, Florida, Louisiana, Mississippi and Texas. Of this sum, American subsidiary BP Exploration and Production was to pay about $7.1 billion for damage to natural resources, $5.5 billion in penalties (to the federal government) for violations of the Clean Water Act and $4.9 billion to the five states settling for damage to their economies. In addition, more than 400 local governments shared about $1 billion. The total amount was the largest compensation paid for environmental damage in American history.

The mass and specialized media covered this outcome extensively, the *New York Times* adding that BP had spent several years in ridding itself of important assets in anticipation of the costs of *Deepwater Horizon* and that the British corporation "now emerges sound and with cash to explore." In an editorial published a week later, the newspaper said the settlement

> will also provide a significant, continuing source of revenue for the repair and restoration of the Gulf of Mexico's marshes, barrier islands, fisheries, deep-sea corals and other vulnerable elements of an ecosystem that had been ailing long before the spill.[10]

By 2017, BP predicted in its annual *Energy Report* that global exploitation of alternative energy will have quadrupled by 2035.

Natural resources for R&D

Much of the world's attention to the supply of rare earths was dramatized in an article appearing in *Scientific American*'s issue for November 2009. Authors Mark Jacobson and Mark Delucci, commenting on the use of scarce materials in the construction of wind turbines, stated, "The most problematic materials may be rare-earth metals such as neodymium used in turbine gearboxes. Although the metals are not in short supply, the low-cost sources are concentrated in China." This suggested that, in future, highly industrialized countries "could be trading dependence on Middle Eastern oil for dependence on Far Eastern metals."[11]

What are rare earths? They are chemical elements (all metals, some of which occur only as trans-uranium or humanly made elements). These substances have a quantitatively modest, but critical, demand in industry; they are relatively costly to excavate and process. Economic happenstance, furthermore, has made them largely exploited in China and little elsewhere so that, since about 2000, China is able to control the export of neodymium, lithium, samarium, ytterbium and similar elements. By 2010, China could delay considerably rare-earth exports to Japan in retaliation for a territorial dispute with Beijing which, China said, was initiated by the Tokyo government. The delay affected the manufacture in Japan of essential automobile components.

Among consumers in the industrialized countries, those of the EU have proved to be the most determined in their reactions to China's potential for economic warfare using the rare earths. Largely at the instigation of Germany, the European Commission drafted a plan, "Tackling the Challenges in Commodity Markets and on Raw Materials," for action by the European Council and the European Parliament so that EU countries could recycle rare earths already produced in manufactured goods such as portable telephones.

During the decade 2002–2011 the price of neodymium increased more than 700 percent: from US$4.30/kg to US$30.00/kg, according to European business media in the early weeks of 2011. Brussels consequently prepared a "more aggressive strategy" toward rare-earth exporters, through the good offices of both the G20 nations and the World Trade Organization. This strategy requires European contracts signed with Chinese partners to include clauses guaranteeing the European signatories access to resources inherently at the heart of Europe's commercial policy – e.g., marketable items such as the rare earths.

This example is a case of incertitude, on the one hand, reinforced by the economic policy of a specific country in regard to its exports, and a restraining policy, on the other hand, to be applied only by a determined geopolitical stance taken by importers to resolve complexity. The rare-earth map, meanwhile, was in process of shifting. Prices dipped markedly by March 2012; *Foreign Affairs* magazine pointed to new sources in Greenland. Stratfor analysts, in a 2013 essay by geopoliticians Robert Kaplan and Mark Schroeder, stated that both China and Japan "have a hunger for African copper, cobalt, rare earths and other minerals" available in eastern Congo. The future promised to resolve this problem of warlike supply and demand through new flexibility in negotiations.

When doubt may prove beneficial to complexity

Made famous by the doubting Saint Thomas, who refused to believe in the return of Jesus until he could touch with his own fingers the wounds suffered by Christ while on the cross (John 20:24–29), doubt's benefit is now both a rhetorical device and a quasi-legal precept. Insufficient evidence, in other words, may be ample cause (at least in many legal codes) for dismissing accusations of wrongdoing – whether crime, misdemeanor or simple disorderliness.

Yet dismissal of guilt may not always settle the issue. Doubt, or most certainly hesitation, pervaded America's involvement in Vietnam when Washington took over by increments the position in Indochina abandoned by France as a result of the battle at Diên Biên Phi'u in 1954. As recounted by political scientist and former army colonel Andrew Bacevich (who served there), by 1965 the American leadership put its "handiwork to the test in Vietnam, the brush-fire war that . . . loomed large as a test of American global leadership."[12] Continuing, Bacevich notes,

> To their considerable dismay, [the leaders in Washington] soon discovered that efforts to douse the fire produced the opposite effect. In attempting to snuff out a small war they produced instead a massive conflagration. Determined to demonstrate the efficacy of force employed on a limited scale, they created a fiasco over which they were incapable of exercising any control whatsoever.

After an enduring struggle that took millions of Vietnamese lives and killed tens of thousands of American troops, Washington decided in 1975 to abandon a lost cause. As to military critic Bacevich, there may be no more severe a judge of the weight of doubt than one who participated in the event concerned.

But benefit of doubt knows other aspects. In early 2011, the Pfizer pharmaceutical group came to the realization that it had missed the boat in marketing its Chantix anti-tobacco drug. Pfizer, the world's largest of its category, might have had a premonition when in October 2010, the Tokyo government raised taxes on cigarettes. Japanese smokers, among the world's most active, rushed by the scores of thousands to see their doctors, asking for prescriptions to cut consumption.

Champix, as the Pfizer product is called in Japan, was high on the list of products prescribed; but the manufacturer failed to react accordingly and augment production. Was it from doubt of the smoking public's seriousness? The Pfizer product was simply not available for many smokers trying to kick the habit,[13] so the demand migrated elsewhere.

Fukushima: shortcomings before, gravest concern after

As the Japanese Diet (parliament), governmental ministries and utility firm TEPCO began their own investigations, a special committee of private citizens undertook analysis of how and what happened at the Fukushima-First power-generating nuclear plant in March 2011. Called the Rebuild Japan Initiative Foundation (RJIF), the committee's chairman was Kitazawa Koichi, formerly chairman of the Japan Science and Technology Agency.

RJIF announced its findings to the public two weeks before the first anniversary of the marine earthquake-tsunami-nuclear conflagration. The committee confirmed that the sea wall intended to protect the oceanside plant should have been built higher (in conformity with historical markers nearby attesting to high-water limits reached by earlier tsunami). Japan's leading actors on the nuclear scene had too long maintained a "security myth." RJIF said, about the nation's farm of nuclear reactors.

There followed a crippling breakdown, if not total dysfunction, in the confidence forthcoming from Japan's governance (beginning with the then prime minister, Kan Naoto), the country's nuclear regulators and TEPCO's management. The public remained inadequately informed of what might happen next – including an unannounced plan to evacuate all Tokyo's inhabitants. TEPCO even proposed forsaking the Fukushima reactors and dispersing all employees, but Prime Minister Kan was able to urge abandonment of such moves.[14]

The brunt of the reconstruction of facts (300 specialists interviewed by a team of 30 investigators) was managed by a science journalist from the *Asahi* newspaper, Otsuka Takashi and by Kitazawa Kay. Kitazawa, trained at the London School of Economics and University College London, specialized in city planning and management.[15] They put their combined experience to work and tallied data to supplant the inaccuracies and vagueness prevailing during the first year after the colossal accident. The highly qualified duo transformed complexity into public comprehension.

Shattered glass

Not long after the cataclysmic events at Fukushima, journalist Nick Bilton helped announce a new product of wearable information technology being introduced to the public. In 2012, Google was at last making known its first marketable mini-hardware conceived and produced in a secret R&D location on its main campus in Mountain View, California. The installation was known to company personnel simply as Google X. It spawned Google Glass, a miniaturized IT system contained within a pair of specially equipped eyeglasses.

These ordinary-looking spectacles could read and send messages, view graphics and do Google-type research directly in front of the eyeballs; they held much promise as a profitable new product. Sergey Brin, co-founder of Google, had even called upon the professional services of New York fashion creator Diane von Furstenberg to design several models of Google Glass.

But success was not to be, according to journalist Bilton, who followed the new product all the way to its removal from the market in early 2015. What had happened? First, the product introduced prematurely to the public was a prototype, with deficient batteries and "other bugs," in need of much work before significant sales could be made. Despite widespread advertising and public relations, the new Glass was slow to enter the marketplace.

Then word got about that clients wearing glasses could threaten activities averse to candid cameras, concealed recording and general prying: in private clubs, casinos and gaming centers and even public toilets.[16] Google Glass had followed in the tracks of Apple's ill-fated Newton personal digital assistant, a generic device of two decades earlier. These PDAs, tried by a variety of manufacturers over very short-lived periods, were the discouraging predecessors of today's successful tablets. Doubt and hesitation joined hands and gave birth to complexity in marketing for profit.

As Apple introduced its watch, more doubts

There were doubts in 2015 even within the firm that the world was ready for a very small-screened wearable computer that would also display advertisements. Earlier watches introduced by LG, Motorola and Samsung Electronics had sold poorly. And although Apple had convened a top A-team that had earlier helped develop prize products such as the Macs, iPad and iPhone, the company then lost some of these designers and engineers who left the watch project to join rival manufacturers. Early market surveys made in 2014 failed to show the intense consumer interest that preceded the appearance, a few years earlier, of the smartphone.

These were all stumbles in engineering and esthetic design. The Apple Watch was set, furthermore, for the production of about 7.5 million units in 2015–2016. "That is peanuts compared with the tens of millions of iPhones that fly off the shelves every quarter," reported a doubting *New York Times*. "In a few advanced industries," commented *The Economist*,

> notably aerospace and industrial-machine production, America exports more than it imports. But many industries that have been strong historically

are now running big trade deficits. America imports about $40 billion more in pharmaceuticals than it exports, and a similar gap appears in semiconductors. Other areas of supposed expertise, like communications equipment and computers, run even bigger deficits.[17]

Despite this informed opinion, both Google and Apple leaked surprises to the consternation of exhibitors at the Geneva Auto Show 2015. Word from Silicon Valley perturbed what could have been a celebratory salon to mark an encouraging resurgence of Europe's automobile industry, although still far from the levels reached in 2007. With no corporate presence at Geneva auto show, both firms intimated future exploitation of their expertise in electronic operating systems to reconceive and manufacture vehicle dashboards, thus competing with the carmakers themselves. The design chief of Daimler – corporate owner of the Mercedes-Benz trademark – publicly dismissed the idea that firms such as Apple and Google might undertake the manufacture of vehicles. "A car is so complex inside and out," Gorden Wagener told the business press, "a smartphone is fairly simple compared to that."[18] Could these be stumbles in the making?

Concretely, a projection of such eventuality is that the IT giants could supply a car's entire electrical system and then attempt breaking into the totality of *electric*-car manufacture. Indeed, word at Geneva contended that Apple alone already had a team of several hundred specialists on hand, preparing to elbow aside automotive proprietary systems. They or other upstarts (e.g., Tesla) *could* build entire vehicles. The threats of other designer/manufacturers are motivating.

Medical teleconsultation via Internet

"Internauts" consult a variety of Internet sources to enquire about signs and symptoms of disease, preventive measures, comparative remedies and patient management. A poll in France taken in 2007 by INSERM, the French national medical-research center, showed that 93.2 percent of Internet users were consulting sources dealing with human health. Sweden, Switzerland, the United States and France have since hailed the 21st century with official authorization for medical advice at distance from physicians for patient guidance.

The French had deliberated the idea of teleconsulting doctors for a decade before decreeing in 2010 authorization for such consultations from January 2011 (an act obscured in the news media, however, as people by the millions demonstrated against concurrent reform of retirement legislation). One Parisian hospital, the Rothschild Foundation, for instance, exchanged views on techniques of ophthalmological surgery via satellite television with New York University's School of Medicine.[19]

The French decree legitimated diagnoses and prescriptions at a distance, according to Sandrine Cabut of the daily newspaper *Le Figaro*, although individual acts were already practiced by physicians such as urologist Guy Vallancien to treat at a distance his patients suffering from prostate problems.[20] Medical "visits" of this kind are reimbursable, furthermore, by public or private health-insurance schemes. The new method came at a welcome moment, as France's population continued to grow.

Physicians remained uncertain, however, about long-distance diagnosis. Dr. André Vacheron, a member of the Académie des Sciences Morales et Politiques, wrote in the daily Le Monde that

> Doubt, an adversary that the physician must first eliminate in order to arrive at a sure diagnosis and appropriate treatment, will persist as a challenge to treating properly the unseen patient . . . An example of difficult decisional problems in public health is [a] recent grippe-A pandemic (H1N1). Alarmingly discordant remarks, or else those too reassuring, raised doubts among the population concerning the reality of its dangers – [which admittedly are] difficult to evaluate . . . This example, among others, demonstrates the heavy responsibility [in approving teleconsultation] placed on political decision makers dealing with in a situation of uncertainty.[21]

Another physician, Anne Fagot-Largeault of the French Academy of Sciences, wrote in the same newspaper that an objective of her profession must be "not to inflate uncertainty." Citing one of her 19th-century predecessors, the innovative physician Claude Bernard, she reminded that her profession "must doubt, but never be skeptical . . . The 'doubter' is the real scientist," she emphasized.

Technical misadventures not by plan

Now back for a moment to industry and engineering in more familiar technological terms. Fallen bridges, collapsed buildings, caved-in roadways happen. Those who conceive and build are human beings. Engineers themselves live in dread of mishaps to their projects (most often caused by natural forces). Such events are far from unknown.

Henry Petroski, professor of engineering and historian of the discipline (at Duke University), is an author prolific with vivid examples of engineering gone wrong. He has published journal articles and a film, When Engineering Fails (1987). In this production, Petroski explains the causes of, among other disasters, the tragic end the year before of NASA's Challenger space shuttle.

Among the 20 or so books to Petroski's credit are To Engineer Is Human: The Record of Failure in Structural Design (1985), To Forgive Design: Understanding Failure (2012), and The Essential Engineer: Why Science Alone Will Not Solve Our Global Problems (2010). His work cites examples far from obscure; they make easy reading and uncommonly good sense. And, as do more and more engineers, he stresses the need to introduce ergonomics, bionics and other environmental compatibility in the planning and execution of engineering projects.

Are some quasi-conclusions feasible?

We have seen the phenomenon of reaction to doubt among deciders take different forms. Sophistry is reasoning that may be plausible yet wrong (Hitler haranguing his generals). It differs from *casuistry* in that the reasoning of casuistry is specific to an instance, applying principles of ethos (the guiding beliefs or ideals of a community or nation) to matters of conscience or morality (our medical and pharmaceutical examples). *Specious reasoning*, a "first cousin" to both sophistry and casuistry, connotes using seemingly valid yet deceptive – and, ultimately, non-functional – arguments to undertake action or not, e.g., the Nokia and probably Pfizer examples.

Demagogy, something we witness daily, is the application of any of these attitudes – with added oratorical appeal to our emotions and ingrained prejudices, usually for political but short-term ends. This chapter has thus shown, using real incidents, how the wrong course of future action can be urged by invoking the "right" means of logic (and often rhetoric) for what purport to be justifiable reasons.

Whose persuasion, then, shall we need in order to evacuate uncertainty? The historian-archeologist Ian Morris, in his sweeping *Why the West Rules – For Now, The Patterns of History, and What They Reveal about the Future*, provides a realistic reply in his claim that, "Sometimes a few different decisions or a little good luck can postpone, reduce, or even head off disaster." Yet the choices we make to emerge from doubt, adds Morris, "change the world."[22]

Learning strategy from the ways of industry

Lane Jennings, futurist and formerly editor at the World Future Society, opines,

> Doubt is part and parcel of practically any decision (*every* decision, if you trust the physicists who assert that randomness and chaos are completely unavoidable). Is there, then, no way to minimize the potentially negative impacts of doubt in making plans? I can think of some possibilities.

Jennings continues (in an e-mail of 13 August 2013),

> One is to design plans with built-in check points, at any one of which the initial decision can be modified or even reversed with relative ease, based on the success achieved so far. Another is to prefer plans that support multiple possible outcomes, perhaps not as perfectly as a single fail-proof plan might do, but at least "covering one's bets." In industry, for example, why not design an innovative device that fills a known market niche, while simultaneously funding research in novel uses for a device that looks much the same (e.g., fits in the same package) but works a bit differently. Say perhaps a portable phone, plus a portable with built-in camera, plus one phone with built-in movie camera, etc.?

He adds,

> Then when it comes time to produce the innovation, choose whichever design appears most likely to 'delight' the public. These two examples may be highly

impractical. My point is one of reassurance that there is not more reason to *worry* about planning, but that making *better* plans is almost always possible.

And why not? Jennings's suggestion conforms reassuringly to what engineers do with the systematic, and error-avoiding, procedural checklist. Inventors, as we saw in the chapter on foresight and innovation, are often just as systematic in their exhaustion of possibilities.

The role of doubt in the processes of planning, optimistically something *different* and *better* than in the past, might be collated and diagrammed as follows – proceeding from inoperability to accomplishment. Your authors visualize the scope of doubt in Table 6.2.

While no shortage of examples will come to the reader's mind for (b) through (f), (a) may incite some head-scratching. But one need think only of French tennis champion Marion Bartoli, in intensive training since the age of 15. After finally "winning Wimbledon" in 2013 as a mother aged 28, she told sports journalists a few weeks later (subsequent to Bartoli's defeat by a Romanian rival) that she could no longer find the energy to overcome acute pain in the Achilles tendon and continue her career. While Bartoli might well retract later, she said she was resigning from the courts once and for all.

Above (a), but not shown, would be the provisional graveyard of otherwise the best of intentions: what simply cannot (yet) be done. Here would lie the trisection of the angle, the alchemical morphing of lead into gold, the ideal system of education and training, untrammeled brotherhood, peace treaties to *guarantee* peace, a UN with supranational authority, and whatever other perfection the reader would care to add. Categories (e) and (f) are reserved, of course, for the most successful of creators and innovators. These exceptional people, accustomed to confrontation with complexity in many forms are discussed in more detail in the chapter devoted to foresight and innovation.

Meanwhile, we encounter complexity at a more universal level, that of the vagaries, excesses, abuses and illegalities devolving from the responsibilities of public servants and others executing professional duties that demand rectitude and integrity.

Table 6.2 Planners, creators, designers and finally doers expect a range of doubtful moments and hesitation in their enterprise

(a)	Conceiver foresees no chance of success for otherwise hopeful idea.
(b)	Conceiver estimates a fair chance for good idea's ultimate success.
(c)	Conceiver evaluates better than even chance for final success of idea.
(d)	Conceiver rejects ultimate possibility of failure: "It should succeed."
(e)	Conceiver disregards even slightest chance of failure.
(f)	Innovative concept so well-received that it proves astoundingly successful.

Yet, as in the case of what Steve Jobs accomplished with the ailing Apple Corporation, this master innovator exceeded the most promising expectations of the firm. Meticulously planned strategy can change both the world and history. The range of doubt for the fate of a "good idea" forms a continuum from assuredness of failure (a) to certainty of success (f).

Notes

1 The term *Anthropocene* dates from the year 2000.
2 O'Brien, K., "Nokia's Success Bred Its Weakness," *International Herald Tribune*, 27 September 2010; ensuing citations convening Nokia are from the same source.
3 Driscoll, T. G., Jr., e-mail received from this conference consultant, 24 January 2015.
4 The *New York Times* reported on Elop's management style on 21 October as did the *Independent*, 22 and 24 October 2010.
5 Rosenthal, E. "U.S. Military Moves to Ramp Up Use of Green Technology," *International Herald Tribune*, 6 October 2010, pp. 1, 7.
6 Daniel Yergin in an authoritative analysis of the world's present and future exploitation of petroleum, "What Happened to the Price of Oil?" in the *International New York Times International*, 24 January2015.
7 RAND (2011), Monograph 969 is cited by J. Baris and L. Van Bubber, page 1 of www.rc.rand.org/pubs/monographs/MGM969.html files.
8 "Indecision and Fear in Oil Rig's Final Hours," by D. Barstowe, D. Rhode and S. Saul, the *New York Times*, 25 December 2019, with cutaways of *Deepwater Horizon*.
9 Pezzulo, G., M. Butz et al., *The Challenge of Anticipation, A Unifying Framework for the Analysis and Design of Artificial Cognitive Systems*, Berlin-Heidelberg, Springer, 2008, p. 13.
10 These remarks appeared respectively in the 1 and 8 July editions of the New York daily, Jacobson, M. and Mark and Delucchi, "A Path to Sustainable Energy by 2030," *Scientific American*, November 2009, p. 42.
11 See Anne Bauer, "Terres rares: Bruxelles prêt à une stratégie plus agressive" (Rare Earths: Brussels Ready for More Aggressive Strategy), *Les Echos*, 2 February 2011.
12 Bacevich, A., *Washington Rules, America's Path to Permanent War*, New York, NY: Metropolitan Books/Henry Holt, 2010, p. 108.
13 Tobacco-Facts.net. "In Japan, Pfizer is short of drug to help smokers," www.tobacco-facts.net/2011/01/in-japan-pfizer, 5 January 2011; see also www.cigarettesflavours/tobacco-control, 4 January 2011, and other mass media of the same dates.
14 Martin Fackler in the *New York Times*, 28 February 2012; Mari Yamaguchi of the Associated Press reporting in *The Denver Post*, 28 February 2012.
15 See http://rebuildjpn.org/en/fukushima and related files, 2012.
16 See "How Google Glass Went from Hottest Thing in Wearables to Ford's Edsel," *International New York Times*, 6 February 2015, p. 15.
17 *The Economist*, "Not Quite What It Seems," 28 February 2015, p. 36.
18 See also interview of Wagener by Matthew Askan, *Cool Hunting*, 14 November 2014.
19 Learned by one of the authors from a principal practitioner involved.
20 The authorization is reported in www.dorffer-patrick.com/article-les-teleconsultations-medicales-autorisees-en-France-59627240.html, 25 October 2010.
21 The citations are taken from two articles signed by the principals in *Le Monde*, 27 October 2013, p. 19.
22 Morris, I., *Why the West Rules – For Now, The Patterns of History and What They Reveal about the Future*, New York, Farrar, Straus and Giroux, 2010.

7 *Philosophia moralis*
Systems stretched to the breaking point

Introduction

The arrival of the industrial revolution brought with it more than change in the crafts of old and the functioning of mill or factory. A novelist and poet of the Victorian period, George Meredith, brought into play social criticism when he condemned selfishness, greed, cronyism, dishonesty and corruption as unwelcome accessories of the sudden novation in the "Systems" of manufacture and commerce. By blaming "systems" Meredith condemned the atmosphere of the age and the new pressures weighing on the citizen.

Today, we try not to overlook the ethical or moral lapses that must be counted among the dishonest or plainly perfidious occurrences within societal institutions and other human systems. The first thief probably stole food from a better-provided neighbor. In our age, large commercial enterprises such as department stores, super- and hypermarkets and commercial malls experience losses through shoplifting and petty pilfering, breaking and entry, management's or employees' inattention, negligence or avoidable sloppiness. Light fingers, even lighter conscience and carelessness are endemic to the tempting influences stemming from industry and trade. Here we try to understand how and why.

The robber barons of North America made fortunes in the 19th century through investment, trading or other commercial undertakings not always orthodox or even legal. Ponzi and pyramid schemes of fraudulent re-investment were current during the "roaring" 1920s, a period of inflated real estate in America leading to the collapse of the New York stock market in 1929. German elections the following year glorified Hitler's National Socialists, and prompted foreign investors to withdraw from the economies of Germany and Austria. Insufficient capitalization of banks in Vienna led to the first bank failure, that of Credit Anstalt in 1931. The two German-language countries tried to form a defensive customs union with money to be borrowed from France, yet the Versailles treaty forbade such moves. These serious stumbles were institutional, not individual, often generating financial calamity elsewhere. The Great Depression was on its way – a financial crisis to be dissipated only by the Second World War and its aftermath of early globalization.

Philosophia moralis 89

By the end of the 20th century a young British investment trader, N. W. ("Nick") Leeson, operating from Singapore, stumbled badly. He managed systematically to lose £827 million for Barings, Britain's oldest merchant bank (founded 1762), effectively condemning this respectable investment house to liquidation. Leeson fled the scene, was caught, tried and imprisoned for a few years. He now advises institutions on measures to avoid disaster by dishonesty of staff.

The free-wheeling nature of work by investment traders in the early years of the 21st century quickly became, again, the basis for disastrous investment house and bank failures in Britain and America – and then elsewhere – leading directly to the global recession of 2007–2009.

A delayed-action bomb

A decade after that economic downturn, the Swiss branch of another great banking entity, London-based HSBC,[1] learned to its dismay that an employee had revealed how its Geneva investment arm, HSBC Private Bank (Suisse), had counseled depositors on methods of income-tax evasion. Not only had the bank urged depositors to exploit tax havens to shelter their savings, but it had illegally refrained from reporting account data to the depositors' respective national tax authorities.

The "whistle-blowing" or alerting employee, a digital-systems engineer named Hervé Falciani, left Switzerland for France, reporting to the tax police there. The worms were out of the tin. French officials conveyed in 2010, under "Project Chocolate," relevant data to the governments of Britain, Spain, Argentina, the United States and other nations. Among the 130,000 tax evaders exposed, the media reported entertainment personalities, business and political leaders, drug dealers and money launderers, and at least one monarch – whose country forbids its citizens to hold accounts abroad.

These events came at an inauspicious moment for Britain, at that time preparing legislative elections scheduled for May 2015. HSBC's former chief executive, Stephen Green, by then a member of Parliament, was mooted for possible appearance before tax authorities. (Green, finally, was not called to testify.) The permanent secretary for Her Majesty's Revenue and Customs, Linda Holmes, however, appeared before the Public Accounts Committee in February 2015. Even Stuart Gulliver, at the time the parent bank's chief executive, concealed from other staff bonus funds equaling $7.5 million he had deposited in a Panamanian tax shelter.[2]

British tax officials reported the recovery, by early 2015, of £135 million in unpaid taxes. All these events were detailed by a non-official body in Geneva known as Swiss Leaks and repeated internationally by several large dailies, among them the *Guardian*, *Le Monde* and the *New York Times*. French, Belgian and Swiss prosecutors began proceedings to charge the Geneva branch of HSBC with encouraging tax evasion.

The sampling of evasion in question, as evidenced by the data made public by Swiss Leaks, is astonishingly widespread. In an infographic analysis made by a historical researcher at the University of Lausanne, Martin Grandjean, the largest number of stakeholders involved reside (in descending order) Switzerland, the United Kingdom, Venezuela, the United States, France, Israel, the Bahamas, Italy, Belgium, India, the Netherlands, Germany, Greece and Russia. Among the smallest accounts were those of residents of Africa, Kuwait, Syria, Lebanon and Eastern Europe.[3]

Sweeping house cleaning catches on

The conflict between what humans *say* publicly, as opposed to what they *think*, has long been handled with a strong sense of responsibility and precaution. This takes form, especially in the arena of public utterance, as one or another type of censorship: self-censure to prevent or correct lapses, guarded words against libel or defamation, censorship based on modesty or moderation, group or institutional censorship and official pre- and post-censorship of media of all sorts.

Didier Regnier, director of the Foundation for Political Innovation (part of the Sciences Po institute in Paris), cites the effects of the arrival of the Internet on what is broadcast through this system of informal but systematized communication. "With the internet, anyone can and does express whatever comes to mind. There are no controls, everything is permitted."[4] The Internet has, in a word, revolutionized communication; even translation has been facilitated through the digital processes.

Regnier's observation helps explain, as well, China's uncompromising restrictions on what is permissible on the Internet and its ancillary networks. The People's Republic has the world's largest, near-homogeneous population. Its leadership applies non-republican, anti-democratic censorship that brooks not the least criticism of totalitarian rule. Yet corruption is not concealed; it is exposed and severely punished.

Liu Han, a Chinese billionaire mining executive, was tried in Hubei province together with younger brother Liu Wei early in 2015 for mafia-style murder. Both were executed, together with three accomplices, after futile appeals. The elder Liu, well known in Australia for his efforts to acquire the iron-ore exploitation firm Sundance Resources, was suspected furthermore of close links with China's security chief, Zhou Yongkang – a key figure in Beijing[5] suspected of colossal graft, behavior totally incompatible with his national responsibilities. Zhou thus became the most senior personality in China to be tried publicly since the judicial proceedings in 1980 of the Gang of Four, defendants who included a former spouse of former leader Mao Zedong, Jiang Qing.

Shortly after the industrial billionaire's prosecution, it was the army's turn. General Xu Caihou had accumulated such a hoard of cash, jade and gold in his Beijing mansion that the loot filled ten truckloads upon its removal. Xu had moved in 1990 from his native northeastern China to become political commissar of 16th Army Group based in the capital. He was later appointed vice-chairman of the Central Military Commission, China's senior military council; he was a Party member and thus qualified for a seat on the Party's Politburo.

Philosophia moralis 91

General Xu retired when he turned 60, but was put under investigation in 2014 for bribery and expelled from the Party. The irony in his case is that he was promoted regularly through the military's political commissar ranks. These are the Party's own controllers of loyalty, dedication and honesty among the officer corps of the army, navy and air force (all three collectively known as the People's Liberation Army).

Influence, misdirected, but high and wide

The PLA has no combat experience since 1980 and has been engaged in business affairs of all sorts, from industrial manufacture to hotel and resort management. "Military corruption, though seldom spoken of so publicly before, has long been a problem"[6] and is a particular target of President Xi Jinping's continuing anti-corruption campaign. A disciplinary method relying on the rectitude of Party members had itself stumbled seriously for decades, denigrating publicly the symbolism of China's single-party concept of governance (see Box 7.1).

Box 7.1   The first socialist emperor?

What is widely accepted among China hands is that Xi [Jinping] is the most powerful leader of China since Deng Xiaoping, with a developing personality cult. Xi is not *primus inter pares* like Deng and Hu [Jintao]; he is simply *primus*. In his recent book, *Chinese Politics in the Era of Xi Jinping*, Willy Wu-Lap Lam, a veteran observer of Chinese elites, explains that "since taking over as general secretary in November 2012 and president of China since March 2013, Xi has centralized power under his leadership to an extraordinary degree, creating and chairing the new Central National Security Commission. [This] has jurisdiction over the army, the police and all foreign-related and national security agencies, along with chairing the Central Military Commission, which comes with his job as [Party] secretary general."

Source: Roderick MacFarquhar, "China: The Superpower of Mr. XI," *The New York Review of Books*, 13 August 2015, p. 32

The plot thickened in 2015, the 66th year of the Peoples Republic. Liu Jian, ex-military officer and grandson of Marshal Zhu De (a respected collaborator of Mao Zedong),[7] made revelations on an official website. Accused was another earlier vice-chairman of the Central Military Commission, former General Guo Zhenggang, also under investigation for corruption. Liu pinned the responsibility for the son's errant ways on the accused's father, Guo Boxiong, who had been appointed and promoted to high PLA posts by no less than two former presidents of China, Hu Jintao and Zhang Zemin.

Commenting on holding a parent in China accountable for an offspring's sins, the American private intelligence service Stratfor had the following to say. Son Guo "could simply have been arrested without this fanfare. So our best guess is that a generalized statement is being made, and that statement is not simply about fathers and sons but [about] the older generation of leaders and the younger" generation.[8] The "older generation" was, by historical evidence, preoccupied with problems of economic development of the nation rather than by the ethics of individual citizens. By the end of 2016, several more high-profile personalities were indicted for corruption.

What is systemic analysis to make of such developments in a country whose sole political party is known for its rigid control of party faithful? Is cultural habit so ingrained from former times that it cannot be shaken from the new order? Any reform would probably have to be framed in what systemists Sweeney and Meadows term an *isomorphic* perspective.[9] A likely explanation of the Chinese purges is that after years of leadership by technocrats (former president Hu Jintao is a certified engineer) and party acolytes, the new chief executive *and* general secretary of the single-party ruling the country – and the first to be elected by all party delegates since Mao Zedong – found himself impelled to clean an infested house.

This he did from 2014 until, in 2016, Xi Jinping was acclaimed by the party's Central Committee as "core leader." This party language was used for only the fourth time since Mao Zedong to express the dominance with which the leader has swept his party clean of its most conspicuous corruptibles.[10] Is there a model here to apply to solutions of other complex problems of the world?

The Xi Jinping approach suggests a reductive, if administratively harsh, means of problem resolution when subordinates default in compliance with official policy. This is to say that if the reality of complying with policy cannot be met through the normal chain of management, then induced (virtual) reality can be assured by authoritarian means, including punitive sanctions. A real-life example, well outside China, is President Donald Trump's selection of an individual critically responding to climate change and the Paris Agreement as director of America's Environmental Protection Agency.

Problem analysis leading to induced reality, far from democratic, would not be the choice in a state calling itself a republic. Bordering on the despotic, this is imposition by a governing minority will upon a majority of likely resistance to cultural and probable costly change. Note, however, that the Chinese model had at least temporary effect and may have set a habit-changing example for the future.

When state enterprises finance political parties

Elsewhere, Brazil – contending with grave problems of water supply and management – deals also with a public hygiene challenge by which more than half the country's dwellings lack proper sanitation. In 2014, the nation's development bank, BNDES, lent to private firms nearly $100 million at below-market rates of interest, while the state-owned petroleum company Petrobras paid out

$50 billion in the form of generous gifts to political parties. High inflation, a slowing economy, diminished purchasing power and seemingly ineradicable slums further plagued the federative republic. The national murder rate, furthermore, costs the population 50,000 lives taken annually.[11]

Roberto Mutta, president of the center-right NOVO political party, wants to change all this after the country's next elections in 2018. But NOVO, whose creed is liberalism, is only one of a half-hundred political parties in Brazil ranging in ideology from center-left to extreme right-wing. The strongest membership is in the centrist Democratic Movement party with its 2.34 million adherents and in unseated President Dilma Rousseff's Workers' Party with 1.5 million voters. Five more parties tally more than a million each, in varying political coloration – making any notion of consensus difficult to grasp. The temptation, here and there, to pay for political favors becomes difficult to resist (see Box 7.2).

Box 7.2   World-level soccer champions too?

Here is the opening of a correspondent's dispatch to the *New York* Times, 13 August 2015.

The president is hearing calls for her impeachment. The speaker of Brazil's lower house is grappling with accusations that he pocketed a $5 million bribe. The former treasurer of the Workers' Party is in jail.

Source: Simon Romero. Reporting

Brazil—the world's seventh largest economy—does not head, however, Latin America's toll of perceived corruption. That award goes to Bolivia and Paraguay, where Transparency International, an NGO, set the "corruption index" records for the year 2014 at 30.2 and 28.1, respectively. This index expresses the share of the population victimized by corruption, on a scale of 1 (least corrupt) to 175 (most corrupt). At the lower end of the ranking, the most favorable Latin American indices were attributed to Chile and Uruguay, respectively at 5.3 and 6.7 on the same scale.[12]

Cause and effect

Who or what are the stumbles in Brazil, also Latin America's most populous country? With a mixture of populations both native (early tribal kingdoms) and immigrants largely from Europe, customs and traditions less than rigorous have often become the norms of public behavior. This has been characteristically the deportment of the largest social institutions: business, political parties and government itself, at both federal and state levels. The republic's previous president, Dilma Rousseff, together with her Workers' Party were frequently criticized by opponents as being too "communist," too lax and indifferent to economic irregularities.

Ms. Rousseff is an economist and served as a guerrilla during Brazil's military dictatorship (ended in 1985). She became minister of mining and energy, later serving as chief executive of Brazil's state-operated petroleum corporation, Petrobras. This firm became implicated in the country's politics with hand-outs of huge sums to many of Brazil's parties as already mentioned.

The media reported many of these irregularities, pointing out Brazil's extreme democracy: 50-some political parties, many of which have neither objectives nor programs but seek the social advantages to be gained from government welfare. The number of parties weakened electoral results so that, in Rousseff's case, she headed a coalition of 15 parties. Angela Merkel succeeded, by contrast, in managing a coalition of Germany's three leading parties.

By early 2016 public clamor, predictably in large part by a strong opposition, demanded the impeachment of Ms. Rousseff. This move toward destitution of the presidency also implicated Luiz Inácio Lula da Silva, a past president also tied to illegal loans from state banks to fill official budgetary gaps (but not for personal gain). While still president, Rousseff moved to safeguard "Lula" by having him designated her chief of staff – a job she once filled during Lula's presidency. But she was foiled by tumultuous protests from opponents. The first step in the impeachment process against Rousseff was a referendum in April 2016, when two-thirds of the lower house of parliament voted for impeachment. A month later, the upper chamber did the same.

Opponents who had known her for many years decried her poor political skills and arrogance, while others claimed that she had too much of a "go-it-alone" personality.[13] In systemic terms, this assessment suggests that the Brazilian president was not playing the role of feedback loop – president to government, then parliament, parties, the public and back to government. Before the year 2016 was out, however, the same feedback loop trapped a former governor of the Rio de Janeiro metropolis (1999–2002). Anthony Garotinho was in the hands of then police on suspicion of rigging a cash-for-votes scheme during his tenure.

In sum, system slippage is again at fault: a phenomenon more common than not in a world of highly diversified political cant. Systemic distraction, in this case diverting attention from Brazil's freshwater shortage and the failing fertility of its soil, are serious stumbling blocks for an otherwise rapidly developing nation. As to judicial disposal of the Lula case, the former president was sentenced in 2018 to 12 years of imprisonment. He thereupon announced that he would run again for the presidency in the elections scheduled for 2019.

Meanwhile, 17,000 km away across Africa and South Asia in the Republic of Korea, that country's first woman president was impeached during the winter of 2016–2017. Park Geun-hye, daughter of a former president, was charged with receiving generous gifts of cash from the country's industrial chiefs, and other irregularities. Her destitution was formalized by the Constitutional Court, ordering her expulsion from the presidential Blue House residence. Only months later, new president Michel Temer faced similar charges of corruption.

The post of Brazilian chief executive seemed to promise incumbents a major occupational hazard.

Of manors and manners

During the first decade of the new century, news items in France reported that near Bordeaux a youngish man had been apprehended by the police and incarcerated for having fraudulently taken possession of others' personal and real property: a scam. The victims were a respected family living reclusively but comfortably in their inherited *château*. As the case developed and came before the courts, the extent of the beguiling suspect's unlawful acquisitions proved to be impressive.

After having wormed his way into the amity and good graces of the owners, who were parents of several children and providers of shelter to other members of their family, the intruder first borrowed money under the pretense of needing to expand his "business." The latter remained unspecified but was. In fact, a series of recurring failures. He also claimed to be a secret agent, sent to protect the family from scheming enemies. The family guest repaid little of the loans received; his excuses were gradually inflated into more elaborate – yet increasingly persuasive – expressions of the need for still more cash. Thus was the family, as it emptied its bank accounts, systematically gulled.

The affair culminated in the fraudster's successful hectoring of the two family principals to make over the deed to their property, its furnishings and equipment, valuable art objects, as well as the land on which everything stood. In all, 11 persons turned over all their worldly goods to a slick operator who is currently serving ten years in penitentiary for abuse of confidence and criminal predation. Stolen objects have been recovered only in part, the rest having already been sold and the money earned spent on high living and casino losses.

Lest the reader think this account spurious, the people and places mentioned were identified by court actions and media reports as the Ghislaine de Védrines-Jean Marchand family, whose property is at Monflanquin in the Lot-and-Garonne department of southwestern France. The name of the wrongdoer is Thierry Tilly, born in 1964 and the son of a civil servant. Finally realizing the breadth and depth of the intruder's deception, Ms. de Védrines told *Le Figaro* newspaper that Tilly "made us his slaves."

The metals trade and structural damage

To the north of São Paulo-Rio de Janeiro and west of France, the once automobile-center of the world suffers other kinds of grief. As the American automobile-manufacturing industry outsourced more and more labor for vehicle assembly and the global slump of 2007 set in, an already resourceful trade in the stealing and resale of used metals thrived in Michigan's largest city. (Honest trading in "junk" metals is also a by-product of the automotive industry.) Community deterioration struck Detroit little by little but massively, with many neighborhoods affected severely as homes and shops were abandoned and taxes were no longer paid.

Detroit and communities elsewhere became increasingly aware of metal theft when cables, copper wiring, municipal lighting systems and even sewer covers were pilfered for resale by organized gangs. (Between 2002 and 2007 the price of copper, for example, rose from $1.30/kg to $8.10/kg, or almost 600 percent.) In America, the Institute of Scrap Recycling Industries protects legitimate dealers through its official relationships with cities, towns and the federal government, as well as monitoring related activities outside the United States.

Detroit and other cities in Michigan were thus not alone, as experience in California, North Carolina and Georgia have proved. In Europe, England, Wales and France began to suffer from the same disease, with the electrical communication systems of the French national railways (SNCF) a choice target of metal thieves. There, even roadbeds have been sabotaged by the stealing of rails and signaling equipment.

This is another model of system breakdown, probably a result of weakened control by citizens themselves: waning civic responsibility, community pride and concern for the public costs of repair or replacement. Streets, railways and their yards, and other communication links cannot be minutely patrolled, so the best defense has been to formulate legislation formerly non-existent. New laws and regulations make the witting receipt of stolen metals a criminal offense – perhaps an inevitable aftermath of population growth and loss of tribal coherence, a form of complexity extensively negative in character.

The media have reported a fast-growing spread of fraud by telephone, much of it in Asia, especially in Indonesia and China. The process is as follows. A victim is contacted by a "tax investigator" or "the police," fully informed about the victim's identity and personal life. Chen Yue, a public relations assistant, had just returned from a tourist voyage abroad to her home in Beijing when she received notice by telephone. The caller identified himself as from such-and-such office of the police, stating firmly that his task was to clear the young woman of suspicions of money laundering. She had accumulated a sizable savings account in her bank, the details of which appeared to "officials" as suspicious.

The prolonged discussion by telephone convinced Ms. Chen, hesitant as most Chinese to challenge authority, that the call was part pf a genuine investigation of the sources of her savings. The caller then persuaded his victim to let his office examine the details of her bank deposits, the account number and other details, all of which was to be done over the Internet and by which her savings would then be returned to her account if everything proved legal and aboveboard. She thus lost the equivalent of $30,000, leaving her penniless and without recourse of the least sort. In China alone in 2014, the police dealt with 400,000 similar cases.[14]

When chaos goes into reverse gear

After the great recession of 2007–2009, the United States– and France-based Alcatel-Lucent Corporation found itself in foundering straits.[15] By 2013, the French telecommunication-engineering manager Michel Combes (born 1962) was named chief executive. The new president ordered reformative thinking of the firm's strengths and weaknesses, its operational culture of technological research and manufacturing, as well as a need for drastic restructuring.

Combes then proceeded to cut the company's staff by 10,000 employees and foresaw the return of good economic times. By mid-2015, the bi-national group was strong enough again to react positively to Combes's request to leave the firm and undertake other pursuits. The firm's board of directors consented and, after only 29 months of service, announced Combes's departure. Also announced were an annual salary and bonus of €1.3 million and stock options available until three years later amounting to another €13.7 million for the departing executive.

Union officials and senior members of the sitting Socialist government protested strongly, the French national association of manufacturers (MEDEF) argued that its own code of behavior regarding executive remuneration was being violated, and the pro-capitalist but Socialist economics minister, Emmanuel Macron, affirmed publicly that such payment was well out of order. Both media and public clamored loudly, recalling past cases of flagrant abuse of executive privilege. In the spring of 2016, Renault automobiles and Sanofi pharmaceuticals announced record compensation for their presidents in 2015, respectively, more than €15 million and €16 million. Union leaders and the major media pressed, unsuccessfully, for a law to limit executive compensation.

Dishonest investors and stock market traders, democratically elected public leaders, civil servants charged with sweeping responsibilities, fraudulent acquaintance, organized theft on a large scale and direct exploitation by telephone and the Internet: these are common charges in court. Controlling managerial elements or individuals no longer function as programmed, whether by custom, professional tradition, law or immediate necessity vital to a firm's survival.

The size and scope of the 400,000 police cases of scam in China would not astonish directors of insurance companies, medical-reimbursement plans and related operations reacting to complaints of fraud and outright theft. The Chinese criminal statistic would be the envy of actors Paul Newman and Robert Redford in their epic film, "The Sting" (1973), a riotous tale of two imaginative swindlers who gain the confidence of a gangster boss in the America of the 1930s.

Technical complexity and the scandal of the new century

The Volkswagen People's Car or "Beetle" was an unqualified success worldwide. Its first prototypes appeared in 1937 but the car was commercialized only after the Second World War. The growing firm became VW Group and the world's second largest automotive manufacturer. It now includes the Audi, Bentley, Bugatti, Lamborghini, MAN, Porsche, Scania, SEAT and Skoda brands. VW Group is Europe's largest car producer, with strong markets also in the United States and China.

The Economist of 26 September 2015 briefed its readers on "systematic fraud by [VW] threatens to engulf the entire industry and possibly reshape it." The 24 September issue of the German weekly newspaper *Die Zeit* read, "It smells and smells and smells." The newspaper stressed the necessity to revisit completely the emission testing of cars.

VW had installed software on 11 million vehicles (8 million of these in Europe) in order to pass emission testing through deactivation of emission control, with particular regard for carbon dioxide and nitrogen oxide (NO_x; Box 7.3), once the cars were on the road. *The Economist* reported that exhaust emissions could have risen to 40 times the level permitted in the United States.

Box 7.3 NO_x – systemic and their emission problems

Nitrogen oxides contribute to global warming and therefore climate change: they help produce acid rain, fine particulates and elevated ozone – all concentrated in the air. They also cause smog, damage to plants and severe respiratory problems including lung cancer and other serious diseases. About 50 percent of poisonous NO_x derives from car exhausts. Of this, some 80 percent comes from diesel engines. NO_x are particularly dangerous in urban areas for children and the elderly. NO_x and ammonia containing gases emanating from intensive agriculture may yield ammonium salts, also known as "secondary particulate matter."

What happened?

According to *The Economist*, VW strategy was to position itself in the American auto market with large numbers of supposedly clean diesel models to outcompete with Toyota as the world's largest automotive producer. *Supposedly clean* meant attachment of anti-pollution measurement, via device known as Swift, directly to engine blocks. By design, Swift read falsely. VW's slogan in the United States, "It's time for German engineering," stands for German quality. VW's general management and its design engineers had set out, in full complicity, to deceive the buying public. As the scandal became a global issue, damage to VW itself could affect subsidiaries Seat (Spain) and Skoda (Czech Republic) as well as the entire car industry.

Loss of jobs at VW could thus be expected, also damage to Germany's exemplary auto industry sector and to the quality seal "Made in Germany." Some 11 million VW cars were affected by deceptive anti-pollution software scandal. Of these, 2.8 million cars were on German roads while another 8 million use roads in the rest of the EU.

Another complexity effect is the financial dimension and multifaceted nature of costs associated with this crisis. These factors relate to fines and financial operations (or "captive finance") charged to VW. It is these that have proven fragile for firms after other crises such as British Petroleum and General Motors experienced. The behavior of depositors, lenders and other capital providers in

VW's "environment" might lead to a debt and liquidity crisis for all of VW. Offers of repayment to VW buyers were made ($10 billion and more). And fines are executed to make the bill for cheating the public enormous.

Remaining unclear is whether installation of the deceiving "switch" software in millions of cars is unique to VW, or if this is only the tip of an immense iceberg. Is there, that is to say, a larger systemic issue within the automotive sector? Before the VW scandal, other car builders (Hyundai, Kia and Toyota) had been accused of claiming false performance in fuel consumption or "malfunction" of their emission-control systems. *Die Zeit* reminded (24 September 2015) that, as early as 1998, six U.S. truck factories, jointly with Renault and Volvo, had manipulated diesel exhausts and in 2003 Toyota had accepted an American fine of $34 million because emission-control systems in several car models functioned improperly.

Sequels the subterfuge

Competition among diesel-car producers in the U.S. market may have been a key factor for manipulating emission data. It remains to be seen what the aftereffects of the scandal may mean for the market landscape of car production, especially the traditionally major players and the industry's new competitors.

A crucial aspect is whether the VW trespass simply reflects fraud. Or does the episode reflect a systemic issue of identifying gaps in current regulations and control practices: disregarding these to lower production costs and maintain a clean image. This may already be a process of anticipating development trajectories in a market increasingly veering into new, environmentally more friendly products with much lower emission rates – or electric cars with zero emissions.

The regulatory bluff is likely to result in global tightening of rules regarding emissions, in particular by diesel-equipped vehicles. New firms (Tesla, Google, Apple) may drastically alter auto markets as they move further into the business. Will new alliances among car builders be forged? (As we write, Peugeot seeks to absorb GM's Opel.) This would drastically transform market patterns and their operations. As discussed in *The Economist* of 3 October 2015, the "modern history of car mergers has often ended in disaster" and complicated economic consequences.

Remaining obscure, very importantly, is the impact on VW's workforce, both in Germany and internationally. Not least is what the gross stumble could mean to the firm's hometown of Wolfsburg, for which VW is economically essential. As great as was VW's shock on public opinion, France's Renault Group had another surprise in store some 18 months later. The public learned from the mass media that some diesel-engine series from Renault had a polluting level almost four times (377 percent) higher than the authorized norm.

A country falls in strategic banditry

The re-Russification of the Crimean Peninsula of March 2014 had its origins in an act of largesse – now seen by many as an error, rather than a merely questionable move – by Nikita Khrushchev in 1954. As a successor to Josef Stalin, Khrushchev already had much experience in the Ukraine as general secretary (twice) of the Communist Party in the Ukrainian S.S.R. During the Great Patriotic war of 1941–1945, Khrushchev served as Party link with the high command of the Soviet Army in Ukraine. There he was active in organizing partisan units against the military occupation by the Third Reich. Rising to the assimilated rank of lieutenant-general, he also served on the Stalingrad front. After Stalin's death in 1953, Khrushchev was named general secretary of the Union-wide Party in the U.S.S.R. in 1954. In the same year he arranged to retrocede Crimea – Russian since Catherine the Great made it so in 1783–1784 – as a gift to the Ukrainian S.S.R. There the Crimean Peninsula remained for 60 years before again becoming part of Russia.

Vladimir Putin's arbitrary act of rejoining Crimea to Russia, termed illegal by the UN Security Council, drew intensive opposition from western Ukrainians bent on having their country join the EU. Russia's grab of territory outside its new borders, especially at the moment when the Winter Olympics were held in and around Crimea's resort center of Sochi. Moscow's surprise move drew string protests within Ukraine and in many parts of the world. Yet the Olympics notwithstanding, "it's entirely within the realm of possibility that [Putin] was already mulling over scenarios for his intervention there well in advance of the [sports] event."[16]

The head of the French Institute of International Relations (Ifri), Thierry de Montbrial, construing the March 2014 referendum held in Crimea that favored union with Russia, observed that "Putin has ably exploited the mistakes of his adversaries [in Ukraine] . . . One and all would do well to recall that we always tend to overestimate short-term changes while we underestimate the long-term ones."[17] Another commentator wrote: "Moscow's goals are more subtle . . . focused on a long-range strategy of preventing Ukraine from escaping Russia's economic and military orbit, according to political analysts, Kremlin allies and diplomats interviewed."[18] And another political analyst:

> Our real challenge is to keep Mr. Putin from any temptation to break up one of the biggest countries in Europe [Ukraine]. It may take years, even decades, of effort . . . to know whether our policy has succeeded. Unless it does, we will have a far more dangerous crisis than the one over Crimea.[19]

It is not possible at present writing to anticipate the sequels to the Crimean transfer. Time may tell, especially in the Baltics and Georgia.

Unceasing vigilance over systems

Our examples are signs and symptoms of system stress if not of near-chaos and system failure, often induced by complexity. This may be especially so if human hands have easy access to system mechanics.

Philosophia moralis 101

Identifying and correcting the defects are possible, as we have seen, provided that the will to do so exists. Any system, whether human or inanimate, requires monitoring and intervention commensurate with the defects found and our capacity to restore order. Rectification, even in a system regulated by self-monitoring such as China's Communist Party, may experience aberration. After his house cleaning during the years 2013–2017, President Xi Jin-Ping seized the autocratic mode when in 2018 he arranged for remaining president for an unlimited period of time.

From the irregularities in individual and group behavior among humans, we turn now to behavior of a vastly different kind: that of water, one of the capital resources of nature, vital to all living things.

Notes

1 Formerly the Hong Kong and Shanghai Banking Corporation, a British establishment founded during the 1880s.
2 A year later the International Consortium of Investigating Journalists (ICIJ) revealed that a law firm in Panama City, Mossack Fonseca, had 14,153 clients worldwide, representing 215,000 industrial or commercial firms. While many clients had broken few or no laws, others were at fault for not declaring offshore benefits to their own governments. The global ICIJ is on the Internet.
3 See "Une évasion fiscale planétaire," Courrier international (Paris), 12 March 2015, p. 41.
4 Speaking on French public radio France Inter, 17 February 2015. "Sciences po" is the popular designation for the Institut d'Etudes Politiques de Paris.
5 The Guardian, from Agence France-Presse, taken from Sina Weiho (the Chinese Twitter), 5 February 2015.
6 "Rank and file," The Economist, 14 February 2015, p. 45.
7 Anonymously written, "China's Anti-Corruption Drive Serves Dual Purposes," Stratfor, 10 March 2015.
8 Ibid.
9 Linda B. Sweeney, Dennis Meadows, The Systems Thinking Playbook, Chelsea Green Publishing, White River Junction VT, 2010, p. 7. In "Xi's History Lessons" (cover editorial), The Economist of 15 August 2015 described on p. 11 China's president's efforts to reconstruct and pay full tribute to the role of the Chinese military in resisting Japan's occupation of China., 1937–1945.
10 See detailed reporting from Beijing by Chris Buckley, the New York Times, 30 October 2016.
11 In 2012, the World Health Organization established a global average of 10 homicides per 100,000 inhabitants, whereas the figure for Brazil was 32 per 100,000: one of the highest.
12 See map, "Democracy to the rescue?" The Economist, 14 March 2015, p. 43.
13 Report from Brasilia by Andrew Jacobs, International New York Times, 3 May 2016, p. 1.
14 "Life savings disappear as fraud surges in China," by Didi Kiesten Tatlow and Patrick Boehler, International New York Times, 19 August 2015, p. 15.
15 This company was earlier formed by the merger of the giant telecommunications builder Alcatel and what had once been the highly innovating Bell Telephone Laboratories.
16 Caryl, C., "Putin: During and After Sochi," The New York Review of Books, 3 April 2014, p. 43.

17 Montbrial, Th., director-general of the Institut Français des Relations Internationales, wrote the commentary "Ukraine: la France a un rôle à jouer" in Le Figaro, 15 March 2014, p. 16.
18 MacFarguhar, N., in a file from Moscow, the *New York Times*, 9 April 2014.
19 Stephen Sestanovich teaches international diplomacy at Columbia University. His comment, "Keeping Putin in Check," appeared in the *International New York Times*, 15 April 2014, p. 9.

8 Water
Simple matter of special complexity

An essential constituent of life

We automatically assign high value to rare objects. Freshwater, a substance vital for life, is indeed a rare resource. Referring to it as "blue gold" suggests that water is special for us humans, not only for us as only one of millions and millions of living organisms on Earth. Water is the basis of all life on Earth and most likely also of other life forms in the universe, should these ever be found. The process of evolution has been a "wet" affair.

All organisms consist essentially of water. Plants and animals comprise 50–95 percent water; human bodies are 60 percent water. Drinking water is essential for our survival and the durability of human settlements. In future a major challenge will be to meet the need for water in all regions, areas which differ markedly in availability of water for human consumption and sustaining ecosystem services. The importance of water is internationally recognized in Agenda 21 of the Earth Summit (1992) and subsequently in the MDGs and the SDGs of the 2030 Agenda for Sustainable Development.

Urban environments, including megacities, house millions of people in comparatively small areas. Since 2007, more than half of humanity lives in urban communities. This percentage is still increasing, especially in Africa and Asia.

Patterns of water use illustrate interdependencies of groups of water users at all scales. For instance, upstream water withdrawal or pollution may severely affect communities living downstream. This can lead to conflicts over water, possibly to political tension if not war. This may occur when water is shared across national boundaries as in the case of large rivers crossing territory of several nation states. For many countries, much or all their water resources originate from neighboring countries.

Since the UN embarked on the process of global and equitable sustainable development the special importance of water has become ever more obvious: its availability is linked to national *per capita* income. As environmentalist Jeffrey D. Sachs pointed out in his book *Common Wealth* (2008), "The very poorest of the poor are found in regions with low average water availability per person, high variability of rainfall, lack of irrigation, and low water storage capacity." This translates into high-water stress in prevailingly arid countries with scarce water resources as in the Sahel Zone of Africa.

This chapter reviews the importance of water for current and future generations. It outlines, in view of continued human population growth and environmental change, efforts to cope with a looming water crisis. We describe the complex setup regarding the water cycle, how humans have affected water quality and availability as well as the specific role the international community will play to develop global solutions to sustaining one of our most important natural resources.

H_2O – special, indeed

Under normal conditions water is a liquid. It may also appear in its solid state as ice or its gaseous state of vapor or steam. Snow, fog, dew and clouds are other forms in which water exists. Our oceans, streams, lakes and rain are made of water, and water is the essential component of all life forms on Earth.

Crucial to our existence is that water absorbs and releases large quantities of heat. Warmer water bodies release heat into a surrounding cooler environment, and they take up heat from warmer surroundings. We know the stabilizing effect of larger water bodies, be they oceans or lakes. Often vital, moreover, is the transport of huge water masses through the oceans, from cooler to warmer regions or the reverse of such transport.

What makes water so particular? Its molecule consists of only two hydrogen and one oxygen atoms, the known chemical formula is H_2O. H-O-H hasn't a linear structure; its hydrogen atoms subtend a 105-degree angle. The molecule is dipolar; its hydrogen atoms have a slight positive charge, whereas the oxygen atom on the other side of the molecule has a slight negative charge. This allows water molecules to form larger crystal structures through hydrogen "bonding." Hydrogen bonds are responsible for the stability of water molecules and the large amount of energy required to change water from liquid to gas.

Because liquid water is denser, ice floats on water rather than sinks. Ice has also an insulating function. It keeps the water below it, as in lakes, in liquid form. This and the density anomaly of water – i.e., that water has its highest density at 3.96°C – are vital for the survival of aquatic life during cold periods. Hydrogen bonds, moreover, are *sine qua non* for the three-dimensional structure of biological macromolecules including the carriers of genetic information, DNA and RNA. The dipolar nature of water also explains why water is a most important solvent, for instance of salts.

The usefulness of water for calibrating our physical world is also reflected in using water as a reference for mass (weight), temperature and energy.

Water on planet Earth

Water, produced in the process of star formation, has been prevalent in the universe almost throughout its existence. It is found in interstellar clouds within our own galaxy, the Milky Way. Most likely, water exists in other galaxies too.

Hydrogen and oxygen, forming the H_2O molecule, are among the most common elements in the universe.

In an article in *Scientific American* about liquid water in our solar system, Shannon Hall (2016) recommended that "It now looks like the solar system is awash with this key ingredient of life." This refers to recent discoveries by NASA of liquid water on Saturn's moons Titan (the largest) and Enceladus and on the Jupiter moons Callisto, Europa and Ganymede, the latter being the largest of Jupiter's icy moons. The planetary oceans confirmed to date add up to 50 times the quantity of water on Earth.

Earth is the blue planet. Visitors from other planets might have baptized ours Water rather than Earth. The first view of our planet from space has changed our perception of our home as to its fragility and singularity in space. The oceans make about 71 percent of Earth's surface. The total volume of water on Earth, the *hydrosphere*, is some 1.3 billion km^3. Some 96.5 percent is ocean water. The remaining 3.5 percent is polar ice and glaciers (1.77 percent); groundwater (1.7 percent); permafrost, lakes, swamps and rivers (0.03 percent); and water in the atmosphere (0.001 percent).

Water and its specific properties have been *sine qua non* in the evolution of life. Life originated in the oceans; it conquered land some 400 million years ago. Water operates as an important dissolvent in organisms and forms an essential element of their metabolism and associated processes. Water is essential for the two most important organismic processes, photosynthesis and respiration. Life is crucially dependent, not only on water itself (see Tab. 8.1 for availability of freshwater), but also on its dynamics within the hydrological cycle.

The water cycle

Cyclic behavior of major processes is a characteristic of Earth systems. Chemical elements including all those essential to life tend to circulate within the biosphere in specific paths between organisms and their environment. These are

Table 8.1 Extremes in water availability: ten countries and territories richest and poorest in water availability (in m^3 per person and year)

French Guiana	812,121	Kuwait	10
Iceland	609,319	Gaza Strip	52
Guyana	316,689	United Arab Emirates	58
Suriname	292,566	Bahamas	66
Congo	275,679	Qatar	94
Papua New Guinea	166,563	Maldives	103
Gabon	133,333	Libyan Arab Jamahiriya	113
Solomon Islands	100,000	Saudi Arabia	118
Canada	94,353	Malta	129
New Zealand	86,554	Singapore	149

Source: Otchet (2003)

two-way processes: from the environment to the organism, and from the organism to the environment. Energy transfer in an ecosystem, however, contrary to that of matter, is non-cyclical.

Cycles of materials are called *biogeochemical cycles*. These include the calcium, carbon, hydrogen, mercury, nitrogen, oxygen, phosphorus, silicon, sulfur and water cycles. Sometimes the rock cycle is also added. Gaseous and sedimentary types of cycles also exist. Cycles of elements or inorganic compounds also essential to life are *nutrient cycles*. The complexity of these systems is illustrated by the following.

- These cycles build hierarchical systems, from localized cycling phenomena to the global cycle level.
- Moreover, cycles are not independent from each other, but they form a system of interacting cycles with interlinked elements and processes. This connectedness has often been overlooked; cycles have been looked at from a global and "one factor" perspective.
- And, lastly, virtually all of these cycles are affected by global climate change. This is generally agreed upon, but we still do not understand how specific changes in climate patterns affect each of these cycles at different spatial and temporal scales.

There may be, furthermore, no general answer to the last statement, although there is agreement that there exist complex interactions among these systems. Human impact, including that on climate, may add further complexity to systems already complex. This is a crucial point when we discuss management issues and options for adapting to global change.

The hydrosphere comprises all water on Earth in all its different states: solid, liquid and gaseous. It includes marine and inland waters and associated *ecotones* such as brackish water systems, groundwater and subterranean water systems as well as ice and water in the atmosphere (and perhaps the lithosphere). Water is found in major reservoir systems – i.e., saline water, freshwater, ice and water in the atmosphere.

Drivers of the water cycle are evaporation, condensation, precipitation, infiltration, runoff and subsurface flow. These processes transport water between reservoirs, in the course of which water may be in all its different aggregate phases: liquid, solid (as ice) or gas (vapor).

Furthermore, the water cycle includes energy exchange which affects climate regimes, water purification and replenishment, transport of minerals, shaping of geological processes such as erosion and sedimentation, and the sustenance of the Earth's life forms and the ecosystems in which they occur.

The water cycle has been affected by human activities, directly or indirectly. Human-induced global climate change is responsible for major changes to the water cycle. The signal from direct human use of freshwater, however, has been estimated four times higher than that from climate change (Vörösmarty et al. 2000; Bogardi, pers. comm.) As stated in the third *UN World Water Development Report* of 2009, there is consensus among climatologists that climate warming will intensify or accelerate the entire hydrological cycle.

Other important anthropogenic changes to the water cycle have been *inter alia* because of agriculture and associated chemical water pollution, industry, dam construction, deterioration and destruction of forest ecosystems, removal of groundwater and river water, and urbanization. This had been summarized by Charles Vörösmarty and his collaborators in an overview of the global threats to human water security and biodiversity, published in 2010.

The river continuum concept

Lotic water ecosystems, such as rivers, form a continuum from their upper reaches down to the sea. This continuum is characterized by changing physical-chemical parameters as well as by biological components. Ultimately the course's gradient determines the system's overall properties. These properties determine, in turn, the gradient's segments, one after the other. A river system has, that is to say, feedback loops upriver and down; but it has even more complexity arising from discontinuities along its course.

Tributaries and their biotic communities affect, for instance, the main river in various parts along the river's course. Thus lotic aquatic systems must be seen as continuous, integrating discontinuities through their systemic elasticity. Flowing water systems are best understood through the interplay between their continuous and discontinuous nature (Schönborn 1992).

For thousands of years these complex systems have experienced drastic changes through human-made impoundments and diversions. Especially since the 1950s, numbers and storage volumes of dams and reservoirs have increased massively (Lehner et al. 2011). There are an estimated 50,000 larger dams (those higher than 15m) in the world. Over 50 percent of all large river systems are affected by dams, affecting systems both upstream and downstream through inundation, flow manipulation and fragmentation (see discussion in Nilsson et al. 2005). Dam construction has led to habitat fragmentation worldwide, with enormous effects on both biodiversity and the structure and function of aquatic ecosystems.

Perennial discharge in oceans has been completely (or almost) stopped for some among the large rivers. This severely impedes or halts sediment transport from land to sea with severe repercussions on nutrient distribution, substrate availability for riverine habitats and microhabitats crucial to biodiversity. Last, but not least, also affected are ecosystems of vital importance to estuarine and coastal communities. Many river deltas are sinking, leading to negative effects also on human population.

Further anthropogenic discontinuities

Specific examples of transboundary effects of river fragmentation are discussed in the third UN *World Water Development Report* (2009). Examples include

- closure of the Jordan River Basin,
- conflicts between agriculture and industry over water in Orissa (India),
- competition for water and downstream impacts in the Indus River Basin, and
- competition between fisheries and hydroelectric power in the Mekong River Basin.

108 Water

In sum, a river or aquifer spanning political territory may lead to competition or even conflict between sectors or countries. Problems become more complex once that large rivers cross several national borders.

Transboundary water issues are dealt with in two UN Conventions, namely the Convention on the Protection and Use of Transboundary Watercourses and International Lakes (otherwise known as the Water Convention) and the Convention on the Law of the Non-Navigational Uses of International Watercourses (otherwise, the Watercourse Convention).

The Water Convention was adopted at Helsinki in 1992 and entered into force in 1996. As of October 2013, it counted 39 Parties which included almost all countries sharing transboundary waters in the region of the UN Economic Commission for Europe (UNECE)[1]. In 2003, the Water Convention was amended to allow accession by UN member states outside the UNECE region. The Watercourse Convention of 1997 entered into force only in 2014.

In his message to the Meeting of the Parties to the Water Convention in November 2012, Ban Ki-moon, UN secretary-general, stated,

> The globalization of the [Water] Convention should also go hand-in-hand with the expected entry into force of the United Nations Watercourses Convention. These two instruments are based on the same principles. They complement each other and should be implemented in a coherent manner.

The "Third Pole"

Unfamiliar to most readers, the Third Pole or Hindu Kush-Himalaya is the mountainous region around the Tibetan Plateau. This region covers over 5 million square kilometers and stretches some 3,500 km (summary information in Box 8.1). Its border in the west is formed by the Pamir and Hindu Kush ranges, in the east by the Hengduan Mountains, in the north by the Kunlun and Qilian Mountains, and in the south by the Himalayas. The Third Pole contains the largest amount of snow and ice outside the Polar Regions, hence the name. This highly complex and dynamic mountain system includes not only more than 100,000 km^2 of glaciers but also Earth's wettest and driest environments. Rising to 8,000 m above sea level, it represents almost all life zones. Most of Asia's major river systems, moreover, are critically dependent on melt water from its glaciers (UNEP 2012).

Box 8.1   A zone of foreseeable calamity

The Third Pole region has enormous socioeconomic and cultural diversity. It is home to many ethnic communities speaking over 600 languages, many more dialects. Endowed with rich natural resources, it contains all or part of four global biodiversity hotspots. Mountain resources provide a wide range of ecosystem services, basis for the livelihood of the 210 million inhabitants of the region, as well as providing services indirectly to 1.3 billion people – one-fifth of the worlds' population – who live in river basins downstream. More than three billion people benefit from food and energy produced in these basins originating high in the mountains.

Source: International Centre for Integrated Mountain Development (ICIMOD), *Help Save the Third Pole* (brochure)

Current and future environmental changes in the Third Pole Region, in particular climate change and associated changes in water, snow and ice dynamics, will not only impact over 1.5 billion people living in the region but also the global climate system in its entirety. Conditions in the region not only affect the Asian monsoon system but also atmospheric circulation patterns in Eurasia and, more generally, in the Northern Hemisphere (UNESCO et al. 2011). Thawing of permafrost may result in massive release of greenhouse gases such as CO_2 and especially methane. This should further increase greenhouse gas emissions. Gas release may have enormous consequences for climate change mitigation and for delimiting global warming to less than 2 °C as agreed upon in the Paris Agreement of the COP 21 conference held in Paris in 2015.

Why "foreseeable" catastrophe?

ICIMOD, in its brochure *Help Save the Third Pole*, also highlights some of the gigantic risks the region is facing, all of them directly or indirectly related to climate change:

Natural disasters: In 2007, seven of the top-ten natural disasters by number of deaths occurred in the Third Pole region, accounting for 99 percent of total deaths. These incidents not only indicate the prevalence of disasters in the region but also the extreme susceptibility of the Third Pole region.

Mountain poverty: Poverty is pervasive in the mountains. The poor access, the complexity and fragility of mountain conditions and the marginalization of mountain communities from the mainstream, coupled with climate stresses and a proneness to natural disasters, all contribute to both high levels of income and food poverty. As a result, mountain people are increasingly exposed to growing physical, social and economic risks.

Vulnerability and livelihoods: Climate change has made the future of mountain indigenous people and their livelihoods more uncertain. Available scientific evidence suggests that climate change will place significant stress on the livelihoods of rural mountain people.

Glacier retreat: The most widely reported massive change is the rapid receding of glaciers and the losses of water storage capacity and reduced melt water in the dry season. These will have profound implications for downstream water resources. Glacier retreat is also likely to lead to an increase in the size and number of glacial lakes, and thus increased risk of glacial lake "outburst floods," with their potential to destroy lives, livelihoods and infrastructure downstream.

Water decline: Glacier recession and reduced snow cover could disrupt the hydrological regime of the river basins. Snow and glaciers play a modulating role in hydrology; changes in the hydrology could lead to an overall decline in water availability. Reduced ice volumes and snow cover mean reduced water storage. Increased temperatures will result in rain falling in the winter instead of snow – no snow left to melt and give water in the spring. Changes in the monsoon regime could also mean less water being available when it is most needed. Decline in water availability may have repercussions on all aspects of the social and ecosystem infrastructure. With water systems going from plenty to scarcity in a few decades, mountain peoples' food production and economic growth will be adversely affected. Local and regional tensions over water supplies may increase.

Biodiversity loss: Mountains are rich repositories of biodiversity with many endemic species, and they provide the ecosystem goods and services on which downstream communities depend. Climate change threatens the continued existence of some of the world's rarest species that occupy small climatically influenced niches; larger and more specialized species are likely to be lost because of habitat destruction.

Food security and agricultural sustainability: Changes in water availability have a direct effect on mountain agriculture. According to the [International] Food Policy Research Institute, the negative impacts of climate change on global cereal production may vary from 0.6 to 0.9 percent, but at the Third Pole this could be as high as 18 to 22 percent. Irrigation water from rivers sustains nearly 55 percent of Asia's and around 25 percent of world's cereal production – feeding over 2.5 billion people in Asia. A UN report, *The Environmental Food Crisis*, warned that melting glaciers and reduced snow could jeopardize world food security and drive food prices at unprecedented levels.

Water, as the world prepares for 2030

Setting the scene

Water has been an essential component of the MDGs. It is going to remain pertinent for all three "classical" pillars of sustainable development: economic, environmental and social.

Water is a stand-alone goal among the 17 SDGs of the 2030 Agenda for Sustainable Development (United Nations 2015): Goal 6 is to "ensure availability and sustainable management of water and sanitation for all." This goal is composed of six interconnected targets; these relate to

1 achieving universal access to safe and affordable drinking water,
2 sanitation and hygiene,

3   reducing water pollution,
4   sustainable use and development of water resources,
5   implementing integrated water resources management, and
6   protecting and restoring water-related ecosystems.

This process draws on 15-year experience with the "MDG approach" (2000–2015) and continues unfinished business and latest developments from consultations and reporting of UN-related agencies.

Tasks ahead are enormous, especially in view of the tight time line for the 2030 Agenda, not far distant in the future. Pressure on water resources and increasing pollution at national and international levels are a result of continued population growth and urbanization, rapid industrialization of the former Third World, and the challenge of meeting the needs to feed the world's expanding population.

UN-Water, in its 2014 report on *A Post-2015 Global Goal for Water*, draws a bleak picture of the current situation. Over 1.7 billion people live in river basins with water usage exceeding recharge rates. Results include the drying of rivers, depletion of groundwater and degradation of ecosystems and their services. Today at least 80 percent of wastewater is discharged without treatment. Potential water demand is estimated to grow by 55 percent until 2050. If current consumption patterns continue, by 2025 two-thirds of humanity could be living in countries experiencing severe water stress. About 40 percent of the human population currently lives in basins transcending national boundaries, stretching across two or more countries. These basins represent 60 percent of global freshwater flow. (Some 2 billion people depend on availability of groundwater.) Crises in regard to water supply have been identified by various sectors in society as one of the highest global risks.

This situation is aggravated by impacts of global climate change on the water cycle and on changing precipitation patterns leading to water-related disasters. This means the most severe disasters in terms of their economic and social effects. An infographic from the UN Office for Disaster Risk Reduction made this clear (UNISDR 2012): Floods, droughts and storms affected 4.2 billion people, equaling 95 percent of all people affected by disasters since the Rio Earth Summit in 1992. The resulting financial damage amounted to $1.3 trillion. These are the costs of 63 percent of all disaster-related damage during that two-decade period of 1992–2012.

As summarized in the UN-Water report of 2014 on an eventual Sustainable Development Goal on water,

> A global goal for water would thus contribute to poverty eradication, gender equality, enjoyment of the human right to water and sanitation, and universal human development while conserving the Earth's finite and vulnerable water resources for current and future generations.

More on water and the UN

The year 2015 was remarkable in many ways. It marked the seventieth anniversary of the UN itself, the time line for the MDGs, the starting point of a new agreement on climate change (the COP 21 meeting held in in Paris), and it set in motion the new 2030 Agenda for Sustainable Development and its SDGs.

The same year marked the fortieth anniversary of the International Hydrological Program (IHP). Better known for its work in literacy, education for all and the world's cultural and natural heritage, UNESCO's scientific undertaking concerning water has been decisive in shaping the global water agenda (overviews in Dumitrescu 2006, UNESCO 2015). Now a worldwide enterprise, the effort arose from the alertness of a physicist and engineer, Michel Batisse. When appointed by UNESCO in 1951, he was stationed in Egypt as science liaison officer and specialist for his organization's Arid Zone project. At first single-handed, Batisse's professional and humanitarian concerns persuaded his superiors to "go water." This UNESCO did.

These actions paved the way for the International Hydrological Decade (1965–1974) and the closer involvement of the UN's World Meteorological Organization as well as several scientific NGOs and numerous national governments. The Decade triggered an expanding capacity-building process in hydrology, a field then poorly understood. (In many countries, *hydrologist* was then still an unknown profession.) By 1975, the scene was set for establishing the IHP and its Intergovernmental Council. The IHP is today a prime endeavor in assessment, research, training and management in freshwater supply around the globe.

The importance of water and the multitude of related activities carried out by various UN entities led to the creation of an inter-agency mechanism: UN-Water, a platform for system-wide coordination and coherence with regard to freshwater and sanitation related matters (Box 8.2).

Box 8.2 UN-Water

UN-Water is the United Nations inter-agency coordination mechanism for all freshwater related issues, including sanitation. Building on a long history of coordination in the UN System, UN-Water was formalized in 2003 by the United Nations High Level Committee on Programs. It provides the platform to address the cross-cutting nature of water and maximize system-wide coordinated action and coherence. UN-Water promotes coherence in, and coordination of, UN system actions aimed at the implementation of the agenda defined by the *Millennium Declaration* and the World Summit on Sustainable Development as it relates to its scope of work. Through UN-Water, the United Nations act as "One UN." The scope of UN-Water's work encompasses all aspects of freshwater, including surface and groundwater resources and the interface between fresh and seawater. It includes:

- Freshwater resources – both in terms of their quality and quantity, their development, assessment, management, monitoring and use (including, for example, domestic uses, agriculture and ecosystems requirements);

- Sanitation – both access to and use of sanitation by populations and the interactions between sanitation and freshwater; and
- Water-related disasters, emergencies and other extreme events and their impact on human security.

The main purpose of UN-Water is thus to complement and add value to existing programs and projects by facilitating synergies and joint efforts, so as to maximize system-wide coordinated action and coherence as well as effectiveness of the support provided to Member States in their efforts toward achieving the time-bound goals, targets and actions related to its scope of work as agreed by the international community, particularly those contained in the MDGs and the Johannesburg Plan of Implementation (World Summit on Sustainable Development).

UN-Water currently counts 31 Members and 38 Partners. Members are UN entities including those responsible for major funds and programs, specialized agencies, regional commissions, conventions, etc. Other organizations outside of the UN system are Partners of UN-Water.

Source: www.unwater.org; accessed 16 November 2016

Means of implementation

Despite considerable international efforts and experience, in particular during the time of MDG implementation (2000–2015), efforts need to be further scaled up in many countries to reach the 2030 targets. This will require massive support from the international community.

UN-Water (2015) has compiled important information on the means required to implement SDG 6 and 17^2. Achieving universal access to basic water, sanitation and hygiene alone would mean costs of about $ 50 billion/year. Seventy-seven percent of the UN's 193 member states would not have the financial means to meet these targets. Almost a technical revolution would be needed to create appropriate environments for the latest technologies in wastewater treatment, Earth observation, weather and river monitoring, as well as exact measurement of agricultural irrigation. There is also a need to build capacity for the implementation of the 2030 Agenda in its entirety. Lastly, complete monitoring systems are required to serve multiple actors at different scales and for different applications.

To this end, for example, under the UN-Water umbrella a new monitoring framework is being setup for water and sanitation related SDG targets. This framework builds on a partnership of seven UN entities. Strengthened and extended partnership-building that optimizes existing alliances (within a revitalized Global Partnership for Sustainable Development) is, finally, what the international community seeks to achieve.

All these means are interconnected. Implementation of SDG 6, for example, should have repercussions on achieving other SDGs. It is now up to countries and their specialized institutions to take rapid action, if necessary with external support. Successful implementation of the water SDG is prerequisite for reaching the other SDGs, especially those related to poverty, food, energy, gender, ecosystems and climate (see UN-Water 2015).

Israel is among the 20 water-poorest countries. The example in Box 8.3 shows new ways of converting seawater to freshwater, meeting demands in Israel and possibly other nations of the region. Will progress in desalination be a long-term strategy to meet water needs globally? Or will the freshwater problem only be postponed, permitting complexity to "strike back?"

Box 8.3 Freshwater as Israel proves

In July 2016 IDE Technologies, a firm in Tzoran-Kadima, Israel, announced most promising results from its desalination system converting water from the Mediterranean to liquid consumable by humans. Through a pipeline 2 m in diameter, IDE's plant at Sorek draws seawater from roughly 1.5 km offshore, filters and desalinates it, ready for human consumption. In one of the world's most arid countries, IDE technologist Edo Bar-Zeev reported that the plant can provide more freshwater than the country needs.

The Sorek plant has been operational since 2013. With a seawater treatment capacity of 624,000 m³/day it is the world's biggest seawater desalination plant.

Sources: Rowan Jacobsen in Scientific American Weekly Review, 20 July 2016, and www.water-technology.net/projects/sorek-desalination-plant, accessed 18 June 2017

The urgent need to re-state the complexity view

Cognizance about water and its relevance for life and the human species is a prerequisite for its environmentally sound management. The water cycle is just one of the many elements of earth's network of interacting systems. Major alterations to the functional properties of the cycle may massively impede on sustaining human well-being. Human-induced climate change on our system of ocean currents may even exacerbate this trend. Oceanic conveyor belts, the so-called global thermohaline circulation, comprising a complex system of currents, may become dysfunctional. This will have disastrous consequences for humankind. It may trigger alterations in the water cycle, the cycle which redistributes not only water around the planet, but which is also responsible for the exchange processes among all water reservoirs – i.e., saltwater, freshwater or water in solid state (ice) or gas form (vapor).

The growing human population and associated water utilization and consumption patterns have led to a change of most if not all our freshwater systems (key examples are presented in Vörösmarty et al. 2004). Agricultural systems have come into being during the last 10,000 years, industry-related water use is not even a 300-year affair, and most recently pollution has reached new dimensions.

For the first time in human history we experienced the global distribution of insecticides such as DDT. What we see now is not only a drastic change to the chemical composition of our Earth system, but a planet with newly synthesized substances released into the environment and distributed through our global water system. Nano-particles and new materials such as plastics or pharmaceuticals have already led to environmental disasters. We have added "us" to the natural complexity of earth's systems and thus even created new complexity, in quality and quantity. As Bogardi and others pointed out in their article on water security (2012), "Water connects several socio-ecological, economic and geophysical systems at multiple scales and hence constitutes a 'global water system.'"

Awareness and knowledge about the current situation is essential for a literate society. Moreover, a precautionary principle could help preventing further exacerbation of anthropogenic impacts on our global water systems. This applies in particular to the multitude of polluting substances which grow in diversity as does in parallel our ignorance of their effects on ecosystems. And last but not least, ever-more decisive for human well-being will be education, technology and research to prevent us from transgressing planetary boundaries and remain within humanity's safe operating space (see chapter on the Anthropocene and planetary boundaries). This not only applies for water but also its interrelationship with the other factors decisive for sustaining the human species.

Strong compulsions from the complexity syndrome

This chapter puts emphasis on the freshwater challenge. The complexity of water needs, however, increased attention in order to deal with water problems systemically. The hydrological cycle needs to be seen as interlinked with other biogeochemical cycles and systems such as the Earth's atmospheric and geological systems, for example. The impoverished state of much of the planet's agricultural soil (especially in African countries), as another example, was evoked pointedly at the COP 22 climate conference (Morocco, November 2016).

Success or failure in meeting the goals and targets anticipated in Agenda 2030 will depend on the degree of coordinated interaction that we can assure among the diversity of systems. The family of problems facing us all reflects complexity indeed, but their prospective solutions remain no less complex. The only road to sustainable development open to humans is a combination of the application of imaginative genius and the conviction that they can "make the system work" – the world system of systems.

Notes

1 The UNECE region includes 56 countries in the European Union (EU), non-EU Western Europe, Southeast Europe, Eastern Europe, the Caucasus, Central Asia and North America.
2 SDG 17: Strengthen the means of implementation and revitalize the global partnership for sustainable development.

References

Bogardi, J. J., D. Dudgeon, R. Lawford, E. Flinkerbusch, A. Meyn, C. Pahl-Wostl, K. Vielhauer and C. Vörösmarty 2012. Water security for a planet under pressure: Interconnected challenges of a changing world call for sustainable solutions. *Current Opinion in Environmental Sustainability* 4: 35–43.

Dumitrescu, S. 2006. The Essence of Life. UNESCO Initiatives in the Water Sciences. In: Petitjean, P., Zharov, V., Glaser, G., Richardson, J., de Padirac, B., and Archibald, G. (eds.), *Sixty Years of Science at UNESCO 1945–2005*, pp. 233–259. UNESCO, Paris.

Hall, S. 2016. Our Solar System Is Overflowing with Liquid Water. www.scientificamerican.com. Accessed 6 January 2016.

ICIMOD (International Center for Integrated Mountain Development). *Help Save the Third Pole* (brochure). www.icimod.org. Accessed 18 June 2017.

Lehner, B., C.R. Liermann, C. Revenga and 12 others 2011. High-resolution mapping of the world's reservoirs and dams for sustainable river-flow management. *Frontiers in Ecology and the Environment* 9: 494–502.

Nilsson, C., C.A. Reidy, M. Dynesius and C. Revenga 2005. Fragmentation and flow regulation of the world's large river systems. *Science* 308: 405–408.

Otchet, A. 2003. The water crisis: How has it come to this? *A World of Science* 1(5): 2–5.

Sachs, J.D. 2008. *Common Wealth*. Penguin, London.

Schönborn, W. 1992. *Fließgewässerbiologie*. Gustav Fischer Verlag, Jena, Germany.

UNEP 2012. *Global Environment Outlook 5. Environment for the Future we Want*. United Nations Environment Programme, Nairobi, Kenya.

UNESCO 2015. *Water, People and Cooperation – 50 Years of Water Programmes for Sustainable Development at UNESCO*. UNESCO, Paris.

UNESCO, SCOPE, UNEP 2011. *Third Pole Environment*. Policy Brief 13, June 2011.

UNISDR (United Nations Office for Disaster Risk Reduction) 2012. *Impacts of Disasters since the 1992 Rio de Janeiro Earth Summit*. www.preventionweb.net/files/27162_infographic.pdf.

United Nations 2015. *Transforming Our World: The 2030 Agenda For Sustainable Development*. United Nations, New York.

UN-Water 2014. *A Post-2015 Global Goal for Water: Synthesis of Key Findings and Recommendations From UN-Water*. United Nations, New York.

UN-Water 2015. *Means of Implementation: A Focus on Sustainable Development Goals 6 and 17*. United Nations, New York.

Vörösmarty, C.J., P. Green, J. Salisbury and R.B. Lammers 2000. Global water resources: Vulnerability from climate change and population growth. *Science* 289: 284–288.

Vörösmarty, C.J., D. Lettenmaier, C. Leveque, M. Meybeck, C. Pahl-Wostl, J. Alcamo, W. Cosgrove, H. Grassl, H. Hoft, P. Kabat, F. Lansigan, R. Lawford and R. Naiman 2004. Humans transforming the global water system. *EOS* 85: 509–520.

Vörösmarty, C.J., P.B. McIntyre, M.O. Gessner, D. Dudgeon, A. Prusevich, P. Green, S. Glidden, S.E. Bunn, C.A. Sullivan, C. Reidy Liermann, and P.M. Davies. 2010. Global threats to human water security and river biodiversity. *Nature* 467: 555–561.

World Water Assessment Programme 2009. *The United Nations World Water Development Report 3: Water in a Changing World*. UNESCO, Paris and Earthscan, London.

9 Biological diversity
Bountiful Mother Nature

The challenge

In the last chapter, we appreciated the many attributes of water, the complications of scale that water can produce and dominate. We deplored the dramatic inequality of water's distribution on Earth and sometimes beyond. Humans, not a diversified species, cannot survive without water. Biodiversity, too, is complex as well but also extremely varied in its ramifications. It is beset with controversy at all levels, from local to global. Loss of the diversity of life on Earth continues to be one of humankind's greatest challenges. This relates particularly to the responsibility of the present to future generations and the need to preserve it for them as well as being fundamental to sustainable development.

As citizens we continue to be ignorant of essential elements of biological diversity such as the number of species on Earth and especially such taxonomic units as fungi, bacteria and archaea.

Curbing the loss of genetic diversity, species and ecosystems requires difficult decisions to be taken by the global community especially in regard to economic and other ecosystem services. Species of all major groups of organisms are of importance to mankind, and many may have benefits yet to be identified such as antibiotic substances, medicinal plants or plant species with food value. The diversity of life has even broader importance as discussed next with its linkage to security, resilience, social relations and freedom of choices and actions.

Biodiversity in a nutshell

Biodiversity refers to the number and variety of animals, plants and microorganisms. It describes variety and variability of life on Earth at genetic, species and ecosystem level.

Biodiversity is unevenly distributed on Earth. In the terrestrial realm it tends to be highest in the tropics whereas in marine environments it is highest along coasts of the Western Pacific and at mid-latitudes in all oceans. Fewer than two million species have been described scientifically. Current species numbers are thought to be some 10 million, scientists also presented estimates of up to 100 million or even higher (overview in Barthlott et al. 2014). Fifty percent of all species may be arthropods, but many of the lower organisms such as fungi, bacteria and other microorganisms are only poorly known. Recently Locey and Lennon (2016) published an amazing estimate of 1 trillion (10^{12}) for the number of microbial species on Earth.

Diversity of life is a product of evolution – i.e., the processes which have created diversity at all levels of biological organization. Evolutionary history of life on Earth has been a history of speciation (formation of new species), changes within species, and loss of species (extinction).

Evolution is explained by the theories formulated by Charles Darwin and Alfred Russel Wallace in the 19th century. Their theory of evolution by natural selection was integrated into the modern evolutionary synthesis through classical genetics and later population genetics. Evolutionary theory is firmly established – based on facts and theories of science, not only from the biological sciences but also from other disciplines.

Earth itself is only 4.5 billion years old. Life already appeared on Earth over 4 billion years ago. More than 99 percent of species that ever lived on Earth are extinct. Five major extinction events have shaped life during Earth's history. The most famous was the mass extinction event some 65 million years ago (the Cretaceous/Tertiary or K/T boundary), which led to the extinction of about 75 percent of all species living at that time and included the demise of the dinosaurs.

Currently, many scientists speak of a sixth mass extinction triggered by the human species. Main causes of current changes in organismic diversity are habitat loss, changes in ecosystem composition, introduced alien species, overexploitation, pollution and global climate change.

Understanding of evolution has translated into enormous contributions to humanity such as in the fields of human disease prevention and treatment, new agricultural products, industrial innovation and for society at large.

Life benefits humankind at all levels of its organization. Benefits at the ecosystem level are called ecosystem services. These include provisional services (e.g., food, water, fiber and fuel), regulating services (e.g., climate, water and disease), cultural values (e.g., spiritual, esthetic, recreational, educational) and supporting services (e.g., primary production, soil formation).

The Convention on Biological Diversity

The Convention on Biological Diversity (CBD of the United Nations 1992) is one of the three "Rio Conventions" emerging from the famous UN Conference on Environment and Development (UNCED, the "Earth Summit") held in Rio de Janeiro in 1992. The other two accords are UNFCCC and the UN Convention to Combat Desertification (UNCCD).

The CBD defines biodiversity, a contraction of "biological diversity," as "the variability among living organisms from all sources including terrestrial, marine and other aquatic ecosystems and the ecological complexes of which they are part; this includes diversity within species, between species and of ecosystems."

CBD came into force in 1993. As stated in the Global Biodiversity Outlook 3 (GBO 3), its objectives are

> the conservation of biological diversity, the sustainable use of its components and the fair and equitable sharing of the benefits arising out of the utilization of genetic resources, including by appropriate access to genetic resources and by appropriate transfer of relevant technologies, taking into account all rights over those resources and to technologies, and by appropriate funding.
> (SCBD 2010)

Currently, there are 196 parties to the CBD (with 168 Signatures), including the EU (www.cbd.int, accessed 18 February 2018).

Setting the biodiversity scene – insurmountable obstacles because of complexity?

Biodiversity – historical remarks

Elliott Norse and Roger McManus first published the term biological diversity and its definition in the 1980 annual report of the Council on Environmental Quality, "Ecology and Living Resources: Biological Diversity." A reduction of *biological diversity*, the notion became well known internationally after the publication of E. O. Wilson's book *Biodiversity*, based on the National Forum on BioDiversity held in 1986 in Washington, under the auspices of the U.S. National Academy of Sciences and the Smithsonian Institution. "Biodiversity" was proposed by Walter G. Rosen who had conceived the Forum. The details of the history of the terminology are found in Farnham (2007).

Biodiversity is an important component of all ecosystems, irrespective of whether these are undisturbed or affected by human activity. Moreover, it is the foundation of all ecosystem services, vital to human well-being. As stated in the *Millennium Ecosystem Assessment (MEA)*, decisions humans make that impact the diversity of life also affect their well-being as well as that of other species. More specifically, "biodiversity contributes to security, resiliency, social relations, health, and freedom of choices and actions."

Despite the enormous increase in global conservation efforts, pressure on biodiversity continues to change virtually all ecosystems on planet Earth. Current species extinction rates, for instance, have most likely increased between 1,000 and 10,000 times the background extinction rates during Earth's history (Pimm et al. 2014; Pimm and Joppa 2015). Scientists speak now of the sixth mass extinction (Barnosky et al. 2011; Kolbert 2014).

Biodiversity 2002–2010

In 2002 the Parties to the CBD committed themselves to the "2010 Target" – i.e., "to achieve by 2010 a significant reduction of the current rate of biodiversity loss

Biological diversity 121

at global, regional and national level as a contribution to poverty alleviation and to the benefit of all life on Earth." This target was endorsed by the World Summit on Sustainable Development, held in Johannesburg in 2002, and by the UN General Assembly.

This target has not been met as clearly illustrated in the Global Biodiversity Outlook 3 (GBO 3), released during the International Year of Biodiversity (2010). The Outlook presented detailed information on the subsidiary targets and progress indicators toward the "2010 Target."

Reasons for not reaching the Target are manifold. One major issue may have been the multifaceted and complex nature of life on Earth, a result of discussions since the CBD was put into place. In the process of "tackling the biodiversity issue," it has become clear that diversity of life does not "evolve" in isolation but in concert with other processes of global concern such as global human development, nature and environmental conservation, food security and health and the increasing connectivity among cultures and civilizations. The last is facilitated through our modern ICT.

For instance, the term *ecosystem services* was first "implicitly used" in the World Conservation Strategy (International Union for Conservation of Nature 1980) and in publications of the late 1980s and early 1990s to reflect the relationship between biological diversity and economy. Explicitly, the term appeared in publications such as Paul and Anne Ehrlich's book Extinction (1981). There the authors stated that, "It is the dependence of human civilization on the services provided by ecosystems that concerns us here" (p. 86). This they illustrated with the examples of climate, freshwater, soils, wastes and nutrient cycling, pest and disease control, pollination, food supply and a "genetic library" of useful organisms and products. The term *ecosystem services* triggered international awareness and debate through the MEA. This evaluation was carried out between 2001 and 2005 (MEA 2005a). It responded to a request for information by the CBD and other international participants. The assessment was targeted at the consequences of ecosystem change for human well-being and the options available to enhance conservation and sustainable use of ecosystems in terms their contributions to human well-being (see MEA 2005b and Box 9.1).

Box 9.1 The *Millennium Ecosystem Assessment* (MEA) – an overview of the 2005 exercise

The MEA was carried out between 2001 and 2005 to assess the consequences of ecosystem change for human well-being and to analyze options available to enhance the conservation and sustainable use of ecosystems and their contributions to human well-being. The MEA responds to requests for information received through the CBD and other international

> conventions (the UN Convention to Combat Desertification, the Ramsar Convention on Wetlands, and the Convention on Migratory Species) and is also designed to meet the needs of other stakeholders, including business, civil society and indigenous peoples. It was carried out by approximately 1,360 experts from 95 countries through four working groups and encompassed both a global assessment and 33 sub-global assessments. An independent Review Board oversaw an extensive review by governments and experts. Each Working Group and each sub-global assessment has produced detailed technical assessment reports.

The MEA was "the largest-ever global evaluation of the relationship between human well-being and ecosystems." In summary, its major findings are (from SCBD 2006):

- Biodiversity is being lost at rates unprecedented in human history.
- Losses of biodiversity and decline of ecosystem services constitute a concern for human well-being, especially for the poorest.
- The costs of biodiversity loss borne by society are rarely assessed, but evidence suggests that they are often greater than the benefits gained through ecosystem changes.
- Drivers of loss of biodiversity and drivers of change in ecosystem services are either steady, show no evidence of decline over time, or are increasing in intensity.
- Many successful response options have been used, but further progress in addressing biodiversity loss will require additional actions to address the main drivers of biodiversity loss.
- Unprecedented additional efforts will be required to achieve, by 2010, a significant reduction in the rate of biodiversity loss at all levels.

It remains to be seen whether and to what extent in 2020, the time line for the current Strategic Plan and for its "Aichi Targets," these issues will still need close attention (see the following).

Cognizance of the "complex nature of the beast" underpins the reasoning provided by GBO 3 for the failure to meet the 2010 Target (SCBD 2010, p. 84): "Actions tended to focus on measures that mainly responded to changes in the state of biodiversity . . . or which focused on the direct pressures of biodiversity loss." Neither the underlying causes nor the sustaining of benefits from ecosystem services have been mentioned in the responses to the loss of biological diversity prior to 2010. That future action should now be extended to "additional levels and scales" may reflect a simplistic picture prevailing in the period 2002–2010 of how to curb loss. In other words, ignorance of the complexity of the subject, or lack of political will to act on the issue appropriately, may have been responsible for missing the Target.

Biodiversity – 2010–2015 and beyond

The assessment of extinction risks carried out by the International Union for Conservation of Nature draws a bleak picture of the status of species assessed to date. The 2017 *IUCN Red List of Threatened Species* (for an overview see Box 9.2) comprises, of a total of 91,523 species assessed, 25,821 species (28.2 percent) as threatened with extinction (IUCN 2017). Two major uncertainties should be considered, *viz.* that despite enormous efforts, the number of species assessed is less than 5 percent of the species known to science and that this may only be a small fragment of the total number of species inhabiting Earth. Insufficiently covered in the *IUCN Red List* are reptiles and fishes of the vertebrate group and – virtually in their entirety – all other major groups of organisms. These include the invertebrates, plants (except for gymnosperms), fungi and protists.

Amphibians are not only the most threatened group of vertebrates with between 32 percent and 55 percent (best estimate, 41 percent) in danger of extinction, but because of a lack of information ("Data Deficient"), a large number of amphibian species cannot be assessed based on IUCN criteria. At the same time new species are being described at a rapid rate. This clearly indicates that true species numbers of amphibians may well be substantially above current figures (Howard and Bickford 2014). For details and future assessments see Erdelen (2014).

Sobering information is also provided by the World Wildlife Fund's *Living Planet Report 2014* declaring that, "The state of the world's biodiversity appears worse than ever." More specifically, the *Living Planet Index*, an indicator of the state of global biological diversity (based on trends in vertebrate populations of species from around the world) shows a decline of 52 percent between 1970 and 2010 (1970–2012: 58 percent according to WWF's 2016 Report) – i.e., the number of vertebrate populations has already been reduced globally by more than half, decreasing even further. Regionally, figures vary between 36 percent for temperate and 56 percent for tropical regions. Of the latter, decline is most dramatic in Latin America at 83 percent.

Terrestrial species declined by 39 percent between 1970 and 2010, mainly as a result of habitat loss and concomitant extension of areas under human land use. Freshwater species decline during the same period was 76 percent. This was a result of habitat loss and fragmentation, pollution, invasive species and changes in water levels and freshwater system connectivity. Marine species declined 39 percent in the tropics and the Southern Ocean. This included marine turtles, sharks and large migratory seabirds.

"If current trends continue to 2020, vertebrate populations may decline by an average of 67 percent compared to 1970" says WWF's *Living Planet Report 2016*.

Box 9.2   The *IUCN Red List* – an overview

The International Union for Conservation of Nature (IUCN), the world's leading conservation organization, has supported species conservation from its very beginnings. This approach was formalized through the establishment of the Species Survival Commission (SSC) in 1950. The first *Red Data Book* was published in 1963 under the leadership of Sir Peter Scott and highlighted the highest-profile species. Since then, the *IUCN Red List of Threatened Species* (at www.iucnredlist.org) has become the most authoritative and internationally accepted system for assessing species' extinction risk. The *Red List* is based on a simple yet robust set of quantitative categories and criteria, with the latest version dating from 2001.

The *IUCN Red List* is constantly updated, and the version launched at the Rio+20 meeting in 2012 included 63,837 species. It assigns species to one of eight categories based on their risk of extinction. Species in the three categories of Critically Endangered, Endangered and Vulnerable are considered as "threatened." The June 2012 version of the *IUCN Red List* included 19,817 threatened species: 41 percent of amphibians, 33 percent of reef-building corals, 25 percent of mammals, 13 percent of birds, and 30 percent of conifers: all indications of the grave threat to species. "Data Deficient" species are those for which inadequate information is available to make an informed assessment. Rates of data deficiency vary wildly among groups, from 1 percent of birds to nearly half of all cartilaginous fishes (sharks, rays and their allies) and freshwater crabs.

To date, comprehensive species assessments have been completed for all the world's amphibians, mammals, birds (most recently in 2012), cartilaginous fishes, reef-building corals, freshwater crabs, freshwater crayfishes, mangroves, seagrasses, conifers and cycads (plants with an appearance midway between palms and ferns). Comprehensive assessments are ongoing for many other taxa in order to remedy known biases in coverage, but even so the majority of described species remain *Not Evaluated* including most plants and the vast majority of invertebrates and virtually all fungi and algae.

Source: IUCN's *Red List of Threatened Species – Strategic Plan 2013–2020*

At the same time, we still do not even know the order of magnitude of the number of species inhabiting our planet. Estimates of the total number of eukaryotic species, for instance, originally ranged between 2 million and 100 million. (The cells of eukaryotic species have cells whose nuclei are *good* or bound by membranes.) To date, some 1.8 million species have been scientifically described and estimates of the total number of extant species seem to converge around 10 million (Mora et al. 2011; for a more recent discussion see Stork et al. 2015). This is a very conservative estimate in view of the fact that well over 80 percent of species are unknown. The so-called lower organisms such as fungi, bacteria and archaea are particularly poorly understood.

Efforts to reduce biodiversity loss have recently been significantly reinforced. This was underscored when the UN declared 2010 the International Year of Biodiversity, a year that mobilized tremendous efforts at all administrative levels for conservation. In that year, heads of state and government for the first time in the history of the UN debated biodiversity issues at the UN General Assembly. At the COP 10 meeting of the CBD, held in Nagoya (Japan), decisive steps were taken for the future of life on our planet. The meeting culminated in the adoption of the Nagoya Protocol on Access to Genetic Resources and the Fair and Equitable Sharing of Benefits Arising from Their Utilization, a new Strategic Plan for 2011–2020 including new global targets (Aichi Targets) and a Resource Mobilization Strategy.

As pointed out in the CBD's technical report on progress toward the Aichi Targets:

> The overarching mission of the Strategic Plan for Biodiversity is to take effective and urgent action to halt the loss of biodiversity in order to ensure that by 2020 ecosystems are resilient and continue to provide essential services, thereby securing the planet's variety of life, and contributing to human well-being, and poverty eradication. Such an ambitious, yet crucial overarching mission requires the implementation of measures across several fronts, structured under five Strategic Goals and supported by the twenty Aichi Biodiversity Targets.
> (Leadley et al. 2014)

The Strategic Goals are (SCBD 2014):

A Address the underlying causes of biodiversity loss by mainstreaming biodiversity across government and society.
B Reduce the direct pressures on biodiversity and promote sustainable use.
C Improve the status of biodiversity by safeguarding ecosystems, species and genetic diversity.
D Enhance the benefits to all from biodiversity and ecosystem services.
E Enhance implementation through participatory planning, knowledge management and capacity building.

It should be emphasized that Goal E is all-embracing and related to the implementation of Goals A–D.

The timeframe for these goals and the corresponding targets is 2020. The fourth Global Biodiversity Outlook (GBO 4) is in fact the mid-term report on the Strategic Plan. GBO 4 highlights that the majority of the targets are still reachable but that this poses several challenges. Greatest successes are (a) the progress toward conserving 17 percent or more of terrestrial and inland water areas and (b) the coming into force of the Nagoya Protocol in October 2014, already ahead of the 2020 time line. Except for Aichi Target 16, related to the Nagoya Protocol, **none** of the other targets seem to be attainable *in their entirety* unless efforts are massively scaled up (see SCBD 2014). Progress has been achieved only among some components of individual targets related to awareness (Target 1), protected areas (Target 11) and knowledge (Target 19).

A difficulty inherent to the system of targets is the lack of quantifiable definitions that could form the basis for measuring success for 2020. Moreover, interdependence of targets, in other words complexity, may be a crucial issue of the system. For instance, the mobilization of financial resources (Target 20) may be decisive for the ability to meet other targets. Tittensor and colleagues could not find significant increases in resources expected to be mobilized by 2020 (Tittensor et al. 2014). The authors also point out other difficulties in reaching the Aichi Targets which may be considered system-inherent properties. For example, these may be (a) time lags before outcomes are detectable, be they positive or negative, (b) the problem of scale (local vs. regional and global improvements) or (c) limitations of taxonomic coverage (see discussion in Tittensor). The authors conclude with the statement that "efforts need to be redoubled to positively affect trajectories of change and enable global biodiversity goals to be met by the end" of the 2010s.

It should be kept in mind that the third Global Biodiversity Outlook was released only in 2010 (SCBD 2010). The report stated that "all major pressures on biodiversity were increasing," which included (a) loss, degradation and fragmentation of natural habitats, (b) overexploitation of biological resources, (c) pollution, in particular as regards nitrogen and phosphorous, (d) impacts of invasive alien species and (e) climate change and ocean acidification.

Given the complexity of "our living systems" and the fact that we may have already transgressed the relevant planetary boundary (see chapter on Anthropocene and planetary boundaries), it reads like *Mission Impossible* to "take effective and urgent action to halt the loss of biodiversity," the mission underpinning the "2050 Vision" of "a world where biodiversity is valued, conserved, restored and wisely used, maintaining ecosystem services, sustaining a healthy planet and delivering benefits for all people" (SCBD 2014).

At the same time, the general conclusions of GBO 4, released in 2014 (SCBD 2014), highlight some of the aspects of the complexity of biodiversity loss and urgent matters related to reaching the Aichi Targets by 2020. Specifically needed is (a) a package of actions to be implemented, (b) a broadened political and general support for the Strategic Plan and for the objectives of the CBD and (c) an "overall substantial increase in total biodiversity related funding." These and other conclusions of GBO 4 are related to a deadline soon upon us: 2020.

Complex setup of biodiversity-related institutional framework

The CBD bundles global efforts toward the conservation of diversity of life on Earth. The multifaceted nature of this endeavor becomes clear from the programs, the major groups and the cross-cutting issues the CBD deals with (Table 9.1). The Conference of the Parties (COP) to the CBD has established seven thematic programs. Key issues are treated in theme-specific programs. Programs are

Table 9.1 Thematic programs, major groups and cross-cutting issues covered by the CBD

Thematic Programs

Agricultural Biodiversity	Island Biodiversity
Dry and Sub-humid Land Biodiversity	Marine and Coastal Biodiversity
Forest Biodiversity	Mountain Biodiversity
Inland Waters Biodiversity	

Major Groups

Business	Parliamentarians
Children and Youth	The Green Wave for Schools
Cities and Local Governments	Universities and the Scientific Community
NGOs	

Cross-Cutting Issues

Aichi Biodiversity Targets	Health and Biodiversity
Access to Genetic Resources and Benefit-Sharing	Impact Assessment
Biodiversity for Development	Identification, Monitoring, Indicators and Assessments
Biological and Cultural Diversity	Invasive Alien Species
Climate Change and Biodiversity	Liability and Redress – Article 14.2
Communication, Education and Public Awareness	New and Emerging Issues
Economics, Trade and Incentive Measures	Peace and Biodiversity Dialogue Initiative
Ecosystem Approach	Protected Areas
Ecosystem Restoration	Sustainable Use of Biodiversity
Gender and Biodiversity	Technology Transfer and Cooperation
Global Strategy for Plant Conservation	Tourism and Biodiversity
Global Taxonomy Initiative	Traditional Knowledge, Innovations and Practices – Article 8(j)

Source: www.cbd.int, accessed April 2017

implemented through the Parties, the Secretariat and relevant intergovernmental, governmental and NGO and regularly evaluated.

Within the context of its communication, education and public awareness (CEPA) program the CBD collaborates with a number of major stakeholders. Lastly, work in the thematic areas listed in Table 9.1 is closely linked to work on key cross-cutting issues. All these efforts aim at implementing the Convention and its Strategic Plan, and achieving the Aichi Targets until 2020.

The complex nature of issues the CBD is dealing with becomes obvious from its website at www.cbd.int. Moreover, biodiversity and sustainable development are inextricably linked: As provider of the Earth's life support systems, this features prominently in the new 2030 Development Agenda and its targets, the SDGs (UN 2015).

The CBD's Strategic Plan for Biodiversity 2011–2020 and its Aichi Biodiversity Targets provide the UN's framework for action. In all, seven global biodiversity-related conventions collaborate. These are the (1) CBD, (2) Convention on

International Trade in Endangered Species of Wild Fauna and Flora (CITES), (3) Convention on the Conservation of Migratory Species of Wild Animals (CMS), (4) International Plant Protection Convention (IPPC), (5) International Treaty on Plant Genetic Resources for Food and Agriculture (ITPGRFA), the (6) Ramsar Convention and (7) World Heritage Convention (WHC).

Mandates of the seven conventions are as follows (from joint statement by the Liaison Group of the Biodiversity-Related Conventions on occasion of the UN Sustainable Development Summit, 25–27 September 2015):

CBD

Provides broad policy framework comprising conservation of biodiversity, sustainable use of its components and fair and equitable sharing of the benefits arising from the utilization of genetic resources.

CITES

Regulates international trade in listed wild animal and plant species to prevent overexploitation through commerce.

CMS

Conservation and sustainable use of migratory animals and their habitats.

IPPC

Supports governments in protecting plant resources from harmful pests.

ITPGRFA

Aims at guaranteeing food security.

Ramsar

Conservation and wise use of wetlands.

WHC

Protection of the world's natural and cultural heritage of outstanding universal value.

These conventions collaborate through their respective partnerships, initiatives and programs with other UN entities and non-UN partners. Thus they reflect the necessity for biological diversity to be linked to other sectors for its sustainable use and conservation. In fact, COP 13 of the CBD (Mexico 2016) was targeted at mainstreaming across a number of sectors and at identifying next steps within the framework of the 2030 Agenda for Sustainable Development.

The future of Earth's biodiversity – a "wicked problem" of complexity?

In 2012, during the run-up to the Rio + 20 Summit, Tollefson and Gilbert (2012) stated in their *Rio Report Card* that "the three conventions have failed to achieve even a fraction of the promises that world leaders trumpeted two decades ago." Is this failure ultimately a result of the complexity of climate change, biodiversity and desertification and the effectiveness of three more or less independent conventions operating in an intergovernmental mode?

A first indicator of tackling this hyper-complex system of interrelated issues has been the setting in place of a "coordinating mechanism" for the three Rio Conventions – i.e., the CBD, the Convention to Combat Desertification and the Framework Convention on Climate Change (Box 9.3).

Box 9.3   Joint Liaison Group of the three Rio Conventions

In August 2001, a Joint Liaison Group (JLG) between the three Rio Conventions was established as an informal forum for exchanging information, exploring opportunities for synergistic activity, and increasing coordination.

The JLG comprises the officers of the Conventions' scientific subsidiary bodies, the executive secretaries and members of the secretariats. At its fifth meeting in Bonn (Germany (2004)), the JLG identified three issues as priorities for joint collaboration: adaptation, capacity building and technology transfer. Options for enhanced cooperation were identified by the three convention secretariats. The options include the following:

- Promotion of complementarity among the national biodiversity strategies and action plans under the CBD, the national action programs of the UNCCD, and the national adaptation programs of action for the least developed countries;
- Collaboration among national focal points;
- Collaboration among the scientific bodies subsidiary to the Conventions;
- Development of joint work programs or plans, of joint workshops (at the international level) and of joint capacity building (including training, and local, national and regional workshops to promote synergy in implementation);
- Case studies on interlinkages;
- Facilitation of exchange of information and experience, including improving the inter-accessibility of available web-based data;
- Cooperation in CEPA programs; and
- Cooperation in the development of advice, methods and tools.

Source: www.cbd.int, accessed 23 April 2015

A second step, specifically on persistent gaps in research policy, has been to establish intergovernmental mechanisms to handle the problem. An early initiative was the formation in 1988 of IPCC, a move by the World Meteorological Organization and the UN Environment Program. Then came the IPBES in 2012, modeled on the IPCC (for an overview of IPBES see Díaz et al. 2015 and www.ipbes. int). In 2013, at its COP 11, UNCCD established a *science-policy interface (SPI)*. SPI "translates current science into policy-relevant recommendations resulting from assessment and synthesis of current science" (see knowledge.unccd.int/ science-policy-interface, accessed 22 January 2018). Contrary to IPCC and IPBES, the SPI is not an intergovernmental body but comprises independent scientists, policy makers and observers.

Establishment of these panels reflects the need to improve work at the SPI concerning climate change, biodiversity and desertification. This is a systemic solution since the setting up of the respective conventions at the 1992 Rio Conference, without doubt, reflects importance, need for normative instruments as well as complexity and complementarity of matters covered.

Despite our venture into the periphery of wicked problems, we have studiously avoided mention of the tipping points so often part and parcel of evolving complexity. The present chapter has concentrated on life forms having evolved on Earth. Some of these may take a million years to appear and evolve, then last for millions of years of repeated major shifts in Earth systems' properties. Pinpointing a moment of biological modification in structure or function, or of size or color – or any other distinguishing properties, becomes an exercise in ignorance. It may prove impossible to be precise in the estimation of the when, where and how tipping points develop in emerging biological diversity.

There is growing evidence that tipping points or rather abrupt changes in system properties have occurred many times during our planet's history. Currently, we are discussing their relevance at all levels of organismic organization, from populations to ecosystems and even higher levels (see chapter on climate change). Here, we cannot embark on an in-depth discussion of how thresholds, tipping points or punctuated systems have shaped our environments, even our own evolutionary past, and how important a feature they are (going to be) in our world of the Anthropocene. Most likely, with our improving comprehension of the diversity of life on Earth, systemic properties may reveal ever more important features than we thought possible when discussing complexity/diversity/stability relationships, as ecologists have done in the last half century or so. Systems science may have broadened awareness of the changes environment "has (co-)evolved with," a process most likely in place since planet Earth's early days.

Conclusions

Concerns about continued loss of the diversity of life on Earth are one of the most pressing issues of our 2030 Development Agenda. Since the term was coined and E. O. Wilson published *Biodiversity* (1988), we have observed a mushrooming of activities at all levels. The 2010 Target was missed, and since 2010 the global community grapples with the CBD's Strategic Plan and its 20 Aichi Targets to be reached by 2020.

Biodiversity is now, since the UN Summit on Sustainable Development held in 2015, being mainstreamed into various sectors (see Kok et al. 2014) and the new scheme of 17 SDGs and their 169 targets. The critical time line for these is 2030 (see UN 2015).

It remains to be seen what will be achieved by 2020 and 2030, respectively, and when we will bring biodiversity loss ultimately to a complete halt. It seems questionable, to say the least, whether this is at all feasible by the time of these deadlines or even by 2050, the time line of the Biodiversity Vision. The 2020 mission statement talks about "taking effective and urgent action to halt the loss of biodiversity," and the 2050 vision is that "biodiversity is valued, conserved, restored and wisely used, maintaining ecosystem services, sustaining a healthy planet and delivering benefits essential for all people" (SCBD 2010). Will that be enough to preserve our natural heritage in a way acceptable to our future generations? We all know that extinction is forever.

Biodiversity, however, is not an issue on its own but closely linked to other major changes in our Earth systems as reflected in the factors for which planetary boundaries have been identified. For some of them we may have already transgressed critical thresholds. In addition, as reflected in latest measures of the ecological footprint humanity would already require 1.6 Earths to meet its current annual demands (WWF 2016). All these different aspects of a complex Earth system and the continued pressing need to implement sustainable development at all levels will be decisive for the quality of life of the current and future generations. This is intimately related to how we "treat" planet Earth in the future and whether there will be something like "Living in Harmony with Nature" or whether we push our Earth system into states which will create a future for humankind we cannot even imagine today.

If the broad topic of biological diversity were not already sufficiently complex, we now dip into a truly gigantic confrontation by the human race: climate change at the global level.

References

Barnosky, A.D., N. Matzke, S. Tomiya, G.O.U. Wogan, B. Swartz, T.B. Quental, C. Marshall, J.L. McGuire, E.L. Lindsey, K.C. Maguire, B. Mersey and E.A. Ferrer 2011. Has the Earth's sixth mass extinction already arrived? *Nature* 471: 51–57.

Barthlott, W., W.R. Erdelen and D.M. Rafiqpoor 2014. Biodiversity and technical innovations: Bionics. In: Lanzerath D and Friele M. (eds.), *Concepts and Values in Biodiversity*, pp. 300–315. Routledge, London and New York.

Díaz, S. and 83 co-authors (2015). The IPBES conceptual framework – connecting nature and people. *Current Opinion in Environmental Sustainability* 14: 1–16.

Ehrlich, P. and A. Ehrlich 1981. *Extinction: The Causes and Consequences of the Disappearance of Species.* Random House, New York.

Erdelen, W.R. 2014. The future of biodiversity and sustainable development: Challenges and opportunities. In: Lanzerath D. and M. Friele (eds.), *Concepts and Values in Biodiversity*, pp. 149–161. Routledge, London and New York.

Farnham, T.J. 2007. *Saving Nature's Legacy: Origins of the Idea of Biological Diversity*. Yale University Press, New Haven and London.

Howard, S.D. and D.P. Bickford 2014. Amphibians over the edge: Silent extinction risk of Data Deficient Species. *Diversity and Distributions* 1–10. Doi:10.1111/ddi.12218.

IUCN 1980. *World Conservation Strategy*. IUCN, Gland, Switzerland.

IUCN 2017. *Red List version 2017.3, update of 5 December 2017*. IUCN, Gland, Switzerland.

Kok, M., R. Alkemade, M.Bakkenes, E. Boelee, V. Christensen, M. van Eerdt, S. van der Esch, J. Janse, S. Karlsson-Vinkhuyzen, T. Kram, T. Lazarova, V. Linderhof, P. Lucas, M. Mandryk, J. Meijer, M. van Oorschot, L. The, L. van Hoof, H. Westhoek and R. Zagt 2014. *How Sectors can contribute to Sustainable Use and Conservation of Biodiversity*. Secretariat of the Convention on Biological Diversity, Montreal, Canada. Technical Series 78.

Kolbert, E. 2014. *The Sixth Extinction: An Unnatural History*. Henry Holt and Company, New York.

Leadley, P.W., C.B. Krug, R. Alkemade, H.M. Pereira, U.R. Sumaila, M. Walpole, A. Marques, T. Newbold, L.S.L. Teh, J. van Kolck, C. Bellard, S.R. Januchowski-Hartley and P.J. Mumby 2014. *Progress towards the Aichi Biodiversity Targets: An Assessment of Biodiversity Trends, Policy Scenarios and Key Actions*. Secretariat of the Convention on Biological Diversity, Montreal, Canada. Technical Series 78.

Locey, K.J. and J.T. Lennon 2016. Scaling laws predict global microbial diversity. www.pnas.org/cgi/doi/10.1073/pnas.1521291113.

Millennium Ecosystem Assessment (MEA) 2005a. *Ecosystems and Human Well-being: Synthesis*. Island Press, Washington, DC.

Millennium Ecosystem Assessment (MEA) 2005b. *Ecosystems and Human Well-being: Biodiversity Synthesis*. World Resources Institute, Washington, DC.

Mora, C., D.P. Tittensor, S. Adl, A.G.B. Simpson and B. Worm 2011. How many species are there on earth and in the Ocean? *PLoS Biol* 9(8). Online. www.plosbiology.org/article/info:doi/10.1371/journal.pbio.1001127.

Pimm, S.L., C.N. Jenkins, R. Abell, T.M. Brooks, J.L. Gittleman, L.N. Joppa, P.H. Raven, C.M. Roberts and J.O. Sexton 2014. The biodiversity of species and their rates of extinction, distribution, and protection. *Science* 344: 1246752. Doi:10.1126/science.1246752.

Pimm, S.L. and L.N. Joppa 2015. How many plant species are there, where are they, and at what rate are they going extinct? *Ann. Missouri Bot. Gard.* 100: 170–176.

Secretariat of the Convention on Biological Diversity (SCBD) 2006. *Global Biodiversity Outlook 2*. SCBD, Montreal, Canada.

Secretariat of the Convention on Biological Diversity (SCBD) 2010. *Global Biodiversity Outlook 3*. SCBD, Montreal, Canada.

Secretariat of the Convention on Biological Diversity (SCBD) 2014. *Global Biodiversity Outlook 4*. SCBD, Montreal, Canada.

Stork, N.E., J. McBroom, C. Gely and A.J. Hamilton 2015. New approaches narrow global species estimates for beetles, insects, and terrestrial arthropods. *PNAS* 112: 7519–7523.

Tittensor, D.P., M. Walpole, S.L.L. Hill, D.G. Boyce and 47 others 2014. A mid-term analysis of progress toward international biodiversity targets. *Science* 346: 241–244.

Tollefson, J. and N. Gilbert 2012. Rio report card. *Nature* 486: 20–23.

United Nations (UN) 1992. *Convention on Biological Diversity*. United Nations, New York.

United Nations (UN) 2015. *Transforming Our World: The 2030 Agenda for Sustainable Development*. United Nations, New York.

Wilson, E.O. 1988. *Biodiversity*. National Academy Press, Washington, DC.

World Wide Fund for Nature (WWF) 2014. *Living Planet Report 2014*. WWF, Gland, Switzerland.

World Wide Fund for Nature (WWF) 2016. *Living Planet Report 2016*. WWF, Gland, Switzerland.

10 Global climate change
Humanity's supreme challenge

Introduction

Global climate change is probably the most pressing problem facing humanity. The way we manage this phenomenon will shape the condition of all life on Earth. As Professor Lord Stern (2009) expressed it,

> We are fast approaching a crisis which requires decision and action now, before we fully experience the dangers we are causing. And let us be clear, these dangers are of a magnitude that could cause not only disruption and hardship but mass migration and thus conflict on a global scale. They concern us all, rich and poor.

In this chapter, we discuss – all related to complexity – what makes climate change so special, how we have come to know about it, when and how the international community took action, and how the most important international instrument, the United Nations Framework Convention on Climate Change (UNFCCC), developed the instruments devised to cope with it. We emphasize the permanent struggle to understand complexity of planet Earth's systems, at a time when anthropogenic interference with the climate system may put the future of humanity at risk.

Climate change is one facet of a broader picture since humans drove the world into a new epoch, the Anthropocene (see chapter on the Anthropocene). The *Amsterdam Declaration of the Global Change Open Science Conference* (2001) stated that human activities now "have the potential to switch the Earth System to alternative modes of operation that may prove irreversible and less hospitable to humans and other life." In other words, we have to cope with a complex Earth system (a "system of systems"), characterized by tipping points at which small perturbations may cause shifting of these systems into qualitatively different states. Climate change, therefore, is a complex process of change in interlinked complexities.

An additional complexifying element is added by the setup of the UN and its member states who take decisions based on consensus. This, again, is part of a bigger picture of the many organizations dealing with climate change mitigation and adaptation on all scales.

Politically and on a global scale, the "hot potato" is the notion of northern (industrialized) states as causal agents of the "climate problem." As major contributors to global emissions of greenhouse gases they impact on nations of the South, in particular vulnerable Small Island Developing States (SIDS) and least developed countries (LDCs). A 2°C limit (to global warming) was decided in 2010, at UNFCCC's Sixteenth Conference of the Parties in Cancun (COP 16). SIDS had favored a 1.5°C limit, indicative of the gravity of the problems that global climate change will cause for island systems.

As stated in the outcome document of COP 16,

> Deep cuts in global greenhouse gas emissions are required according to science, and as documented in the Fourth Assessment Report of the Intergovernmental Panel on Climate Change, with a view to reducing global greenhouse gas emissions so as to hold the increase in global average temperature below 2°C above pre-industrial levels, and that Parties should take urgent action to meet this long-term goal, consistent with science and on the basis of equity . . . the need to consider . . . strengthening the long-term global goal on the basis of the best available scientific knowledge, including in relation to a global average temperature rise of 1.5°C.

The year 2015 was considered crucial for advancing the international development agenda. Expectations were high, and a roadmap of decisive action was urgently required. The necessary steps were expected to be taken at COP 21 in December 2015 in Paris: An adequate agreement, aligned with latest science as a contribution to a viable and equitable future for humanity, was the target, expected within a broader global transformation. This was expressed in *The Future We Choose*, the Declaration of the High-Level Dialogue on Global Sustainability at the Rio+20 Summit, held in Rio de Janeiro (June 2012).

The Earth Negotiations Bulletin of 18 November 2015, released prior to the Climate Summit in Paris, began as follows:

> The world of international climate change governance is a maze of policies, acronyms and jargon. The complexity of the current negotiations is unparalleled among multilateral environmental agreements. Never before was it more important to cut through the complexity. The world looks to Paris in December 2015 where countries are to adopt a new climate change agreement.

What makes climate change so different?

Forest dieback (from the German *Waldsterben*) and the ozone hole, our most pressing global concerns prior to the concern for climate change, were successfully handled decades ago. The case of global climate change, however, is different. International measures to mitigate climate change have not been overly successful, after more than three decades of international scientific research, diplomacy and other efforts.

Wolfgang Lohbeck, co-founder of Greenpeace in Germany, has observed that climate change does not easily enter our hearts and minds. Even rationally it is a problem difficult to grasp. The issue was further specified in an article on climate change in *Die Zeit*, headed "Morgen vielleicht" (Perhaps Tomorrow), written in 2015 by Malte Henk and Wolfgang Uchatius. The text has the following subheading:

> This article does not present a new theme. It deals with a problem everybody knows. Researchers are warning, politicians are holding conferences, newspapers print headlines. Since decades all want to rescue the climate. Nobody is able to do it. Is this due to climate change itself? Or is it rather human nature?

Malte and Uchatius highlight why climate change is so special:

- The problem is intangible.
- It refers to a catastrophe occurring in slow motion.
- Climate change is a phenomenon which does not create new disasters, but only changes in frequency and severity of already known disasters.
- There are no clearly identified victims and many offenders.
- It is a risk perceived as possibly turning into a problem sometime in the future.

This may not only be a reflection of the complexity of climate change; rather, it points to how Earth systems function and how they respond to human interference. Perhaps we have not evolved mechanisms of perceiving such change the right way (they appear "unnatural") or, put more simply: Climate change may be too complex for us to understand, and even the best of science presents only an overly simplified picture of a phenomenon beyond our mental reach.

As a consequence, the warnings of the experts have not been taken seriously enough by the general public and its decision makers. Only slowly do we begin to realize that there are changes in weather patterns, that polar bears are living in a melting environment and that reports, presentations and even Hollywood movies begin to change our mind-sets and attitudes only incrementally.

Meanwhile, uncountable studies and newspaper articles on climate change have been published, climate change has entered education contents at all levels, so many discussions have been held, documentaries have been produced and even Nobel prizes were awarded. At the same time CO_2 emissions continue to rise, new cars are produced in massive numbers, coal extraction and air traffic have increased. As a promising development, civil society and science have put increasing pressure on politicians and decision makers, in particular in industrialized countries. On the other hand, it is worrisome that the discussion has already moved from climate change mitigation to adaptation. Does this reflect the fact that climate change has already massively changed Earth system properties and impacts on humankind are already noticeable? And may this ultimately lead to "post mortem damage control measures" rather than taking the possibility of mitigating and limiting global warming to 2^0C or less as a serious alternative? Have we given up thinking and acting to mitigate, and do we see the solution only in adapting to what is inevitable?

How did it all start?

Early history

Knowledge about weather and climate has been essential throughout the cultural history of mankind. For civilizations such as the sea-faring peoples knowledge about conditions in oceanic regions was vital for the success of their long journeys across the seas. In many belief systems, people saw an intimate relationship between weather phenomena and decisions "made by good or evil forces." Most famous is the association of El Niño phenomena with the Roman Catholic belief system. One of the best examples of the intimate relationship between culture and climate is the relationship between cultures along the River Nile and the periodical fertile floods of the river that actually sustained these cultures.

Ideologically, the conquest of the environment including climate has been part and parcel of Western thought. This is reflected in the idea that it has been the wish, the right and the ability of humans to control the forces of nature. Changes in climate have been claimed responsible for the decline of a number of ancient civilizations, mostly in combination with other factors as discussed in Jared Diamond's book *Collapse* (2005). On the other hand, climate change may also be seen as a driver for human evolution, cultural innovation and societal adaptation. In short, there is no simple, causal link between climate change and the fate of civilizations (more detailed discussion in Hulme 2009).

In the past, climate change was related to environmental changes such as draining of swamps, forest clearing and the like. Climate change was thought to happen on scales mostly irrelevant for humans. Thus thought and planning centered on the idea of a stable climate, only occasionally interrupted by natural disasters such as earthquakes, floods or volcanic eruptions. These perceptions changed drastically with the growth of scientific understanding of the human dimension of climate change. Some of the major contributors to advancing our scientific understanding of what triggered climate during the last 200 years are listed in Table 10.1.

More recent thought

Following the insights of Wallace Broecker in the late 1980s, the perception of climate change experienced a paradigm shift directly related to system complexity. Scientists realized that it was *sine qua non* to understand the climate system

Table 10.1 Important steps in climate research

1824	Jean-Baptiste Fourier	First description of the greenhouse effect
1859	John Tyndall	CO_2, water vapor and ozone may reflect heat radiation and changes in gas composition of the atmosphere may affect climate
1896	Svante Arrhenius	First calculations of global warming from changes in atmospheric CO_2 concentration
1938	Guy Callendar	Global climate is warming due to increased CO_2 concentrations in the atmosphere
1957	David Keeling	First quantitative evidence for increase in atmospheric CO_2 concentration ("Keeling curve")
1967	Syukuro Manabe and Richard Wetherald	First climate model. Calculations indicated that a doubling of CO_2 concentrations might raise global temperature several degrees
1987	Wallace Broecker	Anthropogenic climate change may lead to abrupt rather than gradual change. Increase of greenhouse gas concentrations may destabilize the North Atlantic Ocean circulation

Source: Hulme (2009)

in its entirety. This included the atmosphere and stratosphere, oceans, polar ice caps, forests, lakes and land cover.

On the international stage UN-driven political discussions of global climate change are mostly associated with the Earth Summit of 1992 and major conferences which followed. However, several important events preceded the Summit; in fact, they facilitated its achievements (Table 10.2).

In 1983, a quantum leap in carrying the discussion occurred: Gro Harlem Brundtland, former Environment Minister of Norway, was asked by Javier Pérez de Cuéllar (Peru), then secretary-general of the UN, to establish and chair "a special, independent commission, the World Commission on Environment and Development to formulate a *global agenda for change.*" This was based on a call by the UN General Assembly to

- propose long-term environmental strategies for achieving sustainable development by the year 2000 and beyond;
- recommend ways concern for the environment may be translated into greater cooperation among developing countries and between countries at different stages of economic and social development and lead to achievement of common and mutually supportive objectives that take account of the interrelationships between people, resources, environment and development;
- consider ways and means by which the international community can deal more efficiently with environmental concerns; and
- help define shared perceptions of long-term environmental issues and the appropriate effects needed to deal successfully with the problems of protecting and enhancing the environment, a long-term agenda for action during coming decades and aspirational goals for the world community.

138 Global climate change

Table 10.2 Important climate-related conferences and events leading up to the United Nations Conference on Environment and Development (UNCED), held in 1992

Year	Event	Location	Outcome
1979	First World Climate Conference	Geneva	Initiated the WCRP
1983	WCED established		
1985	Villach Conference	Villach, Austria	Recommended a convention on climate
1987	WCED publishes report *Our Common Future*		
1987	Montreal Protocol		Restricts emissions of ozone-destroying gases (effective 1989)
1988	UNEP/WMO Conference	Geneva	Founding of the IPCC
1989	Nordwijk Conference	Nordwijk (NL)	Declaration on CO_2 emissions
1990	Second World Climate Conference	Geneva	Preparations for Framework Convention; GCOS founded; First IPCC Report
1992	UNCED	Rio de Janeiro	Decision to establish a Framework Convention on Climate Change (UNFCCC)

Abbreviations: WCRP = World Climate Research Program; WCED = World Commission on Environment and Development; IPCC = Intergovernmental Panel on Climate Change; UNCED = United Nations Conference on Environment and Development; GCOS = Global Climate Observing System

As Gro Harlem Brundtland continues in her foreword to *Our Common Future*,

> What the General Assembly asked for also seemed to be unrealistic and much too ambitious. At the same time, it was a clear demonstration of the widespread feeling of frustration and inadequacy of the international community to address the vital global issues and deal effectively with them. . . . In the final analysis, I decided to accept the challenges. The challenges of facing the future and safeguarding the interests of coming generations. For it was abundantly clear: We needed a mandate for change.

The result of the Commission's work was the famous "Brundtland Report," entitled *Our Common Future*, published four years later, in 1987 (WCED 1987). The Report set in motion not only a further discussion on global environmental issues, but more importantly the process of realizing sustainable development, a process which continues until today (see chapter on sustainable development).

Until the late 1980s, climate change was considered essentially from a "greenhouse effect" point of view. Already, some 30 years ago, the World Resources Institute, in a public hearing in 1985 (see WCED 1987) highlighted that

> the ultimate potential impacts of a greenhouse warming could be catastrophic. It is our judgment that it is already very late to start the process of policy consideration. The process of heightening public awareness, of building support for national policies, and finally for developing multilateral efforts to slow the rate of emissions growth will take time to implement.

At that time, major players in the climate arena were the World Meteorological Organization (WMO), the UN Environment Program (UNEP) and the International Council for Science (ICSU).

A key question already phrased in the Brundtland Report and pertinent throughout the climate discussion is: How much certainty should governments require before agreeing to take action? The systemic nature and complexity of climate change and of our political systems is already recognized in the report. This is reflected in phrases such as "inertia in the global [climate] system" or "time lags in negotiating international agreement on complex issues involving all nations," respectively.

It is realized that no nation can address the climate change issue in isolation. A four-track strategy, comprising (1) monitoring and assessment, (2) research, (3) development of international policies and (4) strategies to minimize damage, nowadays referred to as adaptation strategies, was proposed. The need for a convention on climate change was already expressed at the Villach Conference (see Table 10.2).

UNFCCC, the Kyoto Protocol and conclusions from the Bonn Conference (Earth Negotiations Bulletin)

The international political response to climate change began with the 1992 adoption of the United Nations Framework Convention on Climate Change (UNFCCC) at the World Conference on Environment and Development, held in Rio de Janeiro ("Earth Summit"). UNFCCC sets out a legal framework for stabilizing atmospheric concentrations of greenhouse gases (GHG) to avoid *"dangerous anthropogenic interference with the climate system."* The Convention, which entered into force on 21 March 1994, has 197 parties.

The treaty itself sets no binding limits on greenhouse gas emissions for individual countries and contains no enforcement mechanisms. In that sense, the treaty is considered legally non-binding. Instead, the treaty provides a framework for negotiating specific international treaties (called "protocols") that may set binding limits on greenhouse gases. The UNFCCC Secretariat is located in Bonn, Germany.

With the UNFCCC, the UN introduced the Conference of the Parties (COP) system of meetings. COP 1 of UNFCCC took place in Berlin (1995) and was chaired by Angela Merkel, at that time Environment Minister of the Federal Republic of Germany.

In December 1997, delegates to COP 3 in Kyoto, Japan, agreed to a protocol to the UNFCCC that committed industrialized countries and countries in transition to a market economy to achieve emissions reduction targets. These countries, known as Annex I parties under the UNFCCC, agreed to reduce their overall emissions of six GHGs by an average of 5 percent below 1990 levels in 2008–2012 (the first commitment period), with specific targets varying from country to country. The Kyoto Protocol entered into force on 16 February 2005 and now has 192 parties. At COP 16, held in 2010 in Cancun, Mexico, the Cancun Agreement was reached which states that future global warming should be limited to below 2°C relative to pre-industrial level.

Just prior to the Paris conference, a UNFCCC Climate Change Conference took place in Bonn, Germany, from 19–23 October 2015. The meeting brought together over 2,400 participants, representing governments, observer organizations and the media. The Conference was the last in a series of meetings under the UNFCCC in preparation for the twenty-first session of the COP. COP 21 took place in Paris, France, from 29 November to 13 December 2015. It aimed to advance negotiations to meet the mandate to adopt "a protocol, another legal instrument or an agreed outcome with legal force under the Convention applicable to all parties which is to come into force in 2020."

Leaving Bonn 20 years after the adoption, at COP 1 in Berlin, of the "Berlin Mandate" for the negotiations of the Kyoto Protocol, and ten years since its entry into force, parties to the climate regime were still struggling to find a clear path to address the greatest challenge to ever face humankind. The Paris Climate Change Conference was expected to light the way for governments to finally deliver an effective global response to this epochal challenge. At the time of the Bonn Conference parties were far from reaching any agreement. They had but five weeks to consider their options ahead of Paris, including opportunities to engage at the political level at the pre-COP, convening from 8–10 November in Paris, France. During the closing plenary, the French presidency urged parties to prepare for Paris "using all possible consultations that they can create among themselves." As one seasoned observer noted "turbulence is more of a problem when you are coming in for a landing." The only hope was that, despite a bumpy ride, the process would eventually find a safe landing on a Paris Agreement. And in fact, it did.

Retrospective: the complex scenario for COP 21

Despite almost four decades of discussions of climate change, 20 meetings of the Conference of the Parties (COP) of the UNFCCC and several reports of the IPCC we still had no binding agreement on global climate change prior to Paris.

Glaciers are melting away worldwide, corals of the Great Barrier Reef are dying off, the Pacific and other regions experience more frequent extreme weather events and so forth. Greenhouse gas emissions continue to rise and climate change, if not kept below 2^0 C, may lead to unprecedented events in the future of humankind including storms, floods, heat waves, droughts, melting of the pole caps, sea-level rise, epidemic diseases, waves of human migration. – Time is up.

Since 1880, global average temperature has increased 0.85°C. If greenhouse gas emissions continue to rise at present rates, we may have to expect a 5^0C warmer planet in hundred years. This equals the temperature difference between the last ice age and today. Staying within the frequently discussed 2^0C limit would have to translate into releasing *in total* no more than 1,000 billion tons of CO_2 into the atmosphere. This is equivalent to 30 times the current *annual* global emissions. As a consequence, most of our oil, gas and coal reserves must remain unexploited. This would require a total resetting of the global energy sector. This change cannot happen quickly but because of various factors takes quite some time. Therefore, coal-based power supply systems are expected to continue to be our major source of energy for quite some time. A critical issue is the time lag between phasing out of traditional fossil-fuel based energy systems and their replacement by renewable sources of energy, in particular solar energy.

Why were expectations for COP 21 in Paris higher than for previous meetings? Claus Hecking (2015) has published important information in a contribution to a series of articles entitled "Countdown for the Climate" in the German weekly *Die Zeit*. The following discussion is in part based on his article which appeared on 17 December 2015, just after the Paris meeting.

To date, the Kyoto Protocol has not made a difference, essentially a result of a lack of solidarity among parties to the Convention. Several of them refused to accept binding targets for greenhouse gas reductions. The U.S. and China, both responsible for over 40 percent of global emissions, have most recently agreed to reduce their emissions albeit time lines and targets (still) differ.

A second reason to be more optimistic is that these days we have a much broader consensus on the fact that humans are responsible for climate change. This has been a matter of debate for many years, but the IPCC, in particular through its latest reports, has provided sound evidence that human activities are responsible for global climate change as currently observed. Moreover, the fact that environmental changes are noticeable already has massively increased public pressure on policy makers. Quite unexpected but not to be underestimated, is the influence of the latest contributions of the Roman Catholic Church to the debate, in particular through Pope Francis's encyclical *Laudato Si'* and his appearance at the UN General Assembly. As regards climate change the encyclical says,

> The climate is a common good, belonging to all and meant for all. At the global level, it is a complex system linked to many of the essential conditions for human life. A very solid scientific consensus indicates that we are presently witnessing a disturbing warming of the climatic system.

Third, technological progress has led to less costly systems of power generation. Solar modules have become reasonably priced and wind parks provide low-cost energy. Wind and solar energy are also preferred sources of energy by China and the

United States. Decreasing subventions for the use of fossil sources of energy could also massively support the path toward "green energy systems" (see Box 10.1 for the nexus between climate change, emissions of greenhouse gases and energy).

Fourth, a crucial issue is the debate between industrialized nations and countries in transition. The latter are afraid that their development trajectories and opportunities might be impeded by measures of the international community to mitigate climate change. It is hoped that the UN's *Green Climate Fund* can meet their mitigation and adaptation needs and facilitate emission reductions in these countries.

And lastly, the future of various segments of the industry and economy sectors crucially depends on decisions expected to be taken in Paris. It is clear that emissions will have to be reduced, however, knowledge about cuts to be expected is vital for longer term sound planning and the development of investment schemes in these sectors. An eventual shift of the global economy toward environmentally more friendly technologies would have tremendous spin-offs for specific sectors within industry and business. In fact, divestment trends – i.e., diminishing financial support for the coal or oil sector, might already be indicative of a move toward reducing or even terminating coal and raw oil extraction.

Box 10.1   Climate change and energy – an intimate relationship

Climate change generally refers to changes in statistical properties of the Earth's climate system, irrespective of the underlying causes.

Commonly climate change is nowadays referred to as anthropogenic global warming and its related effects.

Of greatest concern is the release of so-called greenhouse gases. These include water vapor (H_2O), carbon dioxide (CO_2), methane (CH_4), nitrous oxide (N_2O), ozone (O_3), and chlorofluorocarbons (CFCs; used, e.g., in refrigeration systems). CO_2 is the most important of them.

CO_2 concentrations before industrialization (c. 1750): Around 280 ppm. 1750–1950: increase of "only" 50 ppm (from 280 ppm). 1950–1985: Further increase of 65 ppm. 2014: Limit of 400 ppm transgressed. 2015: Warmest year since weather recorded (1781).

Terrestrial biosphere and oceans are Earth's major CO_2 sinks. Two major uncertainties: First, exact intake of the oceans and impact of ocean acidification through CO_2 intake is not known. Second, storage capacities and eventual weakening of the sink function in marine and terrestrial ecosystems is only poorly understood.

Burning of fossil fuels and land use change, in particular deforestation in the tropics, are the most important factors contributing to rising CO_2 levels in the atmosphere. Over 90 percent of fossil-fuel combustion derives from liquid (gasoline and fuel oil), solid (coal) and gaseous fuels (natural gas).

> Reduction of greenhouse gas emissions is intimately linked to changing our energy systems toward regenerative (renewable) sources of energy and lowering of energy consumption. Renewables include geothermal, solar, tidal, wind, wave, biomass and gravitation. Innovative fuel substances and technologies will be of the essence. Costs for renewable energy may be substantially lowered, as a result of technological progress and optimization.
>
> Massive change needed in our energy systems takes time. Systems are complex, energy policies need long time perspectives, technology development needed for reduction of CO_2 emissions from coal power plants.
>
> The Paris Agreement is to come into force by 2020. For reaching the 1.5°C goal massive decarbonization is rapidly needed. CO_2 emissions need to be cut by 70–95 percent until 2050; some 90 percent of fossil reserves will have to remain untouched (IPCC). There is little time for implementing the Paris Agreement.

Earth systems interdependencies – pertinent examples

There is an intimate linkage between greenhouse gas concentrations in the atmosphere and global warming. A limitation to 450 ppm is considered *sine qua non* for not exceeding the 2°C limit. We also need to take into account a cumulative effect of greenhouse gases because of their persistence in the atmosphere. Half time of CO_2, for instance, is about 1,000 years. Should we reach the tipping point for the thawing of permafrost enormous quantities of CO_2 and in particular methane, a greenhouse gas much more disastrous than CO_2, would be released into the atmosphere.

Complex interactions exist between the atmosphere and the oceans. Oceans have been absorbing large quantities of CO_2 which has already caused acidification in the marine environment. It is estimated that about 50 percent of additional CO_2, which has been released into the atmosphere because of human activities has been taken up by the oceans. Therefore, quantification of carbon exchange between the atmosphere and the oceans, ocean acidification and its impact on biodiversity and functioning of marine ecosystems is of the essence for understanding the effects of greenhouse gas emissions in their entirety.

The Strategic Plan for Biodiversity and its Aichi Targets has a time line of 2020 (see chapter on biodiversity). Interestingly, and reflecting the pressing nature of the problem, for the multiple anthropogenic pressures on coral reefs and other vulnerable ecosystems impacted by climate change, the deadline for meeting the respective target was advanced to 2015. The target elements are as follows:

1 Multiple anthropogenic pressures on coral reefs are minimized, so as to maintain their integrity and functioning.

2   Multiple anthropogenic pressures on other vulnerable ecosystems impacted by climate change or ocean acidification are minimized, so as to maintain their integrity and functioning.

The first target has not been met and the second target has not been evaluated because of insufficient information available to evaluate the target (SCBD 2014). In other words, a deadline has been advanced because of the seriousness of climate change related impacts only to see that it could either not be met or not be evaluated. To make the importance of the target clear: Target 10 refers to *all* ecosystems vulnerable to global climate change! However, both the Global Biodiversity Outlook 4 and the technical report on Progress Towards the Aichi Targets of the Convention on Biological Diversity (Leadley et al. 2014), essentially focus on coral reefs in their analyses.

There is evidence that climate change may lead to increased levels of aerosols in the atmosphere. This may trigger massive deterioration of air quality and associated effects on human health, thus requiring more rigorous limitation of aerosols to meet air quality standards. Aerosols are also seen as counteracting global warming as they may have a reflecting effect on solar insulation.

The Paris Agreement, what it means

Paris – the dilemma

The twenty-first meeting of the parties (COP 21) to the UNFCCC was decisive in two different but intertwined aspects of the future of our planet, viz., (1) addressing climate change in view of its pressing nature and the urgency for the world community to act and (2) the "functioning" of the world community itself in view of the complex and global threat humankind and its future generations are going to face as a result of climate change. In other words, climate diplomacy would have dug its own grave if the Paris meeting would have turned into a failure – i.e., if the meeting would not have reached a binding climate agreement through which all nations commit themselves to reduce their greenhouse gas emissions in such a way that the 2°C target (or even the 1.5° C) could still be reached. The agreement is however only a first step. It must also be ratified. This had taken eight years for the Kyoto Protocol!

But much more was at stake. Under the leadership of the UN, climate diplomacy has been one of the most transparent processes in international affairs – democracy "at its best." All nation states, under whatever government, have been participating and a practice of one state – one voice has given equal rights to each of them, irrespective of size, economic status or whatever. A failure of the Paris meeting would have put all this at risk. As journalist Nick Reimer (2015) stated in his book on the history and future of climate diplomacy: "COP 21 in Paris will also decide upon whether democracy is able to address 21st century problems of humankind."

The agreement

On 12 December 2015, the Paris Agreement was adopted by the twenty-first session of the COP to the UN Convention on Climate Change, held in Paris, France, from 29 November to 13 December 2015. The conference was attended by over 36,000 participants, over 23,000 government officials and over 9,000 representatives from UN bodies and agencies, intergovernmental and civil society organizations and almost 4000 members of the media.

Prior to the conference, a leaders' event was held to generate political will toward an agreement. The event was attended by over 150 heads of state and government. Decisive was in particular the participation of China and the United States as the two major CO_2 emitters.

The Paris Agreement is a universal legally binding agreement effective from 2020. It includes 29 articles aiming at strengthening the global response to climate change. Most importantly, it includes holding the global average temperature well below 2°C above pre-industrial levels and the pursuance of limiting temperature increase to 1.5°C above pre-industrial levels. Each party to the convention is requested to make nationally determined contributions (NDCs; see the aforementioned), to be communicated every five years. A global stocktaking of efforts is foreseen for 2023 and thereafter every five years.

COP 21 – a brief analysis (based on Earth Negotiations Bulletin Vol. 12 no. 663 of 15 December 2015)

After the failure of the Copenhagen Conference in 2009 expectations for Paris were high and COP 21 was perceived that it "could not afford to fail," as already discussed earlier. Climate governance and environmental multilateralism were at stake.

The Paris Conference was a success which exceeded expectations. As said in the closing, however, it is considered "good, but not perfect."

Through an approach based on five-year cycles of their nationally determined contributions (NDCs), beginning in 2023, parties shall "ratchet up" efforts to keep global temperature rise within the limits as outlined earlier. NDCs, however, are each country's "fair contribution" reflecting its respective capabilities and national circumstances. NDCs were the "mechanism" to ensure universal participation in the "Paris process." Last but not least, the success of the Paris Agreement will depend on how ambitious the contributions of the parties will be to address the issue of emission reductions.

Major criticism centers on the annual USD 100 billion finance mobilization goal to be reached by developed countries by 2020. There is fear that parties may negotiate a new collective goal after 2025. "Developed countries are not bound by the Agreement to increase their mitigation or support efforts beyond existing commitments" (Earth Negotiations Bulletin Vol. 12 No. 663, p. 43).

Great progress has been the inclusion of human rights into the Paris Agreement which makes this the first multilateral agreement that recognizes human rights.

146 *Global climate change*

Whether the Agreement will determine the end of the fossil-fuel era crucially depends on implementation of the Agreement itself, the mobilization of all actors, and the future role of the Convention in the "fast-changing implementation space."

The ratification process was an unexpected success, in particular with regard to the 55 countries responsible for more than 55 percent of global emissions, which had to act before 2020: Less than one year after the conference already 111 countries had ratified the Paris Agreement (by 19 November 2016).

President Trump and the Paris Agreement: a major actor stumbles

Despite complexity, systemic order survives

North of the Equator, the first of June is the beginning of the meteorological summer. The date 1 June 2017 is not forgotten. It is the day when American President Donald Trump announced that "in order to fulfill my solemn duty to protect America and its citizens, the United States will withdraw from the Paris Accord." This suspension would also include stopping American determined contributions [to the Paris Agreement] as well as those to the Green Climate Fund. Under the Obama Administration the United States had committed itself to contributing $3 billion, of which $1 billion had already been transferred to the Fund. Trump added, "But we will start to negotiate and we will see if we can make a deal that's fair."

As stated by Germanwatch, a Bonn-based German NGO, ignoring all the signs of global climate change is cynical. Another point is that the government of the very state, which historically has contributed most to the global climate crisis, disposes of solidarity with the poorest people who have been hit hardest. Barbara Hendricks, German environment minister (until early 2018), declared, "Trump has decided in favor of the past, the rest of the world for the future."

On first of June 2017, the heads of state and of government of France, Germany and Italy jointly stated, "We firmly believe that the Paris Agreement cannot be renegotiated, since it is a vital instrument for our planet, societies and economies." In his address on the evening of President Trump's announcement, newly elected French President Macron referred to Trump's withdrawal as "error for the interests of his country, his people and a mistake for the future." Macron continued, "Don't be mistaken on climate; there is no plan B because there is no planet B."

We are not discussing any implementations and the "reasoning" behind the United States' withdrawing from an agreement which had taken years to become reality – and which has been signed by all parties to the UNFCCC except for Nicaragua and Syria – and perhaps soon also America as the most powerful of world nation states.

Here we briefly highlight a few systemic issues related to the complexity surrounding the process toward such agreements and ultimately their successful implementation. What have we learned from Trump's withdrawal?

First, changes in political leadership in a given country may have repercussions affecting not only global commitments made in the past but also those to be made (or rather not to be made) in the future.

Second, such changes may be tied to the duration of the leadership in question. In the case of the United States and its presidential terms this might be a maximum of eight years, but might be less. In other countries it may relate principally to the cycles of general elections (e.g., four years in Germany), in particular if these result in a change in head of state or government.

Third, irrespective of any corrective measures that might be taken by a new administration in America, impacts of action as announced may trigger an avalanche of similar action by other UN member states thereby torpedoing overall support for the agreement: a cascading effect. Trump's decision may even be seen as damaging multilateralism, especially after the effort invested to reach an agreement affecting the entire world.

Fourth, how can – to prevent such major turmoil – political systems be made robust or resilient against such short-term change linked to electoral results or changes in incumbency of posts decisive for regulating normative instruments? With changes at ministerial level, on the other hand, institutional memory may get lost and with it the reasoning as well behind important decisions. This is a very perplexing question; its answer may be intimately linked to national sovereignty, the rights of heads of state or government, or even basic democratic principles.

Finally, *déjà vu* or does history repeat itself? The first chapter of American physicist Mark Bowen's book *Censoring Science* begins,

> One sweltering June afternoon in 1988 [the year when the IPCC was established, see Tab. 10.2], an Iowan named James Hanson turned global warming into an international issue with one sentence. He told a group of reporters in a hearing room, just after testifying to a Senate committee, "It's time to stop waffling . . . and say that the greenhouse effect is here and is affecting our climate now." At first, it seemed that our policy makers got the message.

What followed under the George W. Bush administration in the early 2000s was amazingly similar to what we describe here for the year 2016 (further details in Bowen 2008 and Hulme 2009). As Bowen wrote, President Bush announced, "that he would abandon a campaign promise to regulate carbon dioxide," and the United States ultimately pulled out of the Kyoto Protocol. Then administrator of the Environmental Protection Agency Christine Todd Whitman considered these movements as "the equivalent to 'flipping the bird,' frankly, to the rest of the world."

In January 2001, when Bush and Vice-President Cheney were sworn in, the IPCC's Third Assessment Report stated, "There is new and stronger evidence that most of the warming observed over the last 50 years is attributable to human activities" and that "the increase in temperature in the 20th century is likely to have been the largest of any century during the past 1,000 years" (Bowen,

p. 105). As Bowen further stated, "The process that produces [the IPCC assessment reports] is arguably the most consensus-driven that has ever been applied to a scientific problem" (p. 107). But that is still another issue.

The rest of the world shows the way forward

The U.S. withdrawal can take effect only less than immediately, because none of the signatories can resign from the agreement before 2020. In addition, it may take at least one year more to complete the exit negotiations. This four-year period coincides with the end of Donald Trump's first term as president of the United States – the United States will have to decide whether he is going to enter into a second term.

In a statement titled *We Are Still In* and signed by 1,790 U.S. governors, mayors, college and university leaders, businesses and investors (as of 11 June 2017) expressed their commitment to the Paris Agreement: "We . . . are joining forces for the first time to declare that we will continue to support climate action to meet the Paris Agreement."

The statement is an open letter to the international community and to all signatories of the Agreement, a plaintive *vox populi, urbi et orbi* signed by leaders of major states, cities and business corporations (Apple, eBay, Gap Inc., Google, Microsoft and Nike among them). These entities represent 122 million citizens, or more than a third of the country's population of some 326.5 million (in 2017). As said in the statement, "The Trump administration's announcement undermines a key pillar on the fight against climate change and damages the world's ability to avoid the most dangerous and costly effects of climate change. Importantly, it is also out of step with what is happening in the United States."

And now?

As worldwide political reactions at first feared, the Americans' withdrawal is generally not seen now as the end of the Paris Agreement. The pact is functionally weakened, in particular through the halt in payments to the Green Climate Fund: the U.S. contribution was one of the highest. To recall, the Fund reflects commitment by countries with the highest GHG emissions to climate change mitigation and adaptation in developing countries. This is considered the centerpiece of action to finance anti-climate change endeavors via UNFCCC, and is expected to reach $100 billion annually by 2020. Not yet clear are the implications of the American withdrawal for the crucial year of 2018. Debate and adoption of further refinements to the Agreement, including additional regulation, were to take place in the same year. Also remaining to be seen is the effect of Trump's decision on U.S. emissions of GHG. Any further increase may seriously impede reaching the less than 2° target. The impact of the statement *We Are Still In*, as well as further – even reinforced – commitment by the international community may prove crucial to resolving the climate change dilemma.

Interim thoughts along the way

The Paris Agreement is the first international treaty on reduction of greenhouse gas emissions, signed by both industrialized countries and countries in transition alike. A leap forward is the dynamic approach of submitting national plans and of strengthening efforts if reaching of the targets should be at risk. As stressed earlier, the need to reduce emissions is tightly linked to a radical change in our energy systems toward renewable sources of energy – i.e., a phasing out of the use of the fossil fuels coal, natural gas and petroleum.

In particular, it remains to be seen whether CO_2 will need to be "priced" in the future. China, the biggest emitter, already plans a system of country-wide CO_2 certificates. It also remains to be seen whether a global CO_2 taxation system will (need to) be introduced and what this may mean for major fossil-fuel exporting countries such as the Emirates, Russia, Saudi Arabia and Venezuela.

In addition, the near future will show whether the Paris Agreement properly caters for the needs of small island states, least developed and other vulnerable countries. A delicate balance will need to be achieved between mitigation and adaptation measures, and there is an inherent danger that the North/South gap may further widen if action needed, in particular of the South, is not adequately financed. This may be seriously affected by the U.S. withdrawal from the Agreement and from its financial commitments, in particular the *Green Climate Fund*.

The Paris package of follow-up action is not only very complex, but implementation is not a question of "sometime in the future" but of coping with an enormous process of change to ensure that the global community will keep global warming as much as possible below the critical threshold of 2°C. As one of the climate scientists present at COP 21 put it, in view of the lack of insight of politicians into what action reaching of the 1.5°C target would concretely demand: "The text as it stands is between dangerous and lethal."

Lastly, climate change is also a threat to global security (see WBGU 2008, for an overview). A temperature increase above 2°C is expected to create havoc to our environmental, economic and social systems – i.e., the ingredients to sustainable development. It will ultimately also affect internal security of nation states and be a decisive factor for future wars, poverty and terrorism (Fabius 2015).

The ethics of climate change are vital to us and our progeny

New software for the human machine

Ethics and its subordinate, deontology, both suffer from negligence or outright disregard. By way of a basic introduction to the importance of ethics in our analysis of complexity, we concentrate here on the critical value of ethics in our management of water, biological diversity and their governing roles in the total environment.

The relation between ethics and climate change became evident when for the first time the following or similar questions were raised in international debates.

- If famine in Africa and problems with agriculture and disasters such as in the Sahel Zone are linked to global climate change;
- If this is related to increased release of greenhouse gases (GHG) into the atmosphere; and
- If this is essentially a "northern phenomenon," isn't then the "north" also responsible for all these problems?
- If true, wouldn't the relevant states have to assume their responsibility and not only assist the South in mitigating and adapting to these problems but to "directly pay for the damage they have caused?"

Or, put otherwise, wouldn't the ethical dimension of climate change have to handle inconvenient questions such as

- Aren't atmospheric concentrations of greenhouse gases and resulting effects putting the further existence of cultures and species at risk?
- Is it acceptable that some countries generate more of these GHGs than others?
- Who will pay for the damages of climate change?
- In protecting nature, are we not safeguarding humanity – all of it?

It is the poorest and most vulnerable segments of the human population who are affected the most by global climate change. This touches on human rights, which are not only recognized in international normative instruments but also are fundamental to the world's religions.

These and other aspects of the intimate relationship between the roles of ethics but also religion and climate change have been discussed *inter alia* in a seminal paper by Paula Posas, published in 2007. She also noted the role of UNFCCC in debating ethics and climate change, in particular with regard to the IPCC's third and fourth assessment reports of 2001 and 2007, respectively, and the *Buenos Aires Declaration on the Ethical Dimensions of Climate Change*. The basis of that document was the white paper of the same title, published by Brown et al. (2006) of the Rock Ethics Institute Program. The program and partner organizations involved were decisive in casting the Declaration. Posas' article has become ever more important in view of recent communications by religious leaders such as Pope Francis and the Dalai Lama on our responsibilities regarding planet Earth. Indeed, organizations related to major belief systems and philosophies dealt with the subject through a number of pronouncements on climate change. All these underscore the importance of the ethical dimension in the discussion and in the process of managing or – even better – solving the climate problem.

One of the authors had also been directly involved in paving the long and winding road leading to a UNESCO *Declaration on Ethical Principles Relating to Climate Change*. This had been a path of heated debate and controversial decisions

Global climate change 151

of that organization's executive board, a forum of 58 member states which is decisive in UNESCO's governance and decision making. Why did UNESCO embark on such a process?

Why UNESCO?

The UN Security Council, created in October 1945 within the framework of the UN Charter, monitors the geopolitical conduct of the worldwide system or relations among its constituent nations. Until the end of the 20th century, there was no official identification or responsibility for general ethical behavior within the system. In most negotiations, traditional diplomatic conformity prevailed. Although this code of deontology or professional ethics pervaded the UN's mission and actions, its specialized bodies (e.g., those for world health, food and agriculture, labor or international finance and banking) exercised their own codes of intercourse.

In 2002, UNESCO decided that ethics would be one of its priority areas of dialogue. This was a result of a longer reflection of the mandate of that organization in S&T as well as its framework of "universal respect for justice, for the rule of law and for the human rights and fundamental freedoms" (Article 1 of its constitution). With the establishment of UNESCO's International Bioethics Committee (1993) and later the Intergovernmental Bioethics Committee (in 1998), S&T-related ethics and specifically bioethics became an integral part of programs and activities. Later development saw the establishment of the World Commission on the Ethics of Scientific Knowledge and Technology (COMEST, in 1998). In 2003, UNESCO established the UN Inter-Agency Committee on Bioethics, including IGOs within and outside the UN system. Since, activities have centered on standard-setting, capacity building, and the raising of awareness in the world of professional ethics (overview and further details in ten Have 2006). Although national academies of science have their own rigorous standards, UNESCO remains the sole global, pluralistic and multidisciplinary forum for bioethics and the ethics of S&T.

COMEST, in its 2005 report *The Precautionary Principle* (a term most likely derived from the German *Vorsorgeprinzip*, Principle of Precaution), stated,

> UNESCO and COMEST will focus on a number of issues that have been identified for the future, such as the impact of *complexity* on the development of scenarios for decision making. . . [D]ealing with complex systems that cannot be fully predicted (for example climate change) requires a shift of attitude from computability of consequences, to the awareness and readiness to face and manage basically unpredictable developments.
>
> (p. 8; italics ours)

In 2010, COMEST published a report, *The Ethical Implications of Global Climate Change*. This says "climate change cannot be dealt with adequately and properly if [its] ethical dimensions . . . are not highlighted, well understood, and taken into account in decisions about responses" and that the report was meant "not to make climate change a (new) theme of ethics, but rather to make ethics a core and necessary element of any debate about climate change and its challenges." An earlier version of the report had catalyzed further work and eventually led to COMEST's recommendation to UNESCO that it "should adopt an ethical framework of principles in relation to climate change." Further negotiation work by COMEST and UNESCO cleared the path to preparation of a normative instrument, a (non-binding) *Declaration on Ethical Principles in Relation to Climate Change*. Text of the preamble sketches thought behind the *Declaration* (Box 10.2).

Box 10.2 Background and framework for UNESCO's normative work: excerpts from the preamble of UNESCO's *Declaration on Ethical Principles in Relation to Climate Change*

Noting with great concern that human-induced climate change is threatening the sustainability of the Earth's living and non-living systems in an unprecedented way, and is already causing harm and entails potentially irreversible adverse consequences;

Recognizing that inaction to address climate change will have devastating consequences and that there is now an urgent imperative for all to mitigate the causes and adapt to the consequences of climate change;

Convinced that the challenge of climate change cannot be met without the participation of all and at all levels: international organizations, States, subnational entities, cities, administrations, private sector, civil society organizations and individuals;

Recognizing the countries taking the lead in sustainable lifestyles and sustainable patterns of consumption and production, and *recognizing* that sustainable lifestyles and sustainable patterns of production and consumption play an important role in addressing climate change;

Aware of the ethical responsibilities of human beings in this regard,

Conscious of the importance of undertaking climate change actions in accordance with the common but differentiated responsibilities principle as reaffirmed in the Paris Agreement; that significant responses should be pursued by all to limit climate change; and of providing support to countries requiring assistance through both financial and technological means;

Recognizing also that the share of historical, current and future global emissions of greenhouse gases is different among nations and various social groups, and therefore that their responsibilities differ;

Noting with concern that the burdens of climate change are unequally distributed among the Earth's nations and various social groups, with

climate change exacerbating other threats to social and natural systems, and placing additional burdens particularly on the poor and vulnerable;
Reflecting on the complexity of the causes and impacts of human-induced climate change;
Convinced of the need to develop effective and comprehensive cross-cutting policies which address the needs of the most vulnerable and which are gender responsive;
Emphasizing the fundamental importance of science, information and education for responding to the challenge of climate change;
Conscious of the different ethical perspectives in regard to climate change; and
Acknowledging that responses to climate change are likely to have many important and variable ethical implications, and that it has become an imperative to place ethics as a core and necessary element in climate change solutions.

Source: UNESCO 2016

Further consultations took place in 2017, followed by an intergovernmental meeting preparatory to issuing the final text of the Declaration, and final approval by UNESCO's general conference of November 2017.

Impact of the declaration on the ethical dimensions of climate change

The final Declaration should, in future, reveal impacts (or lack thereof). The following points underscore the importance of this – albeit long-lasting and tedious – process:

- The Declaration is the first exclusively ethics-related normative instrument of the UN on climate change.
- Its elaboration and adoption will build on and complement the UN's work on climate change, in particular by UNFCCC and IPCC, and it will reinforce the role of ethics in S&T.
- Universal agreement on ethical principles will underpin and strengthen the process of implementing the Paris Agreement, in particular with regard to countries' voluntary commitments.
- Agreement on ethical principles may also contribute to mobilizing stakeholders other than Nation States to contribute to this process such as civil society, academia and local communities.
- Tackling climate change is closely linked to changing our attitudes toward nature and the planet. Such change is, in essence, based on ethical principles, those which are also *sine qua non* for what we desperately need: a new vision of a sustainable future of humankind.

And some accompanying hardware

How realistic (and, of course, affordable) is the use of adapted materials to temper or even reverse the processes of climate change?

What is geoengineering?

Geoengineering is synonymous with *climate engineering* and *climate intervention*. It refers to deliberate and large-scale intervention in Earth's climatic systems, in order to moderate global warming (see e.g. Royal Society 2009).

Geoengineering is seen as a means to limit global warming, in addition to (or sometimes perceived as part of) climate mitigation and adaptation. On a broader level, the technology is "deliberate intervention in the planetary environment of a nature and scale intended to counteract anthropogenic climate change and its impacts" (SCBD 2016).

What are the specifics?

Geoengineering measures may be either related to removing the greenhouse gas CO_2 (or others) from the atmosphere or to lessen Earth's absorption of solar radiation. Whereas carbon dioxide removal techniques address the root cause of climate change by removing greenhouse gases (in most cases CO_2) from the atmosphere, solar radiation management techniques attempt to offset effects of increased greenhouse gas concentrations by causing Earth to absorb less solar radiation.

In its 2009 report *Geoengineering the Climate*, the London-based Royal Society lists the following (major) technical means:

Carbon Dioxide Removal (CDR) methods:

- Land use management to protect or enhance land carbon sinks
- The use of biomass for carbon sequestration as well as a carbon-neutral energy source
- Enhancement of natural weathering processes to remove CO_2 from the atmosphere
- Direct engineered capture of CO_2 from ambient air
- Enhancement of oceanic uptake of CO_2, for example by fertilization of the oceans with naturally scarce nutrients, or by increasing upwelling processes

Solar Radiation Management (SRM) methods:

- Increasing the surface reflectivity of the planet, by brightening human structures (e.g., by painting them white), planting of crops with a high reflectivity, or covering deserts with reflective material (surface-based)
- Enhancement of marine cloud reflectivity (troposphere-based)

- Mimicking the effects of volcanic eruptions by injecting sulfate aerosols into the lower stratosphere (upper atmosphere-based)
- Placing shields or deflectors in space to reduce the amount of solar energy reaching Earth (space-based)

For a more comprehensive and current listing of geoengineering techniques see ETC Group (2017).

Evaluation

A thorough discussion of the pros and cons of the many geoengineering methods is certainly beyond the scope of this chapter on global climate change. Only a few points shall be highlighted here, most if not all of the resources fueling the discussion are publicly available.

First, following the argument in the Royal Society's report, "None of the geoengineering methods evaluated offers an immediate solution to the problem of climate change, or reduces the need for continued emissions reductions."

Second, CDR methods would be preferable to SRM methods as they foster a process of returning the climate system to its natural state. CDR methods, however, are slow and not yet established as cost-effective and affordable and having acceptable side effects. Fewer side effects have CDR methods that do not perturb natural systems and that do not require changes in land use at large scale. Unacceptable side effects may be expected from large-scale manipulation as in the case of ocean fertilization.

Third, SRM methods may be relatively cheap and could have effects in relatively short time (a few years), which may make them look attractive. Uncertainties exist, however, about their risks and consequences. It may not be possible to sustain the right balance between increased CO_2 concentrations and reduced solar radiation in the long run (over centuries).

A specific example of second-order consequences would be use of the sulfates already mentioned as a shield against the heat of solar radiation reaching Earth. The chemical would have first to be lofted into the atmosphere (probably by jet-engine cargo aircraft: more pollution), and the sulfates dispersed in significant volume. New chemical compounds derived from the sulfates' reaction to solar heat would then, at least in part, fall to ground or sea level with perhaps unforeseeable results. (The activities in this respect, of the David Keith Group at Harvard University, are available in detail on the Internet.)

Fourth, as pointed out in the report, there is a serious governance issue and the lack of appropriate international mechanisms associated with managing and regulating geoengineering. The governance needs relate not only to economic, social, ethical, legal and political aspects (not so much the scientific and technical components), but in particular to transboundary activities and effects. The risks could be great, even phenomenal. We have seen elsewhere how British Petroleum's seabed drilling in the Gulf of Mexico got completely out of human control, with costly results in terms of human lives, destruction of aquatic biota and pollution of both ocean and shore.

UK research on removal of greenhouse gases

As discussed in detail in *Carbon Brief*, the United Kingdom has launched what is probably the first research program on how to remove greenhouse gases form the atmosphere. This is a £ 8.6 million project to explore the potential of *negative emission technologies* (NETs) comprising measures related to soil carbon, afforestation, bioenergy with carbon capture and storage (BECCS) and others. NETs are considered to "almost certainly be needed" in delimit with global warming as requested through the Paris Agreement (well below 2°C above pre-industrial levels). It remains uncertain, however, how long it may take to deploy NETs at relevant scales "without causing knock-on environmental and social problems." (A critical note on afforestation: According to the 2016 CBD report, UNFCCC includes under afforestation measures either land which has not carried trees for at least 50 years or land with non-forest native vegetation. Will conversion, accordingly, lead to vegetation cover with non-native species, and shouldn't we aim instead at reestablishing the natural state as it was before human intervention?)

Current carbon pledges seem indeed to fall short of what is needed, with the risk that in a few years only the carbon budget to reach a 1.5°C limit may be used up. In fact, the program is said to be linked to the British commitment to the Agreement and that NETs will be needed to meet its national, legally binding carbon targets. About 100 researchers from 40 British universities and partner organizations should be participating in the research.

The UK initiative reflects the urgency of reducing GHG emissions to meet the goals internationally agreed upon in 2015 in Paris. Stakes are high, research takes its time, and rebuilding the energy and other sectors for a "decarbonized world" is a tedious and time-consuming process. The UK program is designed "only" to "investigate the potential of NETs, as well as the political, social and environmental issues surrounding their deployment."

The world is in a delicate situation: Will it be possible to meet the climate goals through reducing GHG emissions to the extent needed? If this becomes less and less likely, do we need to deploy any geoengineering technologies to implement the Paris Agreement? And if so, what about applying the precautionary principle and being cognizant of all the implications of such a global undertaking? As discussed next, some of these questions are addressed in efforts of the UN and its specialized entities dealing with climate change. With time passing, humankind moves itself into an ever more severe dilemma with what it has itself created.

The UN – controversial views from within?

The UN Convention on Biological Diversity (CBD), in its COP 13, held in Mexico in December 2016, reaffirmed its moratorium on climate-related geoengineering. The moratorium was already agreed upon at COP 10 in 2010. Even earlier, in 2008, the CBD had already issued a moratorium on ocean fertilization. The Secretariat of the CBD has produced two detailed reports on geoengineering and biodiversity, published in its technical series, viz. reports 66 (SCBD 2012) and 84 (SCBD 2016), respectively. The 2016 report is based on an extensive reference base and discusses major international and national syntheses, assessments and reviews of geoengineering. Its key messages and conclusions are mostly critical about geoengineering, in particular with regard to its overall environmental impacts and how it may affect biodiversity in particular.

UNFCCC has "not considered geoengineering . . . in its official agenda . . . with many governments opposing to it," but "geoengineers now attempting to introduce the issue [of geoengineering] into the UNFCCC." The IPCC has somewhat shifted its views on the subject: Whereas geoengineering was seen first as "largely speculative and unproven and with risks of unknown side-effects," the fifth Assessment Report (2014) not only discussed some of the CDR techniques but also considered the extensive use of BECCS. A further shift is notable, furthermore, in the preparations for the 6th Report where geoengineering has not only already been seen as an option worth analyzing but also "to be considered as a cross-cutting issue throughout all working groups" (ETC Group 2017). This changing perception is already meeting strong resistance from scientific media and organizations in civil society.

These controversial discussions about geoengineering, in particular its reflection of a massive humanitarian concern, shed new light on the importance of the UNESCO Declaration with which we began this chapter. The exchanges could eventually trigger major UN engagement and further dialogue on successful implementation of the Paris Agreement.

Conclusion

Professional discourse on complexity, and whether it offers utility or futility in its potential exploitation, promises to remain complicated.

Problem analysis of climate change is a key example of the need for debating ethical dimensions of our global challenges, irrespective of diversity in politics or belief systems. The UNESCO *Declaration* has been a first and stabilizing process toward developing a normative standard, the first of its kind in this domain after decades of debate on global warming. With geoengineering, however, ethical concerns were expressed from the beginning. These resulted not only from a controversial perception but also from a long history and rising awareness of human-caused environmental problems and even disasters. The gravity and (often unknown) consequences of early attempts to manipulate Earth's climate system on a global scale remain precautionary.

The future will show whether what started with a *Declaration* – i.e., a rather weak normative tool – will eventually emerge as stronger instruments governing how geoengineering will develop: Will it be banned in its entirety, or in regard to SRM methods, or some only or not at all? The UK project, already briefly introduced, may indicate that under certain conditions selective approaches to reduce CO_2 levels in the atmosphere may (need to) be used in the future. This will depend on success or failure to implement the Paris Agreement. This could develop through substantial increase of reducing GHG emissions or recourse to geoengineering as a last resort to cope with eventual failure in a global decarbonizing process. Another crucial element is cost. Yet at the moment that a single country is able to obligate $35 billion annually over 2017–2026 decade to purchase of armaments from another single country, the reordering of budgetary priorities should prove feasible.

As pointed out in the ETC Group's briefing on geoengineering for the UNFCCC intersessional meeting in Bonn (2017), "geoengineering must be considered as a political rather than a technical issue" and that "it is essential to strengthen the precautionary approach: experiments in the real world (open air, ocean, land) should not be allowed in the absence of strong governance." The same Group added,

> Geoengineering research should – in line with the CBD decision – be focused on socio-political, ecological, ethical questions and potential impacts and contribute to a debate about whether democratic governance of geoengineering is ever possible, and how. And even more important: funding and research on climate change needs to urgently be scaled up to support implementation of proven and locally adapted ecologically and socially sound solutions to the climate crisis – not speculative and distracting technofixes.

In conclusion, the climate change problem is the most pressing of complex challenges to humans, and radically new solutions may be needed to meet the goals of the Paris Agreement. There seems to exist broad consensus that "Current commitments made by Parties to the UNFCCC would significantly reduce climate change and its impacts . . . but are insufficient to keep warming within 2ºC" (SCBD 2016).

The window of opportunity is rapidly closing for staying within or below this limit through emission reduction only. Stronger measures are essential.

Our next chapter on international relations and diplomacy provides a closer look at how the political machinery works in a variety of different contexts of the complexity factor.

References

Bowen, M. 2008. *Censoring Science. Inside the Political Attack on Dr. James Hansen and the Truth of Global Warming.* Dutton, New York.
Brown, D., N. Tuana, M. Averill and 22 others 2006. *White Paper on the Ethical Dimensions of Climate Change.* Rock Ethics Institute, Penn State University, Pennsylvania.
COMEST (World Commission on the Ethics of Scientific Knowledge and Technology) 2005. *The Precautionary Principle.* UNESCO, Paris.
COMEST (World Commission on the Ethics of Scientific Knowledge and Technology) 2010. *The Ethical Implications of Global Climate Change.* UNESCO, Paris.

Diamond, J. 2005. *Collapse: How Societies Choose to Fail or Succeed*. Viking Penguin, New York.
ETC Group 2017. *Climate Change, Smoke and Mirrors. A Civil Society Briefing on Geoengineering*. ETC Group and Heinrich Böll Foundation, Bonn, Germany.
Fabius, L. 2015. Das Klima der Angst. Zwei Grad können darüber entscheiden, ob es mehr Kriege, Armut und Terrorismus geben wird. Wir brauchen jetzt ein Klima-Abkommen. *DIE ZEIT* of 7 May 2015, No. 19: 11.
Hecking, C. 2015. Wir lassen sie nicht untergehen. Warum der Pariser Gipfel den Durchbruch im Kampf gegen den Klimawandel bringen könnte. *DIE ZEIT* of 24 September 2015, No. 39: 26.
Henk, M. and W. Uchatius 2015. Morgen vielleicht. *DIE ZEIT* of 3 June 2015, No. 23: 15–17.
Hulme, M. 2009. *Why we Disagree about Climate Change. Understanding Controversy, Inaction and Opportunity*. Cambridge University Press, Cambridge.
IPCC 2014. *Climate Change 2014: Synthesis Report. Contribution of Working Groups I, II and II to the Fifth Assessment Report of the Intergovernmental Panel on Climate Change*. IPCC, Geneva, Switzerland.
Leadley, P.W., C.B. Krug, R. Alkemade, H.M. Pereira, U.R. Sumaila, M. Walpole, A. Marques, T. Newbold, L.S.L. Teh, J. van Kolck, C. Bellard, S.R. Januchowski-Hartley and P.J. Mumby 2014. *Progress towards the Aichi Biodiversity Targets: An Assessment of Biodiversity Trends, Policy Scenarios and Key Actions*. Secretariat of the Convention on Biological Diversity, Montreal, Canada. Technical Series 78.
Posas, P.J. 2007. Roles of religion and ethics in addressing climate change. *Ethics in Science and Environmental Politics* 2007: 31–49. Doi:10.3354/esep00080.
Reimer, N. 2015. *Schlusskonferenz. Geschichte und Zukunft der Klimadiplomatie*. Oekom Verlag, München.
Royal Society 2009. *Geoengineering the climate. Science, governance and uncertainty*. Royal Society, London.
SCBD (Secretariat of the Convention on Biological Diversity) 2012. *Geoengineering in Relation to the Convention on Biological Diversity: Technical and Regulatory Matters*. Technical Series No. 66. CBD Montreal.
SCBD (Secretariat of the Convention on Biological Diversity) 2014. *Global Biodiversity Outlook 4*. CBD Montreal
SCBD (Secretariat of the Convention on Biological Diversity) 2016. *Update on Climate Geoengineering in Relation to the Convention on Biological Diversity: Potential Impacts and Regulatory Framework*. Technical Series No. 84. CBD Montreal.
Stern, N. 2009. *The Global Deal. Climate Change and the Creation of a New Era of Progress and Prosperity*. Public Affairs, New York.
ten Have, H. 2006. The activities of UNESCO in the area of ethics. *Kennedy Institute of Ethics Journal* 16: 333–351.
UNESCO 2016. *First Draft of a Preliminary Text of a Declaration on Ethical Principles in Relation to Climate Change*. UNESCO, Paris.
WBGU (German Advisory Council on Global Change) 2008. *Climate Change as a Security Risk*. Earthscan, London.
WCED (World Commission on Environment and Development) 1987. *Our Common Future*. Oxford University Press, Oxford.

11 Diplomacy and foreign trade
Weaving the web of international intercourse

Introduction

We emerge from the complicated field of climate change to what is meant to be the very semblance of order and system among differing populations. The historical relations of geopolitical tracts known as Rome, Carthage, the Levant and the Middle Kingdom (China) took form progressively. They facilitated commercial exchange, averted war or combined with other powers to rival – and sometimes defeat or acquire – still other territories. The system of international communication and conciliation expanded steadily, its complexities ever accessory to other progress.

In 1648, the Peace of Westphalia became a geopolitical accomplishment. The pact convoked the (Germanic) Holy Roman Empire and its princes, together with the kingdoms of France and Spain, the Dutch Republic and the Swedish empire, as well as the sovereigns of free imperial cities in order to halt incessant warfare. While peace did not follow throughout Europe, it was restored between the Dutch and Spanish, between France and the Germanic domains, ending effectively the religious Thirty Years' War and formalizing the existence of nation states. This was the so-called Westphalian sovereignty. The essential feature of this type of rule is self-government, a virtue re-invoked almost three centuries later by the Treaty of Versailles (1919) but hobbled erratically during the two decades of peace that followed.

Self-government translates (or should) in systemic terms as *self-organization* and *adaptation* – essential movers of systems. Governance at the national level interacts with governance in alien states; this becomes the foundation of foreign relations. When relations become strained, two or more parties resort to diplomatic maneuver, the art of interstate compromise. The possession of power by one or more states may succumb, however, to a craving for more power, territory (even maritime) or new material resources for their economies.

When this occurs, according to Robert D. Kaplan, once chief geopolitical analyst at the Stratfor private intelligence firm in the United States, geopolitics replaces peaceful relations and unimpeded diplomacy. Recall Japan's takeover of Chinese Manchuria and the Third Reich's aggression to annex *Lebensraum* taken from Eastern Europe, the Balkans and Soviet Russia. In cases such as these, system sometimes loses its self-adjustment capacity, falls back on and reinforces its

Diplomacy and foreign trade 161

earlier self-reliance, moves more closely to a state of great disorder until involved directly in war – and war is chaos unleashed, total failure of the concept of equity.

The globalization of deliberative dialogue

Here we examine a discrete system, how a nation's diplomatic influence varies with shifts in the globe's power centers, how non-diplomats are doing more and more diplomatic work of high order and, rather specifically, the efforts of the EU to create and manage a multi-nation diplomatic service confronted by ever more complex problems to resolve.

We apply here the more primitive analogy of creating a national diplomatic effort, filling in the obvious gaps by extrapolation or other plausible interpretation needed to form a multi-nation capability in foreign relations. We survey the advantages to be gained and the handicaps of building such capacity. We base our views on the vagaries of recent history (reported extensively by the information media) as well as our own, combined experience of more than 25 years' service in an intergovernmental negotiating body.

The new diplomats include specialists of many kinds drawn from both inside government and outside, responding in part

- by expanding official duties (those of environment, natural resources, energy issues, drug-enforcement measures, monetary controls); and
- to governmental requirements imposed by both the Cold War, the new terrorism, the resurgence of China as a great power, and the changing face of the African continent as well as problems of migration from there and Latin America.

Given the amplitude of the negotiating system, there seem to be adequate sources of qualified personnel for governments to respond to new challenges.

The effects of time on form and function

First, there are more women in a profession that was once the province of males. This is especially so among the industrial democracies, where the glass ceiling is proving itself less and less shatterproof. Today, there are more female ambassadors than at any time before. Yet women are often confronted by difficult opposite numbers, such as American Ambassador April Glaspie and Iraq's Saddam Hussein in the early 2000s.

Developing countries have the most difficulty here, because their cultural constraints tend to keep women remote from their countries' decision-and-power centers. Throughout the world, however, the woman's voice and proven sense of moderation during negotiations are increasingly heard and accepted at and beyond conference tables.

With the digital revolution, diplomatic officers are doing more of their own direct correspondence (on behalf of their ambassadors, of course) with their ministries at home. As in related political and business activity, the traditional "secretary" (usually a young woman), too, is lesser a cog in the administrative machinery than before.

Diplomats today are better educated than those of two or three generations earlier, who usually satisfied entry requirements with a single university degree. Today linguistic ability and a strong formation in political science, economics (including trade and finance), education, environmental protection, public health and security or management are sought among candidates. Training in a national school of public policy is a strong qualification. No longer is political pull or a moneyed family the simpler standard for admission.

Auxiliary diplomats are a phenomenon of the new age of radically changed communication among sovereign states. Given the span of the negotiating system, there are thus many NGOs seeking to influence (or eliminate) a multitude of recommendations, resolutions and novel programs initiated by parliaments constitutionally equipped to devise, introduce and negotiate shifting international accommodation.

The chancelleries hear from science

Since the height of the Cold War, there are other new actors on negotiating staffs: scientists and engineers. The advent of nuclear weapons and other arms of mass destruction is responsible for this change. The world of our natural environment includes some of the oldest and most respected of these NGOs: the IUCN, the World Wildlife Fund and Greenpeace. Other bodies champion diverse kinds of challenge: malnutrition, public hygiene, specialized medical aid, education for girls, protection of children, learning a trade, banking for women, encouraging start-ups and many more.

One of the most effective NGOs strategically may be the curiously named Pugwash Conferences on Science and World Affairs.[1] This unusual initiative followed the publication in 1955 of a manifesto generated by mathematician/philosopher Bertrand Russell and the twice decorated Nobelist in physics, Albert Einstein. The two scientists sought an end to the post-1945 proliferation of nuclear weapons, beginning with public pressure to limit production of new arms.

The movement soon took form as weapon designers from both West and East, often led by American or Soviet scientific personalities, explored technicalities. Their findings and recommendations were often heeded by Moscow and Washington and the Conferees soon took on other sensitive chores – such as the seemingly endless war in the former French Indochina, to whose leaders they proposed war-ending measures. Despite its efforts, however, Pugwash has not succeeded in dissuading North Korea from its ambition to possess thermonuclear weapons or in persuading Israel to admit publicly its status as a power belonging to the nuclear "club."

In another but equally important area of endeavor, the New York Times congratulated editorially France and its diplomats on the success of the COP 21 Conference[2] in the final weeks of 2015. This UN climate change meeting near

Diplomacy and foreign trade   163

Paris of the world's nations engaged debates during a troubling political period in several world regions. There were no incidents of terrorism to mar the event. The assembled nations undertook to prevent a rise in planetary average temperatures, beyond an additional 2°C over present norms, by the end of the century.

Physicist Sidney Passman, once a member of the U.S. Arms Control and Disarmament Agency and later director of UNESCO's Division of Scientific Research and Higher Education, is more than qualified to advance an opinion on science's role in diplomacy.

> The UN and especially UNESCO have been successful in bringing scientific people together, notably in the SESAME synchrotron project. I recall efforts at UNESCO with China and its cultural revolution, and with Burma, Romania, Tunisia, Cuba, and especially North Korea.[3]

The global environment as part of science

The head of the International Institute of Applied Systems Analysis in Laxenburg (Austria), Pavel Kabat, hailed the pledge of the voting governments to try as well to hold temperature rise to a minimal 1.5°C. Commenting further on this resolution, a French journal of agricultural engineering called the COP 21 decision one of "science merging with politics," a real achievement in international relations.

Developing countries are far from forgotten by the science/diplomacy twosome. Alan Leshner, an experienced American diplomat-scientist, wrote in the December 2014 issue of *Science & Diplomacy* of his collaboration in Africa with the American Association for the Advancement of Science (AAAS):

> In 2010 I had the opportunity to lead a group to Rwanda for a workshop on regional cooperation in East Africa. The AAAS-organized workshop brought together senior government officials and scientists from Burundi, Congo, Kenya, Rwanda, Tanzania and Uganda. It was part of a broader political effort undertaken by the heads of state to develop a coherent East African Community. Among a number of other key issues, increasing regional cooperation in science and education was an important goal.

Another theater of informal diplomacy is the world of sports. The resumption of the Olympic Games in 1924 was an effort, in part, to dissipate the effects of war and postwar after the upheaval of 1914–1918. Japan abandoned plans to host the 1940 Olympics after numerous nations had signaled their abstention from the Games because of Japan's military excesses in China. The Games scheduled for 1964 in Tokyo gave Japan the opportunity, on the contrary, to divest itself of the image of a war-mongering dictatorship leading to the Asian-Pacific conflict of the 1940s. The success of the 1964 Summer Games helped the phenomenal growth during the next third of a century (1960s–1990s) of Japan's economy – second only to America's – and Tokyo's rising role in peaceful democracy.

Bilateral ping-pong matches between Mao Zedong's China and the United States first broke the ice that would later emerge as renewed diplomatic relations between the two political giants. Political ice, long since formed on relations between the People's Democratic Republic of [North] Korea and the United States saw bizarre cracks when the north's leaders showed a penchant for basketball; they encouraged top American "cagers" to visit Pyongyang, the north's capital, for exhibition games.

Washington and Moscow, on the other hand, favored absence from the Olympic Games as a strong power play. The Americans avoided Moscow in 1980 because of the Soviet Union's attack on Afghanistan and, in 1984, the Soviet absence from the Games in Los Angeles was a blow of counter-propaganda. The comparative innocence of competitive sports succeeded in providing one-upmanship in self-serving political warfare for both sides.

The present age is witnessing a curious turn-about in North Korea's relations with the rest of the world, China and Russia excluded. The Democratic People's Republic seized the opportunity offered by the Winter Olympics of 2018 held in the Republic to the south in order to 1) have accepted a diplomatic team to negotiate renewed relations between the two halves of the Korean Peninsula and 2) to prepare the ground for an invitation a fortnight later by northern president Kim Jong-un to American President Donald Trump to join him in "denuclearization" talks. The invitation was conveyed through South Korean officials and answered positively in the same way. This after months of exchanged taunts and insults by the two chief executives, but also after 65 years of an armistice not always respected by both sides. Will Pyongyang's overture prove to be simply another kind of "sport," deadlier than most, and little more than continuation of a diplomatic void and worrying phantasm in the world's search for peace?

Culture as affinity among adversaries

In other forms of cultural exchange between differing social systems, music and ballet found an active role to play even during the most bellicose of the years of the Cold War. Symphony orchestras of standing exchanged visits between the East and West of the period, as did ballet troupes and soloists from both concert music and the world of dance. There was no extreme hiatus in this world of rigorously structured entertainment and cultural leisure. Daniel Barenboim, an Argentine-born Israeli pianist and conductor, in a personal contribution to peaceful communication between intensely rival loyalties, formed a symphony orchestra of only Palestinian and Israeli youths. Their performances continue to be well-received, a manifestation of non-complexity within a web of complexity dating from the late 1940s.

Foreign rock bands were not welcome, however, to the Soviet Ministry of Culture, although welcomed with enthusiasm in Czechoslovakia and Poland. The Rolling Stones, on the other hand, helped sweeten re-established diplomatic relations between the United States and Cuba with a public concert given in Havana, summer 2016. In the same year, BBC4 radio marked the 100th anniversary of the birth of violinist Yehudi Menuhin, recalling his many efforts to bring the traditional music of India and South African townships, for example, to western audiences and make western classical music more accessible by audiences in emerging countries. As cultural ambassador, Menuhin performed through the good offices of the International Council of Music, an NGO attached to UNESCO. This is not a world of serious stumbles or perilous tumbles; the cultural-exchange system works rather well.

Diplomacy, as a tested model of intercourse reaching back to the ancient Persians and Chinese, has thus ramified into new forms, responding to changing human perspectives and needs, but sometimes skirting daringly the limits of tradition and order in international exchanges while evading serious disorder.[4]

A matter of poles apart

Humanity's perspective of territory and the imperative to claim proprietary rights on portions of Earth's land and sea is no more evident than claims about the polar stretches. North and south, these areas have been the objectives of exploration since at least the time of the Vikings, although Roman navigators and cartographers were already aware of the nature of the boreal reaches. Today, although the situation is in a state of controlled political flux, the scientific community has been conspicuously present in national claims for authority over polar territories.

In the Arctic, aggressive exploration by mainly the navies of Britain, France, Russia, the Nordic lands and the United States were clearly moves to dominate portions of the frozen expanses. China is currently active, and especially interested in Greenland's natural assets. While there is no continent to cap the "top" of Earth, the search for a northwest passage between northern Canada and the ice-bound winter cover of the northern Pole expanded our knowledge of this part of the globe while sometimes taking the toll of posing entire expeditions and their materiel. No territorial claims were ever fixed by international agreement.

Southwards, the situation was at first similar. Aboriginal explorers from the Pacific archipelagos were roughly aware of the snow and ice cover well to the south. James Cook, naval captain and Fellow of the Royal Society, took note of the frigid regions south of New Zealand and Australia, but contented himself with the acquisition of the Australian continent for London, arranging the first immigrations and introducing exotic biota to Europe. (Cook brought the "mimosa" or Persian silk tree, *Albizia julibrissin*, to England.) Exploration intensified during the 19th century, and during the following hundred years, several South American nations showed growing interest in Antarctica.

In our time, the southern continent with neither human natives nor government, hosts scientific researchers from around 30 countries. The number varies as scientific stations open or close, and their presence is regulated by a series of international agreements known as the Antarctic Treaty System.

The Treaty System was born of a major scientific event, the International Geophysical Year of 1957–1958, one aim of which was to increase exponentially our knowledge of the total Antarctic environment. Scientists collaborated closely with diplomats, diplomatic agents with the research community. The resulting Treaty System functions as effectively as the kinematics of the reciprocating steam and combustion engines; it holds promise.[5] The Geophysical Year also ended a 12-year hiatus in information exchange between scientists of East and West.

Europe unites, somewhat

The ambition of a combined foreign policy for the EU has been a baffling exercise since the days of the Common Market in the 1960s. Because there is no centralized government of the Union, executive authority is managed by a consolidated staff known as the European Commission. Its executive director is called president of the Commission. Above them, there is a supervising quasi-legislature, the European Parliament. This body, after advice from its executive European Council and long hesitation, finally authorized a post of senior representative of the EU for external matters and has since appointed the first and second incumbents. This negotiating agency is the European External Action Service or EEAS.

This unusual innovation in international diplomacy took form as a foreign-service corps, as authorized by the Treaty of Lisbon's Article 27. The EEAS and its staff of functionaries should be ultimately 6,000 strong, serving a total population of a half-billion Europeans. The EEAS operates directly under the authority of the EU Commission's president. The first occupant of the post was Baroness Ashton of the United Kingdom, a Labor party member of the House of Lords with little previous exposure to matters foreign. Her successor, Federica Mogherini of Italy, is a seasoned diplomat.

In founding this novel diplomatic contingent, the European Parliament called upon the supervising European Council and the constituent member states "to reach, with the Parliament's involvement, a comprehensive and consensual plan for the creation of the EEAS." Stated otherwise, the Parliament did not want to leave initiative and authority for action by the EEAS entirely in the hands of the EU's executive arm, the European Commission in Brussels.

Putting the new process to test

In February 2017, major European media reported that the European Commission's president since 2004, Jean-Claude Juncker, would not seek a second term. He explained that after Britain's "Brexit" referendum of 2016, he was doubtful of the EU's future. Union planning called, however, for a new diplomatic scenario to be implemented by way of the Union's representative offices throughout the world – i.e., both in the Union and outside its geographic limits. The EEAS itself will comprise trained nationals coming from each member, assigned to diplomatic tasks of Union-wide scale. These diplomats can be expected to take time to orient themselves and develop the coordination and effectiveness that all member nations expect of such negotiating professionals.

Diplomacy and foreign trade 167

The key limitation has been the lack of historical precedent: this is an effort never before attempted, anywhere. On a scale the size of Europe's, the advantages and shortcomings will have to be weighed by both the Union and individual countries. The societal implications are mainly the strategic and operational consequences that might befall any member-nation and its population. The process achieved should be of learning value, furthermore, to other world regions contemplating a similar initiative: for example, the creation announced in 2015 by Saudi Arabia of a coalition of all 34 Muslim states to combat terrorist jihadism.

A glint in the eye needs body and form, as reflected in Box 11.1. The mass migrations toward Europe of 2015–2016 were to prove a major test of the Union's cohesiveness when confronted by a shared problem. Despite the new External Commissioner's efforts, the EU's member states chose to react independently against the freedom of access provided by what are known as the Schengen agreements. This meant reinstituting border controls dropped earlier and refusing entry to certain migrating travelers. Individual countries proved more effective than the broad, collective will of the Union as a whole – at least on the migratory events of 2015, when Germany alone absorbed almost one million transients from Syria and elsewhere.

Box 11.1 Transition from no plan to first attempt

The original Common Market[6] was without diplomatic arm, since the six founding members thought that none was needed. The lack was regretted as member states grew in number from the original six signatories of the Treaty of Rome, taking effect in January 1958. The shortcoming became more pressing when the relabeled EU found itself concerned more and more with diplomatic/military matters. The Union grappled with external states or other alliances (regarding Kosovan, Bosnian, Serbian and other Balkan links; in Africa, with Rwanda, Congo and later Mali). There was still no one nor a single agency in charge of diplomatic exchange. The Treaty of Lisbon succeeded in establishing the equivalent of a super ministry to bring additional equilibrium and prestige to the Union.

With a growing number of urgencies preoccupying the EU beyond its circumference, the alliance resembles increasingly a philharmonic orchestra seeking to harmonize at once 27 different compositions produced by 27 different artists (one from each nation). While not yet chaotic, developments continue to raise the question: Can differing diplomacies satisfy the Union's national members and their unitary intent? An EU deal with Turkey of March 2016 proved a test of such satisfaction. Its aim was to halt emigrant departures from Turkey toward Europe and relocate for resettlement many migrants already (illegally) in Europe as well as those still on Turkish soil, the combined package costing the Union €6 billion. The harmonization is still under way; only history will assess its quality and, especially, its quantity. Turkey's own agenda, by no means a secret, was its desire to become a full-fledged member of the EU, given that the country has been a participating member of the NATO alliance since 1952.

A problematic menu

In recent decades some of the most pressing issues facing Europe have been of an economic/financial nature, all too familiar to readers since the onset of the recession of 2007–2009. Although fundamentally of a non-diplomatic character, such problems inevitably have diplomatic overtones. The economic/political effects on inter-nation relationships caused by financial anguish in Greece, Spain, Portugal or Italy, as well as the continuing puzzle of unemployment in France, cannot be overlooked by their EU neighbors. These are, in effect, Europe's foreign affairs preoccupations of the new century, exacerbated by the obstacles created within the Union.

The first of these, cited because of its geographic proximity to Europe, occurred in the aftermath of the Arab Spring of 2011. Tunisia, where the fever broke out, is struggling valiantly to re-establish its proven attractiveness to European and world tourism, a critical national industry. Next door, Egypt continues to react to military rule despite the Muslim Brotherhood's electoral supremacy; this country, too, suffers from extensive boycott of its otherwise ancient-world attractions.

Beyond the shores of the Old Continent, other complexities prevail. While not presuming to assign priority – this is impossible – we mention here some of the challenges demanding new scenarios from Europe in its long-term need not to neglect the attention, care and sometimes indulgence necessary in the world of foreign relations. Yemen and even Saudi Arabia suffer from jihadist interference. Iran and Afghanistan are in difficult transition from extensive western attention, but continue as one of the theaters of antagonism between Sunni and Shia. The Saudi public executions in 2016 of 47 "Shiite traitors" was an affront to its neighbor, Iran. Farther west, Libya had its first national elections in 40 years, yielding only second place to confirmed jihadists. Yet new centers of civil conflict emerged in that oil-rich land. Politics in the Muslim world remains complexity-oriented.

Congo and Ivory Coast, for years fractured and in part dismembered, are intermittent dictatorships in economic difficulty. Landlocked Mali is a newer victim, according to economic analyst Benjamin F. Soames of the African Studies Centre in London, "a darling of western donors and hailed as one of the new democracies in the Muslim world." The country is now under pressure from young Islamist officers who displaced President Amadou Touré in 2012.[7]

The Mali situation was aggravated by

- Salafi Algerians in the country since 2002 and calling themselves Al Qaeda,
- native Tuaregs returned from Libya bearing considerable arms, and
- the insurgents' reactions to the cumulative corruption of Touré's entourage.

Benjamin Soames adds that European and American policy makers have "been much too timid in responding to the crisis" although it remains unclear just what the policy experts should or could do. Meanwhile the Tuaregs consolidated their position in impoverished Mali, whose population is twice the size of Libya's, where they are militating for severe limits to monumental and other decorative additions to Islamic tombs. As a former French colony, Mali was long a recipient of French foreign aid before France responded in 2012 to calls for military assistance against all Qaeda-type attacks on the vast, mainly desert nation. French President François Hollande agreed to help provide aid "for a few months." His special-force mission remains in Mali.

The menace of more nuclear potential

A second concern for some time was the acquisition by Iran of nuclear means of warfare. While the Iranians maintained that their R&D were intended for civil purposes only, the "Quartet" formed by the UN, the EU, the United States and the Russian Federation long interpreted Iranian intentions differently. The first three members of the foursome applied paralyzing economic sanctions against Iran, with Russia not at all enthusiastic about penalizing action. The negotiations reached a near-inertial crisis in 2014–2015.

Thus while there may have been active efforts by Iran to nuclearize itself during the drawn-out parleys, a form of conspiracy theory appeared on the part of most of the Quartet. This may have stemmed logically from the endless decades of propaganda and nuclear-strike threats by North Korea against the Republic of Korea, Japan and the United States. Why would not Iran favor such an approach? The conspiratorial thesis may have plagued those prepared to conclude negotiations with Tehran – and may have raised doubts of complicity as well among Iran's patron states of China and Russia. At any rate, negotiating sessions and behind-the-scenes diplomacy between the Quartet and the Iranians finally led to a signed compromise in mid-2015. "Behind-the-scenes" also suggests, unhappily, intrigue and skull duggery. There is, in fact, little of this today, yet public impressions persist (Box 11.2).

Eighteen months later, as the new occupant in the White House, one of the first public utterances of President Donald J. Trump was to condemn the deal with Iran made during President Barack Obama's final term.

Box 11.2 Conspiracy theory and system resilience

The fate or complexity of social systems may be positive or else erosive and destructive, as we recognize throughout this book. When a logical solution to a problem fails (such as legislated control of personal firearms), other means may succeed. *The Random House Dictionary of the English Language* defines conspiracy as "an evil, unlawful, treacherous or surreptitious plan formulated in secret by two or a combination of persons for a secret, unlawful, or evil purpose."

These goals may be the overthrow of the leader or of an entire government; the formation of an illicit trust to regulate the flow of needed resources or a final product, or rules and regulations to exclude categories of membership in associative bodies or religious groups. Here a minority of humans seek, in other words, to assert control over the free choice of others – e.g., the passers who offer the fleeing Syrian emigrant with an exfiltration route in exchange for an exorbitant fee. The dictionary's definition fails, however, to accommodate conspiracy as also a willful act to restore the rule of law, justice and public safety.

Associated with the Iranian nuclear challenge was the Iranian government's publicly stated preference for the elimination of Israel as a nation-state. To counter these pronouncements from Tehran, Israel uttered a series of barely muted threats to take independent, military action against Iran to deprive it of any nuclear capacity that might be amassed. The American government, ever protective of Israel, continued throughout this shouting match to play its additional role of principal dissuader of Israeli intentions to use military means to neutralize Iran's nuclear undertaking.

By 2014–2015 much of the world's attention shifted, focused now on Syria, a Muslim and Arab country, that a century earlier was a territorial objective of British and French imperial diplomacy. (But politics, like the weather, changes; see Box 11.3). The Arab Spring there took on a new and prolonged agony of its own with the UN joining the EU (especially France and Britain) to pressure Shi'ite leader Dr. Bashar al Assad to desist from armed oppression of his country's Sunni "rebel" majority.[8] In 2011–2012 much of Europe's attention (and Moscow's) had turned to relations abroad, notably the Syrian internal dispute. When former UN secretary-general Kofi Annan proposed a diplomatic settlement through Assad's negotiations with the rebels, both sides agreed to the proposal but failed to implement it.

Box 11.3   The Moscow-Tehran-Damascus rationale

"Washington's focus on the Muslim world" since September 2001 "has not only given Russia more room to reassert itself in its own former Soviet periphery, but has given Moscow substantial leverage over the United States and the West on security measures in Europe due to [Russian] ties to Syria and Iran," as reported by Stratfor in an analysis of 2012.[9] This leverage culminated in 2013–2014 when Vladimir Putin unilaterally re-annexed Crimea by force, taken from sovereign Ukraine – and succeeded in "getting away with it." Yet the western sanctions against Russia that followed had economic effects. Western boycott left much Russian petroleum unsold, and the cost of food supplies for the Russian consumer doubled between 2014 and 2016.[10]

Diplomacy and foreign trade 171

A UN Security Council effort to assign an international peacekeeping force in Syria failed, with Russia seconded by China voting three times against the Security Council resolution to monitor the move. The Russian/Chinese explanation, according to Russian ambassador to the UN Vitaly Churkin, was that the Security Council's resolution would facilitate western European/ American military intervention in Syria. Meanwhile Syrian insurgents continued their aggressive opposition, with arms funded by Saudi Arabia and several Gulf states – small nations motivated in part by their hostility to Iran's backing of the Syrian presidency. Damascus remained far from, yet so near to, Brussels. (Baroness Ashton of the EEAS took part in the Security Council deliberations.)

Disparities home-grown by the Union itself

Since the Schengen accords of the 1990s sought elimination of transborder restrictions within the EU's periphery, we have seen that the Union thereby virtually invited terrorists to free access to haven within its member countries. To succeed in such access, the procedure to follow is to worm one's way (usually with false passports) into one of the Union's border nations, then move gingerly into the false migrant's target country. Two such transgressors made their way from Syria to mainland Europe and took part in the Parisian street side killings of November 2015. They died within their own slaughter.[11]

The newly arrived migrant may qualify as political refugee or find illegal employment in a labor category much in demand. Here begins the contest between right and wrong since entry into any given country may be legitimate or under false pretenses (see Box 11.4). An example arena is Austria, which during the Cold War was a much-sought target for defectors from the Marxist-Leninist nations. A country of 9 million, Austria is an attractive place to land and seek a new life. The Vienna daily *Kurier* illustrated in mid-summer 2012 how the illegal-immigration picture affected Austria the previous year; the figures published did not include tourists and other legal travelers visiting the small and hospitable Alpine country.

Box 11.4 Illegal entry to Austria from neighboring states (in percent, 2012)

Germany 7   Italy 44
Hungary 25 Slovakia 6
Other 18

At the time the greatest proportion of nationalities arriving illegally in Austria originated in more distant Afghanistan, the Russian Federation, Pakistan and Somalia, and in that order. The fewest illegals came from Turkey, Iran, Iraq and Syria, in that order.[12] Migration statistics would change drastically within five years.

A variant of the worming-one's-way infiltration is found in a member-state's recalcitrance as a nation hesitating to comply with standards set by the European Commission for the entire Union. Romania has been a consistent offender in this respect, with its nationals frequently traveling by bus as tourists to nearby European countries. Once arrived, some sightsee or shop; a few beg, pick pockets, steal or rob. There have been occasional cases of murder abroad by unwelcome visitors.

When cloth frays at the edges

The EU's welcoming attitudes began wearing thin with the migrations induced by the Arab Spring, especially the violence in Libya preceding the death of President Muammar Kaddafi in 2011. There followed by the deadly civil war then beginning in Syria. Italy, Greece and Spain took the brunt of receiving illegal entrants crossing the Mediterranean. Some of the transients originated in Mali, Sudan, Somalia, Eritrea and far-off Afghanistan, all seeking a better life in the El Dorado of Europe.

Spain, Italy, Greece and the legendary political refuge of France admitted few as legitimate political exiles, cloistering the balance in improvised detention areas and repatriating as many as possible by special commercial flights. *The Economist* (6 February 2016) treated this topic editorially with a cover-story title, "How to Manage the Migrant Crisis, and Keep Europe from Tearing Itself Apart." The journal's solution: continue to admit refugees but regulate the flow inwards rigorously.

A start in this direction would have to be in Turkey, where the Ankara government had little taste for launching a thorough and costly vetting process (and where the crossing trade had become a flourishing industry). A subsequent effort would be made in countries whence the migrants originate. Millions of political and economic exiles have left in waves from Iraq and Syria to escape the barbarism imposed by Daesh (Daesh in Arabic, ISIS or ISIL in Britain and North America), the so-called Islamic State in Iraq and Syria. Daesh has made it publicly clear that it will brook no dialogue with states governed by infidels, so that "diplomatic relations" take on new meaning: a vacuum between even neighboring nations. One cannot imagine how to envisage "negotiations" with such prejudiced adversaries; the complexity will remain.

A future diplomatic nut very hard to crack?

The grand strategy of the Islamic State today seems clear to its victims, as well as to the watchful EU and United States. The new caliphate seeks to destroy the world's civilizational structures and values that it assesses as incompatible with Islam. Today the initial targets are in Europe, probably because of its geographical access from Daesh's core in Iraq and Syria under leader Abu Bakr al-Bagdadi or else his chief spokesperson. Al-Bagdadi has been reported several times as killed; he lives on. This self-proclaimed chief of state has stated repeatedly that there is no room for negotiation with the "infidel" world, that the Islamist persuasion will ultimately be supreme.

There should come a time, perhaps before it could be anticipated, when economic and energy needs will prove essential to the Daesh and its subsidiaries: all 34 Islamic states. Fabricated complexity has its limits. If not, how then would jihadism's new world co-exist with other planetarians? So the devious yet combined counsel of Machiavelli and Nietzsche, together with the orderly neo-Platonists and Montesquieu, might surge to influence world leaders. This would surely aid national leaders to find a state of non-war, synthesizing near-harmony between conflict ideologies. Only one thing is certain – the effort would be worth a trial.

Vetting filtration to exclude the unwanted subsumes, too, enthusiastic cooperation within the EU and by non-EU nations along the Union's boundaries: a further complexity in itself. Violence broke out against refugees in Germany, Hungary and Greece, and in Macedonia, Serbia and Croatia. Pending coherent and collaborative action by the EU, Austria and nine other European/Balkan countries faced an influx of another 200,000 migrants arriving on the continent in the first two months of 2016. The adamant stand taken by Poland, Hungary and Slovakia for total exclusion was reinforced by a closing of the frontiers of the small nations, newly affiliated to preclude further intrusion by the unwanted.

Other causers of intra-European misunderstanding reflect day-to-day incidents having unsought repercussions. There exist contrast reality and illusion even between governments, as we note in Box 11.5. When country A decides to close automobile assembly plants in country B, for example Germany's Opel factory in Britain, the bad taste of an unemployment-creating scenario can last for some time. When France's new Socialist government declared in 2012 its intention to raise taxes on individual incomes exceeding €1 million annually to 75 percent, the British prime minister urged those affected to move to his country in order to avoid increased levies on income. This met a derogatory response from French officials and mass media, one not to be mitigated even by the most diplomatic of efforts at damage control.

Box 11.5 Action and consequences

The illusion that one has understood the past feeds the further illusions that one can predict and control the future. These illusions are comforting. They reduce the anxiety that we would experience if we allowed ourselves to fully acknowledge the realities of existence. We all have a need for the reassuring message that actions have appropriate consequences, and that success will reward wisdom and courage.

Source: Nobelist (in economic sciences) Daniel Kahneman on believing that we understand, in *Thinking, Fast and Slow*, New York, Farrar, Strauss and Giroux 2011, p. 204

174 *Diplomacy and foreign trade*

In foreign relations, their attendant diplomacy – and sometimes knotted complexity – and "illusion that one can predict and control the future" seems also endemic in aid and assistance to other countries. These are usually emerging economies, where finances may be corrupt and thus remote from real needs. Such conditions have frequently led major states to make critical errors in their lending, or giving outright and receiving accountability. The empires of centuries past knew this problem, one that does not vanish with time.

The Calais camping-ground drama

As a consequence of the mass migration to Europe in 2015–2016, a problem that found its way to quasi-solution was complex to the degree of frustration. This was the informal, nomadic and squatter mores of a slum improvised by migrants arriving from the Mediterranean at the northern French port of Calais. They sought illegal passage to Dover on the Channel's opposite shore. British immigration officials would not hear of allowing entry to these migrants (none of whom had visas), impatiently assembled on the French side.

The would-be immigrants to Britain came mainly from the Middle East and Afghanistan; they were mostly men and boys, some under ten years. They resisted efforts by local and national governments in France to resettle or deport them. Charitable organizations and private citizens provided succor in the form of tents, meals, improved sanitation and other caring help. Complexity grew from these relief complications for all concerned. Police then broke up the "Jungle," as it was nicknamed, a bivouac of misfortune and desperation. Only more time would permit finding better solutions, one hoped, and approaching equitability for all concerned.

But the nerves of Calaisians and the government in Paris lost their steadiness. Officials finally dispersed the 3,500 or so aspiring immigrants to England, assigning them to shipping containers and cabins in various holding centers in the French north. With a referendum scheduled to decide within a few months whether the United Kingdom would remain a member of the EU, French minister of economics, industry and digital technology Emmanuel Macron publicly challenged the prime minister in London, David Cameron, to help ease the dramatic pressure weighing on the Calais region.

Otherwise, Macron proclaimed, once Britain should opt out of the EU, then so would end French efforts to prevent detained migrants from leaving France: a challenge of extreme defiance. Yet two days later, in a conference between Cameron and Hollande, London agreed to aid France with a transfer of £22 million to the French treasury as relief in the crisis.

Had Minister Macron's threat been carried out, at least three emerging complexities could have been foreseen.

- With Britain self-excluded (by referendum) from the EU, the future of the Union itself might be in grave doubt.

Diplomacy and foreign trade   175

- The remaining Union could attempt to isolate Britain (as it did Russia upon her re-annexation of Crimea) from much commercial and financial exchange with the remaining 27 national markets of the EU.
- *In extremis*, a state of unconcealed political warfare could develop between France and Britain.

During the same few days of the London-Paris arrangement, Poland's Donald Tusk, president of the European Council, made a public plea to migrants headed for Europe. He told them, during a speech made in Brussels, "there is nothing here for you." Shortly after, Chancellor Merkel, President Hollande and Prime Minister Cameron then applied soft-power pressure on Turkish President Recep Tayyip Erdogan to make a concerted effort to prevent would-be emigrants from transiting Turkey toward the Mediterranean Sea and Greece. As a result, the Balkan route was minimized, and refugees sought other possibilities. In one incident, mainly African migrants tried effecting a ship-to-ship transfer on the high seas between Libya and Italy in order to reach Alexandria (Egypt) instead of Greece. The transshipment effort failed tragically as more than 500 individuals perished in stormy seas.

Stumbles in the globalization of export/import

Foreign commerce is a complicated objective in the foreign relations of many countries. Such trade is, in fact, a dynamic and continuously self-adjusting system in the development and exploitation of a typically modern nation's foreign policy. Selling or buying with profit merchandise and services originating in economies alien to one's own requires information and know-how to deal successfully with others' economy and culture. Your authors have experienced these conditions while residing, working and studying in South and East Asia, Africa, the Americas and Europe.

The 44-nation UN Monetary and Financial Conference, also known as the Bretton Woods conference of July 1944, gave birth in 1947 to the 23-nation UN General Agreement on Tariffs and Trade (GATT). GATT in turn became the 120-country World Trade Organization in 1994. The body's mission remained largely unchanged: to rationalize and regulate as equitably as possible commercial exchanges between sovereign states.

Trade grew, sometimes disrupted by economic sanctions imposed by one country or a group of nations against commercial partners whose political forays abroad met with disapproval. Subsequent sanctions did economic harm, for instance, to the new China, Taiwan and later North Korea, Iran and Russia among others. By the second decade of the 21st century, regional trade agreements were sought by the United States and transatlantic, as well as transpacific correspondents. These trade and investment partnerships were designed, largely at American insistence, to circumvent courts of justice in case of contractual discord, the courts being replaced by arbitrational panels: fewer lengthy proceedings, lesser fines.

The U.S. wanted agreements by January 2017, but there were stumbles. Germany and Austria, whose economic backbones are formed by extremely active small and medium enterprises feared unfair competition and arbitration that would be abused by pressure from industrial and service-sector giants. Successful traders also wanted to preserve their economic culture of rigorous apprenticeship as practiced in their homelands. France, in an altogether different key, feared commercial invasion by unacceptable products: chemical pesticides, bleach-rinsed poultry, hormone-enhanced beef and genetically modified organisms. France also feared impingement on traditional product names as in the case of bovine meat and certain cheeses.

During a multi-nation trip to Europe in April 2016, President Barack Obama visited the annual industrial fair in Hanover to meet and converse directly with European traders and concerned NGOs, such as the European Economic and Social Committee. These groups demanded that the EU's Commission assess what impacts the TTIP could have on national economies and their different sectors. The process continues with Canada and Europe signing a related pact in February 2017, but over extremely rough ground since the arrival on the scene of a strongly opposed American president.

Patronage and beneficence from rich to less rich

Besides the perfectly balanced, yet still theoretical *quid pro quo* of commercial intercourse between sovereign states, there is further transfer of economic benefits and brain power among the almost 200 national sovereignties of the world. This is the know-how financial assistance made available to the less endowed by nations able to some of their own riches. This system is not, however, one without its stumbles and tumbles. One of the first acts of incoming American president Donald J. Trump in 2017 was to suspend all action on the Atlantic and Pacific versions of this trade pact. His reasoning was that agreement of this nature was not putting "America First." There was, in effect, too little *quo* returned for the *quid* invested; see Box 11.6. The system stumbled again, falling into immobility.

Box 11.6   How much does foreign aid cost?

Total world costs of foreign aid and assistance, also called official development assistance (ODA), are not computable with accuracy, although valid statistics are available from the most generous countries. These are the members of the Organization for Economic Cooperation and Development (the most advanced industrial democracies) or the EU or both. In the 28 full-membership OECD countries, where most migratory activity took place during the second decade of this century, refugee costs in 2015 doubled those of 2014. All calculable costs in 2015 totaled $131.6 billion (dollars are OECD's currency of accounting). This sum represents a rise from the approximately $80 billion allocated for the same purpose in 2000. The funds came from the members of OECD or of the EU, or of both. This figure is exclusive of private donations and the grants and services provided by NGOs: the International Committee of the Red Cross, Doctors without Borders, Handicap International, Amnesty International, Transparency International and hundreds more. We estimate that the gross sum for the year 2016 was in the neighborhood of $225–250 billion.

OECD reported that Europe's most provident donors were, in terms of percentage of national income, Norway, Sweden, Luxemburg, Denmark and the United Kingdom. The six most modest contributors, in the same terms, were Slovenia, Greece, the Czech Republic, Poland, Slovakia and Iceland.

International giving or lending may cause, in addition to the relief or help intended, the creation or worsening of political relationships with the recipient country. The world's poorest countries expect more help from the UN itself, already plagued by extraordinary operational costs; see Box 11.7. Parliaments are traditionally watchful of this hazard, but by the time audits are received by lenders (or givers) avoidable damage may have been done – a loss sometimes to the discredit of the donor. Experienced diplomats, too, are apprehensive of this risk, although most realize that when aid has been fed into the maw of another bureaucracy, the desire for true accountability may be little else than wishful thinking. Good foreign relations thus count, ineluctably, on diplomacy, not diplomacy on strong foreign relations.

Box 11. 7   Where is the UN in the world's foreign aid?

A UN Economic and Social Council report in 2016 had the following response (paraphrased). Each year, ECOSOC's Operational Activities for Development reviews UN policies, including the implementation of the General Assembly's four-yearly policy review. This guides the UN cluster of development funds and programs. They include the UN Development Program, the UN Children's Fund, the World Food Program, UN Women and others working directly with countries around the world – making progress in all the dimensions of sustainable development.

Complex, without much doubt, such are the ways between not only the haves and have-nots of the world but also among solidly sovereign states and the associated, welcome bureaucracies (both UN and NGO) at intergovernmental level.

178 *Diplomacy and foreign trade*

Yet this fails to explain why aid funds seem better spent in some countries and sometimes wasted elsewhere. In an analysis by *The Economist* using 2014 data from the World Bank, OECD and Freedom House, a country's poverty and sound governance counted strongly: states small in size and not populous appeared to make aid results readily visible.

Nations in the small category included in alphabetic order Bhutan, Kosovo, Samoa, São Tomé and Principe and Vanuatu. While more populous lands (also alphabetically) such as Bangladesh, India, Indonesia, Nigeria, Pakistan and the Philippines manifested much less visibly the results of per person foreign aid. Samoa, for example, received $4,658 per person. Much larger India commanded $3,669 per head, with fewer apparent results. "That is where [the money] goes," observed the London weekly. The aid given is not a question of errant alms.[13]

In the next chapter, we move on to when deepening conflict turns to war and delayed conditions of peace.

Notes

1 The native Amerindian Mi'kmaq name Pugwash derives from that of a small estuary in Nova Scotia, on whose shore Canadian-American industrialist Cyrus Eaton invited the first exchanges on science and a peaceful world in the late 1950s. The site is now a memorial to those early consultations.
2 This was the twenty-first annual meeting of the Conference of Parties examining and debating workable solutions for the multiplying problems of the damage to nature caused by climate change: a UN initiative. Earlier COP reunions, notably that of 2009 in Copenhagen, had failed to make significant headway.
3 In e-mail exchanged with the authors, 13 March 2016. Project SESAME, Synchrotron-light for Experimental Science and Applications in the Middle East, is headquartered in Jordan.
4 The literature on the inner workings of diplomatic life are usually analyses at the level of macro politics, such as Henry Kissinger's Diplomacy of 1991. Public accounts of the give-and-take within diplomatic teams, at the ministry or by its representatives stationed abroad, are rare. A recent tell-all example is Viêcent Jaubert's La face cachée du Quai d'Orsay, Enquête sur un ministère en dérive (The Hidden Face of the Quai d'Orsay, Investigation of a Ministry Adrift), Paris: Robert Laffont, 2016.
5 The daily life of researchers in Antarctica is well reported by Rebecca Priestley in "Seal Barks and Scientists," *New Zealand Listener*, 21 January 2017.
6 Known in its early years as the European Economic Community, the later "Union" derived from the voluntary rationalization of Europe's coal and steel industries after the Second World War.
7 See "Timbuktu's Tomb Raiders," the *New York Times*, 8 July 2012.
8 President al Assad graduated from Damascus University as a doctor of medicine. He did post-doctoral studies in ophthalmology in London.
9 A Stratfor analysis, "Russia's Mixed Signals regarding Syria" (via Internet), 12 July 2012.
10 According to public broadcaster France Inter radio, 14 April 2016. *The Economist*, commenting on the guiding role of the governor of the Central Bank of Russia, concluded, "The Russian economy is in a bad way, but [Governor] Elvira Nabulina has saved it from worse" (16 April 2016, p. 56).

11 For a thorough retrostrategy of the murderous events in France in the eventful year of 2015, see Gilles Keppel and Antoine Jardin, Terreur dans l'Héxagone, Paris: Gallimard, 2015. The "hexagon" is the topographical form of France, akin to the "boot" shape depicting Italy.
12 Kurier (Vienna), "Höchstrichter bremsen Asylbehörde" (Stronger Asylum-Agency Constraints), 12 July 2012, p. 17.
13 "Misplaced Charity," The Economist, 11 June 2016, pp. 54 and 55.

12 The military
Risk management-plus, not perversity

This chapter takes us from alien idiosyncrasies faced by a government's civil service to the vagaries to be encountered by its uniformed services. In both settings, complexity can play a major role. It is usually the military, however, who experience complexity to its most devastating degree: war. We examine here three cases of the wreckage which may result from overbearing management of resources.

Our goal is to understand how and why spreading complexity in selected engagements failed despite experienced, aggressive leadership. Using reliable historical accounts, we analyze the conception, planning and strategy, execution and the effects of a series of critical actions. There the application of strategy missed its principal goals. Our admitted prejudice, however, is that the sources used may be subject to omission, misinterpretation or flaws in scholarship. Our primary constraint is imposed by length of text; a book would prove more complete in argument than a single chapter.

If war can be mismanaged, so can the main societal tasks of public order in times of peace, allowing rational use of resources, a sense of public well-being, and sustainable development of the human condition. Our review may also be among the first to explain the tools of the futurist to analyze the mechanics of faulty military leadership. This is to say that misunderstood complexity may cause casualties too.

When complexity defied belief

Readers may note that the recapitulation which follows could be, perhaps crassly, a refashioned profile of the entire 20th century. (See later under the heading "Finality by Folly.")

In autumn 1941 Third Reich forces were given a month-to-finish-by-winter deadline to compensate for the failure of Operation Barbarossa several weeks earlier. That action was to capture Moscow and bring the U.S.S.R. to its knees. An ambitious plan – also one facing obstacles of immense scale – was developed but executed unsuccessfully. Historian David Stahel (2014) tells a tale of unquestionable determination and perseverance that will furrow the complexity brow of any system planner or manager analyzing retro-strategic detail, military or civil.

Code-named Operation Typhon (Typhoon), a mass of 1.9 million Wehrmacht troops launched on 2 October 1941 a veritable storm against a seemingly unlimited yet unready Red Army.[1] The operation stalled before October's end because of rain, mud, cold, snow and unexpected Soviet resistance. Author Stahel's perspective is largely from the German side, paying remarkable attention to the often-adverse German point of view, as recorded in operational accounts, letters home, diaries and later reconstructions, by individual Wehrmacht troopers in the assault force. The German effort, organically, was that of Heeresgruppe Mitte (Army Group Center), a swarm of four field armies – the Second, Fourth, Ninth and Panzergruppe 2. Group Center was further broken down into 19 army corps, comprising a dizzying 67 divisions and supporting units.[2] At the time a German army division averaged 15,000 officers and men.

Commanding Group Center was Field Marshal Fedor von Bock, aged 61, a *Junker* whose oversight responsibility was the largest field command within all German armed services. Typhoon followed and proved itself ancillary to the ill-fated Operation Barbarossa launched the previous June, with Germany's surprise declaration of war on the Soviet Union. War's outbreak as well as its end remains, even today, an incalculable probability (see Box 12.1).

The renewed German effort in October 1941 lost much of its dynamism, however, during its encirclement of Kiev (Ukraine). Hitler insisted on driving ahead to Moscow, however, and taking that capital no later than New Year's Day of 1942. Such was the Führer's confidence in a quick victory that troops and equipment were not winterized (indeed, they were still very much in summer gear): an environmental and logistical failure that would ensue at a staggering price. Typhoon bogged down further during its enveloping actions around Viaz'ma and Briansk, forestalling the planned push to Moscow. In the critical pocket "at Viaz'ma the Soviets lost multiple armies to save their capital."[3]

Lengthening German supply lines overland quickly reduced fuel resources for armored and transport vehicles, while resupply by Luftwaffe aircraft was permanently inadequate. Thus, only a year after the Battle of Britain between the German air fleet and the Royal Air Force, unceasing Luftwaffe sorties against the Soviets enabled pilots on the Soviet side at least "to gain invaluable experience . . . every German loss reduced [German] superiority" in the air war.[4]

Box 12.1 When *if* should have counted more than *how*

"The victory of Nazi Germany [over Soviet Russia] was assumed from the outset, and planning for how that was to be achieved was undertaken at the expense of a more important consideration, concerning if that could be achieved."[5] – Complexity was disregarded.

Generals named mud and ice

The massive charge forward to the Soviet capital quickly foundered in expanding immobility. Unceasing autumn rains turned roads and fields into knee- and axle-deep *rasputitsa* (quagmire), soaked summer uniforms, affected distribution of rations and medical support, and impeded sleep and rest. The resupply of munitions as well as engineering and medical materiel became as problematic as insufficient fuel. What aerial support there was proved to be as rare as the sunshine.

Soviet scorched-earth policy compounded the increasingly chaotic conditions by denying improvised shelter to soaked and growingly exhausted German units. Fire-fights with both artillery and automatic arms took a terrible toll of life. Fast-diminishing troop strength forced the hurried recomposition of regiments and brigades on both sides. As to the sustained perversity of the weather, the author explains[6]:

> [T]here was nothing unusual about the onset of the Russian *rasputitsa* by mid-October. It was the German command, beginning with Hitler but including all of the army's leadership, which proved consistently impervious to any negative influence threatening to derail their plans . . . Suddenly it appeared that the only thing to stop the German soldier was his own lack of determination to impose himself upon his enemy . . . An indomitable will to succeed, always exemplified by Hitler's own struggle to win power and "save" Germany, was the touchstone of Nazi and, increasingly, military rationale.

With the German advance stalled, Stalin reassigned Marshal Georgi Zhukov from a front in the north, charging him with the defense of Moscow. The capital prepared for the worst which, finally, did not occur. German attempts to take and hold Russian ground failed regularly – as had earlier attacks by Charles XII of Sweden at Poltava in 1709 and Napoleon in 1813, even after the latter had invested Moscow for an entire month. Over the centuries, the land of Russia had become a revolving disc for intruders arriving from many sides (Box. 12.2).

Box 12.2   Flashback: "no, general, no complex strategies"

Alexander I to General Prince P. I. Bagration, commanding Russia's Second Western Army near Vitebsk, 5 July 1812

"[We] are still opposed by superior numbers at every point and for this reason we need to be cautious and not deprive ourselves of the means to carry on an effective campaign by risking all on one day. Our entire goal must be directed towards gaining time and drawing out the war as long as possible. Only by this means can we have the chance of defeating so strong an enemy."

The Tsar's recommended algorithm to his prince was plain: "Keep it simple, soldier!"

Source: Lieven 2010

Hitler and his marshals had learned little, driven by their creed that all Slavs are *Untermenschen* (subhumans) and deserve nothing better than to serve another, master race. This was Germany's politico-military compulsion for the drive through Poland after having seized Czechoslovakia, with a culminating conquest of "inferior" Soviet Russians to serve the victors. After this major calamity of the German war against the U.S.S.R., "even Hitler could not hope to pass over the scale and cost of fighting in the east, and he admitted that Germany had been caught unawares."[7]

Comparative evaluation (later called net assessment) of *Homo sovieticus* by the German invaders – even if it was attempted – did not materialize.[8] A year later, from November 1942 until February 1943, Germany's top military managers repeated the same scenario at Stalingrad on the lower Volga River.

Supply and resupply

Hitler said, *Unawares*. Few staff studies of Soviet Russia as adversary – potential or active – were undertaken by Nazi Germany during the 1930s. Nor had objective appraisals of the worth of the Soviet soldier together with his equipment and tactics in comparison with the German counterparts, essential elements in net assessment. On the contrary, according to author Stahel, traditional German military lore combined fatefully with the "Nazi mind." The latter demanded,[9]

> the power of individual "will" [amounting] to a determination to overcome all obstacles and opposing forces. Failure to do so was a reflection on the individual, not the circumstances. The requisite "will" to carry out an order or achieve an objective was therefore accorded decisive importance. Logistics had been a major problem throughout the summer campaign . . . but the fact that the most immediate objectives had been met allowed [the German high command] to overlook the gravity of the problem. By ordering another large-scale offensive to the east, [the high command] merely delayed throughout the summer campaign the worst of the logistical crisis, and that was all before the weather affected movement so adversely.

The logistics of Typhoon was the direct charge of Major-General Eduard Wagner, the army quartermaster-general, a man of

> blind devotion and professional incompetence. . . [G]iven Wagner's many shortcomings and failed promises, his survival in the post of

quartermaster-general only confirmed the support he, and his judgments, often enjoyed. Importantly Wagner was an enthusiast for all manner of Nazi ideals, including the power of individual "will," which asserted the power of the spiritual over the tangible.

Stahel's analysis continues:[10]

> Following this line of Nazi mythology, German troops, regardless of the supply situation, could conquer Moscow so long as they remained determined to do so. The folly of such belief should have been apparent during Operation Barbarossa, but the absence of a learning curve within the German high command doomed Operation Typhoon to repeat many of the previous mistakes,

including those of Napoleon and other would-be conquerors of the Russians.

What the irresolution of complexity signified

Although the author does not specify total casualties suffered by Army Group Center (they may not be available), there are German figures known for the 3 million-man *Ostheer* (Eastern Army). This was the overall command of the Wehrmacht in Eastern Europe and the western Soviet Union and of which Field Marshal Bock's forces were part. Barbarossa itself, until the start of Typhoon, had cost Nazi Germany 185,000 lives.[11] During the October weeks of Typhoon, German dead averaged 1,300 daily, or about 40,000 for that month only, making the toll of the summer-autumn campaigns a costly 225,000 combat fatalities. There were many more wounded to be added to those killed, missing or taken prisoner.

As to losses in transport, both wheeled and tracked, "[f]rom a starting total of 600,000 vehicles at the beginning of Operation Barbarossa the *Ostheer* was down to just 75,000 serviceable vehicles by mid-November 1941.[12]" Bock's forces needed a minimal daily reprovisioning of 6,500 tons of all stores but were lucky if they received half that amount because of shortages of everything including favorable weather conditions (see Box 12.3).

Historian Stahel, thanks to his linguistic access, gives readers a good notion of many original documents in German – unit reports and journals, private diaries and letters to families, as well as postwar revelations. This contributes to balanced retro-strategic analysis: the systemic deboning of an operational plan that was futile from its conception through its execution and results. Typhoon was a matter of learning by making serious mistakes, of course, but also one of lessons not learned.

Box 12.3 "Climate change" helps subvert massive invasion

The failings of the Third Reich's Russian offensive combined faulty command; overly ambitious targets, goals and their timing; inadequate air support and logistics; and the German forces' own "climate change" dilemma. Meteorological data were known by military elders because a generation earlier German forces spent three full winters in Russia after their success at the battle of Tannenberg (1914), before Russia withdrew from the war during its revolution of 1917. Hitler himself knew the rigors of cold and mud during the four winters his regiment spent in the Franco-Belgian border region.[13] In 1941, Hitler adamantly refused to alter war plans as rainy October became snow-bound November. Reason had no role to play, so disaster took charge.

Finality by folly

What could have been the genesis of such astuteness? Hitler's decision to go to active war against France, Britain and their neighbors in 1940 proved ultimately to be a wrong road. In official military documents presented at the war crimes trials in Nuremberg after the Second World War, the Führer was shown to have explained his decision during a meeting with his generals on 23 November 1939, as recorded in a postwar memoir by Allen Dulles (1947).

> Wars today are different from those of 100 years ago. Today we can speak of a racial fight. Today we fight for oil fields, rubber, treasures of the earth . . . The decision to strike was always in me. Earlier or later I wanted to solve the problem . . . The permanent sowing of mines on the English coast will bring England to her knees. However, this can only be done if we have occupied Belgium and Holland. It is a difficult decision for me. No one has ever achieved what I have achieved. My life is of no importance in all this. I have led the German people to a great height, even if the world does hate us now. I am gambling everything.

Such is one rationale, citing actions in the world system involving vandal-like destruction. The emergence of factors Hitler enumerated proved thus to be race, natural resources and the armed blockading of enemy territory and seizure of the adversity's neighbors. He failed to interpret these as stumbling eventualities as well. Hitler interpreted his own motives as selfless, original and daring. His narcissism later found, nonetheless, a scapegoat, Field Marshal Walther von Brauchitsch, the army commander-in-chief who had planned every German campaign of 1940–1941 (all successful). Brauchitsch turned 60 as Typhoon bogged down; Hitler forced him into retirement.

Chain of command, or linkage not to be broken

Now to other tales of military miscalculation and its contribution to complexity of consequences. These events are also of scale.

In autumn 1944 General Dwight Eisenhower convened a decision-making conference in Saverne (near Strasbourg), France. Attending were senior commanders Omar Bradley, Bernard Montgomery, George Patton and Jacob Devers. The last, Devers, leading the American-French Sixth Army Group, had moved unexpectedly quickly and effectively through the Rhone River valley after landings made equally efficiently along the French Riviera in August 1944. In close pursuit of the Wehrmacht's decimated Fourteenth Army, Devers was poised to be the first among the western Allies to cross the Rhine and enter on German soil.

This key operation had been reserved by Eisenhower, however, for Bradley and Montgomery as a special honor for occupying – and denying its further use by Germany – the industrialized Ruhr Basin farther north. The Basin was the Third Reich's heartland of design and manufacturing for its military needs. Devers had taken great pains, in fact, to plan and prepare his force for deployment across the Rhine, even creating in eastern France two river-crossing schools before attempting to traverse the border's swift-flowing stream.

Once that Eisenhower had evaluated Devers's initiative, the supreme commander ordered Devers to stay where he was. The decision made it possible, in turn, for the Germans under Field Marshal Gerd von Rundstedt to begin concentrating troops, armor and logistics only a month later for an ultimate effort in the Rhineland against the western Allies: the battle of the Bulge. Devers thus failed to realize his hopes of first-across-the-Rhine.

Eisenhower's decision to stick to preconceived strategy was tantamount to subordinating Devers's "system" to his own, a clash between two large-scale strategies that was resolved by the classical managerial expedient of a straightforward, top-down order. While two discrete orders of battle had conflicted momentarily, their respective concerns were then arbitrarily integrated into a single, major goal maneuver.

The stumble or tumble, if this is what it was,[14] was absorbed by system resilience. Devers did what he was told to do. But other objectives suffered, according to military historian David Colley.[15] According to this specialist, historical analysis has shown that maintaining the Eisenhower-favored strategy cost the Allies some 200,000 more deaths by the end of winter 1944–1945 and hundreds of thousands more wounded or taken prisoner.

In all probability, the war might have been shortened by a few months, and more concentration-camp lives saved, had Jacob Devers been permitted to do what he had devised and was prepared to accomplish. Top management bent the system, so to speak, to accommodate subsidiary considerations rather than major goals. Complexity had been contrived, unnecessarily.

Two-way mirror, when defense becomes offense

We tread now, again, the ground where hundreds of studies have searched the how and why of the surprise strike by Japan that destroyed much of the U.S.

Navy at Pearl Harbor in 1941.[16] A young Japanese historian, Eri Hotta, has taken another tack (Hotta 2013). Few analyses made outside Japan in languages other than Japanese have relied extensively on material published in the Japanese language. Ms. Hotta has produced an analysis in English, based chiefly on sources in her native tongue. This approach leaves readers with not only a strong sense of source authenticity but also with sufficient confidence that one is penetrating the minds of the planners, strategists and deciders of Japan's war "system" against China and the West during the 1930s-1940s.

After the conflict ended, some of the Japanese policy makers were tried internationally as war criminals and executed. But a plurality of the architects of the war lived on, wrote their memoirs or were interviewed by mass and specialized media; some even rose high in postwar government. Their eyewitness accounts, still growing in number every year, are the unofficial record – together with Hotta's contribution – of what took place.

Japan began extending its empire in the 1890s with the annexation of Formosa (today's Taiwan), won a war with Russia in 1904, and then gained concessions in mainland China. It annexed Korea in 1910. Japan took part in the Paris peace conference of 1919 (Macmillan 2001), but failed to have integrated within the League of Nations' covenant (as Japan strongly desired) any allusion to racial equality among League members.

Japan's delegation, although capably led and staffed, deemed itself very much a second-class, yellow-skinned group trying to function among predominantly white-skinned diplomats representing well-established and powerful countries. As a former wartime Allied nation itself, however, Japan managed to keep control – under official League mandate – of strategically situated island clusters in the north-central Pacific formerly held by Germany (the Marshall, Marianas and Caroline groups), as well as of China's Shantung peninsula.

Disassembly of system of governance

Japan's navy, as senior service (because of its remarkable defeat of two Russian Imperial fleets in 1904), together with a few leaders of the army's conscripted mass had the emperor's ear. Constitutionally the emperor reigned; he did not rule. This was anathema to young officers of both services. As witnesses to Japan's emergence from the long feudalism, they wanted their country strong and resistant to foreign encroachment (note Box 12.4). Yet his senior uniformed subjects made sure that their views were the primary counsel the crown received. A future of intensely aggressive warfare thus became Japan's foreign *and* domestic policy: this policy was even the system's goal. Prince Konoe Fumimaro, a scion of the historic Fujiwara clan, served several times as prime minister; he vacillated repeatedly, however, regarding a possible war with the West. Despite his rank and responsibilities, Konoye proved to be an erratic adviser to his emperor.

> **Box 12.4   Gekokujô, or "I beg to disobey, sir!"**
>
> Characteristic of an emerging Japan in the 1930s was a culture of intended insubordination, especially in the middle ranks of the Empire's officer corps. Gekokujô, written with three ideograms signifying *juniors overriding seniors*, was a method of manipulating official policy by mainly young army officers – often from rural backgrounds and economically depressed families – who deemed that Japan was moving too slowly in finding its rightful place in the world. Heated incidents of this tolerated insolence sometimes led to dramatic assassinations.
>
> Source: Adapted from Richardson, J., "Japan's Sino-Pacific War: A Conflict Unplanned, Lacking Both Means and Foresight?" *Foresight*, Vol. 10, No. 1, 2008, p. 67

Spurred on by a hunger for both territory and regional power, Japan hardened its position in China by seizing Manchuria in 1931. This land grab between two member states was immediately condemned by the League of Nations. Japan left the League in 1933, and in 1937 extended its military operations deeper into China. With Germany's defeat of France in 1940, Japan occupied northern Indochina (today's Vietnam, Cambodia, Laos) and threatened to move farther into Southeast Asia, with an eye to taking control of British Malaya and the Dutch East Indies (now Malaysia and Indonesia) with their riches in metals, rubber and petroleum. Japan's territorial holdings rapidly became vast, distant from home, managerially challenging and complex.

By the late 1930s the Second World War was becoming reality. President Franklin Roosevelt began a campaign of economic warfare against Japan's empire-building, banning American exports of petroleum, iron and rubber to Japan (action taken in 1940–1941). The economic pressure severely affected the strategic reserves of fuel for Japan's naval and air arms. The signing of the Tripartite Pact, or the Berlin-Rome-Tokyo "axis," in September 1940 encouraged Japan to believe that Nazi Germany would come to its aid in case the growing rivalry with Washington for hegemony in the Pacific should lead to armed conflict.

A state (nation, country, land) is a system representing an organized society capable of maintaining and defending itself against the excesses of other societal systems nearby and some natural disasters. (Today, in an era of failing and failed states – complete breakdowns of otherwise dynamic models – one wonders why there have not been more such failures throughout human history.)

If a large, self-governing societal systemist undergoes the analysis described by historian David Unger (2012) in his *The Emergency State, America's Pursuit of Absolute Security at All Costs*, the system will manifest a struggle to pit incertitude against risk. (See Chapter 3.) This also presents a welcome opportunity to engage in *back casting*[17] better to understand cause and effect. David Unger is convinced that America has overlooked, from 1940 until the present, the rule of law in its

The military 189

own republic, violated its constitution and endowed its president with authority that the founding fathers sought to avoid. How justified was such a turn of events?

Now back to Japan and the Pacific

Rivalry dating from the results of the First World War transformed itself into rising tension. Japanese sabers had left their scabbards in China in the 1930s and, as the belligerent decade of the 1940s loomed, prominent figures in Japan's army and navy clamored at home for expanding warfare across international waters. Envisaging two possible scenarios, the army's leadership favored a northern engagement with the U.S.S.R., itself soon perilously locked (summer 1941) in a desperate war against Hitler's Germany. Japanese naval leadership, on the other hand, favored making a major move southward to acquire strategic materials and – by anticipation – ultimately to engage in further confrontation with America and the three other "ABCD" powers, Britain, China and the Dutch.[18]

Was dissent within Japan possible? Author Hotta asks this question more than once in her account. In retrospect, it is amazing how few individuals became the deciding elements in planning a war that could bolster or wreck the hegemony that Tokyo sought in the greater Asian-Pacific region.[19] Those responsible numbered, including the emperor, not more than a few dozen in a Japanese population of 100 million. The military prevailed among those responsible for strategic foresight, whereas civil society (the nation as a whole, including educators and the professions, religious and associative institutions, and in this case industry and commerce) was neither consulted nor much heard.

In a search for root causes of Japan's war in East Asia and the Pacific and its failed strategy, there are several methods of retro-reflection available to the planning analyst and historian. Successful strategies are not often put under the microscope for such enquiry, although political parties and the advertising/public relations industry with their post-campaign appraisals and the military with their after-action critiques offer useful guides for critical retro casting. Here the method that we have selected is *causal layered analysis*, a stratified raking apart of why and how planning may have fallen short.

One analytical method

Causal layer analysis or CLA is a *post facto* dissection-by-tiers of both endemic and external factors having a bearing on the emergent features of a given event, process or system.[20] The four layers of disassembly are presented in Box 12.5, following the order in which they are analyzed.

Box 12.5   Disassembly by layers of reasoning

a – *Litany*, the unchallenged, official view of reality by the system's authors
b – *Societal or systemic causes* of such concepts of reality

> c – *Worldview*, deeper assumptions and ideological certainties
> d – *Metaphor/myth*: subconscious perspectives, yet capable of generating review of **a, b, c** and thus of **d** itself
>
> *Short-term gains* – – > *to* – – > *More sustainable change*

When we probe the first or *litany* (**a**) level among Japanese military leaders (the Emperor included), we recall that the purpose of Japan's grand strategy combined a basic desire to (i) rid the region of white-faced (i.e., Western) intrusion, (ii) obtain more living space and through this, (iii) gain access to new natural resources needed to sustain a wartime (and ulteriorly a peacetime) economy. In this multi-step process, Japan should be able, furthermore, to (iv) acquire political leadership of the entire region. In other words, Japan would reign supreme in East Asia and the western Pacific. No time-table was specified although, with steeply rising losses in manpower, the Japanese leadership was in a hurry to accomplish (i) through (iii) as quickly as possible.

The *systemic* (**b**) level of analysis reflects Japan's severe lack of nearly every resource, including the energy required by a competitive industrial nation. Goaded by her earlier victory over Russia and the experience at the Paris Peace Conference, Japan repeatedly re-assessed its role in East Asia and the Pacific as one of indisputable leadership – even if this must be imposed by force of arms. And here it was the senior-most military management that would assist the imperial authority in showing the way.

The outside *worldview* (**c**) interpreted Japan's position very differently, beginning with its condemnation by the League of Nations for aggression against China. Soviet Russia maintained a highly defensive posture in Siberia, lest a Japanese assault occur there – as a serious one did, along the Russian-Manchurian border in 1939. After the war in Europe became a shooting conflict in early 1940, Japan's intentions toward French, British and Dutch territories in Asia complicated Tokyo's relations with these colonial powers with whom it might otherwise have remained peaceful. Japan's prolonged conflict with China, against both Nationalist and Communist forces, as well as its notoriously harsh treatment of urban and agrarian populations alike, also had worldwide repercussions harmful to Japan.

Appraisal of Japan's behavior at level (**d**), *metaphor* or *myth*, was tantamount to an aggravation of intensity of the three previous levels (**a, b, c**). Ripostes from her main enemies in the Pacific and on the Asian mainland effectively left Japan in complete isolation by 1943–1944. It desperately required raw materials and energy to continue waging war, all the while addressing the needs of a starving and increasingly homeless population, combined with a military establishment incapable of abandoning a war no longer to be won. Author Hotta, through her use of authorative sources, makes repeatedly clear that instead of complexity having reached a zenith, the expansionist process found its nadir.

How systemic is system?

This question needs to be asked, whether it concerns the aforementioned method of examining causes in layers or another. We know from fault-tree analysis (see end of footnote 20) and similar parsings of failure that no system can be perfect; any system will ultimately manifest defects, or stumbles. The Western Allies' conflict in the Near East during the First World War was, for example, despite its almost random organization, a system. The concentrated effort by the British and French to involve the desert clans and tribes of the northern and central Arabian Peninsula against German-Turkish influence was an intensive enterprise in military operations and tactics – but rather patchy in strategy and logistics. Yet the effort proved effective, perhaps ineluctably, by further weakening already frail Ottoman power and governance.

Japan's war-effort system between 1931 and 1945 yielded, as Eri Hotta also makes inarguable, no lasting results. By the late northern winter of 1944–1945, the Japanese leadership ordered its diplomats to find ways to end the Pacific war with the best terms possible. Because communication with the United States, China and Britain was now inoperative, special envoy Hirota Kôki (a trained diplomat, former foreign minister and prime minister) called on Soviet ambassador Yakov Malik (in temporary refuge in the mountains at Hakone from air raids on Tokyo). Japan's Foreign Office also appealed in Tokyo to Danish minister Lars Tillitze to communicate with Copenhagen to seek intercession by the Nordic states. The Japanese themselves canvassed Sweden and Switzerland. Their chief concern, should the war end in defeat, was to preserve the imperial monarchy. Tokyo thus ordered its ambassadorial network to seek *in extremis* means to save empire and emperor, and prevent military occupation by foreign forces. The effort failed, surrender followed.

These intensive overtures yielded no productive responses, so the Foreign Office pressed its envoy in Moscow, Satô Naotake, to intervene through foreign minister Vyacheslav Molotov with Roosevelt and Churchill. Stalin planned, however, to fulfill his promise made at the Potsdam conference of July 1945 to enter the conflict against Japan no later than 15 August 1945 – which he did. Japan's scouring of the horizon with peace feelers proved of no avail whatsoever.

A scenario foreordained?

Author Hotta stresses in her very readable text that the finality of Japan's policy scenario was circumscribed from the outset. And yet there were respectable, demurring voices at the highest levels of government. We have seen that Prince Konoe, a distant relation of the Emperor and former prime minister, was of half a mind to avoid war with China and the West. One of the most consistent protests was from elder statesman Saionji Kimmochi, lord privy seal and very much Europe-oriented. (Prince Saionji had headed Japan's delegation to the Paris Conference in 1919.) Another articulate voice was that of Admiral Yamamoto Isoroku, part of whose career was spent at Harvard University and as naval attaché at the Japanese embassy in Washington. He had opposed the invasion of China in 1931 and then the continuation of the war in mainland Asia, but he remained unheard. While a "great bluffer" (in Hotta's words) but always a loyal son of Nippon, Yamamoto warned his navy's general staff as late as September 1941 that "a war [against the United States] with so little chance of success should not be fought" (again Hotta, verbatim). Most ironically, it was this same distinguished flag officer who designed and meticulously followed through the devastating attack on Pearl Harbor the following December. The beginning of the war also signaled the ending of Japan's dream of a regional empire.

Japan's "war system" proved remarkably resilient, literally through much thick but not much thin in terms of the conflict's intensity. Both the leadership and the public adjusted with unceasing resolution to a consistently desperate combination of factors: air and sea wars with no hope of victory, immense casualty rates both military and civil during endless island-hopping, feeding and housing anywhere near properly Japan's native and acquired populations, aggravated destruction of the munitions industry, no succor or even temporary relief to turn to in any direction (66 cities lay in ruins), and finally victimization to the first nuclear weapons.

This was a war that, even through the slightest rustling of a restless samurai's sword, should never have been.

Some near-conclusions on military history

We have passed in review a series of faulty scenarios. First, the combined German operations Barbarossa-Typhoon, a massive effort to take Moscow in record time, failed for lack of proper preparation. There complexity prevailed, only to be undone by determined inhabitants on their own soil. Toward the close of the Second World War, supreme Allied commander Dwight Eisenhower made a wrong strategic decision based on his preference of subordinate personalities: an option that would prove inordinately costly in human lives. Finally, we examined Japan's intentions and capabilities during the same major conflict, when geopolitical ambitions in Tokyo commandeered the complex process of economic support of military decision and erred totally. The circumstances of nascent military engagements are more easily recognized in retrospect than as they occur, so that tipping points may fail to be self-evident. The tipping points in this chapter's three cases, as moments in a process, remain fuzzy in all three, the "points" probably were synchronous with decisions leading to unintended complexities. These, in turn, became identifiable episodes of human history.

When intentions are undermined by insufficient capacity to implement them, in civil as well as military life, failure if not disaster is almost sure to follow. This may be a lesson learned as we try to master degraded conditions in the processes of swelling populations and urban growth, climate change, water supply or the contracting variety and number of things that grow. Sustainable development is a prime goal among these major problems, so in the next chapter we turn to a current and poignantly disruptive contributor to complexity: Unexpected, massive and broad-impact migration.

Notes

1. In 1942 Moscow changed official terminology from Red Army to Soviet Army.
2. See Stahel (2014), Table 2, pp. 46–48.
3. Stahel (2014), op. cit., p. 158.
4. Ibid., p. 61.
5. Ibid., p. 27.
6. Ibid., p. 98.
7. Stahel (2014), op. cit., p. 57.
8. During the decade preceding the Second World War, the German Defense Ministry had a military procurement mission stationed on Soviet soil for several years.
9. Stahel (2014), op. cit.,p. 21.
10. Ibid., p. 65.
11. Ibid., p. 1.
12. Ibid., p. 24.
13. Hitler enlisted, 1914, in the 16th Reserve Regiment of the Bavarian army. Wounded, he was made a "runner" (messenger), a lance corporal, and remained in service until 1920.
14. One of your authors, still a reserve officer serving after the war's end, recalls hearing it bruited that as cadets Eisenhower had been hazed by Devers, an upperclassman at the U.S. Military Academy. Devers was three years Eisenhower's elder. Was Saverne a case of spite?
15. This section on the Saverne decision is adapted from Richardson, J., "Wishful Thinking, A Serious Risk Factor in Planning and Strategy," World Future Review, No. 3, 2013, p. 48. See esp. Colley, D., Decision at Strasbourg: Ike's Strategic Mistake to Halt the Sixth Army Group at the Rhine in 1944. Annapolis, MD: Naval Institute Press, 2008, particularly final chapter.
16. Some of the thorough authors include Bix, H., *Hirohito and the Making of Modern Japan*, New York, NY: HarperCollins (2000); Iriye, A., *The Origins of the Second World War in Asia and the Pacific*, London and Harlow: Longman-Pearson Education (2000); Tohmatsu, H. and Wilmott, H., A *Gathering Darkness: The Coming of War to the Far East and the Pacific 1921–1942*, Lanham MD, SR Books (2004); and Watanabe, T. (Ed.), Who Was Responsible? From Marco Polo Bridge to Pearl Harbor (in English), Tokyo: Yomiuri Shimbun (2006).
17. As opposed to forecasting.
18. In an e-mail of 20 March 2014, a former chief historian of the U.S. Air Force, Col. Dr. Stanley Falk, told the authors that Japanese army and navy planners "compromised by adopting both plans." There was no joint planning, according to Falk, "but rather joint bargaining sessions."
19. See Hotta's list of Main Characters, p. xv of her book (Hotta 2013).
20. CLA is an epistemological/philosophical invention of Pakistan-born futurist Sohail Inayatullah, a university professor in Australia and Taiwan. Instead of predicting the future, CLA delimits "transformative spaces for the creation of alternative futures" at four levels of reality (as perceived during the process of analysis). "The challenge is to conduct research that moves up and down" Inayatullah's four layers; each tier embraces different forms of knowing. (See *The Futurist*, January–February 2014, p. 20.) Fault-tree analysis is another what-went-wrong analytical method, from which CLA is in part derived, and originally introduced by the aerospace-engineering industry. It is not pertinent here.

References

Dulles, A. 1947. *Germany's Underground*. Macmillan, New York.
Hotta, E. 2013. *Japan 1941, Countdown to Infamy*. Alfred A. Knopf, New York.
Lieven, D. 2010. *Russia against Napoleon, The True Story of the Campaigns of War and Peace*. Penguin/Viking, New York, p. 151.
Macmillan, M. 2001. *Paris 1919: Six Months that Changed the World*. Random House, New York, pp. 311–314.
Stahel, D. 2014. *Operation Typhoon: Hitler's March on Moscow, October 1941* (with Index). Cambridge University Press, New York.
Unger, D. 2012. *The Emergency State, America's Pursuit of Absolute Security at All Costs*. Penguin Press, New York.

13 Migration
When exit becomes exodus

Introduction

In the last chapter we wrote about the hordes, usually males, transported away from home to fight enemies. Here we scrutinize the phenomenon of hundreds of thousands of men, women and children leaving home for very different reasons; they seldom return to their places of origin. We explain the motives for and against displacement from certain countries to others, highlighting the often complex consequences of these shifts. Using a soft system analysis, we cite specialists in migratory movement and evolving attitudes reflected in different nations' experiences, economic and political policy, culture and religion. Our analysis reviews how population displacement in the early 21st century differs from such movements in the 20th century. Box 13.1 defines by indirection who in such movements is not a migratory inhabitant of this world.

Box 13.1 Who is a migrant?

The UN's International Organization for Migration (IOM) defines a migrant as any person who is moving or has moved across an international border or within a State away from his/her habitual place of residence, regardless of (1) the person's legal status; (2) whether the movement is voluntary or involuntary; (3) what the causes for the movement are; or (4) what the length of stay is.

IOM concerns itself with migrants and migration-related issues and, in agreement with relevant states, with migrants who are in need of international migration services.

A director of London's Institute for Public Policy Research, Dhananjayan Sriskandarajah, has noted that each day in the early 2000s, Great Britain's immigrant population rose by 1,500 persons (mostly from Asia) while its departures numbered about a thousand. He adds that today "there are more Brits abroad than there are foreigners in Britain." About one in ten British passport holders lives abroad, whereas the proportion is far less for American, Australian, Canadian, French, German and New Zealand citizens.[1]

The reason most often proffered for exodus is that the relative cost of living abroad is less onerous than at home. The search for El Dorado may be a less articulated impulse than others such as disagreement with the ambient political scene and the inability to help change it. The El Dorado syndrome applies widely; it is a powerful magnet for the poverty-stricken, the less poor and even those more comfortably off – whether in affluent or developing countries.

Policy researcher Sriskandarajah thus confirms that the economy is responsible for much of the influx of new citizens into receiving countries. Solid economic growth between 1995 and 2005 in Britain, for example, was stoked, he says, by "immigrant workers coming to fill unmet labor demand. One in two doctors and nurses recruited to the Health Service – and, if you believe the newspapers, every plumber in Britain – [came] from abroad." The last refers to a popular pleasantry supposedly explaining why the French population voted against adoption of the European Constitution in 2005: Why should France, with its high unemployment, call in plumbers from a half-continent away to come repair clogged sinks and defective toilets?

The net result of home-grown departures from Britain is that since 1980, some 1.4 million skilled individuals have left its shores. The loss has been balanced by an intake of 1.5 million, according to the Organization for Economic Cooperation and Development (OECD). By January 2015, France had an immigrant population of 4.5 million, almost 9 percent of the national census; 30 percent of these leave France annually to go elsewhere. At the same time, French citizens living abroad numbered 3.5 million.[2] A direct consequence of this exchange of populations, as any visitor to France and Britain readily notes, is the ethnic/cultural diversity brought by the newcomers during the last two or three generations – including a visible increase in the number of mosques.

There was once a beginning

Some populations look askance at such demographic evolution. Dominique Moïsi, a principal adviser to the Institut Français des Relations Internationales in Paris, construes the continuing migrations as evidence that Samuel Huntington was "more right than wrong" in supposing that the world is faced increasingly by a clash of civilizations. Moïsi emphasizes,

> it would be more correct to speak of a clash of emotions. The Western world displays a culture of fear, the Arab and Muslim worlds are trapped in a culture of humiliation, and much of Asia displays a culture of hope. The Muslim world . . . has been obsessed with decay for centuries. Muslims saw the creation of the state of Israel in the midst of Arab land as the ultimate proof of their [own] decline.[3]

Perhaps we should mention that, contrary to Huntingdon, we do not have a situation where the "Rest is polarized against the West" but where alliances of states play a major role. Examples are Russia, Turkey, Iran, the United States and France. We do not have religious wars, but wars of power seeking hegemony. (As to fear of such, there is more next.)

Migration derived largely from humankind's earliest efforts better to sustain itself in an environment from which it needed increasingly to extract nourishment and shelter. The hunter-food gatherer moved from meadow to forest in search of cyclical harvests of nuts, berries, other edibles and water. Once that meat-eating *Homo sapiens* appeared, the primitives sought farther and more widely – throughout entire regions and continents and finally beyond ocean barriers – food, water and animal feed. Survival was and is paramount for both man and beast.

The situation today is far more complicated. Population growth makes new demands on resources and leaves the job market increasingly dubious for populations not yet strongly influenced by the scientific, industrial and information revolutions. The poor want to improve, rising from subsistence to more provident environments; the poorest are willing to move to areas vacated by other poor, merely upgrading somewhat the level of manual labor left behind. There is a further dimension to be envisaged that could (and some say will) complicate the situation: environmental flight. The French environmentalist Nicolas Hulot, writing in the Parisian weekly review *L'Obs*, alerted readers to the very real possibility of waves of "climate refugees" seeking haven from low-lying regions flooded by the melting of Greenland's ice cap, glaciers and Antarctica.[4]

This becomes much more complex (see Box 13.2) as climate change also affects food production and security, thus causing refugee situations whereby even farmers can no longer sustain themselves. Climate refugees and associated migration (intra- and transnational) may grow into a global phenomenon.

Thus survival remains the basic push forward. Displacement is today relatively easy, too – when not impossible because of immigration or citizenship restrictions – and less costly than ever before when normal means of transport are available.

Box 13.2 The coherence of (western) inconsistency

"We have been taught that the collapse of the Roman Empire was brought on by, and itself encouraged, great influxes of barbarian peoples. . . [T]he temptation to draw impressively thick lines on maps leads us to overstate the migrations or invasions of discrete 'tribes.' Movement of peoples and cultures is likely to have been a more piecemeal affair, a continual drift born out of never-ending changes in circumstance."

Source: Roger Osborne, *Civilization, A New History of the Western World*

The haven-seeking and survival factors account largely for the concrete, material motivations of determined migrants. The material aspect has a complement, an abstract factor that pushes populations to decide to move elsewhere, quickly and now, whatever the obstacles. This is the acceptance of dooming foresight: *There is no future here for me, for you, for any of us. It is time to go!*

A migrant may emigrate to a country where he or she will remain, unnaturalized, a foreign resident (who may be taxed). Or he/she may become naturalized, a full citizen usually subject to taxation. The two cases may generate funds to be transferred, at least in part, to the migrant's country of origin to ease the economic burden of those remaining behind.

Once migrants have adjusted to their new circumstances, funds sent home can be substantial. Philippine women working as nurses or household help in affluent spots such as Hong Kong, or Central American families picking fruit in North American orchards, for example, transfer not insignificant amounts annually to help relieve poverty back home. (Male chauvinism in certain societies, one should add, is also a factor inciting the emigration of women to more tolerant soil.) The irony and unfortunate complexity here is that these migrants often earn next to nothing, with little or no social protection, in high-income and so-called advanced national economies.

Pressure and counter-pressure

Continuing our analysis (see also Box 13.3), a result of the existence of migration is "immigration is not merely a way out of an impasse; it is also the exercise of freedom of movement."[5] In the minds of many, this kind of freedom, moreover, has become more of a *right* and less of a *privilege*.

Box 13.3   Factors influencing population movements, 1987–2006[6]

- Increased urbanization in emigration-inducing countries
- "Metropolization" of migrants (literate urbanites feel squeezed out)
- Consumerism/freedom as attraction offered by rich countries
- Expansion of free-circulation space: EU, U.S./Canada, Nordic states[7]
- Encouragement by successful migrants of those still "back home"
- Extension during 1990s of refugee status and rights to African Great Lakes, Algeria, Balkans, Kurdish zones and southwest Asia in general, Sri Lanka, Central America: "imposed" immigration for willing host countries
- Growing facility of exit from disadvantaged or deprived countries; female employment is easier in the democracies; evolution of a "transit economy"

- Family and development-association stimulus; cultural and religious solidarity
- New globalization networks unrelated to earlier colonial patterns. The reader will note that these urge-to-move-on factors were operative before the economically depressed years of 2007–2009 and the Arab Spring of 2011.

The rise in urbanization mentioned at the top of the list in Box 13.3 is complemented by a diminution of rural populations. France's minister of the environment during François Hollande's presidency, Ségolène Royal, maintained excellent diplomatic relations with various sub-Sahelian governments in Africa. Commenting on demographic issues preparatory to France's hosting of the COP 21 world climate change conference in 2015, Royal told a public broadcaster that for every bloc of 20 million in Africa's rural population, there are 1.5 million (7.5 percent) who regularly abandon the countryside to swell urban areas.

There are other sorts of displacement. Political chaos and failing states, for example – including Libya, Somalia, Syria and Venezuela – are adequate reason for massive departures to safe havens elsewhere. The great influx to continental Europe of refugees/migrants/terrorists from the Middle East and the northern regions of Africa, 2014–2017, is treated in Chapter 11 on international relations and diplomacy.

This is no longer a hide-and-seek game between immigration police and some clandestine groups dispatched by ingenious traffickers. The massive nature of . . . departures [from Africa], the determination of those leaving, the sophisticated gear used (GPS with compass for successful navigation), the entire effort shows that the phenomenon under way is an historic one.

And by such massive departures, "these men and women are perhaps obeying a survival instinct. As yesteryear in Europe, there were millions in successive waves leaving Europe to colonize America."[8] Several years ago, three unemployed young men encountered one of your authors in a fishing village near Dakar, Senegal. Conversation revealed that all three had their first degrees in agricultural engineering, yet they had been unable to find work at that level. Proud of their training, they refused to accept lesser jobs, preferring continued unemployment and hand-outs from their families. Young people such as these are candidates for travel far from home.

It must be added that, after having paid unscrupulous traffickers often several and sometimes many thousands of dollars for passage on unsafe craft with little life-saving equipment aboard and equally little to eat and drink, most would-be immigrants are (for the time being) apprehended upon arrival at their destination and usually treated decently, but are sequestered and may be scheduled for return to their countries of origin or embarkation.

At the same time, the frictions and violent protest generated by immigration events can be harmful to the democratic processes so carefully nurtured in many nations during the last two centuries. If we look at anti-minority politics in California of the 1990s, for instance, we find not a few political operators involved. When California's Propositions 187 (restricting immigration) and 209 (abandoning the U.S. policy of affirmative action) were to be voted, organized lobbies "with the backing of some politicians took the issue outside the political parties and the legislature . . . and waged a costly television campaign. They won, and both propositions became law."[9] The victory, for America's conservative Republican Party, was achieved with neither legislative debate nor compromise.

Movements on the right in the EU successfully thwarted admission of refugees in Hungary, Slovakia, the Czech Republic, Austria and Poland despite overall EU policy favoring such entry. The tipping points, whether real or imagined, in all these immigration complexities was the taking of jobs of natives by alien arrivals seeking work – any work.

Migration and asylum policy

In the case of California's Proposition 187,

> the Republican victory backfired completely, since it branded [the party] as mean-spirited, anti-immigrant and anti-minority – the last a bad label to be stuck with in California . . . The proposition was also badly written, so that most of [Proposition] 187 has since been knocked down by the courts. . . [and] even if one were in favor of both propositions, the manner in which they were enacted into law was crude and counterproductive. The centuries-old method of lawmaking [on the other hand] . . . produces laws that are regarded as legitimate even by people who disagree with them,[10]

whereas "laws that pay no attention to the forces of supply and demand end up as costly failures."[11]

During the German presidency of the EU in 2007, Berlin wanted to see the EU veer toward a more coherent policy regarding immigration and asylum. One recalls that a policy implemented during the days of the country's economic miracle of the 1960s was massive importation of factory labor, primarily from Turkey. In 2007, the German government expressed its readiness to cooperate more closely with the European Commission and its visa policy, to help combat illegal migration and visa abuse.

Among the questions linked to migration inwards, Germany has sought

> a coherent policy integrating analysis of the motivations for [refugee] flight, humanitarian cooperation and development, the struggle against poverty, and the requirement of re-admission [of refugees] by countries of origin and

transit . . . The EU must pursue dialogue with countries of [refugee] origin and transit, especially with neighbors to the east and southeast.[12]

This represents part of the formidable background for the welcoming reception in 2015–2016 of an unexpectedly large influx of migrants. In its 8 November 2015 edition, the New York Times Magazine reported that in war areas "nearly 60 million people were displaced" from their roots by war and persecution – "more than at any time" since the Second World War. Children, furthermore, made up half this number.

In contrast to German procedures intended to rationalize the process of immigration, Japan has assumed a stance of prolonged hesitation on the subject. With the national birth rate in steady decline for decades, the Japanese population is quickly growing disproportionately older. As seniors become top-heavy on the demographic bell-curve, it is clear that future birthrates are not likely to meet the country's economic needs 20 to 40 years hence. But Japan remains adamant about a national policy of almost zero immigration, resisting what it calls *gaiatsu*, or external pressures (although some recent court decisions have tended to favor the would-be immigrant). The alien remains, for the foreseeable future, the victim of established prejudice: what the British historian Roger Osborne terms "constricting human diversity by rejecting 'outsiders.'"[13]

Is the immigrant an intruder?

Former French President Nicolas Sarkozy has stressed that no nation belonging to the EU should have the unilateral authority to "regularize massively its illegal immigrants" without prior consultation with other member states of the EU.[14] Note also the remarks in Box 13.4. Sarkozy has also championed the setting up by the EU of processing and filtration centers outside the EU – although he failed to suggest how to negotiate and finance these. Such centers would be, quite obviously, of little attraction to countries about to lose part of their own population, and therefore appear non-negotiable. Emigration standards should be observed, in other words, to the letter of international agreements.

Box 13.4   The chances of immigrants for employment[15] (in the years before the 2014–2017 immigration to Europe)

Male income differences in	Italy are	30 percent less than those of native-born.
	France	22
	Spain	18
	Australia	12
	Germany	8

Employment probability in	Denmark is	25 percent *less than* for the native-born.
	France	23
	Germany	12
	Austria, Spain and Finland	9

The newcomer in a given society is inevitably viewed with curiosity: sometimes with expectations, sometimes with apprehension and occasionally with revulsion. The arrival on the scene of the immigrant has become, not infrequently, a reaction locally of outright fear. After the surge of terrorist attacks on commercial aircraft that began in the 1970s, the "foreigner in our midst" often became the object of more concern than mere curiosity. Since the attacks in the United States of 11 September 2001, an aim of some societies has become one of not simply anticipating the next attack, but preventing something that is "different from the threat of full-scale invasion by a great power. More important, what we face [years later] is likely to be a permanent condition, and this means we need new rules." If we fail to "think through the basic structure of rules, rights and protections that we want, every new attack will produce creeping but permanent limits on freedom."[16] Such trends led *The Economist* to publish, somewhat later, a cover editorial titled "The New Political Divide," meaning the distinction between those states displaying welcome signs to newcomers and those declaring "Keep out."[17]

Changes at home are therefore a preoccupation of those hostile to non-selective immigration (or, in extreme cases, to any immigration). An Australian critical of his government's revised stand on immigrants claimed that "at issue" is the government's desire to change the way Australia deals with migrants. Christopher S. Mulligan of Sydney wrote to the press,

> [Prime Minister John] Howard's government has . . . abandoned the policy and use of the word "multiculturalism," with its connotation of pluralism and diversity, in favor of the newly sanctioned policy of "integration," which promotes strict, paternalistic adherence to Australian values. . . [including] equality and respect.

Mulligan expressed doubt that "a nationalistic exam will make new migrants better citizens."[18]

Realities of attitudes toward migratory movement

Public sentiment for or against immigration may be as migratory as the migration statistics themselves. According to strategic analysts by OECD and within the French prime minister's office, by 2005 – 13 years after the signing of the

Schengen "open frontiers" accords – statistics responding to the challenge of migration included the following:

- The EU nations welcomed 75 percent of migrants; Europe was the primary destination, followed by the Asia-Pacific region and North America.
- Women comprised 49.6 percent of all migrants.
- Settling migrants earned permanent papers for reasons of family consolidation, professional qualification or asylum in Australia, Canada, New Zealand and the United States.
- Labor migration (contractors, trainees, seasonal help, and employees of transnational firms) in Europe numbered 6.4 million in 1990; the figure rose to 9.6 million in 2005 (within a total foreign population of 20 million).
- Family migration, especially in Europe, accounted (as one example) for more than 70 percent of migrants to France from 1990 to 2002.
- Refugees and asylum seekers diminished from 18.5 million in 1990 to 13.5 million by 2005.
- Illegal migrants, 12 million of them in the United States alone, may have numbered as many as 20 million throughout the world.

The data noted earlier as well as the details in Box 13.5 are subject to change sharply since the appearance of the new "boat people" in the Mediterranean and the continuing displacement – sometimes, when not at sea, entirely on foot – of hundreds of thousands of people. They flee war zones and religious persecution in the Middle East and economic privation or political oppression in Africa: the mass migrations of 2014–2017.

Box 13.5 Highlights of UN *International Migration Report* 2015

The number of international migrants worldwide has continued to grow rapidly over the past 15 years reaching 244 million in 2015, up from 222 million in 2010 and 173 million in 2000.

Nearly two-thirds of all international migrants live in Europe (76 million) or Asia (75 million). Northern America hosted the third largest number of international migrants (54 million), followed by Africa (21 million), Latin America and the Caribbean (9 million) and Oceania (8 million).

In 2015, two-thirds (67 percent) of all international migrants were living in just 20 countries. The largest number of international migrants (47 million) resided in the United States of America, equal to about a fifth (19 percent) of the world's total. Germany and the Russian Federation hosted the second and third largest numbers of migrants worldwide (12 million each), followed by Saudi Arabia (10 million).

In 2014, the total number of refugees in the world was estimated at 19.5 million. Turkey became the largest refugee-hosting country worldwide, with 1.6 million refugees, followed by Pakistan (1.5 million), Lebanon (1.2 million), and the Islamic Republic of Iran (1.0 million). More than half (53 percent) of all refugees worldwide came from just three countries: the Syrian Arab Republic (3.9 million), Afghanistan (2.6 million), and Somalia (1.1 million).

Women comprise slightly less than half of all international migrants. The share of female migrants fell from 49 percent in 2000 to 48 percent in 2015. Female migrants outnumber male migrants in Europe and Northern America, while in Africa and Asia, particularly Western Asia, migrants are predominantly men.

The median age of international migrants worldwide was 39 years in 2015, a slight increase from 38 years in 2000. Yet in some major areas, the migrant stock is becoming younger. Between 2000 and 2015, the median age of international migrants declined in Asia, Latin America and the Caribbean and Oceania.

Most migrants worldwide originate from middle-income countries (157 million in 2015). Between 2000 and 2015, the number of migrants originating from middle-income countries increased more rapidly than those from countries in any other income group. The majority of migrants from middle-income countries were living in a high- income country.

In 2015, of the 244 million international migrants worldwide, 104 million (43 percent), were born in Asia. Europe was the birthplace of the second largest number (62 million or 25 percent), followed by Latin America and the Caribbean (37 million or 15 percent) and Africa (34 million or 14 percent).

In 2015, India had the largest "diaspora" in the world (16 million), followed by Mexico (12 million). Other countries with large diasporas included the Russian Federation (11 million), China (10 million), Bangladesh (7 million), and Pakistan and Ukraine (6 million, each).

Between 2000 and 2015, positive net migration contributed to 42 percent of the population growth in Northern America and 32 percent in Oceania. In Europe the size of the population would have fallen between 2000 and 2015 in the absence of positive net migration.

The ratification of UN legal instruments related to international migrants and migration remains uneven. As of October 2015, 36 Member States had ratified all five of the UN legal instruments related to international migration, while 14 Member States had ratified none of the relevant instruments.

Since the 1994 International Conference on Population and Development, the issue of international migration and its relation to development has risen steadily on the agenda of the international community. The 2030

Agenda for Sustainable Development not only includes several migration-related targets but also encourages countries to disaggregate targets by, inter alia, migratory status. An attitude of firm determination confronted (Box 13.6) a risk factor no less daunting.

Source: UN DESA 2016

EU figures released on the number of all arrivals in the first nine months of 2015 totaled 770,000, adding to an EU population in the same year of about 508 million. Of the total transients, there were 63 percent men, 25 percent women and 12 percent children, although these figures remain subject to continuing adjustment after the event.

Box 13.6   Unexpected complexities

The extraordinary resettlement of migrants in Germany . . . met unexpected results for Chancellor Angela Merkel. Her long and successful mandate as her country's leader was marred by resistance to the newcomers and pressure from a combination of the extreme right and populist groups to halt their inflow. Merkel responded publicly with the remark that "We can handle [the situation], and we will."

Source: *Time* (European ed.), 2 May 2016, p. 67

Current numbers notwithstanding, it is of more than passing interest that the *rate* of migration has diminished during the past century. Catherine Wihtol de Wenden, a specialist in migration and citizenship at the Centre National de Recherche Scientifique in Paris, using UN statistics, calculates that 5 percent of the world's population in the early 1900s was migratory. The figure for today is 3 percent which, when translated into absolute numbers, comes to the 190-million total cited for the year 2005 (see Box 13.5). Wihtol de Wenden mentions also that 2007 was the year that the International Convention on the Protection of Migrant Workers and Their Families (2003) came into force, although ratified that far by only 34 governments. These states, she asserted, are now "ready to cooperate in order better to manage a flow that will, at any rate, continue."[19]

New impulses, obstacles, indirect results

Although we have barely looked at the migratory phenomenon as the soft system we called it earlier in this chapter, it is a system, and recognized as such by the

UN's International Organization for Migration (IOM) and the UN High Commissioner for Refugees (UNHCR), both based in Geneva, Switzerland. The IOM alone, tending to the mass logistics (e. g., temporary shelters for the populations in transit through numerous countries), does what it can with an annual budget in the $2 billion category and a staff of some 8,000 specialists. The UNHCR limits the scope of its concerns to the plight and resettlement of people in *bona fide* flight from political or police oppression and violence, although, as we write, the UNHCR may henceforth narrow the definition of what a *refugee* is (and, therefore, is not).

Prevention of abuses at the source – thereby thwarting the would-be migrant's impulse to flee – is a measure not easily undertaken by the most well-meaning of nations. Such action would be repudiated as interference by outside influences in a country's internal affairs. Yet the aspirations of migrants exist and will continue, permutating into a host of factors particular to families or individuals: economic, social, cultural, moral/religious, and often any number of these in combination. If, of the statistic of 770,000 individuals evoked earlier, each person has two sound reasons to pull up stakes and go elsewhere, we immediately face the challenge of helping to satisfy about 1.5 million discrete motivations. (The total, real number of personal reasons is obviously much higher.)

What are the effects on the countries left behind by migrants? Other than a reduced demographic count, the combined loss of many pairs of hands with brain drain will leave economic and cultural scars. Time will probably heal these, but the period required could be costly in terms of a country's facility to master its overall development and civilizational advance.

As to receiving countries, their established division of labor – and their attitudes and policies regarding employment – will dictate, for the most part, where to place whom and how many, as well as where in terms of economic sector. As a result, there will likely be a swelling of the host country's menial-labor force because jobs for street sweepers and waste management staff will be quickly filled, as will those on construction crews, for lesser hospital staff and in food-handling establishments.

We have seen that the strategy and planning of today's determined migrants may be matched by resistance in the countries accepting them. Nevertheless, policies of host nations are essentially welcoming, with the exception of the few countries selecting their immigrants according to vocational utility to the national economy or, as in the case of several central and eastern European states during the crush of migration in 2015, on the basis of migrants' religious convictions.

Extended significance

After the almost unrestrained globalization of the years 1990–2007, "[p]oliticians and their constituents in the United States, Europe and China [grew] increasingly nervous about letting capital, goods, and people move freely across their borders," emphasize two specialists commenting in *Foreign Affairs*.[20] "Although globalization as a process will continue to sputter along," they add,

> The idea of unrestrained globalization will wane in force . . . As the integration of national economies stalls, maintaining the high degree of openness already established will require deft management . . . to ensure [that its benefits] are distributed more equally.

This is an opinion shared today by many; it is logically an extension of the complexity of the migratory "system."

In a January 2007 report titled *Migration and Remittances*, the World Bank had pointed out that funds sent home by migrant workers abroad can be an impressive portion of a migrant-exporting country's GDP. In Haiti, Tonga and Moldova, remittances from abroad exceed 25 percent of GDP. In countries of the former Soviet bloc, remittances from abroad vary from about 12 percent of GDP in Serbia and Tajikistan to over 4 percent for Hungary and Macedonia. Another view is that displacement compelled by the lure of emigration is not likely to ease very soon. Economist Philippe Legrain, in his book *Immigrants: Your Country Needs Them*,[21] supports open borders and emphasizes that the net advantage of money sent from abroad – instead of finding its way into tax-haven bank accounts – goes straightaway, and advantageously, into the pockets of the local poor.

As the global population heads to some 9.5–10 (or even 11 billion) billion by the year 2050, Bruno Hérault, recently of the French government's Strategic Analysis Center, notes that while refugees and asylum seekers were down in number by one-third between 1990 and 2005, there are currently more than 20 million illegal workers throughout the world.[22] The facility of movement ensured by the globalization process probably means a further increase, although guesswork projection must be avoided. The Greek government stated in this respect, on the eve of the new year of 2016, that over 3,000 Syrian refugees were still making their way to Europe daily through the Turkey-Greece gate of entry.

There is, however, an unavoidable omission in our analysis here because we are unable to compute blemishes on a largely irregular and formless but continuing system: namely, how many fabricated refugees and other false migrants may be camouflaged among those legitimately displaced and eager to move on to auspicious resettlement. We include in this category some traffickers, themselves ever seeking new opportunities to exploit the defenseless, as well as terrorists with special missions or agendas. The Belgian, British, French, German, Spanish, Turkish and other governments know such subterfuges. The process can be mystifyingly complex – one to be attacked by sound police work, although stumbles will surely remain in what there is of system in the migratory world.

Both the UN and regional groupings such as the EU and the OECD urge developed countries to broaden their efforts to integrate immigrants, not only in the workforce but in society as a whole. The Paris-based OECD, for example, stresses how migration alleviates labor shortages; migration's effects on tax revenue; and the relationship between migration, demography and general economic growth.

As for the EU, we explained in the chapter on international relations and diplomacy the studied attention lent in decades past to the orderly assembly and function of this ambitious alliance. With London's Brexit decision of 2016 and President Donald Trump's (initially) critical views of the EU, combined with new hesitations by other Union members, the future of the EU may be shaky. If this multi-nation undertaking should fail, one of the major contributing factors will have been the large-scale anomalies engendered by the migratory initiatives of the young 21st century.

Concluding the inconcludable

There is a reverse side of the coin, however. In North America and Western Europe, invasive job seekers divest native jobholders of much welcome and sympathy for the new arrivals. Under the supervision of the OECD's Director-General José Ángel Gurría, that institution has made problems of migration one of its currently four major priorities, together with development, health care and water supply.[23]

The topic of migration complexity cannot be left without reference to citizen-generated aid and relief offered to new arrivals. Civic associations and other voluntary groups in Germany, France, Italy and elsewhere rolled up their sleeves to provide language lessons, household effects and, above all, enrollment in schools of the immigrants' children. Jobs would come later, as official regulations often prohibit the acceptance of work before the expiry of six months.

Migration is human activity at its most hopeful; it is also one of luck. Hazard or, accident, its complications and complexity seem unlimited. The unraveling of such knots needs as much imagination and dynamism from those helping to find solutions as the migrants themselves have energy and aspirations. Within the perimeter of the OECD, the socioeconomic onus of the migratory movement across the Mediterranean falls on the shoulders of the EU. By July 2017, another 84,000 arrivals appeared in Italy during the previous six months. The unending flow caused the Rome government to convene with officials from Paris and Madrid, calling on the latter and other EU capitals to open their ports to illegal crossers. Despite continuing EU reluctance, mounting pressures could lead to new solutions: the prosecution abroad of passers, voluntary restraining measures imposed by countries of departure (such as Libya) to limit the outbound flow, marked improvement of living conditions in circum-Sahelian Africa – almost certainly with financial subsidies provided by a hesitant EU. But any such moves will consume time.

From the maze of uncertainty and doubt which so often characterizes the world of migrants, we move on now to an area of human enterprise better known for its intentionable order and systematic approach to its own complexities: the realm of sustainable development.

Notes

1 Dhananjayan Sriskandarajah, "Britain at the Corssroads," *International Herald Tribune*, 15 December 2006, p. 8.
2 According to the National Institute of Statistics and Economic Research (INSEE), Paris, 12 October 2015.
3 Dominique Moïsi, "The Global Clash of Emotions," *International Herald Tribune*, 15 December 2006, p. 8. Moïsi evokes the same theme in a major article in the January–February 2007 issue of *Foreign Affairs*.
4 See cover article, "Climate, the Planetary Challenge" (in French), *L'Obs*, 12 November 2015, pp. 37–41.
5 Philippe Fargues, "Afrique et Moyen-Orient: migrations en quête d'une politique" (Africa and the Middle East: Migrations in Search of A Policy), *Politique étrangère*, no. 4, 2006, p. 1022.
6 Bruno Hérault, "Mondialisation et migrations internationales," *Dossiers de la mondialisation*, no. 5, November–December 2006, Paris: CAG, pp. 2–3.
7 Family members of Sweden's [then] minister for integration and gender, Nyamko Sabuni, were admitted to Sweden as political refugees from the Democratic Republic of Congo when Sabuni was 12 years old. In 2005, Sweden processed 2,330 immigration applications from Iraq, 8,951 in 2006.
8 The text is by Modou Mamoune Faye, as reproduced in *Courrier international*, 19 October 2006, p. 36.
9 Fareed Zakaria, *The Future of Freedom, Illiberal Democracy at Home and Abroad*, New York, NY: W.W. Norton, 2003, p. 195.
10 *Ibid*, pp. 195–196.
11 Fareed Zakaria, "Time to Solve Immigation" (editorial), *Newsweek* (European ed.), 8 January 2007, p. 23.
12 "EU 2007, Ensemble, nous réussirons l'Europe" (Together, We Shall Succeed with Europe), Programme de la présidence 1er janvier-30 juin 2007 [French version of official German government document], December 2007, pp. 18–19.
13 Roger Osborne, *Civilization: A New History of the Western World*, New York, NY: Pegasus Books, 2006, p. 211.
14 Reported extensively in the mass media on 15 January 2007.
15 Hérault, *op. cit.*, p. 4.
16 Fareed Zakaria, "Habeas Corpus on the Ropes in A Shadowy War" (review), *International Herald Tribune*, 16 December 2006, p. 8.
17 See *The Economist* of 30 July 2016.
18 In a letter to the editor, *International Herald Tribune*, 30 December 2006, p. 5.
19 Catherine Wihtol de Wenden, "Un monde en migrations" (A World in Migration), *Les Echos*, 16 January 2007, p. 21.
20 Rawi Abdelal and Adam Segal, "Has Globalization Passed Its Peak?" *Foreign Affairs*, January–February 2007, pp. 104–105.
21 Philippe Legrain, *Immigrants: Your Country Needs Them*, London: Little, Brown, 2006.
22 Hérault, *op. cit.*, p. 4.
23 As specified in French public radio reporting on world migration, Paris, 6 December 2006.

14 Sustainable development
Homo sapiens' Holy Grail

Introduction

We leave the errant human being, whether mass peregrinations be voluntary or forced to analyze our species' well-being in a world confronted by a growing population and the concerns of everyone about the acceleration of consumption of nature's richness.

The year 2015 was decisive for future development of today's globalized society. The year had been the time line for the MDGs and the kick-off for their successor aims, the Sustainable Development Goals (SDGs), approved by the UN General Assembly also in 2015. The second most important event was the 21st meeting of the Conference of the Parties (COP 21) to the UN Framework Convention for Climate Change (UNFCCC), held in December 2015 in Paris. Thirdly, 2015 marked the mid-point of the time line of the Strategic Plan for Biodiversity of the CBD and its associated Aichi Targets (2020).

All these efforts are part of a bigger picture: A pressing need of the global community to secure a sustainable future for humankind through translating sustainable development into reality at all levels of socioeconomic evolution. Sustainable development has been the Holy Grail during the last decades when environmental problems, globalization and above all a continuously growing population raised serious questions about the carrying capacity of humans on planet Earth. These are well reflected in the title of the book published by Joel Cohen, a mathematical biologist at the Rockefeller University in New York and at the Earth Institute of Columbia University, in 1995, *How Many People Can the Earth Support?*

Almost 45 years ago the famous report to the Club of Rome, entitled *The Limits to Growth* (Meadows et al. 1972), identified global challenges for the future of mankind and reached the following conclusions:

1 If the present growth trends in world population, industrialization, pollution, food production and resource depletion continue unchanged, the limits to growth on this planet will be reached sometime within the next 100 years. The most probable result will be a rather sudden and uncontrollable decline in both population and industrial capacity.

2 It is possible to alter these growth trends and to establish a condition of ecological and economic stability that is sustainable far into the future. The state of global equilibrium could be designed so that the basic material needs of each person on earth are satisfied and each person has an equal opportunity to realize his individual human potential.
3 If the world's people decide to strive for this second outcome rather than the first, the sooner they begin working to attain it, the greater will be their chances of success.

This report was preceded by earlier debates, based on cybernetics and systemic thinking or systems analysis, both disciplines which were in their early stages of development, stimulated by Jay W. Forrester of MIT. Forrester was a specialist in computer simulations, later followed by the German economist and mechanical engineer Eduard Pestel. Pestel spoke of meta-problems and put emphasis on five factors affecting humanity in its entirety: population development, food production, industrialization, natural resources, and environmental contamination (for further details of the "gestation process" of the report see, e.g., Grober 2010). Complexity was already perceived as an important facet of global development and built into the models of Dennis Meadows and his co-workers. In fact, *Limits to Growth* has been one of the most influential environmental books. As Meadows outlined at the Smithsonian 2012 event on the occasion of the 40th anniversary of *Limits*, the book was meant to be an exercise in thinking. Today it has more serious readers than when it was first published.

In 1993 a 20-year update of *Limits*, the book *Beyond the Limits*, was published. In 2004, *Limits to Growth: The 30-Year Update* came out. No official update was published in 2012, but Jorgen Randers, one of the co-authors of *Limits*, brought out the book *2052: A Global Forecast for the Next Forty Years*. In 2015 Dennis Meadows hit the nail right on its head when stating that the issues raised in *Limits* and these subsequent reports "are not themselves problems; they are symptoms. The problem is continued material growth on a physically finite world" (Meadows 2015).

From a historical perspective, the modern movement toward sustainable development started with global concerns about the environment in the 1960s and saw several major events up to the present. Some of these events are presented next. The processes underlying this path toward sustainable development ultimately reflect how a multi-stakeholder setup copes with different facets of an overly complex issue.

From environmental concerns to sustainable development – before the "Rio Process"

The concept of sustainable development evolved along two major lines. First, the notion of sustainability was created by the German forester Hans Carl von Carlowitz in the late 17th century. He was tasked with sustaining wood supply for the mining sector in Saxony. In his major work *Sylvicultura oeconomica* he

212 Sustainable development

outlines the principles of sustainable forest utilization. This is described in detail in the account of the cultural history of the term sustainability published by the German journalist Ulrich Grober in 2010. The second major impetus came from serious environmental concerns, in particular with regard to environmental pollution during the 20th century. A few of the many contributions to the debate of environmental issues which eventually led to the development of the modern concept of sustainable development and its international recognition follow.

1962. Silent Spring

A landmark publication was Rachel Carson's 1962 publication *Silent Spring*. The title was meant metaphorically, suggesting a bleak future for the whole natural world. Carson expressed serious concerns about agricultural practices and in particular the use of synthetic pesticides and their impacts on plants, animals and humans. Two factors were of concern, viz. the building up of critical pollution in the environment and the geographic spread of DDT, through the food chains and through systems interlinked from local to global scales. The accumulation and residual character of DDT and its detection at almost global level for the first time showed in a very drastic manner the connectedness of our ecological systems. The book had an enormous response and influenced thinking on the environment to an unexpected degree. Most notably, Al Gore wrote the introduction to the 1992 edition of the book. As Dorothy McLaughlin, in an article for the American Public Broadcasting Service put it, "Despite attempts by the chemical industry to dismiss Carson's science, her work is credited with beginning the American environmental movement, the creation of the Environmental Protection Agency, and the 1972 ban on DDT."

1968. The Biosphere Conference

In 1968, UNESCO held its *Intergovernmental Conference of Experts on the Scientific Basis for Rational Use and Conservation of the Resources of the Biosphere* or in short: The Biosphere Conference. The meeting not only introduced the term *biosphere* to the international community, but it was the first global scientific and intergovernmental meeting focusing on environmental problems and their growing importance. The conference report amply illustrates the comprehensive range of issues brought to the fore among delegates from over 60 countries, representatives of 14 intergovernmental organizations, 13 NGOs and other participants (see Hadley 2006a, for further details). In fact, the Biosphere Conference was the first intergovernmental forum to introduce and promote what is now called *sustainable development* (Hadley 2006b). This was 24 years prior to the 1992 UN Conference on Environment and Development (UNCED, see the following).

1972. UN Conference on the Human Environment

The UN Conference on the Human Environment or *Stockholm Conference* not only developed ideas raised in UNESCO's Biosphere Conference further, but is seen as a key meeting preparatory to the emergence of *sustainable development*. The conference was shaped by pollution and acid rain problems – i.e., issues of the North ("industrialized country concerns") rather than the problems the South was facing. Nevertheless, the conference led to the establishment of many national environmental protection agencies and most importantly it created UNEP, the UN Environment Program (for details see Johnson 2012). Although included only in a few of its recommendations the conference saw environment and development as an integrated whole, and UNEP was – contrary to the proposal of the Secretariat of the Conference – designed **not** to be another intergovernmental organization but rather a "program" (Adams 2009). This has been a recurring issue since then. The needs of developing countries were addressed only in meetings to come after the Stockholm conference.

1980. World Conservation Strategy

In 1948, UNESCO, the Government of France and the Swiss League of Nature convened a conference in Fontainebleau, France, which gave birth to the International Union for Conservation of Nature (IUCN). At that time it was called IUPN, the International Union for the Protection of Nature and Natural Resources (1948–1956), followed by International Union for the Conservation of Nature and Natural Resources (IUCN), World Conservation Union (1990–2008), and now known (again) as the International Union for Conservation of Nature or IUCN (for details of the context see Hadley 2006a).

In 1980, IUCN published the *World Conservation Strategy* (WCS), a milestone in the process toward "globalizing" sustainable development (IUCN 1980). This was preceded by debates on conservation and development at IUCN General Assemblies in 1969 and 1972 and the formation of the Ecosystem Conservation Group in 1975. The Group comprised UNEP, UNESCO, FAO and IUCN. UNEP commissioned IUCN to draft the Strategy. What was originally cast as a conservation-related document was changed into a text including aspects of population growth, resources and development. IUCN, UNEP and WWF finally published the document including amendments by FAO and UNESCO. The World Conservation Strategy was born of the environmental thinking of the 1970s and focused on sustainability rather than the development trajectory (details Adams 2009). It was also criticized for failing to "come to grips with the central issue of economic growth, as the motor behind development" (Redclift 1987, p. 52) and "to recognize the political nature of the development process. . . [and] was also simplistic in what it had to say about economic development" (Adams 2009, p. 74).

Nevertheless, the Strategy not only contained a section on Sustainable Development but also contributed importantly to spreading the notion as comprising economic, social and environmental dimensions, despite its focus on conservation rather than environment. Moreover, the Strategy had already anticipated what was later to be named *ecosystem services*. The term became widely known through the MEA (see the following).

214 *Sustainable development*

Before the Brundtland Conference took place, progress since the publication of the World Conservation Strategy was summarized, and it was proposed to revise the document. This revision appeared in 1991 entitled *Caring for the Earth: A Strategy for Sustainable Living* (IUCN 1991). Ideas and content were directly used in the process of preparing for the upcoming conference in Rio and its associated statements (for details see Adams 2009).

1987. Brundtland Report

The next milestone following the World Conservation Strategy was the well-received Brundtland Report, *Our Common Future*, published in 1987. Major environmental issues between the publication of the Strategy in 1970 and the report were the detection of the Antarctic ozone hole (1985) and the Chernobyl disaster (1986).

The Brundtland Report of the World Commission on Environment and Development (WCED), established in 1983 and chaired by then Prime Minister of Norway, Gro Harlem Brundtland. As she wrote in the foreword to the book: "I was being asked to help formulate a third and compelling call for political action: After Brandt's *Program for Survival* and *Common Crisis*, and after Palme's *Common Security*, would come *Common Future*." The "Brundtland definition" is probably the most frequently used and cited definition of sustainable development: "Sustainable development is development that meets the needs of the present without compromising the ability of future generations to meet their own needs." This translates into a *trans-generational responsibility* for each human generation. The report also realized the interconnected nature of our global problems: environmental crisis, development crisis and energy crisis. The report referred to them as "interlocking crises" (p. 4) thus anticipating that systems from different domains are interconnected.

Commission members realized that development trajectories of the time led to increased poverty and vulnerability and at the same time further degradation of the environment. The new development path to be taken should ensure "sustained human progress not just in a few places for a few years, but *for the entire planet into the distant future*" (italics ours). *Our Common Future* put enormous emphasis on fostering economic growth. It did not consider balancing growth against demands in energy and raw materials or how to cope with pollution and decouple economic growth from continued impacts on natural ecosystems and associated loss of their biodiversity.

The "Rio Process"

1992. UNCED

In 1992, the UN Conference on Environment and Development (UNCED), also referred to as *Earth Summit*, took place in Rio de Janeiro, Brazil. This was five years after the release of the Brundtland Report and meant to look into progress made since. It was one of three mega-conferences to come, named aptly the Rio

Conference, Rio+10 (2002, Johannesburg), and Rio+20 (2012, again in Rio). The five years following *Our Common Future* was a time of intense preparations for UNCED conferences, meetings, reports on issues related to environment and development. There were five meetings of the Preparatory Committee. At each of them all member states of the UN were represented. Attendance was enormous. At the conference 172 member states were present including 116 heads of state or government, 8000 delegates, 9000 representatives of the press and over 3000 representatives of NGOs were accredited (Adams 2009).

Achievements of the Earth Summit were among others:

1 Documents:

- *Rio Declaration on Environment and Development*
- Agenda 21: Program of Action for Sustainable Development
- Statement on Forest Principles (non-legally binding)

2 The three "Rio Conventions":

- Convention on Biological Diversity (UNCBD; entry into force: 1993)
- Framework Convention on Climate Change (UNFCCC), 1994
- Convention to Combat Desertification (UNCCD), 1996

3 The setting up of the UN Commission on Sustainable Development (UNCSD)

UNCSD comprises government representatives and was tasked with examining progress in the global implementation of Agenda 21.

UNCED deserves an extensive analysis but we have chosen to focus only on aspects of relevance here.

NGOs met in a Global Forum which was "physically and psychologically distant from the main conference" (Adams 2009). Only the most powerful NGOs, mostly from the North, had influence on the outcome documents. The conference saw a dichotomy of interests and priorities between industrialized and non-industrialized countries ("N/S problematique") related to potential interference of the North with development processes in the South. More specifically, this related to the difficulties of cutting down on greenhouse gas emissions in developing countries and (international) restrictions imposed with regard to using their natural resources such as forests. The latter concern was a result of the non-existence of a binding document on the Forest Principles (recommendations for management, conservation and sustainable development of all types of forests); only a statement was produced. Several elements of the *Rio Declaration* were discussed in a controversial manner reflecting the different views and aspirations of developing and developed countries (see Adams 2009, for further details).

The global effort of Rio brought to the fore complexity at various levels and scales:

- With time, the subject of sustainable development turned into an ever more complex theme.

216 *Sustainable development*

- This translated into an array of issues related to the political consensus process underpinning the UN's decision-making machinery.
- Taking into account the diverse stakeholder interests, in particular as regards governments and NGOs, proved to be a major challenge for producing concrete and consensus-based outcomes.
- The evident "need" to handle themes such as biodiversity, climate change and desertification through normative (binding) instruments such as conventions reflected urgencies in these respective domains.

2000. The Millennium Summit

The Millennium Summit was meant to debate the role of the UN in the upcoming 21st century. Throughout their history as far back as 1945, the UN has been in a permanent process of reforming itself.

As put in the relevant UN General Assembly resolution, the summit aimed at seizing "a unique and symbolically compelling moment to articulate and affirm an animating vision for the United Nations." The Summit was the largest gathering of world leaders by that time. Its outcome document is the *Millennium Declaration* which was translated into a framework for future development, the so-called MDGs (Box 14.1). This was in our view the first time that – at global level – targets with a defined time line (2015) were agreed upon by the global community of nation states.

In retrospective, the report *Transforming Our World* of the 2015 UN Summit on Sustainable Development says,

> Almost fifteen years ago, the Millennium Development Goals were agreed. These provided an important framework for development and significant progress has been made in a number of areas. But the progress has been uneven, particularly in Africa, least developed countries, landlocked developing countries, and Small Island Developing States, and some of the MDGs remain off-track, in particular those related to maternal, newborn and child health and to reproductive health. We recommit ourselves to the full realization of all the MDGs, including the off-track MDGs, in particular by providing focussed and scaled-up assistance to least developed countries and other countries in special situations, in line with relevant support programmes. The new Agenda builds on the Millennium Development Goals and seeks to complete what these did not achieve, particularly in reaching the most vulnerable.

Box 14.1   The Millennium Development Goals

Goal 1: Eradicate Extreme Hunger and Poverty
Goal 2: Achieve Universal Primary Education
Goal 3: Promote Gender Equality and Empower Women
Goal 4: Reduce Child Mortality
Goal 5: Improve Maternal Health

> Goal 6: Combat HIV/AIDS, Malaria and Other Diseases
> Goal 7: Ensure Environmental Sustainability
> Goal 8: Develop a Global Partnership for Development
>
> For further details, see United Nations Millennium Project (2005) and individual task force reports.

2002. The World Summit on Sustainable Development

Ten years after the Rio Summit (Rio+10) another mega-conference took place in Johannesburg, South Africa: The World Summit on Sustainable Development (WSSD). WSSD focused on the so-called WEHAB themes: Water, energy, health, agriculture and biodiversity. As Kofi Annan, former secretary-general of the UN noted,

> These five areas make up an ambitious but achievable agenda, in which progress would offer all human beings a chance of achieving prosperity that will not only last their own lifetime, but can be enjoyed by their children and grandchildren too.

The focus on these themes, however, lost momentum on the road from Johannesburg "back to Rio" for the Rio+20 Summit in 2012 (see the following).

The outcome of WSSD:

- The Johannesburg Declaration on Sustainable Development, a political declaration and the main outcome document.
- The Johannesburg Plan of Implementation as an action plan for the future focusing on already existing targets such as the MDGs and a few new commitments.
- The Type II Partnerships – i.e., some 300 non-negotiated partnership initiatives as key means to implement the MDGs by governments and non-government stakeholders.
- Endorsement of the 2010 Biodiversity Target of the Convention on Biological Diversity (further discussed in our chapter on biodiversity).

Since UNCED many problems related to sustainable development had worsened, including the global poverty situation, the gap between the north and the south, regional famines, the financial support for implementation of Agenda 21 and other actions agreed upon at Rio, the lack of expected changes in activities of international companies, and the issue of sovereignty over genetic resources.

Nitin Desai (2002), UN Secretary-General of the Johannesburg Summit and Under-Secretary-General for Economic and Social Affairs, made specifically critical remarks with regard to the implementation of Agenda 21:

> While Agenda 21 remained a powerful, long-term vision that was still valid, there were four main reasons for the implementation gap that has plagued

progress toward sustainable development. Specifically, it [the Secretariat's report of December 2001 on the implementation of Agenda 21] referred to a *fragmented and uncoordinated approach; too few resources; a lack of political will; and continued wasteful patterns of production and consumption.*

(Italics ours)

Adams (2009, and references therein) presented more general critical remarks on the Rio Process:

> The Rio Conference failed to reconcile the different demands of industrialized and developing countries, and failed to bring about the kinds of changes demanded since the Brundtland Report fifteen years before . . . To a large extent momentum was lost . . . policy evolution through the 1990s was grindingly slow.
>
> (p. 108)

Despite all the criticism expressed, WSSD also came up with several achievements. These included *inter alia*

- the broadening and strengthening of the concept of sustainable development by reinforcing the three interdependent and mutually reinforcing economic, social and environmental pillars,
- a clear understanding of the interlinkages between poverty, human rights, biodiversity, clean water and sanitation, renewable energy, and the sustainable use of natural resources,
- the inclusion of targets and timetables into the WSSD Plan of Implementation on key issues such as poverty, unsustainable patterns of consumption and production, biodiversity loss and global health challenges,
- the launch of more than 300 voluntary "Type II" partnerships between governments, NGOs and the business sectors to support efforts to implement sustainable development, and that
- education was reaffirmed as the foundation of sustainable development and the foundation was laid for establishing a UN DESD (2005–2014).

2005. Millennium Ecosystem Assessment (MEA)

The year 2005 was decisive in carrying further work related to sustainable development. This included the entering into force of the Kyoto Protocol, an international treaty to reduce greenhouse gas emissions, and the completion of the *Millennium Ecosystem Assessment*.

Initiated in 2001, the objective of the MEA was "to assess the consequences of ecosystem change for human well-being and to establish the scientific basis for action needed to enhance the conservation and sustainable use of ecosystems and their contributions to human well-being" (MEA 2005). The MEA has involved the work of more than 1,360 experts worldwide.

Sustainable development 219

The main findings of the MEA were (UNEP 2005):

- Over the past 50 years, humans have changed ecosystems more rapidly and extensively than in any comparable period of time in human history, largely to meet rapidly growing demands for food, freshwater, timber, fiber and fuel. This has resulted in a substantial and largely irreversible loss in the diversity of life on Earth.
- The changes that have been made to ecosystems have contributed to substantial net gains in human well-being and economic development, but these gains have been achieved at growing costs in the form of the degradation of many ecosystem services, increased risks of non-linear changes, and the exacerbation of poverty for some groups of people. These problems, unless addressed, will substantially diminish the benefits that future generations obtain from ecosystems.
- The degradation of ecosystem services could grow significantly worse during the first half of this century and is a barrier to achieving the MDGs.
- The challenge of reversing the degradation of ecosystems while meeting increasing demands for services can be partially met under some scenarios considered by the MEA, but will involve significant changes in policies, institutions and practices that are not currently under way. Many options exist to conserve or enhance specific ecosystem services in ways that reduce negative trade-offs or that provide positive synergies with other ecosystem services.

2012. Rio+20

Twenty years after the Rio Summit world governments and a huge NGO community convened in Rio de Janeiro in June 2012 for the so-called Rio+20 Summit. Sustainable development had meanwhile been accepted as a guiding principle for governments, the business sector and civil society and the implementation process has included ever more of the many elements of the "stakeholder community," in particular with regard to involvement of business and NGOs.

Representatives from 191 UN member states and observers, including 79 heads of state or government, engaged in the general debate, and approximately 44,000 badges were issued for official meetings, a Rio+20 Partnerships Forum, Sustainable Development Dialogues, SD-Learning and an estimated 500 side events in RioCentro, the venue for the Conference itself. In closing the Conference, UNCSD President Dilma Rousseff (Brazil) stressed that Rio+20 was the most participatory conference in history and was a "global expression of democracy." Taking place in parallel to the official events, approximately 3,000 unofficial events were organized throughout Rio de Janeiro, Brazil (as reported in Earth Negotiations Bulletin Vol. 27 No. 51, 25 June 2012).

The outcome document of Rio+20 is entitled *The Future We Want* (UN 2012).

There was additional outcome:

- The idea of a green economy was carried, albeit with a "very defensive and highly qualified text in this section of the [outcome] document."
- The agreement reached to launch a process to develop universal Sustainable Development Goals (SDGs) was one of the most important political decisions of the Conference, given its centrality in helping to define the post-2015 development agenda.
- International recognition that humans have become the main driver of global change – i.e., the beginning of a new era called the Anthropocene and the concept of planetary boundaries and its associated notion of a "safe operating space for humanity."
- The launch of the *Future Earth initiative* (see Box 5.6).
- The quest for a new contract between science and society on the issue of sustainable development and the resulting need for a fully integrated science-based approach built on partnerships between the public sector, private sectors and civil society. The relevant Declaration *The Future We Choose* (www.uncsd2012.org, accessed on 1 December 2015), signed by Elders (an independent group of global leaders), Nobel laureates and members of the UN Secretary-General's High Level Panel on Global Sustainability states: "Such an integrated model which reflects the scientific consensus and is guided by the principles of responsibility and equity will and must provide a **systemic solution** that ensures the wise stewardship of the planet and its people" (bold ours).

In the run-up to Rio+20, nevertheless some persistent critical elements came to the fore again. These were compiled by John Drexhage and Deborah Murphy of the International Institute for Sustainable Development (IISD) in their background paper prepared for the first meeting of the High Level Panel on Sustainability, held on 19 September 2010:

- The concept [of sustainable development] remains elusive and implementation has proven difficult.
- Unsustainable trends continue, and SD has not found the political entry points to make real progress.
- Over the last 20 years SD has often been compartmentalized as an environmental issue although supposed to comprise a social and economic pillar as well.
- Development is mostly [still] seen as economic growth only. This is the classical paradigm of developed countries which is being followed by an increasing number of rapidly developing countries.
- There continues to be a huge gap between the multilateral processes and action at the national on-the-ground level.

Drexhage and Murphy (2010) also highlight some of the causes underlying the complex process of realizing sustainable development: Twenty years may have been too short a time to implement the changes required. What is needed is "systemic change ... in the way the world does business." They even argue about a *new sustainable development paradigm* and conclude their executive summary with a remarkable statement: "The opportunity is ripe to move beyond incrementalism to real systemic change."

Both authors, in their concluding chapter, provided almost a blueprint for the Rio+20 Summit. Only the headings of their conclusions are presented here:

- Taking sustainable development out of the environment "box."
- Fundamentally shifting how we develop and evaluate the health of economies.
- Moving to actual implementation, with real accountability.
- Encouraging transparency and accountability in actions.
- Using partnerships between government, business and civil society.
- Effectively communicating sustainable development successes, policies and learning.

The 2015 Summit on Sustainable Development – MDGs, SDGs and the 2030 Development Agenda

The Rio+20 Summit paved the way for casting the post-2015 development agenda including its most essential element, the Sustainable Development Goals (SDGs; Box 14.2). These build upon the MDGs and aim at completing by 2030 what has not been achieved in "areas of critical importance for humanity and the planet" – i.e., the five "Ps": People, Planet, Prosperity, Peace and Partnership (preamble of *Transforming Our World*, see the following).

As highlighted in the report of UN secretary-general Ban Ki-moon on the post-2015 development agenda (UN 2014):

> The cornerstone for the current global process of renewal was established in Rio de Janeiro in June of 2012, with the adoption of the outcome document of the UN Conference on Sustainable Development *The Future We Want*. The document described the lessons learned from two decades of development experience, and provided an extensive assessment of the progress and gaps in the implementation of the sustainable development agenda.

In September 2015, a UN Summit was held in New York, at the UN Headquarters. This Summit adopted the 2030 Agenda. The respective document is entitled *Transforming Our World: The 2030 Agenda For Sustainable Development* (UN 2015a).

As declared by member states in the outcome document of the Rio+20 Conference *The Future We Want* (UN 2012):

> SDGs should be action-oriented, concise and easy to communicate, limited in number, aspirational, global in nature and universally applicable to all countries while taking into account different national realities, capacities and levels of development and respecting national policies and priorities.
>
> (Paragraph 247)

Box 14.2 Sustainable Development Goals and their target areas (bold ours)

Goal 1   End **poverty** in all its forms everywhere
Goal 2   End **hunger**, achieve food security and improved nutrition and promote sustainable agriculture
Goal 3   Ensure **healthy lives** and promote well-being for all at all ages
Goal 4   Ensure inclusive and equitable quality **education** and promote lifelong learning opportunities for all
Goal 5   Achieve **gender equality** and empower all women and girls
Goal 6   Ensure availability and sustainable management of **water and sanitation** for all
Goal 7   Ensure access to affordable, reliable, sustainable and modern **energy** for all
Goal 8   Promote sustained, inclusive and sustainable **economic growth**, full and productive employment and decent work for all
Goal 9   Build resilient **infrastructure**, promote inclusive and sustainable **industrialization** and foster **innovation**
Goal 10 Reduce **inequality** within and among countries
Goal 11 Make **cities** and human settlements inclusive, safe, resilient and sustainable
Goal 12 Ensure sustainable **consumption and production** patterns
Goal 13 Take urgent action to combat **climate change** and its impacts*
Goal 14 Conserve and sustainably use the **oceans**, seas and marine resources for sustainable development
Goal 15 Protect, restore and promote sustainable use of **terrestrial ecosystems**, sustainably manage forests, combat desertification and halt and reverse land degradation and halt biodiversity loss
Goal 16 Promote **peaceful and inclusive societies** for sustainable development, provide access to justice for all and build effective, accountable and inclusive institutions at all levels
Goal 17 Strengthen the means of **implementation** and revitalize the global partnership for sustainable development

* Acknowledging that the UNFCCC is the primary international, intergovernmental forum for negotiating the global response to climate change.

As stated in the 2030 Agenda:

- We are announcing today 17 SDGs with 169 associated targets which are integrated and indivisible. Never before have world leaders pledged common action and endeavor across such a broad and universal policy agenda (para 18.).

- The new Goals and targets will come into effect on 1 January 2016 and will guide the decisions we take over the next 15 years (21.).
- The SDGs and targets are integrated and indivisible, global in nature and universally applicable, taking into account different national realities, capacities and levels of development and respecting national policies and priorities. Targets are defined as aspirational and global, with each government setting its own national targets guided by the global level of ambition but taking into account national circumstances. Each government will also decide how these aspirational and global targets should be incorporated in national planning processes, policies and strategies. It is important to recognize the link between sustainable development and other relevant ongoing processes in the economic, social and environmental fields (55).

The report furthermore elaborates on implementation, the role of a revitalized global partnership for sustainable development, and the follow-up and review of the Agenda laid out in the report of the 2015 Summit. The SDGs are but a starting point with a time line of 15 years during which an enormous scaling up of activities at all levels is of the essence to meet the Goals and reach the associated targets.

Complexity pervades the sustainable development process along several different but interlinked axes. These are:

1 Consideration of the three dimensions of SD (economic, environmental, social).
2 The SDG system as an interconnected system requiring a "holistic, multisectoral and multidimensional" approach.
3 The highly dynamic science-policy interface and emerging issues.
4 The nexus approach to address differentiated interconnectedness among SDGs.
5 Issues which cut across SDGs (e.g., disaster risk reduction and resilience building).

The International Council for Science (ICSU) has developed a framework for the interactions among SDGs and their targets (Nilsson et al. 2016a, 2016b; ICSU 2017). The framework consists of a scoring system based on a seven-point scale of interactions among SDGs (from inextricably linked to canceling each other out; see example in Box 14.3). This scale should "help policy makers and researchers to identify and test development pathways that minimize negative interactions and enhance positive ones." The authors stress the importance of context – i.e., national circumstances and levels of development – for applying their system of interaction scores. It is furthermore of the essence to consider differences in geography, governance and technology systems rather than relying on generalized knowledge.

> **Box. 14.3   Interactions among SDGs and targets. Example: "The wins and losses en route to zero hunger in sub-Saharan Africa"**
>
> Ending hunger (SDG 2) interacts positively with poverty eradication (1), health promotion (3) and achieving quality education for all (4). Addressing malnourishment is indivisible from addressing poverty. Tackling malnourishment reinforces educational efforts because children can concentrate and perform better in school. Not addressing food security would counteract education when the poorest children have to help provide food for the day.
>
> Food production interacts with climate change mitigation (13) in several ways because agriculture represents 20–35 percent of total anthropogenic greenhouse gas emissions. Climate mitigation constrains some types of food production, in particular those related to meat (methane release from livestock constitutes nearly 40 percent of the global agricultural sector's total emissions). Yet food production is reinforced by a stable climate. Securing food from fisheries is also reinforced by protecting the climate, because that limits ocean warming and acidification.
>
> In some parts of sub-Saharan Africa promoting food production can also constrain renewable energy production (7) and terrestrial ecosystem protection (15) by competing for water and land. Conversely, limited land availability constrains agricultural production.
>
> *Source*: Adapted from Nilsson et al. 2016b

The nexus approach

A nexus is "a cluster of issues that are linked in such a way that interventions focusing on one issue are highly likely to have positive or negative impacts on other issues within the nexus" (Jungcurt 2016; for an in-depth discussion of synergies and trade-offs between SDGs and patterns at global and country level see, e.g., Pradhan et al. 2017). Jungcurt presented the following examples, all of which had been the subject of major science-policy conferences:

- Water, energy and food security
- Infrastructure, inequality and resilience
- Oceans, seas, marine resources and human well-being
- Water, soil and waste
- Health, poverty, gender and education
- Education, health and water
- Education, health and food

In his policy update Jungcurt (2016) also provided an overview of tools for understanding linkages among SDGs, targets and issues for developing strategies for policy coherence. These tools are meant to facilitate an integrated implementation of the "SDG System." This process comprises several steps, beginning with (1) the lessons learned from the MDG experience. This is followed by (2) a mapping of the network of interactions among SDGs and targets and (3) the use of a nexus approach as sketched earlier. (2) and (3) are applied to contexts at the individual country level. (As already outlined in the UN Global Sustainable Development Report 2015b, countries in special situations are LDCs, landlocked developing countries and SIDS.)

Knowledge of the interlinkages between SDGs and targets should support policy makers in diversifying and amplifying policy impact. Additional tools which have been made available are the *Integrated Sustainable Development Goals Planning Model (ISDG)*, the OECD's *Framework for Policy Coherence for Sustainable Development*, The UN Development Group's *Reference Guide to UN Country Teams* and its report on partnerships and actions for SDG implementation at the country level (for further details and references see Jungcurt 2016 and SEI 2014).

Why do we elaborate on this? Simply, because these different aspects reflect the complexity of what at first sight may seem to be – after a tedious process of reaching consensus – just a "list of goals and targets to be achieved." Rather implementing Agenda 2030 means informed decision making, based on a sound understanding of how the planet's systems work, and how we can cope with the changes we have made to our own world.

Foreseeable problems of the future?

The concern expressed in *The Future We Choose*, the declaration from the High-Level Dialogue on Global Sustainability, reflects the complex setup of intertwined and pressing issues to ensure quality of life for present and future generations:

> We are on the threshold of a future with unprecedented environmental risks. The scientific evidence is unequivocal. The combined effects of climate change, resource scarcity, loss of biodiversity and ecosystem resilience at a time of increased demand, poses a real threat to humanity's welfare. Such a future generates unacceptable risks of undermining the resilience of the Earth system including all its inhabitants. We have generated our own geological epoch, the Anthropocene. In this epoch, there is an unacceptable risk that human pressures on the planet, should they continue on a business as usual trajectory, will trigger abrupt and irreversible changes with catastrophic outcomes for human societies and life as we know it.

On the more positive side, there is also hope that our generation can make a difference which eventually benefits future generations and meets our intergenerational responsibility, the core element of our perception of sustainable development. This is expressed in the "we believe" paragraph of the same declaration.

> With bold and courageous leadership, and determined action, a transition to a safe and prosperous future is possible. But both will be essential and time is running critically short. Every delay now closes off opportunities for progress and increases the burden of inequity and poverty, not only for future generations, but for those who are alive today. Yet, our generation is the first to have the privilege of understanding the full complexity of the challenges that confront us and we already have at hand the knowledge, technology and finance required to ensure a sustainable future. Indeed, the application of these tools and with a focus on social and economic inequalities, empowering women and ensuring good governance, is a prerequisite to living within safe planetary boundaries.

Conclusions

The slowness of the "sustainable development process" may reflect complexity at various scales as a basic property of systems. It starts with complexity in the natural world and our continued poor understanding of the functioning and interlinkages among our planetary systems. We need a more in-depth scientific approach which improves our knowledge of these systems. At a second level, we urgently require a better understanding of the systems we humans have created since we have begun to interfere massively with natural systems – i.e., since the beginning of the Anthropocene. And lastly, decision makers and policy makers in our societies need to make informed decisions on these complex issues, based on appropriate education and capacity building processes. It is re-emphasized that the decisions they take are embedded in the global patterns and processes of the functioning of our political systems at all levels.

Inequality among developing countries, those in transition and industrialized nations persists, in short, the North/South divide. Climate change, wars and associated refugee and migration phenomena may exacerbate these divides and impose financial demands from the poorer and more vulnerable segment of nation states.

Finally, a note on the SDGs. As with the sustainable development process during the last decades and its outcome, these are also critically perceived. Some say they are not ambitious enough; others question their timeliness. Some of the targets may already seem unrealistic if to be reached by 2030. It is also suggested to prioritize certain goals. For instance, the education goal is proposed to be elevated, because its achievement would directly benefit poverty reduction, health improvement and inclusive growth thus lessening inequality within and between countries. (For the interested reader we suggest consulting the UN secretary-general's progress reports on SDG implementation and UNDP's guidance note, a living document, first published in 2017).

Sustainable development 227

A crucial, overarching issue is the interdependence among SDGs and their respective targets. Experts indicate, for instance, that without progress on Goal 6 (water and sanitation) the other goals and targets may not be reached; tackling climate change will be possible only if the other SDGs are met as climate and development are inextricably linked to each other. Lastly, the choice of indicators against which to measure progress toward the targets is crucial to ensure that we meet them.

In conclusion, the next 10–15 years should show whether "this time" we will have advanced and within such a short period, by undertaking the decisive challenges associated with making sustainable development reality.

References

Adams, W.M. 2009. *Green Development. Environment and sustainability in a developing world.* Routledge, London.

Annan, K. 2002. Introduction. In *Johannesburg 2002 – Challenges and Partnerships*, pp. 4–5. Agenda Publishing, Newcastle upon Tyne.

Cohen, J.E. 1995. *How many people can the Earth support?* Norton & Company, New York.

Desai, N. 2002. Making it Happen. *Johannesburg 2002 – Challenges and Partnerships, 13–17.* Agenda Publishing, Newcastle upon Tyne.

Drexhage, J. and D. Murphy 2010. *Sustainable Development: From Brundtland to Rio 2012.* Background paper prepared for consideration by the High Level Panel on Global Sustainability at its first meeting, 19 September 2010. United Nations, New York.

Grober, U. 2010. *Die Entdeckung der Nachhaltigkeit. Kulturgeschichte eines Begriffs.* Kunstmann, München.

Hadley, M. 2006a. The early years of UNESCO's environmental programme, 1945–1965. In: Petitjean, P., V. Zharov, G. Glaser, J. Richardson, B. de Padirac and G. Archibald (eds.), *Sixty Years of Science at UNESCO 1945–2005*, pp. 201–232. UNESCO, Paris.

Hadley, M. 2006b. The Man and the Biosphere (MAB) Programme. In: Petitjean, P., V. Zharov, G. Glaser, J. Richardson, B. de Padirac and G. Archibald (eds.), *Sixty Years of Science at UNESCO 1945–2005*, pp. 260–296. UNESCO, Paris.

ICSU (International Council for Science) 2017. *A Guide to SDG Interactions: From Science to Implementation.* D.J. Griggs, M. Nilsson, A. Stevance, D. McCollum (eds.). ICSU, Paris.

IUCN 1980. *World Conservation Strategy: Living Resource Conservation for Sustainable Development.* IUCN, Gland, Switzerland.

IUCN 1991. *Caring for the Earth: A Strategy for Sustainable Living.* IUCN, Gland, Switzerland.

Johnson, S. 2012. *UNEP – The First 40 Years. A Narrative.* UNEP, Nairobi.

Jungcurt, S. 2016. *Towards Integrated Implementation: Tools for Understanding Linkages and Developing Strategies for Policy Coherence.* IISD Reporting Services (Germany), Policy Update # 35.

McLaughlin, D. 1998. Fooling with Nature: Silent Spring Revisited. *Frontline.* PBS. Accessed 22 November 2015.

Meadows, D. 2015. *Growing, Growing, Gone: Reaching the Limits.* Interview by Allen White, Great Transition Initiative (June 2015).

Meadows, D. H., D.L. Meadows, J. Randers and W.W. Behrens III 1972. *Limits to Growth.* Universe Books, New York.

Millennium Ecosystem Assessment (MEA) 2005. *Ecosystems and Human Well-being: Synthesis*. Island Press, Washington, DC.

Nilsson, M., D. Griggs, M. Visbeck and C. Riegler 2016a. *A Draft Framework for Understanding SDG Interactions*. International Council for Science (ICSU). Paris, France.

Nilsson, M., D. Griggs and M. Visbeck 2016b. Map the interactions between sustainable development goals. *Nature* 534: 320–322.

Pradhan, P., L. Costa, D. Rybski, W. Lucht and J. Knopp 2017. A systematic study of sustainable development goals interactions. *Earth's Future* 5: 1169–1179.

Redclift, M. 1987. *Sustainable Development – Exploring the contradictions*. Methuen, London.

SEI (Stockholm Environment Institute) 2014. Cross-sectoral integration in the Sustainable Development Goals: A nexus approach. Discussion Brief. Stockholm Environment Institute, Stockholm, Sweden.

UN 2012. *The Future We Want*. United Nations, New York.

UN 2014. *The Road to Dignity by 2030: Ending Poverty, Transforming All Lives and Protecting the Planet. Synthesis Report of the Secretary-General on the Post-2015 Agenda*. United Nations, New York.

UN 2015a. *Transforming our World: The 2030 Agenda for Sustainable Development*. United Nations, New York.

UN 2015b. *Global Sustainable Development Report: 2015 Edition*. United Nations Department of Economic and Social Affairs, Division for Sustainable Development. United Nations, New York.

UNDP (United Nations Development Program) 2017. *Institutional and Coordination Mechanisms. Guidance Note on Facilitating Integration and Coherence of SDG Implementation*. UNDP, New York.

UNEP (United Nations Environment Program) 2005. *Overview of the Millennium Ecosystem Assessment*. www.unep.org. Accessed 1 December 2015.

United Nations Millennium Project 2005. *Investing in Development: A Practical Plan to Achieve the Millennium Development Goals. Overview*. United Nations, New York.

15 Risks, new departures, global solutions
Challenges of a complex frontier

Winding up

We have presented diversified models of problem solving, in nature and among humans, where complexity plays a significant role. We have reviewed the vagaries, whether delight or hazard, of our communal home. We have shown with vivid examples the contrariness of human behavior – while not overlooking the foresight and innovation of which *Homo sapiens* is remarkably capable. The whole presents an exercise in problem analysis that leads to the question: Are there solutions to the major problems facing humanity?

Yet we live in an era when humanity faces increasing challenge at all levels. Poverty, hunger, violent dissent, terrorism, war, unregulated international migration, natural disasters where and when they are unexpected, epidemics, climate change, loss of the diversity of life. All make the daily headlines of our mass media.

Throughout the chapters we emphasized the practical, problem-oriented way of understanding complexity. We do not have answers to all the questions raised, but we hope we have illustrated how to accommodate, adapt and live agreeably in an increasingly complicated world. This is the universe in which a great-ape species, one hopes rightly classified as *sapiens*, struggles to make the future work.

Being aware of the interconnected and globalized nature of our world is the first step toward sensitizing ourselves to make the "right" or evidence-based decisions. It would be interesting to reckon what bias might lie behind what we consider "right." Currently provocative thought is to speak even of "wicked problems" for which there are only clumsy solutions.

We should hope, nevertheless, to build up the capacities needed to deal with issues in the most effective manner. This is important at a time when global change dynamics defy systems of national governance and point toward a development trajectory possessing strengthened international collaboration and new systems of global governance.

As we have seen, complexity is by no means a static phenomenon. Interdependencies, especially in regard to our economic systems, are becoming stronger. Globalization has accelerated and is creating new, interlaced systems of complex interdependence. No wonder we see a blurring of national and international politics/policies throughout virtually all sectors and societies. Humans have created a hyper-system blending elements of remaining natural and anthropogenic environments and their products. In the early 21st century, through the MEA, we have learned about the service function of ecosystems surrounding us or of which we are part.

On goals and targets

Since the WSSD, held in 2002 in Johannesburg, "targeting" has become an approach to tackle our global worries. The Summit had agreed upon the 2010 Target for Biodiversity. We missed this target. In the International Year of Biodiversity (2010) the new 20 Aichi Targets were declared. Another targeting example was the eight MDGs (2000–2015). Since 2015 these have been succeeded by the 17 (global) SDGs (time line: 2030).

We saw in the chapters on industry and migration that goals and targets fail to be set with precision or else are not set at all. This lack of a fairly finite strategy leads to stumbles and, at times, serious tumbles. The chapter on diplomacy pointed out the need for exactness in goal- and target-setting, despite the frailty of our existing system of international relations. The fact that goals and targets can be identified, and consensus aimed at is already enormous progress in international diplomacy, even though targets may be either too ambitious, not reachable within identified time lines, or both. In the military chapter, we witnessed strategy fail too often under critical circumstances. Unfortunately the bane of all staff planning, even when undertaken with minute preparation, care and reliable intelligence, is its sudden uselessness the moment the first shots are exchanged.

It remains to be stressed that targeting is a time-consuming and sometimes frustrating process. The context of the 2015 negotiations on climate change and the extensively negotiated 2-degree Celsius limit of global temperature rise is a good example. Added to the hardships emanating from complexity are the ethical, moral and religious inhibitions that create fences that then serve as barriers to problem solving.

Complexity is part of the recognition procedures at various scales. First, the issues debated are themselves complex: biodiversity, climate change, sustainable development, macro- or micro-economics, if not corruption itself, and the assurance of safety and security. Secondly, they each stand for complex systems of systems; these possess inherent management difficulties (those "wicked problems"). Thirdly, they are all interlinked. Fourthly, addressing them successfully translates into proper functioning of globalized political systems and their decision-making models. Complex systems are thus forming the backgrounds to all the problems as well as the mechanisms underpinning the finding of alternative results. Lastly, the solutions – although the problems are global in nature – are not restricted to particular levels. They must be sought at every tier of authority and decision, from local to global. This may explain why progress in these spheres is frequently painstakingly slow despite the pressing nature of the issues at stake.

Risks, new departures, global solutions 231

What makes resolution even more difficult is that the processes outlined here are associated with major changes to be made in the way we exploit our resources, meet our energy demands and how we produce and consume. In other words, we need to change from existing complex systems such as economic growth, industrial production and lifestyles to other complex or even more complex systems to facilitate the changes needed to ensure that humanity sustainably lives *on* and *with* the Earth. In industrial production, for example, are the sacrosanct targets of GDP and GNP growth and increased market share truly justified incitements to "do better?" As Joseph Stiglitz, economist and Nobel laureate, pointed out at the World Economic Forum in Davos in 2016, "GDP is not a good measure of economic performance, it's not a good measure of well-being." Or in food supply, reduced meat consumption seems a realizable goal (at least for those of us who do not go hungry), from the dual imperatives of health maintenance and sustainable agrarian growth. As the learners that we are, a proximate goal will be to learn how to use the future better than we did yesterday and are doing now.

Complexity versus stable evolution of the environment

In this book we have dealt to a considerable extent with sustainable development and its many UN-related aspects. Readers may better understand this by referring to our past professional relationship with the UN or, more specifically, to UNESCO. It is true as well that we see the UN and other intergovernmental and NGO institutions trying to grapple with a diversity of large-scale problems as they seek solutions to the complexity of the tasks before us. Either this is a weak point of multilateralism or it indicates the need of *new forms of multilateralism* as suggested by Frank Biermann in his book *Earth System Governance* (2014).

Complexity may have become a non-word in terms of obstructing rather than finding solutions. Policy- and decision makers often seem not overly motivated by (a) discussing the complexity of issues they contend with, and (b) second-order difficulties accompanying decisions to satisfy societal needs and aspirations or (c) being unaware of the downstream consequences of actions taken. They may even feel paralyzed rather than energized to address multifaceted and complex questions. Ultimately this may cause a dragging out of international meetings and delaying or impede consensus-based outcomes.

Perhaps understanding of complex systems, of which today we are all part, is now an integral factor in assuring quality of life in the Anthropocene. Our world, interconnected, globalized together with fast, effective communication webs to provide us with an endless yet immensely useful data. From these, we need to select and exploit what is most pertinent to the world that we wish to occupy as a rewarded and free society – one not relying on false premises, "fake news" and erroneous conclusions.

But first, a current, and even counterproductive, constraint. By now, readers will have wondered: why do not the authors evoke the most evident and complicated problem of all – limiting the world's growth in population? The response

232   Risks, new departures, global solutions

is simple in words but utterly complex in values and the spiritual dimension. Its cultural dimensions are so varied and different that codification is a giant task in social anthropology. Countries with high or exceptionally high birthrates do not want to be singled out during international assemblies.[1] As a consequence, the topic is by common consent out of bounds, off limits in international public debate. We humans, acting in concert, simply do not refer to curbing the mammalian impulses to reproduce our kind. Least of all is the matter a subject for dialogue in the international conference halls or corridors of influence.

More functional limitations and the press of time

All the rest of the complexities, therefore, include the diversity of values and value systems making up the world's civilizational variety. Despite all efforts, this diversity has not been recognized as an essential pillar of sustainable development. It was advocated for many years by UNESCO, the only UN entity charged with a cultural mission. The concept of cultural differences would then be transformed into mechanisms or normative instruments of the international community. There its civilizing worth would blend equally with other factors (educational, environmental, ethical) to make development truly sustainable.

Although the authors have presented complexity in an array of human activity yet in a limited number of topical areas, the fields chosen fall within the scope of our experience and familiarity. Other fields have not been further elaborated, although they are important. For instance, public health, gender and methodologies of complex systems analysis are not included. Energy has not been given the space it deserves. Urban systems, husbandry, soil quality and agriculture as major elements of our anthropogenic environment since mankind abandoned hunter and food-gatherer lifestyles have not been explored here. The same *nostra culpa* applies to complexity in banking and finance, transport networks, transformative postal systems, architectural and monumental degradation, erosive mechanical wear, design complexity, the increasing problem of cyber threats, and still more zones of simplicity transformed into complication and complexity.

We thought of responding to this question early in our final chapter, although suggestions for the way forward appear throughout the text. Our first concern is the enormity of the stake in unearthing responsible solutions, and finding them quickly: the very future of humanity. Secondly, while time is not on our side, our problems are widespread as well. Solutions to the critical environmental hazards need to be in place within the next 10 to 25 years. For biological diversity, by way of example, the extinction clock ticks mercilessly and needs to be stopped. Extinction remains irreversible. And yet time delays may be preprogrammed in everything we try to stabilize: whether the human population, forest degradation, waste management. All these processes are inevitably linked to complex systems involving feedback loops and delayed reaction.

What is the most effective way to respond? We of the complexity school have not wished to present cookbook solutions. There are few, if any, magical ways to proceed. Perhaps compiling a handbook, one that we could have titled *A Guide to*

Risks, new departures, global solutions   233

Surviving in the Cosmos. We preferred instead to sensitize readers and the decision-making communities to (a) understand complexity and (b) make the best use of its quality as indispensable for the future progress and well-being of all in our novel environment of lifelong learning. And yet *complexity literacy* cannot be met by awareness alone. Targeted coaching, training and learning show the pragmatic way to the apprehension of *complex* and *complexity*. Complex matters, in all their aspects, are interpretable by an expertise of its own, exploiting an ample supply of case histories, innovative methods of process simplification, as well as improved models for problem resolution.

Pondering solutions

Coming up with solutions to global problems is not simple. We can sketch here only a few ideas on the way toward solutions, rather than the solutions themselves (which may not exist to date). Complexity of process is reflected in the efforts of the international community, especially since the end of the Second World War, when the UN came into being. Since then the concept of sustainable development has taken shape, and the world of nation states has tried not only to manage increasing complexity but an increasing number of problems at all levels. In the chapter on climate change we described the history of scientific understanding of the phenomenon, the quest for the mechanisms responsible for climate change, and the global efforts, in particular of the UN and its systematically and intelligently organized programs leading to solutions. These and related processes are directly influential on the future of humanity.

We are living in the information age, in knowledge societies. Modern **ICT** and the Internet make us much more effective in acquiring the data we need to be literate in a "landscape of global change, challenges and problems." For instance, if one searches the Internet for "solutions to climate change," responses include *decarbonization, renewable sources of energy, circular economics, stopping greenhouse gas emissions* and the like. Through the media, we are constantly informed about what is happening on our planet. We can literally access any information on any subject, at anytime and anywhere. Through the social networks and hundreds and thousands of fora we can express our opinion, join like-minded groups to create political momentum and change "the system."

In the past, information was not readily available, nowadays we are confronted with the options of selecting and using accurate data pertinent to a given question or problem. There are several steps (and associated time lags) between retrieving and analyzing specific information for local, national and international decision making and policy making. As outlined in the executive summary of the UN Report *A World That Counts. Mobilizing the Data Revolution for Sustainable Development* (UN 2014a), "Governments, companies, researchers and citizen groups are in a ferment of experimentation, innovation and adaptation to the new world of data, a world in which data are bigger, faster and more detailed than ever. This is the data revolution." The report continues, "There are huge and growing inequalities in access to data and information and in the ability to use" them. This data revolution ineluctably translates into new partnerships and fora in order to harness the sustainable development process and its 2030 Agenda.

Our systems can and should be better adjusted, moreover, to meet our needs. There are certain **mechanisms** at our disposal; we should make better use of these. They include *capacity building* in all its dimensions and through all segments and age classes of society, through teaching and learning and training. There are also awareness raising, with special emphasis on youth and women, as well as on the ethical and legal aspects related to problem solving. As pointed out repeatedly, we need to embrace a new concept of literacy to ensure informed decision making and cognizance among both policy makers and those applying policy. Box 15.1 presents a concept of media and information literacy.

Box 15.1   UNESCO's conception of the five laws of media and information literacy

The laws embrace the different sources of informed knowledge available largely from journalism. The specialized literacies designated in the present book as "scientific literacy" or "complexity literacy" are positioned within the context of Laws 4 and 5 – themselves the product of academic learning or vocational or professional training.

Law 1

Information, communication, libraries, media, technology, the Internet as well as other forms of information providers are for use in critical civic engagement and sustainable development.

Law 2

Every citizen is a creator of information/knowledge and has a message. They must be empowered to access new information/knowledge and to express themselves. MIL is for all – women and men equally – and a nexus of human rights.

Law 3

Information, knowledge and messages are not always value neutral, or always independent of biases. Any conceptualization, use and application of MIL should make this truth transparent and understandable to all citizens.

> **Law 4**
>
> Every citizen wants to know and understand new information, knowledge and messages as well as to communicate, even if she/he is not aware, admits or expresses that he/she does. Her/his rights must however never be compromised.
>
> **Law 5**
>
> MIL is not acquired at once. It is a lived and dynamic experience and process. It is complete when it includes knowledge, skills and attitudes, when it covers access, evaluation/assessment, use, production and communication of information, media and technology content.
>
> Source: www.unesco.org/new/en/communication-and-information/media-development/media-literacy/five-laws-of-mil/, accessed 20 March 2017

Knowledge created anew from scientific research should enter much faster the different kinds and levels of education systems; education needs to be better aligned with current and potential issues humankind is continuing to face. In sum, our learning environments should be more closely aligned with Anthropocene awareness: more visionary problem solving, ever in search of creative and innovative knowing-how.

A special domain within the broad field of capacity building is *institutional capacity building*. Do we have the appropriate structures with the capacities needed to manage current and future problems? Isn't the fact that we discuss new forms of governance and institutional reform indicative of a vast change process needed to assure that our species moves within the adequately identified *safe operating space* and does not transgress critical *planetary boundaries*? While the question may seem theoretical, the responses that it begs are incontrovertibly pragmatic.

Arithmetic upwards

We think several mechanisms should be considered within this context of institutional capacities – all related to facilitating and accelerating a trajectory toward sustainable solutions. First, there are many ways of improving performance of existing institutions. Second, collaboration could be considerably scaled up for improving cooperation to create synergistic, mutually reinforcing networks. Third, we may need to re-create extant entities. These should focus on problem-related matters and operate in emerging fields. Examples of the latter are the many think tanks which have been created in recent years, specialized in matters such as sustainability, questions of the environment, energy, the advent of robotics and bionics, and the future of employment. Fourth, we need to remember that in all cases we are dealing with systems: orderly mechanisms that perform only as do their constituent elements.

An example of the first two points is the strengthening of UN-Habitat, the UN program dealing with our urban future; cities are where the fate of decisions on sustainability will be put to test. To this end we need to invent a new urban model with clear objectives and a roadmap for implementation and better linkage to the climate change and sustainability agendas. This – to make urbanization a key issue of world politics – was strongly suggested by the German Advisory Council on Global Change, following the Habitat III Conference held in Quito in 2016 (WBGU 2017).

Promising examples leading to bold solutions may pave the way for speeding up what has been a slow process. Realizing bold visions may stem from "incremental negotiation and redefined circular motion," a critical comment on the world's handling of urgent environmental issues, published in an editorial of *Nature* just prior to the Rio+20 Summit. More recently Pope Francis and the Dalai Lama discussed an ecological and ethical agenda, respectively, similar to the Earth Charter. They promote a new global ethics that would eventually allow transcending boundaries as set by "classical" belief systems (part of our third point noted earlier). Another example is E. O. Wilson's initiative *Half Earth* which aims at setting aside and protecting half the planet for future generations. As he writes in his book, "The declining world of biodiversity cannot be saved by the piecemeal operations in current use alone," and "The only proven way to halt the destabilization of the living world is to protect the largest possible reserves and the native biodiversity surviving within them." Our current trajectory of hugely increasing numbers and coverage of protected areas at all levels is promising, but the future will show whether we will get close to the vision one of our most eminent biologists had in mind with those words in 2016.

Sometimes we feel a dire need for more prescient thinking as found among classical science fiction writers and others who presented scenarios for an "ideal" future world. Being drowned in problems overshadows the quest for ideals. Nature-based technologies and innovation such as in fields like bionics or biomimetics are examples of many which could provide long-term and environmentally friendly solutions for some of humankind's challenges (overviews in Barthlott et al. 2014, 2016). (Biomimetics is the imitation of models, systems and elements of nature for the purpose of solving complex human problems.) To date, this enormous potential has not been given adequate attention, for example in biodiversity fora and in the technology landscapes discussed in the 2016 Global Sustainable Development Report of the UN (UN 2016).

In our increasingly urbanized world, development solutions, including innovative (low carbon) transport and energy systems would essentially be developed in cities (WBGU 2016). Several attempts have been tried to make the city of the future look more "organic" compared to our prevailing urban concrete jungles. A good example of what can be done is Singapore. Perhaps the sustainable city of the distant future will more closely resemble a forest in terms of structure and

Risks, new departures, global solutions   237

system-internal cyclical processes. Harnessing technology and innovation may not be the ultimate fix for all our problems, but it would certainly be a facilitating mechanism to cope with the most pressing of our knotty situations.

System readiness

In terms of solutions already in place, we have examples of good practice or role models proven successful. Many of them at the same time have never become widely known. Good ideas are either not communicated or local solutions remain local despite their potential to solve problems at national or international levels. We need a method of better disseminating success stories or better adapting and applying solutions to a broader spectrum of challenges.

Money rules the world and therefore also the processes toward a sustainable future of mankind in all its ramifications. Indicative of this has been all the **financial mechanisms** the international community set in place for its major efforts related to biodiversity (e.g., Japan Biodiversity Fund), climate change (Green Climate Fund), sustainable development (Addis Ababa Action Agenda as integral to the 2030 Agenda), and others. These mechanisms should work at two levels, (a) the thematic area for which they had been put in place, and (b) all "types" of nation states (industrialized countries, countries in transition, both developed and developing; in short, overcoming the North/South divide). The key term in this context is clearly "*Development Aid.*" An interesting question is: What will be the role of nation states in the future? What will be the ultimate result of the problem analysis of poor versus rich societies or society-internal disparities?

It has been clearly recognized that successful implementation of the new 2030 Agenda and its SDGs requires international and domestic funding vastly exceeding the limits of official development assistance (ODA). Development financing has diversified. Although for poor countries ODA and other official flows continue to be essential, other kinds of international and domestic resources have overtaken ODA. As discussed in *Beyond Aid*, a publication of the American Center for Strategic & International Studies, "Successful implementation of the new [2030] agenda will require that international cooperation proceed in new ways that transcend the traditional aid-centered paradigm" and "Financing for development must overcome the tendency to regard official development assistance as if it were the principal instrument of development cooperation" (Michel 2016).

We need a paradigm change from today's governance systems to those of the future. Key words are **global governance, Earth system governance** or even a new **(bio-) geography of governance**. The chapters of this book and in particular paragraphs in this chapter indicate a strong need for such changes in the way humans interact with each other and with our planetary systems. In view of our current challenges governance systems on all scales would need to be scrutinized as to their extant structural and functional properties – as opposed to those needed for sustaining a healthy global system and well-being of its dominating change agent, *Homo sapiens*. One of the best examples remains, therefore, all kinds of transnational environmental issues.

Possibly with the release of Rachel Carson's *Silent Spring* the global community for the first time became aware of our global impact on the environment (see our chapter on sustainable development). DDT had entered our food chains and become globally distributed. This has meanwhile developed into a serious broader situation of global pollution. A recent IUCN report estimated that globally 1.5 million tons of primary microplastics, largely from laundering of synthetic textiles and abrasion of tires (while driving) are annually released into the oceans (Boucher and Friot 2017). Also on a global scale, a plethora of new substances are entering – at increasing rates – our ecosystems. Yet we have hardly a clue about their potential or actual environmental impacts, including those on the human species.

A possible second time was the period when consciousness spread that nature does not follow political boundaries. Rather the contrary applies. Many political limits do neither sustain the confines of natural systems nor the historic geography of ethnic communities. One example is national boundaries reflecting colonial heritage. As Tim Marshall put it in *Prisoners of Geography* (2016), "colonial powers drew artificial borders on paper, completely ignoring the physical realities of the region" or, in his chapter on Africa, that ethnic conflicts within African countries are evidence that the "European idea of geography did not fit the reality of Africa's demographics." In almost all domains of the environment, furthermore, it is now realized that successfully (meaning sustainably) managing natural systems follows transnational management. Put differently, solutions and sustainability are intimately linked to simultaneously working at local, subnational, national and international levels.

Models for succeeding

A fine example is that water management can no longer rely on segmented views but should rather apply integrated or holistic approaches at river basin or watershed levels (see chapter on water). And for biodiversity preservation we need to look into how life is distributed on Earth, the domain of biogeography (transboundary protected areas and conservation networks of natural systems rather than of isolated fragments). Climate change provides us with a challenge without borders, except for our planet being itself the ultimate border.

These are workable models for management related to "big systems" or systems of systems. In addition, such management often requires not only new governance modalities (as discussed next) but also a new geography of competencies bundling capacities from the spatial unit to be managed. Take, for instance, the management of a TBR (Transboundary Biosphere Reserve; see UNESCO's Man and the Biosphere Programme, for further information). All national stakeholders involved should provide expertise and design as well as operate the required policy frameworks in a close joint effort. All this should, moreover, be part and parcel of what TBRs are meant to be globally in order to develop guidance for their further development.

The TBR concept has never been static. Starting from an already open concept for conservation which no longer excludes the human factor, as was the case in many of the traditional approaches to nature conservation, biosphere reserves have evolved into testing sites for sustainable development, including education, energy and conservation in its classical sense, to grappling with climate change, and embracing in fact all three dimensions of sustainable development (environmental, economic and social). They are part of a globally representative *World Network of Biosphere Reserves* (originally designed on the basis of the Earth's biogeographic regions), both for building global capacity and for monitoring global change.

TBRs are thus a good example of the need for transnational collaboration, from the grassroots level to the highest political levels of heads of state or government. The (bio-) geography of institutional networks including all institutions and organizations of relevance is what counts for managing a particular system or problem area. Stumbles and even tumbles happen, but the TBR is directing its practitioners to new thinking in terms of "geographies of institutional landscapes." This applies particularly to both ends of scale, the national level and below, as well as the transnational level. Structures and processes may require revamping in our time of the Anthropocene, during which humans have begun to reshape planetary systems at unprecedented scales and rates.

In addition to discussing the need for new schemes of global governance or Earth system governance (overview in Biermann 2014), we may need a new geographic approach and thinking about the *geography of governance*, in fact in its broadest sense a *Biogeography of Governance*. The "bio" in what is possibly a new descriptor relates both to the main actor in the Anthropocene, *Homo sapiens* and to the distribution of other life forms on Earth and their endangerment. Both these elements may be directly related to all we refer to as *current global challenges*. Why geography? Because geography is "an all-encompassing discipline that seeks an understanding of the Earth and its human and natural complexities – not merely where objects are, but how they have changed and come to be."[2]

Systems, complexity and making the future work

Through the interlinkage with our planetary or Earth systems we arrive at what is commonly referred to as the classical notion of *global governance* (for a history of the term see Weiss and Wilkinson 2014), "the totality of institutions, policies, norms, procedures and initiatives through which States and their citizens try to bring more predictability, stability and order to their responses to transnational challenges" (UN 2014b). As Thomas G. Weiss, initiator of the UN Intellectual History Project (1999–2010), wrote in 2009, "The story of global governance remains an unfinished journey" (Weiss 2009). In our jargon it may be one of the most important examples of complexity issues to be addressed for the future of mankind. Needless to say that the UN plays a capital role in global governance, with its three-body setup: UN member states, UN professional secretariats, and an increasingly important "Third UN" comprising non-state actors such as regional organizations, NGOs, academics, independent commissions and other organized and compatible groups (*sensu* Weiss and Jolly 2009; see also our chapter on sustainable development).

As stressed in the 2015 report *Confronting the Crisis of Global Governance* of the Commission on Global Security, Justice & Governance (initiated by The Hague Institute for Global Justice, the Netherlands, and the Washington-based Stimson Center), "these increasingly global actors can work together in a network approach to governance towards inclusive and innovative solutions to some of the world's most complex and pressing global issues" based on an "effective strategy for reform [requiring] smart coalitions of like-minded states or non-state actors to mobilize and sustain support for change." On the occasion of the UN's 75th anniversary in 2020 the same report proposes a *World Conference on Global Institutions*, that is to say, a "multi-stakeholder and formal multilateral negotiation on global institutional reform."

Is this an ambition which "could serve as a rallying point for smart coalitions and simultaneously generate political momentum for multiple, urgent global reforms?" Is such ambition excessive in a world already somewhat uncomfortable with "globalization" – not to overlook the renewed form of local warfare, often by single assailants, that we call terrorism?

Notwithstanding the orderliness of the UN and its approaches to complex problems and, conversely, the irregularity and often chaos of terrorism, the risk of system abuse will not disappear. The Cambridge Analytica-Facebook scandal of 2018 serves as an intimidating marker of excess. Personal data of 87 million Facebook users came into unauthorized exploitation for commercial or political purposes without the knowledge of those whom the information portrayed. Facebook's users numbered about 2.2 billion logged-in subscribers at the end of 2017. Expressed otherwise, almost 30 percent of the planet's population of 7.6 billion had their descriptions and preferences used without their permission.

Or are there still further complexities for Earth's inhabitants on their trajectory towards a "sustainable global society founded on respect for nature, universal human rights, economic justice, and a culture of peace" (preamble of the Earth Charter)?

Notes

1 Of the world's 12 most prolific countries in 2015, with a birth rate roughly twice that of the international average, 11 are on the African continent. Source: www.statista.com, accessed 17 March 2017.
2 Wikipedia, The Free Encyclopedia, https://en.wikipedia.org/w/index.php?title=Geography&oldid=837864381. Accessed 5 June 2018.

References

Barthlott, W., W.R. Erdelen and M.D. Rafiqpoor 2014. Biodiversity and technical innovations: Bionics. In: Lanzerath, D. and M. Friele (eds.), *Concepts and Values in Biodiversity. Routledge Studies in Biodiversity Politics and Management*, pp. 300–315. Routledge, London and New York.

Barthlott, W., M.D. Rafiqpoor and W.R. Erdelen 2016. Bionics and biodiversity – bio-inspired technical innovation for a sustainable future. In: Knippers, J. et al. (eds.), *Biomimetic Research for Architecture and Building Construction*, Biologically-Inspired Systems 9. Springer International, Switzerland. Doi:10.1007/978-3-319-46374-2_3.

Biermann, F. 2014. *Earth System Governance: World Politics in the Anthropocene*. MIT Press. Cambridge, MA.

Boucher, J. and D. Friot 2017. *Primary Microplastics in the Oceans: A Global Evaluation of Sources*. IUCN, Gland, Switzerland.

Commission on Global Security, Justice & Governance 2015. *Confronting the Crisis of Global Governance*. The Hague Institute for Global Justice and Stimson Center, The Hague and Washington, DC.

Marshall, T. 2016. *Prisoners of Geography. Ten Maps that Tell you Everything you Need to Know about Global Politics*. Elliott and Thompson Limited, London.

Michel, J. 2016. *Beyond Aid. The Integration of Sustainable Development in a Coherent International Agenda*. Center for Strategic & International Studies. Lanham.

UN (United Nations) 2014a. *A World That Counts. Mobilizing the Data Revolution for Sustainable Development*. United Nations, New York.

UN (United Nations) 2014b. *Global Governance and Global Rules for Development in the Post-2015 Era*. United Nations, New York.

UN (United Nations) 2016. *Global Sustainable Development Report 2016*. United Nations, New York.

WBGU (German Advisory Council on Global Change) 2016. *Humanity on the Move: Unlocking the Transformative Power of Cities*. WBGU, Berlin.

WBGU (German Advisory Council on Global Change) 2017. *New Urban Agenda: Implementation Demands Concerted Effort Now*. WBGU, Berlin.

Weiss, T.G. 2009. The UN's role in global governance. *UN Intellectual History Project, Briefing Note Number* 15: 1–6.

Weiss, T.G. and R. Jolly 2009. The "Third" United Nations. *UN Intellectual History Project, Briefing Note Number* 3: 1–3.

Weiss, T.G. and R. Wilkinson 2014. Rethinking Global Governance? Complexity, Authority, Power, Change. *International Studies Quarterly* 58: 207–215.

Further reading

Atlan, H., *Le vivant post-génomique ou qu'est-ce qu'une organisation?* (Post-Genomic Life or What Is an Organization?), Paris: Edition Odile Jaco, 2011. The author is a physician, cellular biologist, biophysicist and philosopher concerned with complexity.

Avery, J.S., *The Need for A New Economic System and Selected Works* (Vol. One), 66891 Ed (Sweden), Irene Publishing. A quantum chemist tackles international economics.

Clemens, W.C., Jr., *Complexity Science and World Affairs*, Albany, NY: SUNY Press, 2013. The consciousness and context of complexity in international relations will also help planners, strategists and progress evaluators outside diplomatic pursuits.

Ettleman, L., "A Historian's View of America's Long Debate on Immigration," *Time*, 23 October 2006. The United States has many of the same concerns with immigrants today as when the 100th millionth American citizen was recorded in 1915.

Fisher, M.H.L., *Migration, A World History*, New York, NY: Oxford University Press, 2014.

Freedman, L., *Strategy, A History*, New York, NY: Oxford University Press, 2013. See Chap. 13, The Rationality of Irrationality, p. 156.

Gleick, J., *Chaos, Making a New Science*, New York, NY: Penguin Books, 1988.

Godet, M., *From Anticipation to Action, A Handbook of Strategic Prospective* (in English, trans., from the French), Paris: UNESCO Publishing, 1993.

Godet, M., *La boîte à outils de prospective stratégique* (Toolbox for Strategic Prospective), *Cahier no. 5*, Paris: CNAM/LIPSOR, 2001: 102 pages of common sense to minimize doubtful choices.

Fukuyama, F., *Political Order and Political Decay, From the Industrial Revolution to the Globalization of Democracy*. New York, NY: Farrar, Straus and Giroux, 2014, See esp, pp. 276–283.

Harari, Y.N., *Sapiens. A Short History of Humankind*, New York, NY: HarperCollins, 2016.

Hinas, A. and P. Bishop, *Thinking about the Future, Guidelines for Strategic Foresight*, Washington, DC: Social Technologies, 2006.

Holland, J.L., *Complexity: A Very Short Introduction*, New York, NY: Oxford University Press, 2014.

International Migration Outlook (formerly *Trends in International Migration*), OECD, Paris, 2006. A novel treatment is a chapter on "Managing Migration – Are Quotas and Numerical Limits the Solution?" The International Institute of Applied Systems Analysis (IIASA, in Austria) announced in July 2016 a partnership with the EU's Joint Research Center in Brussels "to provide science-based knowledge on migration and demography to support EU policy."

Further reading 243

Johnson, N.F., *Simply Complexity: A Clear Guide to Complexity Theory*, London: Oneworld Publications, 2009. See Chap. 1, Two's Company, Three Is Complexity.

Johnson, S., *How We Got to Now, Six Innovations that Made the Modern World*, New York, NY: Random House/Riverhead, 2014.

Kahneman, D., *Thinking, Fast and Slow*, New York, NY: Farrar, Straus and Giroux, 2011.

Kastoryano, R., *Quelle identité pour l'Europe? Le multiculturalisme à l'épreuve* (Which Identity for Europe? Putting Multiculturalism to Test). Paris, Presses de Sciences Po, 2005.

Maldacena, J., *Black Holes, Wormholes and the Secrets of Quantum Time*, Scientific American, November 2016, p. 20. Black holes may entangle despite space-time separation.

Mari, J.P., *Les bateaux ivres* (The Drunkenly Erring Boats), Paris: J.C. Lattès, 2015.

Martin, J., M. Abella and M. Kuptsch, *Managing Labor Migration in the 21st Century*, New Haven CT and London: Yale University Press, 2006. Emigrants also head for prosperous developing countries such as Thailand.

Meadows, D.H., *Thinking in Systems – A Primer*, White River Junction VT: Chelsea Green Publishing, 2008.

Millett, S., *Managing the Future, A Guide to Forecasting and Strategic Planning in the 21st Century*, Axminster, Triarchy Press, 2011.

Millett, S.M., *Managing the Future, A Guide to Forecasting and Future Planning in the 21st Century*, Axminster, UK: Triarchy Press, 2011. See esp. Chap. 3, Futuring and Visioning, p. 62.

Milmo, C., "The Flood of Immigrants that Failed to Materialize," the *Independent*, 3 January 2007. When Bulgaria and Romania joined the EU, the "feared flood of workers" failed to appear at Heathrow Airport. (This article appeared well before the migrant floods to Europe of 2015–2016.)

Mitchell, M., *Complexity, A Guided Tour*, New York, NY: Oxford University Press, 2009. This volume, with enclosed DVD, is intended as a primer for the very young.

Miyamoto, M., *A Book of Five Rings* (trans. Victor Harris), Woodstock, NY: The Overlook Press, 1974. Written in 1645, this book is an early guide to management strategy. The book is called by its publisher "Japan's answer to the Harvard MBA."

Morin, E., *Science avec conscience*, Paris, Editions du Seuil, 1962.

Mueller, J., "Is There Still a Terrorist Threat? The Myth of the Omnipresent Enemy," *Foreign Affairs*, September-October 2006.

Narayanamurti, V. and T. Odumosu, *Cycles of Invention and Discovery: Rethinking the Endless Frontier*, Cambridge, MA: Harvard University Press, 2016. The authors are researchers at Harvard's Belfer Center for Science and International Affairs.

National Research Council and the National Academies of Science, Engineering and Medicine, *Diplomacy in the 21st Century, Embedding a Culture of Science and Technology throughout the Department of State*, Washington, 2015. A handbook that could serve many other countries.

Oreskes, N. and E. Conway, *Merchants of Death: How A Handful of Scientists Obscured the Truth on Issues from Tobacco Smoke to Global Warming*, New York, Bloomsbury Press, 2010: authoritative voices create doubt in the public mind.

Pezzulo, G., M.V. Butz, C. Castelfranchi and R. Falcone (eds.) *The Challenge of Anticipation, A Unifying Framework for the Analysis and Design of Artificial Cognitive Systems*, Berlin Heidelberg: Springer-Verlag, 2008.

Richardson, J., *Science and Governance: Scientists as Actors on the International Political and Social Stage* (unpublished monograph), Paris, UNESCO and ICSU, presented at workshop organized by the two sponsors at Visegrad (Hungary), June 1990, p. 366.

Seaman, J., *Rare earths and clean energy: Analyzing China's upper hand* (*Note de l'IFRI*, in English), Paris, Institut Français des Relations Internationales, September 2010, p. 38 explain an economically complex strategy.

Trump, D.J. and T. Schwartz., *The Art of the Deal*, New York, NY: Advance Publications (Random House), 1987. Although diplomacy may be wanting in some business negotiations, the author explains his principal tenet of "thinking big."

UNDESA (United Nations, Department of Economic and Social Affairs, Population Division) 2016. International Migration Report 2015: Highlights (ST/ESA/SER.A/375).

United Nations Industrial Development Organization (UNIDO), *Networks for Prosperity, Connecting Development Knowledge Beyond 2015*, UNIDO, Vienna, 2012.

Vuillerme, J.L., *Miroir de l'Occident, le Nazisme et la civilisation occidentale* (Mirror of the West, Nazism and Western Civilization), Paris: Toucan, 2014. Well-researched monograph on simplicity: How Third Reich dogma relating to "exterminationism" was looted from earlier models, all western but non-German in origin.

Williams, K., "Immigrants a Driving Force Behind Start-Ups," *The Washington Post*, 4 January 2007, p. D05.

Index

Note: Page numbers in **bold** indicate a table. Page numbers followed by b indicate boxes.

50 Years of Education (UNESCO) 44
2010 Target 120–122, 130
2013 World Social Science Report (ISSC and UNESCO) 58
2030 Agenda for Sustainable Development: biodiversity and 127–128, 130; decision-making in 24; environmental education and 47, 49–50, 55; financial mechanisms 237; science, technology and innovation (STI) and 68; sustainable development and 112, 221–223, 225; water in 103, 110–111, 113

actions and consequences 173, 173b
Adams, W. M. 218
adaptation 160
adaptive interaction 2, 57
aerosols 144
Agenda 21 47, 103, 215, 217–218
agricultural systems 115
Aichi Biodiversity Targets 122, 125–127, 131, 143, 210, 230
al Assad, Bashar 170
al-Bagdadi, Abu Bakr 172
Alcatel-Lucent Corporation 96–97
alternative energy: exploitation of 79; military and 76–77; technological progress in 141–142
American Association for the Advancement of Science (AAAS) 163
Amsterdam Declaration of the Global Change Open Science Conference 133
Anderson, J. L. 29
Andromeda Strain, The (Crichton) 29
Annan, Kofi 170
Antarctic Treaty System 165–166

Anthropocene: beginning of 17, 19b; biosphere and 19–21; complexity and 231–232; concept of 15–18, 24; criticism of term 17–18, 19b; global recognition of 220; humankind and 18, 133; planetary boundaries and 21, 24; stratigraphy and 17, 19b; use as communication tool 19
anthropogenic biomes (anthromes) 19–20
Apple 82–83; iPhone 74–75
applied sciences 60–61
Arab Spring (2011) 71n3, 168, 172
atmosphere 143–144
attractor 23
Austen, I. 75
Austria 171, 171b, 176
Autin, W. J. 17–18, 19b
automobile industry: competition in 99; exhaust emissions fraud and 98, 98b; fraud in 97–99; metal theft and 95–96; outsourcing in 95
Averill, M. 150

Bacevich, A. 80–81, 87n12
back casting 188
Ban, Ki-moon 47, 108, 221
Barabási, Albert-László 4
Barenboim, Daniel 164
Barings 89
Bartoli, Marion 86
Bar-Zeev, E. 114b
basic sciences 60–61
Batisse, Michel 112
Begon, M. 23
Behrens, W. W. 35, 210–211
Bell Telephone Laboratories 35
"Berlin Mandate" 140

Index

Bernard, C. 84
Bertalanffy, Ludwig von 4–5
Beyond Aid (Michel) 237
Beyond the Limits (Meadows et al.) 211
Biermann, F. 231
Big World Small Planet (Rockström and Klum) 21
Bilton, N. 82
biodiversity: complexity and 129; decline in 35, 60, 110, 122–123, 130, 236; defining 118–120; distribution of 118–119; economy and 121; ecosystems and 120; ecosystem services and 119, 121, 126; extant species estimates 124; extinction risks 123, 123b–124b, 131; geoengineering 157; institutional framework 126–127, **127**; intergovernmental mechanisms for 130; loss reduction initiatives 120–122, 125–126, 130–131, 236; sustainable development and 127; tipping points in 130; UN conventions on 127–129, 129b, 131
Biodiversity (Wilson) 120, 130
Biodiversity Vision 131
bioethics 60, 151
biogeochemical cycles 106
biogeography of governance 237, 239
biological diversity *see* biodiversity
biosphere: anthropogenic biomes (anthromes) 19–20; components of 21; concept of 212; integrity of 22
Biosphere Conference 212
BlackBerry 75
BNDES 92
Bock, Fedor von 181
Bogardi, J. J. 115
Bogdanov, Alexander 4
Boileau, J.-J. 39
Boole, George 35
Bowen, M. 147–148
Boyce, D. G. 126
BP Exploration and Production 78
Bradley, Omar 186
Bradshaw, C. J. A. 20
Braje, T. J. 19
Brauchitsch, Walther von 185
Brazil: corruption in 92–93, 93b, 94; public hygiene in 92
Bretton Woods conference 175
Brexit referendum 166, 208
Brin, Sergey 82
British Petroleum (BP) 77–79

Broadgate, L. 22
Broecker, W. 136
Brook, B. W. 20
Brookhaven Symposium 23
Brown, D. 150
Brundtland Conference 214
Brundtland, G. H. 137–138, 214
Brundtland Report 138–139, 214
Buenos Aires Declaration on the Ethical Dimensions of Climate Change 150
Bush, G. W. 147
Butz, M. 78

Cabut, S. 83
Calais, France 174
Cambridge Analytica-Facebook scandal 240
Cameron, David 174–175
Cancun Agreement 140
capacity building 41, 234–235
Capra, F. 1, 5
Carbon Brief 156
carbon dioxide removal (CDR) methods 154–155
Caring for the Earth (IUCN) 214
Carlowitz, Hans Carl von 211–212
Carpenter, S. 24
Carson, Rachel 34–35, 212, 238
casuistry 85
causal layer analysis (CLA) 189–190, 193n20
Cearreta, A. 18
Censoring Science (Bowen) 147
censorship 90
Center for the Fourth Industrial Revolution (of WEF) **74**
Challenge of Anticipation, The (Pezzulo and Butz) 78
chaotic behavior 2, 57
Chen, Y. 96
Cheney, Dick 147
China: alternative energy in 141; centralized power in 91b; CO_2 emissions 141, 145, 149; corruption in 90–92; Internet censorship 90; Paris Agreement and 141, 145; rare earths and 79–80; sanctions against 175; sports diplomacy 164; Syria and 171
Chinese Politics in the Era of Xi Jinping (Lam) 91b
Chu, D. 1
Churchill, Winston 191
Churkin, Vitaly 171

Index   247

CITES *see* Convention on International Trade in Endangered Species of Wild Fauna and Flora (CITES)
civil society: geoengineering and 157; globalization and 60; governments and 66; science and 135, 220; sustainable development and 219–221
Clarke, A. C. 29
climate change: adaptation and 136; alternative energy and 141; certainty and 139; civilization and 136; complexity and 133, 135–137, 139; as core boundary 22; early history of 136; education and 46–47; energy and 142b–143b; ethics of 149–154; geoengineering 154–155; global North contributors to 134, 150; global security and 149; greenhouse gas emissions and 139–142, 142b, 148; human impact on 106, 111, 114, 133, 135–136, 141, 143–144; impact on global South 134, 150, 226; international measures to mitigate 133–136; international political response to 139–142; migration and 197; perceptions of 135–136; permafrost thawing and 109, 143; research history **137**; temperature increases 141; Third Pole and 109–110; tipping points in 143; UN global agenda for 137–138, **138**, 139; water-related disasters and 109–111
climate diplomacy 144
climate refugees 197
CMS *see* Convention on the Conservation of Migratory Species of Wild Animals (CMS)
CO_2 emissions 141, 145, 149, 154–155
Cohen, J. 210
Collapse (Diamond) 136
Colley, D. 186
Combes, M. 96–97
COMEST *see* World Commission on the Ethics of Scientific Knowledge and Technology (COMEST)
Common Wealth (Sachs) 103
communication, education and public awareness (CEPA) program 127
complexity: biodiversity and 22; capacity building and 234; data and 233–234; defining 1–3; doubt and 80–82; exposure to 5; foresight and 28, 34, 39; humans and 6–8; institutional capacity building and 235–236; mathematical manifestations in 5; mechanisms and 234–237; military and 180–181, 181b, 182, 182b, 183, 183b, 184–186; nature and xv, xvi; obstruction and 231; of process 233; profiting from 13–14; recognition process and 230; in science 57, 59; system stability and 23; value systems and 232
complexity literacy 233
complex systems: adaptive interaction 2, 57; Anthropocene and 231–232; attractor 23; chaotic behavior 2, 57; characteristics of 2; defining 2; emergence in 57; fat-tailed behavior 2, 57; problems and 230–231; resolution of 8–9, 230–231; science-policy interfaces in 6; self-organization 2, 57; tipping points in 7, 23, 130, 133
complication 8–13
computers, development of 35–36; *see also* information and communication technologies (ICT)
Conference of the Parties in Cancun (COP 16) 134
Conference of the Parties (COP) Paris 2015 *see* Paris Climate Conference 2015 (COP 21)
Conference of the Parties (COP) system 139–140, 178n2
Conference of the Parties (COP) to the CBD 125–126
Confronting the Crisis of Global Governance (Commission on Global Security) 240
conspiracy theory 169b–170b
Convention on Biological Diversity (CBD) 119–121, 125–127, **127**, 128–129, 131, 156–158, 210, 215
Convention on International Trade in Endangered Species of Wild Fauna and Flora (CITES) 128
Convention on the Conservation of Migratory Species of Wild Animals (CMS) 122b, 128
Convention on the Law of the Non-Navigational Uses of International Watercourses (Watercourse Convention) 108
Convention on the Protection and Use of Transboundary Watercourses and International Lakes (Water Convention) 108
Convention to Combat Desertification (UNCCD) 119, 122b, 129–130, 215

248 Index

Coombs, P. H. 44, 54
COP 21 *see* Paris Climate Conference 2015 (COP 21)
Copenhagen Conference (2009) 145
coral reefs 143–144
corruption: in Brazil 92–93, 93b, 94; Chinese punishment of 90–92; finance and 89; industry and 88; in Korea 94; Latin American 93; military 91–92; tax evasion 89–90
Coursera 51
Crichton, M. 29
Crimean Peninsula 99–100, 170b
Crutzen, P. 16–18, 19b, 21
cultural clash 34
cultural differences 232
cultural exchange 164–165
cybernetics 4

Daesh 172–173
Daimler 83
Dalai Lama 150, 236
dam construction 107
Darwin, Charles 119
data 233–234
DDT 115, 238
Decade of Education for Sustainable Development (DESD) 46–48, 50
decision-making: doubt and 85; impediments to 34; military leadership and 186
Declaration on Ethical Principles Relating to Climate Change (UNESCO) 150, 152, 152b, 153, 153b, 157
Declaration on Science and the Use of Scientific Knowledge 59
Deepwater Horizon disaster 77–79
deliberative dialogue 161
Delors International Commission on Education for the Twenty-First Century 45
Delors, J. 44
Delucci, M. 79
demagogy 85
Deng, Xiaoping 91b
Derry, G. N. 70
Desai, Nitin 217
desalination 114, 114b
DESD *see* Decade of Education for Sustainable Development (DESD)
Detroit 95–96
Deutsch, L. 22
de Védrines family 95

developing countries: education and 50; environmental challenges and 59b, 137; impact of climate change on 148; inequality and 226; science/diplomacy and 163; women in 161
Devers, Jacob 186, 193n14
Diamond, J. 136
diplomacy: climate 144; cultural exchange 164–165; developing countries and 163; education and 162; European Union 166–167, 167b; foreign aid and 177; influence of 161; macro politics and 178n4; migration and 174–175; scientists and 162–163; specialists in 161; sports and 163–164; women and 161–162
directional drilling 76
disassembly: causal layer analysis (CLA) 189–190; of governance system 187–190; layers of 189–190; litany 189b, 190; metaphor/myth 190b; societal/systemic causes 189b; worldview 190b
displacement 197, 199, 203, 207
dissipative structures 5
Disturbing the Universe (Dyson) 30
DIVERSITAS 67
Division of Scientific Research and Higher Education (UNESCO) 163
doubt: complexity and 80–82; decision-making and 85; innovation and 82; planning and 86; science and 84; scope of 86, **86**
Dräger, J. 51
Drexhage, John 220
Dudgeon, D. 115
Dulles, A. 185
Dyson, F. 30

Earth Charter 236, 240
Earth Summit of 1992 46–47, 111, 119, 139, 214–216
Earth system governance 237, 239
Earth System Governance (Biermann) 231
Earth systems: anthroturbation and 18; climate change and 133, 135–136; complexity and 24–25; extinction events and 119–120; fragility of 23; human impact on 1, 3, 15–20, 20b, 21, 64; insecticides 115; interconnectedness and 64–65; planetary boundaries and 21, 23–24, 131; population and 20, 25; systemic solutions and 66; tipping points in 24, 133; water cycle 105–106, 114

Earth System Science Partnership (ESSP) 67
Eastman, G. 73–74
Eastman Kodak Co. 73–74
ecology 4, 22–23
economy: biodiversity and 121; circular 70; green 70, 220; migration and 196, 198b, 206; sustainable development and 142
Ecosystem Conservation Group 213
ecosystem ecology 4
ecosystems: biodiversity and 120; pollution in 238; stability in 22–24
ecosystem services 119, 121, 126, 213
Edison, Thomas 36
education: challenges for 53–54; climate change and 46–47; defining 42; environmental change and 41, 43–51, 54; equitable access to 52; globalization and 41, 43–45, 50, 54; higher 53–55; history of 42; information and communication technologies (ICT) and 41, 51–52, 54–55, 62–63; innovation and 40; intergenerational 44; interrelationships in stages of 55; pedagogy and 42; purposes of 42–43; science and 62; social networks and 41; subject-specific approaches in 45–46; sustainability and 43–44, 48, 53, 55
Education for All (EFA) 46–47, 50, 53
Education for Sustainable Development (ESD) 44, 47–48, 48b–49b, 50–51
education technology 51–52
EEAS *see* European External Action Service (EEAS)
Ehrenfels, Christian von 4
Ehrlich, A. 121
Ehrlich, P. 121
Einstein, Albert 162
Eisenhower, Dwight D. 186, 192, 193n14
El Dorado syndrome 196
Elop, S. 75
emergence 57
Emergency State, The (Unger) 188
emergent behavior 2
energy: alternative 76–77, 79, 141–142; climate change and 142b–143b; renewable 76, 143b; solar 39, 141; wind 141
engineering 84
environment: awareness of human impact on 212, 238; education and 41, 43–51,
54; interlinked problems of 59, 59b; transboundary issues in 61
environmental disasters: compensation for 78–79; predictive actions and 77–78
environmental education 43, 47, 50
environmental flight 197
Environmental Food Crisis, The (UN) 110
environmental pollution 238
Environmental Protection Agency (EPA) 212
Erdelen, W. 63
Erdogan, Recep Tayyip 175
Erlandson, J. M. 19
Escrigas, C. 54
ESSP Transitions into "Future Earth" 67
Ethical Implications of Global Climate Change, The (COMEST) 151
ethics 149–154, 236
European Commission 79, 166, 172, 200
European External Action Service (EEAS) 166
European Union: Brexit referendum 166, 208; combined foreign policy 166; diplomacy 166–167, 167b; diplomatic services 161; economic issues 168; economic sanctions against Iran 169; false migrants and 171–172; foreign relations and 168–169; Great Britain and 174–175; migration and 167, 172–174, 200–201, 203, 205, 208; Syria and 170, 172; terrorism and 171
evolution 119
executive compensation 97
exhaust emissions 98, 98b
expediency 75–76
extinction: biodiversity and 123, 123b–124b, 131; mass events 119–120; risk assessment 123, 124b
Extinction (Ehrlich and Ehrlich) 121

Fagot-Largeault, A. 84
Falciani, Hervé 89
Farnham, T. J. 120
fat-tailed behavior 2, 57
fault-tree analysis 191, 193n20
Faure Commission 44
Faure, E. 44–45, 45b
Ferreira, P. 3
financial mechanisms 237
Fjelland, R. 1
Fleytas, A. 78
Flinkerbusch, E. 115
foreign aid 176, 176b, 177, 177b, 178

foreign commerce 175–176
foreign relations: diplomacy and 161, 168, 174; financial assistance and 176, 176b, 177, 177b, 178; foreign commerce and 175–176; governance and 160
foresight: complexity and 28, 34, 39; framing 34; horizon scanning 34; innovation and 35–37; interpolation in 31; predictive approaches of 29–30, 78; rejecting the assumed and accepted 34; science fiction and 28–29; strategic 31–34, 34b; systematic 30–31; techniques 34–35
Forrester, J. W. 211
Foundation for Political Innovation 90
fracking see hydraulic fracturing (fracking)
France: economic development in 38; innovation in 38–39; migration and 196; trade agreements 176
Francis, Pope 33–34, 34b, 141, 150, 236
fraud 96–99
Fukushima-First nuclear plant 81
Funtowicz, S. 59
Future Earth 64–65, 67, 220
Future We Choose, The 66, 220, 225
Future We Want, The (UN) 48, 66, 219, 221

Gaffney, O. 22
Gaia concept 4
Gallopin, G. C. 59
Garotinho, Anthony 94
General Agreement on Tariffs and Trade (GATT) 175
General Systems Theory 4
geoengineering 154–155, 157–158
Geoengineering the Climate (Royal Society) 154
geopolitics 160–161
Germany: education in 51; innovation in 38; migration to 167, 173, 200–201, 205b; political parties 94; Schlieffen Plan 32–33; and Second World War 180–189; trade agreements 176; VW scandal 98–99
"Gestalt" 4
"Gestaltproblem" 4
Gilbert, N. 129
glacier retreat 109–110
Gladwell, M. 23
Glaspie, April 161
Global Action Plan 48

Global Action Program (GAP) on Education for Sustainable Development 46
Global Biodiversity Outlook 3 121–122, 126
Global Biodiversity Outlook 4 125–126, 144
global ethics 236
Global Forecast for the Next Forty Years, A (Randers) 211
global governance 237, 239–240
globalization: complexity and 229–230; education and 41, 43–45, 50, 54; inequality and 43; migration and 206–207; remittances from abroad 207
Global Monitoring Report for Education for All (UNESCO) 53
global science 58; see also science
global security 149
global sustainability: developing economies and 66; partnerships in 67, 67b; research in 65b, 67, 67b; see also sustainable development
global thermohaline circulation 114
Global University Network for Innovation (GUNI) 54
global warming: emissions and 143; emissions reduction targets 140; geoengineering 154–155; nitrogen oxides and 98b
Goethe, Johann W. von 34
Google 82–83; Google Glass 82
Gore, Al 212
governance: biogeography of 237, 239; civil society and 66; climate change 69, 112, 134, 140–142, 144–149; disassembly of 187–190; Earth system 237, 239; foreign relations and 160; geopolitics and 160–161; global 237, 239–240; multilateralism and 66, 231
Grandjean, Martin 90
Great Britain: emigration from 195–196; immigration to 195; see also United Kingdom
Greece: emigrant departures from 207; European Union 168; migration to 172–173, 175; schools in 42
Green Climate Fund 142, 146, 148
greenhouse gas emissions: climate change and 139, 142b, 150; fossil fuels and 142; global warming and 143; increase in 140–141; northern industrial states and 134; permafrost thawing and

109; protocols for limits on 139, 141;
reductions in 143b, 154, 156, 158;
removal of 156; research on 137;
treaties for reduction of 144, 149
Greenpeace 162
Green, Stephen 89
Griggs, D. 224b
Grinevald, J. 17
Grober, Ulrich 212
Gulliver, Stuart 89
Guo, Boxiong 91
Guo, Zhenggang 91–92
Gurría, José Ángel 208

Haeckel, Ernst 4
Half Earth (Wilson) 236
Hall, S. 105
Harper, J. L. 23
Hazelkorn, E. 53
Hazen, R. 61
Hecking, C. 141
Heijden, C. van der 32
Heinlein, R. A. 29
Help Save the Third Pole
  (ICIMOD) 109
Hendricks, B. 146
Henk, M. 135
Hérault, B. 207
higher education 53–55
High Level Panel on Global Sustainability
  220, 225
Hill, S. L. L. 126
Hindu Kush-Himalaya (Third Pole) 108,
  108b, 109, 109b
Hirota, Kôki 191
Hitler, Adolf 181–183, 185, 185b
Holbrook, J. M. 17–18
Hollande, François 39, 169, 174–175, 199
Holmes, Linda 89
Holocene 16–17, 21
Hoover, H. 30
Hotta, E. 187, 189–192
Howard, John 202
How Many People Can the Earth Support?
  (Cohen) 210
HSBC Private Bank (Suisse) 89
Hu, Jintao 91, 91b, 92
Hughes, T. P. 24
Hulot, N. 197
human-environment interactions:
  Anthropocene and 18, 24; anthropogenic
  biomes (anthromes) 19–20; chronology
  of major impacts 20b; complexity in
15, 106; planetary boundaries and 24;
  population and 20
humankind: challenges for 229; energy
  consumption 20; planetary boundaries
  and 235; population 20, 31; safe
  operating space 235; salient
  actions of 7–8; systems of 8
human rights 145
Humboldt, W. von 51–52
Huntington, S. 196–197
Hus, J. 41
Hussein, Saddam 161
Huxley, Julian 44
hydraulic fracturing (fracking) 76–77
hydrosphere 105–106

ICIMOD *see* International Centre for
  Integrated Mountain Development
  (ICIMOD)
ICSU *see* International Council for
  Science (ICSU)
ICT *see* information and communication
  technologies (ICT)
IDE Technologies 114b
IGBP *see* International Geosphere-
  Biosphere Program (IGBP)
IISD *see* International Institute for
  Sustainable Development (IISD)
Immigrants (Legrain) 207
Incheon Declaration for Education 2030
  49–50
India: foreign aid and 178; immigrants
  from 204b; solar energy in 39
information and communication
  technologies (ICT): access to 52;
  communication and 54; education
  and 41, 51–52, 54–55, 62–63; global
  connectivity and 121; knowledge
  and 233, 234b, 235, 235b; media and
  information literacy (MIL) 234b–235b;
  science and 61
innovation: cause-and-effect process 37;
  complexity and 36, 39; doubt and 82;
  education and 40; emergences in 73, **74**;
  failure and 74–75; foresight and 35–39;
  permanent process of 73; protection
  and 37–38; research and development
  38–39
insecticides 115
Insisting on the Impossible (McElheny) 74
institutional capacity building
  235–236
intellectual property 38

Index 251

252 Index

Intergovernmental Bioethics Committee 151
Intergovernmental Panel on Climate Change (IPCC) 64, 65b, 130, 141, 147–148
Intergovernmental Platform on Biodiversity and Ecosystem Services (IPBES) 130
International Bioethics Committee 151
International Centre for Integrated Mountain Development (ICIMOD) 109, 109b
International Convention on the Protection of Migrant Workers and Their Families 205
International Council for Science (ICSU) 59, 64, 65b, 66, 67b, 139, 223
International Council of Music 165
International Geophysical Year of 1957–1958 165–166
International Geosphere-Biosphere Program (IGBP) 16, 67
International Human Dimensions Program on Global Environmental Change (IHDP) 67, 71n4
International Hydrological Decade 112
International Hydrological Program (IHP) 112
International Institute for Applied Systems Analysis 31
International Institute for Sustainable Development (IISD) 66, 220
International Institute of Applied Systems Analysis 163
International Migration Report 2015 203b–205b
International Organization for Migration (IOM) 195b, 206
International Plant Protection Convention (IPPC) 128
International Social Science Council (ISSC) 67b, 71n4
International Treaty on Plant Genetic Resources for Food and Agriculture (ITPGRFA) 128
International Union for Conservation of Nature (IUCN) 121, 123, 123b–124b, 162, 213
International Union for the Conservation of Nature and Natural Resources 213
International Union for the Protection of Nature and Natural Resources 213
International Union of Geological Sciences (IUGS) 16

International Year of Biodiversity (2010) 121, 125, 230
Internet: censorship of 90; information and 233; medical teleconsultation via 83–84
interpolation 31
IOM *see* International Organization for Migration (IOM)
IPCC *see* Intergovernmental Panel on Climate Change (IPCC)
IPPC *see* International Plant Protection Convention (IPPC)
Iran 168–170
Islamic State 172–173
Israel: Iranian threats to 170; water in 114, 114b
ISSC *see* International Social Science Council (ISSC)
ITPGRFA *see* International Treaty on Plant Genetic Resources for Food and Agriculture (ITPGRFA)
IUCN *see* International Union for Conservation of Nature (IUCN)
IUCN Red List of Threatened Species 123, 123b–124b
IUGS *see* International Union of Geological Sciences (IUGS)

Jacobson, M. 79
Jäger, Jens 3
Jakhu, Ram 36
Japan: disassembly of governance system 187–190; foreign policy and 187–188, 191–192; governance in 187; intended insubordination in 188b; migration and 201; war-effort system 187–192
Jaspers, Karl 8
Jennings, L. 85–86
Johnson, N. 13
Joint Liaison Group (JLG) 129b
Jouvenel, B. de 32
Jouvenel, H. de 32
Juncker, J.-C. 166
Jungcurt, S. 224–225

Kabat, P. 163
Kaddafi, Muammar 172
Kan, N. 81
Kaplan, Robert D. 80, 160
Keplinger, Y. 78
Khrushchev, Nikita 100
Kim, J.-U. 164
Kitazawa, Kay 81
Kitazawa, Koichi 81

Klum, M. 21–22
Konoe, Fumimaro 187, 191
Kopnina, H. 50
Korea: corruption in 94; diplomacy and 164; North Korean threats to 169
Kyoto Protocol 140–141, 144, 147

Lam, W. 91b
Land, E. 73–74
Lawford, R. 115
leadership analysis 34; *see also* military leadership
League of Nations 187–188, 190
Learning (Delors) 44
Learning to Be (Faure) 44–45, 45b
Leeson, N. W. 89
Legrain, P. 207
Lennon, J. T. 119
Leshner, A. 163
Limits to Growth, The (Meadows et al.) 35, 210–211
Linked (Barabási) 4
litany 189b, 190
literacy 41
Liu, Han 90
Liu, Jian 91
Liu, Wei 90
Living Planet Index 123
Living Planet Report 2014 (World Wildlife Fund) 123
Locey, K. J. 119
Lohbeck, W. 135
lotic water ecosystems 107–108, 111
Ludwig, C. 22
Luisi, P. L. 5

Macron, Emmanuel 97, 146, 174
Malik, Yakov 191
Mao, Zedong 91–92, 164
Marshall, T. 238
mass extinction 119–120
massive open online course (MOOC) 52
mass migration: Calais camps 174–175; European Union and 167, 172–173; men and boys 174; prevention strategies 175; *see also* migration
Mayor, F. 44
McElheny, V. K. 74
McLaughlin, D. 212
McManus, R. 120
McNeill, J. 17
MDGs *see* Millennium Development Goals (MDGs)
Meadows, D. H. 35, 210–211

Meadows, D. L. 35, 92, 210–211
mechanisms 234–237
media and information literacy (MIL) 234b–235b
medical teleconsultation 83–84
Menuhin, Yehudi 165
Merkel, Angela 94, 140, 175, 205b
metal theft 96
Meyn, A. 115
migrants: defining 195b; employment and 200, 201b–202b, 206, 208; funds sent home by 198, 207; illegal employment 171; protests against 200; violence against 173
migration: benefits of 208; characteristics of 203, 203b–205b; citizen-generated relief 208; economy and 196, 198; environmental flight and 197; European Union and 167, 171–172, 175, 203, 205, 208; factors influencing 198b–199b; Great Britain 195–196; historical 197, 197b; impacts of 206; political causes of 199; politics of 200; population growth and 197; prevention strategies 175; rates of 203b–204b, 205, 207–208; survival and 197–198; system of 205–206; terrorism fears and 202; urbanization and 199; war and 201; women and 198, 203, 204b
military corruption 91–92
military leadership: climate change data 184b–185b; disassembly in 187–192; failed strategy in 186, 189, 192; individual will and 183–184; intended insubordination in 188b; misunderstood complexity in 180–181, 181b, 182, 182b, 183, 183b, 184–185; net assessment and 183; systems in 191; tipping points in 192
Millennium Declaration 216
Millennium Development Goals (MDGs) 24, 31, 50, 53, 65b, 103, 110–111, 113, 216, 216b–217b, 221, 230
Millennium Ecosystem Assessment (MEA) 120–121, 121b, 122, 122b, 218–219
Millennium Summit 216
Modern Express cargo ship 11–12
Mogherini, F. 166
Moïsi, D. 196
Molotov, Vyacheslav 191
Moltke, Helmut von 33
Montbrial, T. de 100
Montgomery, Bernard 186
Moore, G. 35

254 Index

Moore, H. 63
Morin, E. 1
Morris, Ian M. 7–8, 85
mountain poverty 109
Müller-Eiselt, R. 51
Mulligan, C. S. 202
multilateralism 66, 231
Murphy, Deborah 220
Mutta, R. 93

Nagoya Protocol 125
National Academy of Sciences 120
National Forum on BioDiversity 120
nationally determined contributions (NDCs) 145
natural disasters 109
net assessment 183
networks concept 4
Nilsson, M. 224b
Nobre, C. A. 65
Nokia 74–75
Noone, K. 21, 23
Norse, E. 120
North Korea 37, 162, 164, 175
nuclear energy 18, 36, 73, 81
nuclear weapons 37, 162, 164, 169–170
nutrient cycles 106

Obama, Barack 169, 176
oceans: acidification of 21–22, 43, 126, 142b, 143–144; atmosphere and 143; biodiversity and 118; climate change and 114, 142b; discharge in 107; fertilization of 154–155, 157; pollution in 156, 238; renewable energy and 30; stabilizing effect of 104; volume of 105
O'Connor, M. 59
official development assistance (ODA) 176b, 237
Olympic Games 100, 163–164
O'Neil, W. D. 33
open systems 5
operational analysis 30
Operation Barbarossa 180–181, 184, 192
operations research 30–31
Operation Typhon (Typhoon) 181–185, 192
Organization for Economic Cooperation and Development (OECD) 176b, 177, 177b, 196, 207–208
Orr, D. W. 43
Orwell, G. 52
Osborne, R. 201

Otsuka, T. 81
Our Common Future (Brundtland) 138, 214–215

Pahl-Wostl, C. 115
Paris Climate Conference 2015 (COP 21): adoption of 145–146, 210; China and 141, 145; climate change governance and 69, 112, 134, 140–142, 144–149, 163; diplomacy and 144, 162–163; global warming limits and 109, 156; human rights in 145; implementation of goals in 143b, 146, 157–158; nationally determined contributions (NDCs) 145; Trump and 92, 146–148; U.S. and 92, 141, 145–149
Park, Geun-hye 94
Passman, S. 163
Pasteur, Louis 38
patents 38
Patton, George 186
Peace of Westphalia 160
Pearl Harbor attack 187, 192
pedagogy 42
People's Liberation Army 91
Pérez de Cuéllar, Javier 137
permafrost thawing 109, 143
Pestel, E. 211
Petrobras 92, 94
Petroski, H. 84
Pezzulo, G. 78
Pfizer 81
planetary boundaries: Anthropocene and 21, 24; biodiversity and 126; categories of 21–22; concept of 15, 21, 24, 64; defining 23; hierarchical patterns of 22; institutional capacity building and 235; local and regional levels of 22; policy and 22; thresholds in 22; tipping points in 22–23, 69, 131
Planet Under Pressure Conference 64–65, 65b
planning 86
Polaroid Co. 73–74
polar territories 165–166
policy: capacity building and 41; education and 54; planetary boundaries and 22; science and 6, 59, 65–66, 68–71, 130
political systems 147
pollution: automobile industry and 97–98; biodiversity loss and 123, 126, 214; chemical 21–22, 77, 107; environmental 35, 115, 212, 238;

impact of 210; water 12, 103, 107, 111, 156
population: Earth systems and 20, 25; foresight and 31; limits on 231–232; migration and 197; order and systems in 160; rates of 207; sustainable development and 220; water use and 104
Posas, P. 150
Post-2015 Global Goal for Water, A (UN-Water) 111
Precautionary Principle, The (COMEST) 151
predictive actions 77–78
Prigogine, Ilya 5
Prisoners of Geography (Marshall) 238
problem analysis 92
Proposition 187 (California) 200
Pugwash Conferences on Science and World Affairs 162
Putin, Vladimir 100, 170b

Qingdao Declaration 52

Ramsar Convention 122b, 128
Randers, J. 35, 210–211
rare earths 79–80
Ravetz, J. 59
Rebuild Japan Initiative Foundation (RJIF) 81
refugees 167, 172–175, 197
Regnier, Didier 90
Reimer, N. 144
Renault Group 99
renewable energy: climate change and 143b; food production needs and 224b; initiatives for 218; military and 76
research and development (R&D) 38–39, 63
Resilient People, Resilient Planet 68
Revkin, A. 19b
Richardson, J. 16
Rio+10 Summit of 2002 215, 217
Rio+20 Summit of 2012 48, 64–65, 65b, 66–67, 129, 134, 215, 217, 219–221
Rio Conventions 46–47, 119, 129, 129b, 214–215
Rio Declaration on Environment and Development 215
Rio Earth Summit (1992) 46–47, 111, 119, 139, 214–216
Rio Report Card (Tollefson and Gilbert) 129

river systems: human impact on 107–108; transboundary issues 107–108; wastewater discharge 111; water demand in 111
Rockström, J. 21–24
Roosevelt, Franklin D. 30, 188, 191
Rosen, W. G. 120
Rosenthal, E. 76
Rousseff, Dilma 93–94, 219
Royal Dutch Shell 31–32
Royal, Ségolène 199
Royal Society 154–155
Ruddiman, W. F. 17
Rundstedt, Gerd von 186
Russell, Bertrand 162
Russell, W. H. 34
Russia: Crimean Peninsula and 99–100; economic sanctions against Iran 169; innovation in 39; Muslim world and 170b; sanctions against 170b, 175; Syria and 171
Russian Airbus A-321 explosion 9–11, 13

Sachs, J. D. 103
Sadin, E. 29
safeguard systems 77–78, 86
Saionji, Kimmochi 191
Sarkozy, Nicolas 201
Satô, Naotake 191
Schätzing, F. 29
Scheffer, M. 24
Schengen agreements 167, 171, 203
Schlieffen, Alfred von 32–33
Schlieffen Plan 32–33
Schoemaker, P. 32
schools 42; *see also* education
Schrödinger, Erwin 7
Schroeder, M. 80
science: 21st century 58, 58b, 63–64; access to knowledge 235; basic and applied 60–61; communication of 61b–62b; complexity and 57, 59; defining 57–58, 70; diplomacy and 162–163; doubt and 84; education and 62; global challenges and 63–67; indigenous and local knowledge in 61; information and communication technologies (ICT) and 61; polar territories and 165–166; policy and 6, 59, 65–66, 68–71, 130; science fiction and 28–29; sustainable development and 59, 66, 220, 226; synthesis in 43; terminology 60; *see also* global science

Science Agenda – Framework for Action 59
science and technology (S&T) 63
science fiction: foresight and 28–29; prescient thinking in 236; science and 28–29
science-policy tnterface (SPI) 6, 59, 65, 130, 223
Science sans conscience (Morin) 1
science, technology and innovation (STI) 58, 65, 68, 70
science, technology, engineering, mathematics (STEM) education 63
Scientific Advisory Board (SAB) 68–70
scientific literacy: communication and 61b–62b; defining 61; importance of 62–63; information and communication technologies (ICT) and 62–63; sustainable development and 41
Scott, P. 124b
SDGs *see* Sustainable Development Goals (SDGs)
Second World War: climate change data 184b–185b; Japan in 187–192; Operation Barbarossa 180–181, 184; Operation Typhon (Typhoon) 181–185; Pearl Harbor attack 187, 192; Russian offensive losses 184; Tripartite Pact 188
self-government 160
self-organization 2, 57, 160
Shannon, Claude 35
Silent Spring (Carson) 35, 212, 238
Silva, Luiz Inácio Lula da 94
sixth mass extinction 119–120
Small Island Developing States (SIDS) 134
Smithsonian Institution 120
Soames, B. F. 168
social networks 41
solar energy 39, 141
solar radiation management (SRM) methods 154–155
sophistry 84
Soviet Union: Crimean Peninsula and 100; German army and 181–184; Japanese army and 190; nuclear weapons and 162; sports diplomacy and 164
Species Survival Commission (SSC) 124b
specious reasoning 85
sports diplomacy 163–164
Sriskandarajah, D. 195–196
Stahel, D. 180–181, 183–184
Stalin, Josef 182, 191

Statement on Forest Principles 215
State of the Planet Declaration 64–65
Steffen, W. 16, 17, 19b, 21–23
STEM education *see* science, technology, engineering, mathematics (STEM) education
Sterling, S. 44
Stern, N. 133
STI *see* science, technology and innovation (STI)
Stiglitz, J. 231
Stockholm Conference 212–213
Stoermer, E. F. 16–17
Strand, R. 1
Strategic Forecasting, Inc. (Stratfor) 39, 80, 92, 160
Strategic Plan for Biodiversity (CBD) 125, 127, 131, 143, 210
strategy 1
Stratfor *see* Strategic Forecasting, Inc. (Stratfor)
Stromberg, J. 16, 19b
sustainability 211–212
sustainable development: biodiversity and 35, 60, 127; complexity and 220, 223, 226, 230–231; complexity-stability in 23; concept of 211–212; defining 214; ecosystem services and 213; education and 43–44, 48, 53, 55; environmental concerns and 212; financial mechanisms 237; global ethics and 236; global initiatives for 65b, 210, 213–226, 231; goals and target areas 222, 222b, 223–224, 224b, 225–227, 230; interactions in 224, 224b, 225, 227; models for 238–239; movement toward 210–213; multilateralism and 231; nexus approach 224–225; science and 59, 66, 68, 220, 226; systemic solutions and 220–221, 235–237; transnational collaboration in 238–239; water in 110–114
Sustainable Development Goals (SDGs) 24, 55, 103, 113–114, 127, 210, 220–221, 222b, 223, 224b, 225–226, 230
Swan, Joseph W. 36
Swarm, The (Schätzing) 29
Sweeney, L. B. 92
Sylvicultura oeconomica (Carlowitz) 211
Syria 170–172, 207
systematic fraud 96–99
systemic distraction 94

systemic solutions 220–221, 235–237
systems: adaptation and 160; conspiracy theory and 169b–170b; corruption in 88–89, 92–94; cultural exchange 164–165; defining 1; failure in 73–74, 95–96; fraud in 96–99; infirmity in 8; problem analysis 92; safeguard 77–78, 86; self-organization and 160; slippage in 94; vigilance and 100–101
systems thinking 4

Taiwan 175
tax evasion 89–90
telephone fraud 96
Temer, Michel 94
territory 165
terrorism: climate change and 149; coalitions against 167, 240; diplomacy and 161; education and 41; European Union 171; migration fears and 199, 202, 207; Schengen agreements and 171
theft 95–96
"Theories of Complexity" (Chu, Strand, and Fjelland) 1
Third Pole: biodiversity in 109b; biodiversity loss 110; climate change risks 109–110; cultural diversity in 108b; food security and agricultural sustainability 110; glacier retreat 109–110; mountain poverty 109; natural disasters 109; vulnerability and livelihoods 109; water decline 110; water resources in 108–109
Tillitze, Lars 191
Tilly, Thierry 95
Tipping Point, The (Gladwell) 23
tipping points: climate change and 143; complex systems and 7, 23–24, 130, 133; defining 22; history of 130; migration and 200; military leadership and 192; planetary boundaries and 22, 69
Tittensor, D. P. 126
Tollefson, J. 129
Touré, Amadou 168
Townsend, C. R. 23
Tracing Complexity Theory (Ferreira) 3
trade and investment partnerships 175–176
Transboundary Biosphere Reserves (TBR) 238–239
transboundary issues 61; water issues 107–108

Transforming Our World (UN) 43, 216, 221
Treaty of Versailles 160
Trefil, J. 61
Tripartite Pact 188
Trump, Donald J. 92, 146–148, 164, 169, 176, 208
Tuana, N. 150
Turing, Alan 35
Turkey: emigrant departures from 167, 172, 175, 207; EU membership and 168; factory labor from 200
Tusk, Donald 175

Uchatius, W. 135
UN Conference on Environment and Development (UNCED) 46, 119, **138**, 214
UN Conference on the Human Environment 212–213
UN Economic Commission for Europe (UNECE) 108
UN Educational, Scientific and Cultural Organization (UNESCO) 44–45, 47–48, 50, 53, 59, 68, 70, 112, 151–152, 152b, 153, 153b
UN Environment Program (UNEP) 130, 139, 213
UNEP *see* UN Environment Program (UNEP)
UNESCO *see* UN Educational, Scientific and Cultural Organization (UNESCO)
UNESCO Science Report 68
UN Expert Committee on Climate Change 47
UNFCCC *see* United Nations Framework Convention on Climate Change (UNFCCC)
UNFCCC Climate Change Conference 140
Unger, D. 188
UN-Habitat 236
UN High Commissioner for Refugees (UNHCR) 206
UN Inter-Agency Committee on Bioethics 151
United Kingdom: Brexit referendum 166, 208; greenhouse gas removal 156; migration to 174–175; *see also* Great Britain
United Nations: biodiversity-related conventions 119–121, 125, 127–128; economic sanctions against Iran 169; education and 44–48; foreign aid and 177, 177b; global governance and 240;

population estimates 31; science and 68–70; Syria and 170–171
United Nations Framework Convention on Climate Change (UNFCCC) 46, 46b, 119, 129, 133–134, 139–140, 145, 148, 150, 157, 210, 215
United States: alternative energy in 142; CO_2 emissions 141, 145; economic sanctions against Iran 169; foreign relations and 168–170; Kyoto Protocol and 147; Muslim world and 170b; Paris Agreement and 141, 145–149; regional trade agreements 175–176; rule of law and 188–189; sports diplomacy 164
Universal Declaration of Human Rights 42
UN Office for Disaster Risk Reduction 111
UN Secretary-General's High-Level Panel on Global Sustainability 68–69
UN Security Council 100, 151, 171
UN Summit on Sustainable Development 131
UN-Water 111, 112b, 113, 113b
UN World Water Development Report (2009) 106–107
urban environments: migration and 198b, 199; water use and 103

Vacheron, A. 84
Vallancien, G. 83
value systems 232
Vielhauer, K. 115
Visbeck, M. 224b
visioning technique 34–35
Visser, J. 48
Vom Ursprung und Ziel der Geschichte (Jaspers) 8
Vörösmarty, C. 107, 115
VW Group 97–99

Wagener, G. 83
Wagner, Eduard 183–184
Walker, B. 24
Wallace, Alfred Russel 119
Walpole, M. 126
wastewater discharge 111
water: agricultural systems and 115; availability of **105**, 115; chemistry of 104; complexity and 115; demand for 111; desalination 114, 114b; human impact on 107–110, 114–115; hydrosphere 105–106; implementation of goals 113–114; importance of 103–105, 112–114; lotic ecosystems 107–108, 111; national per capita income and 103; pollution 12, 103, 107, 111, 156; prevalence of 104–105; resources on Earth 104–105, 108–109, 114–115; sustainable development and 110–114; UN initiatives 110–112, 112b–113b; urban environments and 103
Water Convention 108; see also Convention on the Protection and Use of Transboundary Watercourses and International Lakes (Water Convention)
Watercourse Convention 108; see also Convention on the Law of the Non-Navigational Uses of International Watercourses (Watercourse Convention)
water cycle: Earth systems and 105–106, 114; human impact on 106–107
Waters, C. N. 17–18, 20b
WCED see World Commission on Environment and Development (WCED)
WCS see World Conference on Science (WCS)
We Are Still In statement 148
Web of Life, The (Capra) 1
WEF see World Economic Forum (WEF)
Weiss, Thomas G. 239
What Science Is and How It Works (Derry) 70
WHC see World Heritage Convention (WHC)
whistle-blowing 89
Whitman, C. T. 147
Why the West Rules – For Now (Morris) 85
wicked problems 54, 129
Wiener, Norbert 4
Wihtol de Wenden, C. 205
Williams, M. 17, 20b, 21
Wilson, E. O. 120, 130, 236
wind energy 141
WIPO see World Intellectual Property Organization (WIPO)
Wise, R. 29
women: diplomacy and 161–162; migration and 198, 203, 204b
World Climate Research Program 67
World Commission on Environment and Development (WCED) 137, 214

World Commission on the Ethics of
  Scientific Knowledge and Technology
  (COMEST) 151–152
World Conference on Education for
  Sustainable Development (2009) 47
World Conference on Environment and
  Development 139
World Conference on Global Institutions 240
World Conference on Science (WCS)
  59–60, 60b, 61
World Conservation Strategy (IUCN)
  121, 213–214
World Conservation Union 213
World Economic Forum (WEF) 36,
  74, 231
World Educational Crisis (Coombs) 44, 54
World Education Forum 49
World Heritage Convention (WHC) 128
World Intellectual Property Organization
  (WIPO) 38

World Meteorological Organization
  (WMO) 112, 130, 139
World Resources Institute 139
World Summit on Sustainable
  Development 112b, 121, 217–218, 230
World That Counts, A (UN) 233
World Trade Organization 175
World Wildlife Fund 123, 162

Xi, Jinping 91b, 92, 101
Xu, Caihou 90–91

Yamamoto, Isoroku 191–192
Yergin, D. 77

Zalasiewicz, J. 17–18, 20b, 21
Zhang, Zemin 91
Zhou, Yongkang 90
Zhu, De 91
Zhukov, Georgi 182

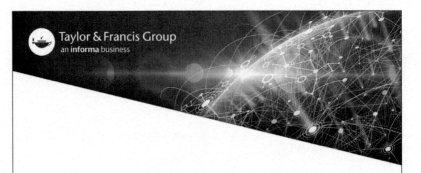